Ida van Zijl

Gerrit Rietveld

Ida van Zijl

Gerrit Rietveld

Contents

Foreword

In late 1988 I visited Han Schröder, Truus Schröder-Schräder's youngest daughter, in Richmond, Virginia. I wanted to interview her about the Rietveld Schröder House, its furniture and contents, and the archive amassed by her mother, which had been transferred to the stewardship of the Centraal Museum in Utrecht a year earlier. 'You cannot understand the house unless you're aware of my mother's views and how she actually lived there,' she said as soon as the formal niceties were out of the way.

For two days I peered through a kaleidoscope of memories into a life animated by her mother's idealism. For most of the time we spoke about the house and Truus, and only as I was leaving did Han bring up the subject of Gerrit Rietveld. 'You're doing an awful lot for Rietje,' she said. Until that moment I had not fully realized that the guardianship of Truus Schröder's estate, besides entailing an obligation on the part of the Centraal Museum in Utrecht, was also a personal commitment for me, a debt of honour that I hope has been repaid in part with this book.

Truus Schröder always firmly believed that the house and archive had to be preserved intact in order to guard the legacy of Rietveld's work and ideas and their deserved reputation. Much has been achieved on all fronts in the twenty or so years since the transfer of his legacy. Important milestones were the publications about the Rietveld Schröder House edited by Paul Overy in 1988, the two volumes about De Stijl edited by Carel Blotkamp from 1982 and 1996, and the Rietveld biography by Frits Bless from 1982. In 1992 the Centraal Museum staged a major retrospective exhibition of Rietveld's work, which subsequently toured to museums around the world. A catalogue raisonné compiled by Marijke Kuper and myself was produced to accompany this exhibition. In the interim there have been several publications about specific aspects of Rietveld's oeuvre. Interest in his work burgeoned. Several houses by Rietveld have been restored and examples of Rietveld's furniture are now to be found in important design collections. A high point in the recognition for Rietveld's oeuvre was the inscription of the Schröder House on the UNESCO World Heritage List in December 2000.

A monograph that presents Rietveld's most important designs and ideas along with relevant facts about his life as a cohesive whole has until now been lacking. Despite the materials at my disposal, filling this lacuna proved to be less straightforward than anticipated. One considerable difficulty was the absence of an extensive personal archive. Thus far I have been unable to find even something as basic as a photograph of the young Rietveld with his parents and siblings. Extensive correspondence, diaries or other documents in which Rietveld recorded his thoughts and ideas are not available. He published articles on a regular basis from the 1930s, but many of these texts are limited to fairly general arguments about the visual arts and his outlook on life. In the literature a great deal of attention has been devoted to the period when Rietveld was involved with the De Stijl circle. His significance for the architecture and design of the inter-war years and the period after World War II, in the Netherlands as well as abroad, has still barely been touched upon. This volume does not claim to be exhaustive either, but it is an attempt to present a more balanced picture, intended as an introduction for those intrigued by the Red-Blue Chair and the Schröder House who want to discover more about Rietveld and his work. At the same time I hope that it will spur others to undertake research into his oeuvre and its significance in a broader context.

While writing this book I have made grateful use of the findings of earlier research by Bertus Mulder, Marijke Kuper, Paul Overy and Peter Vöge. Besides discussions about Rietveld's work with these authorities, my conversations with Rob Dettingmeijer, who provided a commentary on the initial draft of the manuscript, Jurjen Creman, Gerrit Oorthuys, Marie-Thérèse van Thoor and many others have broadened my insight and understanding. A text does not automatically become a readable book, so I am also grateful to Molly Faries, Willemijn Fock, Felice van Marrewijk and Karlijn Stoffels for their suggestions and editorial comments. My colleagues at the Centraal Museum, including Bauke Aardema, Maarten Brinkman, Renger de Bruin, Cecile Ogink, Dea Rijper and Marije Verduijn, provided huge support in the gathering of material. Andrew May took on the difficult job of translating into concise English a Dutch text on a very Dutch subject in an even more Dutch context. Special thanks are due for his sensitive rendering of the many quotations from Rietveld and his contemporaries that is as faithful to their words as to the spirit of the times. There are two other people whose contribution I wish to mention specifically: Jaap Oosterhoff, who as guardian of the Rietveld Schröder Archive has for many years been a prop and stay in my research into Rietveld, and Nora Schadee, who has helped to style my texts with humour, precision and where necessary her own astute input.

And all of that for Rietje. – *Ida van Zijl*

Rietveld receiving an honorary doctorate from the Technical College in Delft on 11 January 1964

1. Conviction and vision

It's not religion that guides or has guided me.
It's not idealism that compels me. It's pure egoism,
the realization of my own existence.[1]
– Rietveld, 1964

The members of the audience in the auditorium of the Technical College in Delft (Technische Hogeschool te Delft), the predecessor of Delft University of Technology, must have pricked up their ears when Rietveld spoke these words on the acceptance of his honorary doctorate on 11 January 1964. If someone else, such as Le Corbusier (1887–1965), had stated something of similar import, the audience would probably have laughed and thought, we knew that already, but he's daring to say it out loud, all the same. Things sat differently with Rietveld. To those present, he represented the idealist *pur sang*, someone who concentrated on mass production and public housing because he believed that everyone had the right to fine surroundings. He was someone who had persevered, despite setbacks and a lack of recognition, someone whose political leanings were far to the left. So religion was not his mainspring? That was to be expected from a half-baked communist, but to assert that he was not an idealist? That smacked of false modesty, something that people were not accustomed to from Rietveld. Whether the tenor and meaning of these three phrases could have been conveyed to the audience in the limited time-span of a speech of thanks is debatable, but perhaps that was not Rietveld's main concern. He was probably more interested in taking stock for himself.

'It's not religion that guides or has guided me'

It seems so self-evident, but in the secularized Dutch society of today religion is much less a motive for someone's actions than it was for Rietveld's generation. At the dawn of the twentieth century, a broad spectrum of religiously or ideologically inspired emancipation movements was emerging. In the Netherlands the labour movement and the women's movement have been etched in the collective memory, but the various religious sects were also stirring. Within the Protestant church there was a groundswell of groupings that were pressing for autonomy and, just like the Catholics, were demanding equality in society. This development led to the 'pillarization' of Dutch society, a compartmentalization of the population based on religious or political ideology. Each pillar had its own social institutions, from church and political party to sports club and housing association, even its own particular shops, schools and hospitals.

Religion was also an all-defining factor in Rietveld's parental milieu. At the age of twenty he became a confirmed member of the strictly Calvinist Netherlands Reformed Church, a step that is not taken lightly or without conviction: a member of the congregation thereby declares that he or she subscribes to the doctrine as professed in that church, and can henceforth take part in the celebration of the Last Supper. The Netherlands Reformed Church was one of the main Protestant denominations in the country, though the formation of offshoots within this denomination was also fairly commonplace.[2] The reasons for such schisms are often difficult to understand for outsiders, but in essence the majority of conflicts revolve around the degree of personal responsibility for one's deeds. Many of these deeds, actually everything in which humankind takes pleasure, were wrong. 'The heart of the sons of men is fully set in them to do evil,' to quote Ecclesiastes. This sense of sin would colour Rietveld's younger years. The strict Calvinistic milieu in which Rietveld grew up was not, however, hidebound, closed or conservative in every respect. The vehemence of theological disputes went hand in hand with a highly developed sense of personal responsibility, the search for truth could prompt a great thirst for education and schooling, and the engagement with the world was expressed in a missionary urge to convince others. Development of one's talents was a duty, because the talents given by God had to be used for the common good, and ultimately one had to answer for one's deeds as an individual before the almighty Creator. This attitude moulded Rietveld's character and gave him the strength to search for his own path. This is how, as a seventy-year-old, he looked back on his youth:

From very early on I was also … aware of the relativity of everything, what we observe, appreciate and appraise … What my mother found most beautiful and best in life was considered bad and sinful by my father … We were raised with the duty to do the right thing and to shun evil, the material was base and bad whereas the spiritual, which I have never understood, was elevated and good. When this unfulfillable duty to elevate everything to the spiritual plane fell from my shoulders, through the understanding that all our actions are just incidental phenomena in the great scheme of things, then life became lighter for me. Then I understood that (pretence or no pretence) for us nothing can be more important than the delight in the temporal growth and temporal perpetuation of the separation of ourselves and the surroundings![3]

He failed to explain how or why this moral obligation was lifted from his shoulders. He never mentioned with whom he talked about such matters. It may have been Rietveld's private tutor in architecture, the architect P. J. C. Klaarhamer (1874–1954), who was responsible for sowing the first seeds of doubt. Klaarhamer had belonged to the same Church as Rietveld, but later renounced it.[4] Another possible interlocutor was Willem, Rietveld's younger brother by two years, who read classics at Utrecht University and in 1914 attended seminars in Leiden given by the philosopher G. J. P. J. Bolland, a neo-Hegelian whose ideas made a big impression on artists. Rietveld may also have become acquainted with the work of Spinoza and Kant, Hegel, Schopenhauer and Nietzsche via his brother.[5] One of Rietveld's first clients, H. G. J. Schelling (1888–1978), an architect for the Dutch Railways (Nederlandse Spoorwegen), was certainly an important conversation partner. He introduced Rietveld to the work of the Indian sage Rabindranath Tagore, which Rietveld was fond of quoting later on. Rietveld tried to involve his wife, Vrouwgien Rietveld-Hadders (1883–1957), in his personal development and wanted her to distance herself from traditional religion. 'Ger, what will you give me in return?,' was her alleged response.[6] Such a step would, in her eyes, cause nothing but misery. For his part, Rietveld sawed off the ornaments on the harmonium that he and Vrouwgien played when singing psalms and hymns, and once he ejected the minister from the house in a somewhat less than mild-mannered fashion.

It was no empty slogan that he did not allow himself to be guided by religion, even in his work. Over and against international, secular Modernism stood a conservative movement inspired by national traditions. From the 1930s to the mid-1950s, this traditionalism was prevalent in Dutch architecture. The Catholic architects from this school very much wanted to see religious conviction reflected in buildings. Their most outspoken representative was M. J. Granpré Molière (1883–1973), who was appointed professor at the Technical College in Delft in 1924. His work and that of his students was therefore denoted as the 'Delft School', a term later applied to all traditionalist architecture.[7] Two months after receiving his honorary doctorate at Delft in 1964, Rietveld was to be made an honorary member of the Association of Dutch Architects (Bond van Nederlandse Architecten, or BNA), at the same time as Granpré Molière.[8] Some of those listening to Rietveld's address in Delft were undoubtedly already aware of this piquant detail.

'It's not idealism that compels me'

That was a deliberate statement. When Rietveld produced his first experimental designs the world was awash with idealists, from advocates of world peace – the League of Nations was established on 25 January 1919 – to the supporters of the Third International, in which socialists, communists and anarchists were united in the struggle to bring about the socialist world revolution. All were convinced their utopias were within reach. In a similar vein, the founders of De Stijl wanted nothing less than to create new art for a new society. 'The new consciousness is prepared to realize the internal life as well as the external life,' reads the fourth precept of the De Stijl group's 1918 manifesto that was signed by Theo van Doesburg (1883–1931), Vilmos Huszár (1884–1960), Anthony Kok (1882–1969), Piet Mondrian (1872–1944) and Jan Wils (1891–1972).[9] It was formulated so generally that the painter Mondrian, whose ideas were inspired by theosophy, as well as the architect Wils, a hardline communist, felt that they could put their signatures to it.[10] From 1919 Rietveld was closely involved with this avant-garde group. For the first time he felt he belonged, and the idea that he was crazy, which he mentioned in an interview many years later, evaporated.[11] He threw himself into a world that unremittingly propagated the new. With hindsight it is difficult to ascertain the beliefs that Rietveld adhered to at the time. In his furniture designs the focus was already fixed on their spatial character, but whether this had social implications, and if so then what, remains unclear. In later texts his attitude towards De Stijl was somewhat detached, portraying De Stijl as a necessary phase in the renewal of visual art and architecture.

In the 1920s the circles in which Rietveld moved were expanding thanks to the publication of his work in the *De Stijl* journal. This exposure prompted Bruno Taut (1880–1938), Kurt Schwitters (1887–1948), El Lissitzky (1890–1941) and Mart Stam (1899–1986) to visit him in Utrecht. These avant-garde figures were driven by high-minded ideals. El Lissitzky and Stam were confirmed communists; Rietveld was a 'fellow traveller'. He never became a member of the Communist Party or, for that matter, any other political movement, but he was certainly active in clubs and associations that maintained close ties, officially or otherwise, with the left wing of the political spectrum, such as the Netherlands-New Russia Fellowship (Genootschap Nederland-Nieuw Rusland). Many Dutch artists and intellectuals, including the architect H. P. Berlage (1856–1934), were members of this society, which effectively danced to the tune of the Communist Party of the Soviet Union. In 1928 Rietveld became the architecture editor of the fellowship's journal and designed its vignette and cover.[12] Rietveld also sat on the board of the Utrecht chapter of the Dutch Film League (Nederlandse Filmliga), alongside the architect Sybold van Ravesteyn (1889–1983) and *jonkheer* M. R. Radermacher Schorer (1888–1956), a minor aristocrat who was director of an insurance company and a patron of the arts. This association was founded by the author and critic Menno ter Braak and the filmmaker Joris Ivens in 1927 to organize the private viewing of films not screened by the commercial cinemas.[13] Rietveld also organized lectures and took it upon himself to bring important exhibitions to Utrecht. All of this demonstrates his profound concern about developments in society, especially where these pertained to culture in general or his profession in particular. Rietveld had a close personal relationship with the architect J. J. P. Oud (1890–1963), co-founder of De Stijl, particularly in the 1920s and 30s.[14] In their correspondence, Rietveld reveals a side to his character that is much more emotional than his public appearances and published texts might suggest. The opening words of his first postcard to Oud, dated 19 August 1919, read, 'Esteemed Sir, I thank you for your letter and understand very well that you find it rather expensive.' Oud had asked Rietveld to furnish a model home in the blocks of housing he had designed for Rotterdam's new residential district of Spangen. Their correspondence soon became less formal in tone. On 23 January 1920, Rietveld wrote, 'Dear Oud (I will simply omit that Sir, which sounds so strange now) and I will simply write in the familiar form, which I do in my thoughts also – if that is not alright then just put me in my place – I can cope with just about anything.'[15] Rietveld regularly asked Oud for information and his opinion on a diversity of matters, while in return telling him his personal views on these topics and letting him know what he was working on. He often extolled the virtues of Oud's work and at that time Rietveld probably looked up to him as a role model. Oud was already internationally renowned for his public housing projects in Rotterdam and kept up an extensive network of contacts all over the world.

In the period 1920–40 Rietveld took an especially active and vocal interest in all kinds of social and

G. Rietveld

elke ware schepping (of ze in den vorm van uitvinding, gebouw, schilderij, dans of muziek verschijnt) verandert het inzicht, de eischen en de behoeften van den tijd en komt in botsing met nog heerschende eischen en behoeften uit vorige perioden.
een schepping moet dus de plaats **veroveren** in plaats van te beantwoorden aan de geldende eischen en de nood-zakelijkheid.

rietveld.

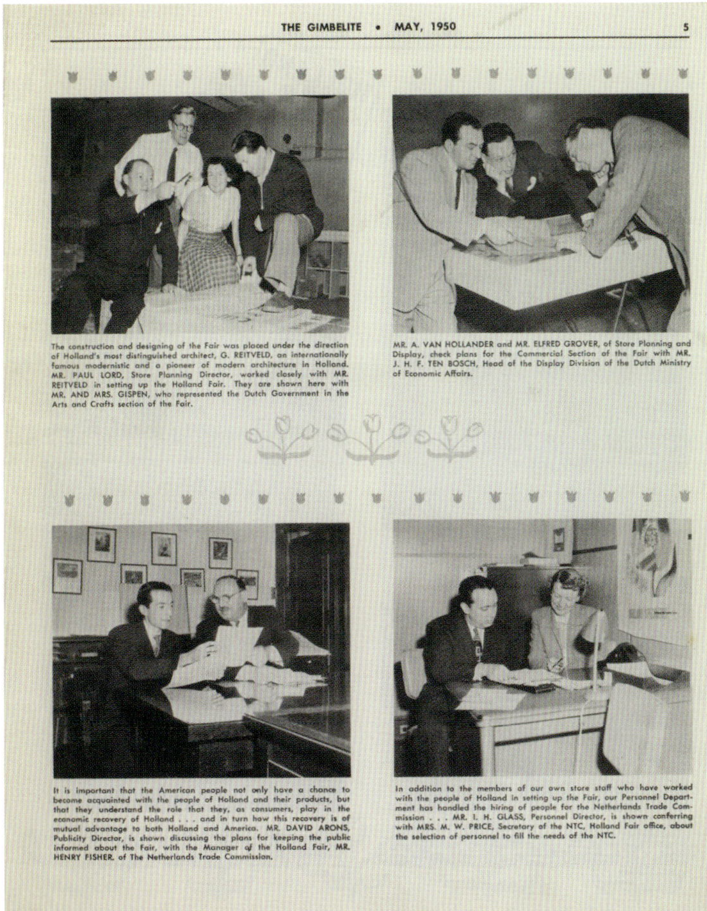

THE GIMBELITE • MAY, 1950 5

The construction and designing of the Fair was placed under the direction of Holland's most distinguished architect, G. REITVELD, an internationally famous modernistic and a pioneer of modern architecture in Holland. MR. PAUL LORD, Store Planning Director, worked closely with MR. REITVELD in setting up the Holland Fair. They are shown here with MR. AND MRS. GISPEN, who represented the Dutch Government in the Arts and Crafts section of the Fair.

MR. A. VAN HOLLANDER and MR. ELFRED GROVER, of Store Planning and Display, check plans for the Commercial Section of the Fair with MR. J. H. F. TEN BOSCH, Head of the Display Division of the Dutch Ministry of Economic Affairs.

It is important that the American people not only have a chance to become acquainted with the people of Holland and their products, but that they understand the role that they, as consumers, play in the economic recovery of Holland . . . and in turn how this recovery is of mutual advantage to both Holland and America. MR. DAVID ARONS, Publicity Director, is shown discussing the plans for keeping the public informed about the Fair, with the Manager of the Holland Fair, MR. HENRY FISHER, of The Netherlands Trade Commission.

In addition to the members of our own store staff who have worked with the people of Holland in setting up the Fair, our Personnel Department has handled the hiring of people for the Netherlands Trade Commission . . . MR. I. H. GLASS, Personnel Director, is shown conferring with MRS. M. W. PRICE, Secretary of the NTC, Holland Fair office, about the selection of personnel to fill the needs of the NTC.

Opposite page: Rietveld as a young man, c.1905 (top left); Rietveld with his wife, Vrouwgien Hadders, shortly after their marriage in 1911 (top right); Rietveld with his three oldest children, c.1920 (bottom left); Rietveld in *De Stijl 7*, 1927 (bottom right)

This page: Rietveld in *The Gimbelite*, May 1950 (top left); Rietveld with Willem Sandberg, c.1955–60 (top right); Rietveld with his great-grandson in the living area of the Schröder House, c.1963 (bottom)

cultural questions. 'It's not idealism that compels me' was primarily a declaration that he felt no need to exchange one creed for another, and in this he was just like Klaarhamer, about whom Rietveld would later write that this 'son of a minister, having outgrown the Calvinistic milieu, also shunned any other partisan affiliation'.[16] The relativism of human existence, of which Rietveld had become so convinced, translated itself into a marked open-mindedness. He maintained contact with all kinds of people and was incensed by individuals who claimed to be in the right and on those grounds denounced the work of others.

In 1940 he wrote to the editors of *De 8 en Opbouw*, a journal that was the mouthpiece of the Functionalist movement in Dutch architecture:

Having now resigned as a member of De 8 and the congress, I felt stubborn and stupid for going and separating myself from friends with whom I have nevertheless always felt the closest affinity of all. I can do nothing about this, but I think that the way in which art is being treated herein is terrible.

He was referring to an article in the journal about the 'Holland van 1859' Fire Insurance Company's headquarters in Dordrecht. The baroque extravagance of Van Ravesteyn's architecture here, when as an architect for the Dutch Railways he had initially produced highly functional buildings, elicited a scathing critique from the reviewer: 'This building reflects neither the common man nor the élite, i.e. [it speaks of] a haughty disdain for the great mass of afflicted humanity, for whom at this present time a great love is awakening.'[17] A year later, after joining a group excursion to 'De Kunstmin' theatre in Dordrecht, a project also designed by Sybold van Ravesteyn, Rietveld was laudatory in his comments about the building. His article concluded, 'It was therefore all the more agreeable that when viewing this playhouse conversion we were able to observe that mutual understanding and appreciation among architects with such diverse social priorities proved to be possible there.'[18]

By 1964, in his speech of thanks on receiving his honorary doctorate in Delft, Rietveld probably did not want to make any claim to idealism, because in practice the lofty ideals of his friends led to the destructive denunciation of anyone who thought differently. He considered it his duty as an architect to contribute to other people's opportunities for self-realization. To his audience he explained that he believed he could achieve this by realizing architecture that stirs the senses to activity and makes people aware of their personal existence. He also thought it important to encourage a way of life that is as little as possible at other people's or indeed the whole world's expense. He wanted to simplify the production process and gear it to new technological possibilities so that the heavy toil of the worker would be rendered obsolete. In that endeavour he tried to respect the ideas and wishes of each individual. In 1927 he therefore suggested to Oud that he place a questionnaire in *i10*, a Dutch avant-garde journal:

Mrs Schröder and I (and hopefully you, too) would thus like to make it possible for everyone, who must by necessity have an abode and cannot have a house built themselves, to contribute nevertheless to determining the new dwelling, group of dwellings or urban expansion.'[19]

Almost thirty years later Rietveld was still putting this idea into practice. In 1956 he punctiliously noted down all the observations and remarks voiced at residents' meetings in Hoograven, a new residential district in Utrecht for which he designed 388 housing units in 1954–57, and tried to resolve as many complaints as possible.[20] If that isn't idealism, then what is?

'It's pure egoism, the realization of my own existence'

Without a certain conviction it is impossible for someone to make choices or, as Rietveld formulated it, 'In order to be able in life to say yes in some cases and no in others, a more or less explicit stance is necessary, though I don't see how this can be anything but very relative.'[21] He was keen to convey this unequivocally to his audience in Delft:

It would be narrow-mindedly unnatural to imagine that our will and efforts (good or bad) (stupid or sensible) can be anything other than a sort of side-effect in the immeasurable and intangible cosmic happening ... This liberating thought, which at the same time destroys all our endeavours, does not, however, release us from the duty to limit our necessities of life to a minimum … There is, for example, joy in the creation and appreciation of works of art, in which the sensory value is not dependent on the quantity of material. And in architecture, in which greater functional merit can be ascribed to the quality of empty space than to the built mass.[22]

Rietveld was not an egoist, even though he claimed to be one, but he did have an irrepressible urge to express himself in his work. The fulfilment of this creative vocation did, however, present Rietveld with a real moral dilemma. It propelled him into a different world and he turned his attention to a new future, which resulted in him and his wife drifting apart. In 1924 he moved his studio to the ground floor of the Schröder House and a love affair blossomed with the house's commissioner, Truus Schröder. He tried to limit the negative impact of this selfish and in 'Reformed' eyes sinful choice by dividing his time and attention. It was, of course, no more than an uneasy compromise.
The private circumstances in which he found himself were as muddy as his work was lucid. The relationship with Truus was taboo and his circle of acquaintances took this public secrecy in their stride. Anecdotes and reminiscences about Rietveld commend his modesty, simplicity and cheerfulness. He was a cordial man. Seldom was there mention of the tensions in his private life and the inevitable disappointments in his career as an architect. He did not keep a diary and much personal correspondence is no longer extant, with the exception of the scrawl-filled postcards to Oud, but there, too, the content is basically limited to work and related matters. There is little to be read about his private affairs and Rietveld even continued to convey greetings from his wife to Oud, long after the permanent nature of his extra-marital relationship had become obvious. The taboo about their liaison meant that Rietveld and Schröder, who were both fairly introvert anyway, kept to themselves even more and were fairly isolated from the outside world. Truus's daughter Han wrote about this in 1986:

She made his position in our family and her relationship to him insufficiently clear to me, so that a sort of thin, transparent separation, a veil, developed between us, which was never broken down or resolved … M[other] was a sort of shadow figure her whole life, alongside and behind (but primarily behind) Rietveld. And that was a darned difficult position, of a complexity that he perhaps did not always understand.[23]

They most probably made a conscious choice to maintain this status quo. In the 1920s a divorce was indeed a scandal, but not impossible. In the avant-garde circles in which he moved, Rietveld would certainly not have become a pariah if he had chosen this course of action, but he remained with his wife and their six children. For them it was 'Father Rietveld', 'Mother Rietveld' and 'Aunt Schröder'.[24] Rietveld presented Truus Schröder to the outside world as his business partner or she remained in the background.[25] He moved in with her following his wife's death in 1957. Nevertheless, during a guided tour he gave for his 1959 exhibition at the Stedelijk Museum in Amsterdam, Rietveld still referred to Truus as a 'female interior architect who had very radical ideas about the employment of space … but also possessed spatial intuition', with whom he had built the Schröder House.[26] For her part, Truus Schröder kept silent about the nature and duration of her relationship with Rietveld for many years after his death. The first time she allowed something to be written about it openly was in 1974, in an interview with the journalist B. Kroon: 'There was more going on. Between the young architect and the young woman a rapport had developed … from which a love affair grew that would last for their entire lives.'[27] According to her daughter Han, it was a relief for Truus Schröder to admit this so openly. Rietveld never uttered a word about this aspect of his life. Perhaps his reticence about this development had something to do with the associated consequences for his relationship with his wife and children. For Bep, his eldest daughter, the tensions between her parents meant the end of a carefree, happy youth. Etched in her memory is receiving far less attention than she was accustomed to from that time forward. Rietveld's pedagogical view that you may be able to feed children but cannot actually raise them probably contributed to this as well.[28]
In practice, 'the realization of my own existence', as Rietveld termed it so finely, meant for him an uncertain livelihood as an architect and an extra-marital relationship with a woman who understood him,

stimulated him in his work and in addition supported him financially. If that isn't egoism, then what is? Those in the lecture hall who were familiar with Rietveld's personal history would certainly have been able to place this egoism. This does not mean that Rietveld's choices left him cold, but he believed that people had to create joy in their own lives; this was 'healthy egoism'.[29] He probably felt no compulsion to justify a choice once he had made it, nor to dwell for long upon the difficulties he encountered as a consequence. A rendering of account can be an implicit solicitation for approval, something that Rietveld was not seeking. He wanted, for once, to elucidate his ideas and worldview, and this speech of thanks provided him with the platform to do that.

'The reality that architecture can create is space'

The first fairly long text about architecture by Rietveld dates from 1928 and bears the title 'Inzicht' (Insight).[31] The article reads like a profession of faith. In short, almost autonomous, statements he formulates his philosophy of life and his beliefs about architecture. Here he first uses the definition of architecture as the creation of space. By then he was already forty years old. In later texts he expands upon these ideas, sometimes also mentioning people who inspired him or approvingly quoting some philosopher. A fundamental principle is that a human being becomes aware of the world and his or her ego, the self, through direct sensory experience. The development of this awareness is the essence of human existence.

Sight is the most important of the senses, which explains Rietveld's great interest in the functioning of the eye. Seeing can be divided into form, colour and space. With form we distinguish between concave, convex and flat, with colour between red, blue and yellow, and with space between in, around and between.[31] The purpose of art is to make possible that direct sensory experience and the 'becoming conscious' that ensues from this. According to Rietveld, the visual arts, namely painting, sculpture and architecture, correspond to the three elements of seeing: painting to colour, sculpture to form, architecture to space. However, when the senses are stimulated simultaneously, the experience of reality is less intense. He was therefore not a proponent of the merging of the visual arts, an approach long advocated by Van Doesburg; each discipline must seek its own path. The combination of miscellaneous sensory stimuli in a single art form is fundamentally wrong, hence his categorical condemnation of film with sound and his attempts to design a stereoscopic cinema where the image becomes three-dimensional. This principle, which implies a negation of the narrative character of the medium of film, had many supporters within the Dutch Film League.

Architecture also had to concentrate on a single sense: the eye, the organ through which space is perceived. Space as a concept made its entrance in the final decade of the nineteenth century in German treatises about visual art and architecture.[32] Berlage was the first person in the Netherlands to introduce space as a fundamental quality of architecture.[33] In the 1920s the concept was already so well established that it could mean anything and everything to the beholder, and every architect attached a personal significance to it. Rietveld's views on this cannot be traced back to a single source.[34] It is, however, unequivocal that space formed the crux of his work from as early as 1918. The analogy between his early furniture pieces and the work of the painter Bart van der Leck, with its emphasis on space that remains uninterrupted, suggests that the germ of Rietveld's preoccupation with space was sown in the studio shared by Klaarhamer and Van der Leck, albeit through the work that Rietveld was exposed to there rather than by theoretical treatises. Nor is it possible to deduce any all-embracing theory about architectonic space from Rietveld's texts. He repeatedly quoted an aphorism by the Indian sage Tagore: 'Through limitation of the limitless, truth becomes reality.' He also mentioned Schopenhauer's statement – 'Die Farbe ist die qualitative Teilung der Tätigkeit der Retina' (Colour is the qualitative division of the activity of the retina) – as the foundation on which he could continue to build in his work.[35] This does not necessarily imply that Rietveld had extensively studied or fully grasped the concepts of these two philosophers or any other mentioned in his notes. They primarily evoke the character of an era, a popularized philosophical context that influenced architectural discourse in the early twentieth century. In his texts Rietveld comes across as an intelligent mind, a keen-witted observer, someone who thinks about his words and actions, and needs to place his work in a broader social context. Rietveld was not, however, a profound thinker, neither as a writer nor as a speaker. In this respect he is no exception among his confrères, either then or now. He used texts and sometimes just individual sentences that offered him some footing or provided an explanation for his own experiences and transformed these into a theoretical foundation for his work. The sources from which Rietveld drew his ideas are in the final analysis not that interesting; what matters was that for him the sum total constituted a coherent whole in which he found a justification for the choices he made in his life and work. This applies as much to the task he set himself as an architect as it does to the methods he employed.

'designing as well … as possible'

For Rietveld the work of the architect possessed a moral dimension: 'The unity of all the requirements that people can justifiably ask of architecture is an elementary spatial experience; no goal whatsoever can be in conflict with this. This is the joy that architecture can bring. Material and the method of working must be subordinate to this.'[36] Every human being must have the possibility of experiencing reality and through becoming aware of it achieve personal growth. The perception of space is central to the architectural task, but on moral grounds Rietveld came to the conclusion that the architect's primary task is the improvement of the living conditions of the masses. Industrial production is a prerequisite for this. The experiments with which he entered the public arena were therefore the design of public housing and furniture production based on industrialization and prefabrication.

Industrial production with the sole objective of mass production for mass consumption was, however, anathema to Rietveld:

If we think about the masses of things that are produced en masse every day for no other reason than that they can be sold, without it being certain to what extent they are useful to our society, we shall not without scruple cooperate in stimulating the sale of all these things even more by designing them as well as possible.

To this he added that everyone must search his own conscience in order to determine 'to what he definitely wants to contribute and to what he does not'.[37] Rietveld made no pronouncements about the political implications of his social beliefs, though his membership of various associations and participation in all kinds of activities clearly nailed his colours to the mast. He did not, however, regard it as his task or expertise to serve as a mouthpiece:

Here I deliberately avoid mentioning the social changes, which have occurred wholly in parallel with innovations in architecture; I do this first of all because these changes cannot be treated as incidental events, and secondly because I was to talk about architecture and I want to deal with this based entirely on the considerations of the architect. These considerations are however always dominated by social necessity.[38]

Nevertheless, personal development ought not to be achieved at other people's expense, at least not at too great an expense. Perhaps this outlook has its roots in Rietveld's Christian background, although he insisted with almost desperate tenacity that this was an objective social law rather than a moral conviction. In a letter dating from 1954 he wrote:

Social justice arises, irrespective of the struggle of political and other idealists, as a necessary consequence of the use of the machine. i.e. as a necessary consequence of human ingenuity, regardless of the underlying motive which activated this ingenuity: selfishness or love of one's neighbour.[39]

Rietveld's ideas and views are not that remarkable and their theoretical basis is weak, but as a whole they offer insight into his position and conduct. It is certainly unique that he made the experience of space central to his work so early on. It is something of a coincidence that, as the son of a cabinetmaker, he made the obvious choice to conduct his experiments in this domain, but this did enable him to penetrate to the very core. 'Small things offer more possibilities to develop a style,' he commented in an article about Oud's work in 1951.[40] That is what makes Rietveld's position in the twentieth century unique.

Rietveld and the staff of his workshop on Adriaen van Ostadelaan, Utrecht, 1918. Rietveld is seated in an uncoloured armchair. Around 1923 he began to paint his furniture in several colours, including the famous Red-Blue version of this chair.

2. Summer 1918

The chair is also gradually freeing itself of its complicated past, because mechanical production methods mean that new materials and new constructive discoveries are becoming more important than differences in form.[1]
– Rietveld 1930

The photographer has gone to stand in the road in order to fit the whole group into the frame. Five pairs of eyes peer into the lens: three teenagers in aprons and smocks, cigarettes between their fingers, lean nonchalantly against the sill of the large workshop window; a kid with a hoop, intrigued by all the goings-on, stands next to them; in the middle sits the cabinetmaker, who is also wearing a smock and holding a cigarette. He does not smile, but stares intently towards the photographer. The scene's *pièce de résistance* is the chair in which Rietveld is seated, an armchair constructed from wooden slats and boards. He wanted to send photographs of his work to a new periodical, *De Stijl*, and this decision to step into the limelight was a crucial moment. Rietveld was unsure whether it would succeed and nobody could foresee where it would all eventually lead, but he must have sensed how important a moment it was. Hence this official portrait of the cabinetmaker and his chair, of the artist and his manifesto.

Rietveld had taken this step on the advice of the architect Robert van 't Hoff (1887–1979), who had recently built a summerhouse in the village of Huis ter Heide, about 10 km (6 miles) east of Utrecht. This villa-like design was strongly influenced by the work of Frank Lloyd Wright (1867–1959), whom Van 't Hoff had visited the previous year in the United States of America. The house's owner, J. N. Verloop, had ordered furniture from Rietveld for the house: copies of Wright's chairs for the Coonley House and designs by Rietveld himself. Van 't Hoff was keen to see the result and therefore visited Rietveld's workshop at the Adriaen van Ostadelaan in Utrecht. Rietveld gave an account of this encounter some forty years later. 'Well, that's good … that could have turned out worse,' was Van 't Hoff's reaction to the Wright furniture, Rietveld related in a later interview. This approval encouraged him to inform his client that the things he made himself were quite different: 'He simply had to see them, so I went to fetch them, and then he said: "We've just set something up … a movement. You belong to it."'[2]

The little boy from Utrecht, by his own account a shy dreamer, born on 24 June 1888 and brought up in a respectable, strictly Calvinist, lower-middle-class milieu, had grown into a self-assured thirty-year-old, brimming with ideas and the proprietor of a business with three employees. Rietveld's father, Johannes Cornelis Rietveld, was a cabinetmaker, and his mother, Elisabeth van der Horst, was a housewife. They had two daughters and four sons and from 1891 lived above the furniture-making workshop at Poortstraat 98 in Utrecht. Gerrit Thomas Rietveld was their second child. It was taken for granted that the boys would go and work in the business; the girls would remain at home until they married. An exception was made for Willem, Gerrit's younger brother by two years: he was a sickly child but had a fine head on his shoulders and went to university. Gerrit left school at the age of eleven and a half and his first assignment as an apprentice in his father's workshop was to design a small suite of furniture for the gatehouse of Castle Zuylen, close to Utrecht, and

Table and three chairs for the gatehouse of Castle Zuylen, Oud-Zuilen, c.1906. These items were designed and manufactured by Rietveld while he was working at his father's workshop.

Rietveld with other draughtsmen in C. J. A. Begeer's workshop, Utrecht, c.1913

assist with its execution. His father supplied furniture, wainscoting and complete interiors in any desired style, in keeping with the prevailing fashion. Rietveld learned all the finesses of the trade, including complex carpentry skills, such as the carving of ornaments, veneering and French-polishing. It was hard work, he would comment later.

In 1904, aged sixteen, he enrolled for evening classes in the industrial arts at The Utrecht Museum of Applied Arts (Het Utrechtsch Museum van Kunstnijverheid), where he attended courses in drawing, painting, anatomy, the theory of proportions, modelling, technical drawing and the theory of style and ornamentation. One of his teachers was P. J. Houtzagers (1857–1944), a reputable architect in Utrecht.[3] Houtzagers' projects included the design of detached villas in the lanes around the Wilhelminapark, which had been opened in 1898. This residential district, intended for the well-to-do middle classes, was one of the first planned urban expansions at the end of the nineteenth century; it was not far from the Rietveld family home.

Rietveld made a good impression at school. In the course year 1907–8 he received a prize as a highly promising student. The training bore fruit. For the conference room of the Utrecht Mortgage Bank (Utrechtse Hypotheekbank, similar to a building society), which was restored and renovated by Houtzagers, Rietveld's father supplied the furniture and wainscoting, while Rietveld painted the tympanum above the doors with putti depicting the four classical elements: water, fire, earth and air.[4]

Rietveld's training after primary school was typical of a pattern in which an increasingly emancipated working class is supported by the more enlightened middle classes. Important businesspeople, including the Van Beuningen and the Fentener van Vlissingen and Begeer families, were intent on modernizing the city swiftly. Their liberal views and approach meant that every talented individual was welcome to contribute. Carel J. A. Begeer (1883–1956) in particular presented Rietveld with many opportunities. This cultural entrepreneur, who in 1910 became director of the C. J. Begeer Royal Utrecht Silverware Factory (Koninklijke Utrechtsche Fabriek van Zilverwerken

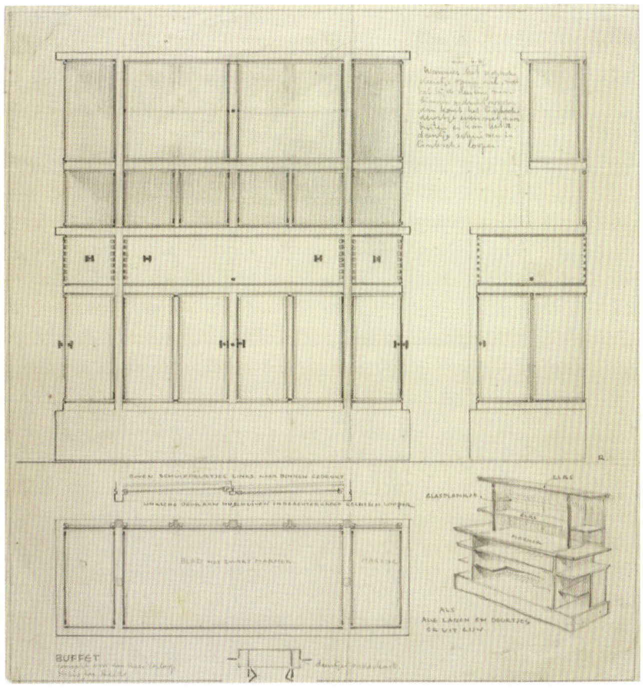

Design for a sideboard for J. N. Verloop, 1915–17, in the style of Frank Lloyd Wright

Upright armchair, 1908

Portrait of Anthonie Begeer, 1910–12

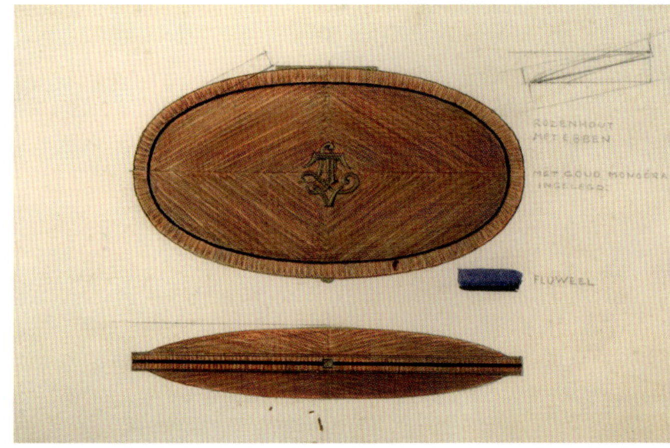

Design for a jewellery box, c.1905–15

Conference room, Utrecht Morgage Bank, Utrecht, c.1906. The furniture and panelling were executed in Rietveld's father's workshop. Rietveld had a large part in both the design and its realization, and he executed the paintings.

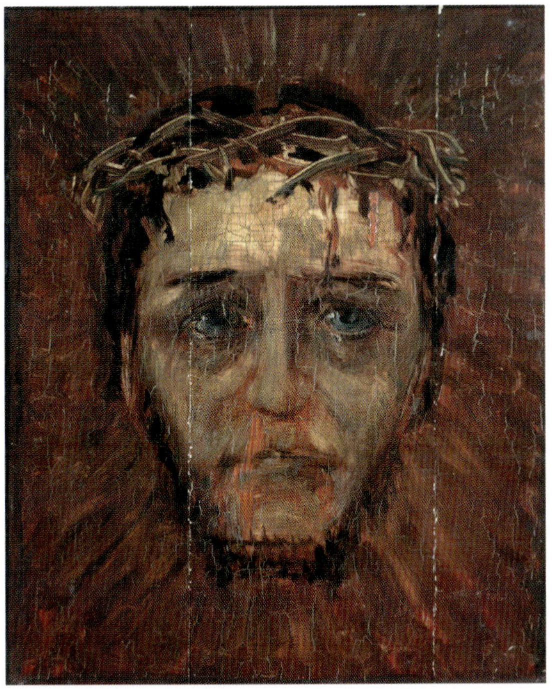

O Haupt voll Blut und Wunden, painting, 1911–12

Showroom for C. J. A. Begeer, Utrecht, c.1910

Wordrobe (top), table (bottom left) and cupboard (bottom right), all 1911. These three items, designed for Rietveld's own home, in Utrecht, demonstrate the range of his work at this time. The wardrobe is relatively conventional, while the drop-leaf table has the idiosyncratic combination of a wooden tabletop and iron legs. Most unusual is the white painted cupboard; its very cheap material and painted accents are distinctively new elements that Rietveld would continue to develop in his pursuit of cheap mass-produced furniture with a more clearly spatial composition.

C. J. Begeer) and was a creditable designer himself, worked with various artists and designers. He saw potential in the promising young man. Immediately after the project for the Utrechtse Hypotheekbank, he commissioned Rietveld to make two showrooms, one in Louis XIV style and the other in Louis XV style. Between circa 1909 and 1913 Rietveld was employed by him as a draughtsman and modeller for medals, silverware and other decorative objects.[5] Around this time Rietveld also painted the portrait of Carel Begeer's father, who had died in 1910, and designed the tombstone for E. Nijland, former headmaster of the boys' section of the Dutch Reformed High School (Nederlandsch Hervormde Burgerschool) in Utrecht. A year after his marriage, Rietveld became a member of the Utrecht association for visual artists, the 'Love of Art' Painting and Drawing Society (Schilder- en teekenkundig genootschap 'Kunstliefde'). For the members' exhibition that opened on 12 April 1912 he submitted three portraits and the dramatic painting, *O Haupt voll Blut und Wunden* (O Sacred Head, now wounded).[6]

Rietveld's tutor, the architect P. J. C. Klaarhamer, was the first person to open the adolescent's eyes to a totally new and fascinating world. This is what Rietveld wrote in his 'In Memoriam' for Klaarhamer in 1954:

It is to the architect Klaarhamer that I personally owe the basis of my professional expertise, because I was one of the few people permitted to be his student for several years. Although he had no high expectations of me, he would work with me in his study at the Korte Janstraat until deep in the night. When I first met him, around 1910, the painter B. v. d. Leck and Klaarhamer both had a workspace in a middle-class house on the Herenstraat in Utrecht. The narrow rooms grew, in my mind, into panoramas of the future.[7]

It was in these years that Rietveld produced his upright armchair, probably the first piece of furniture that was made for his personal pleasure rather than on commission. In all its simplicity it is a splendid example of Rietveld's radical originality. The pinewood components, devoid of any decoration, are affixed to each other at right angles with mortise-and-tenon joints. The backrest, a strip of leather, is affixed to the rear posts with copper tacks. The seat's unattached covering of leather is cut away at the corners and thus remains in place. The chair is structurally robust because of the panel of the seat and the armrests that connect the front and back legs. A horizontal strut between the back legs gives it additional rigidity. It could hardly have been simpler and was at that time unprecedented, with the exception of traditional stools and benches that were used in the countryside and in workshops. For Rietveld simplicity was not an aesthetic ideal, which is how he differed from other 'modern' furniture designers of the time, who used quality oak for simple furniture and introduced subtle decorations in the structure by adding black painted studs.

In 1911, at the age of twenty-three, Rietveld married Vrouwgien Hadders, who was five years his senior. They went to live at Oude Gracht Tolsteegzijde 61 (now Oudegracht 231) in Utrecht and moved to Ooftstraat 23 some two years later, where their first child was born on 26 October 1913. The family grew at regular intervals until there were six children in all: Bep (Elisabeth, b. 1913), Egbert (b. 1915), Tutti (Vrouwgien, b. 1918), Jan (Johannes Cornelis, b. 1919), Gerrit (b. 1921) and Wim (William, b. 1924). It goes without saying that Rietveld made the furniture for his own home. An octagonal table and a tall, slender cupboard echo the style of contemporary furniture of the 1910s: a frame with panelling of plain oak. More idiosyncratic are the iron cuffs used to attach the legs to the seat of a long bench and a drop-leaf table with a chassis of curved iron bands. Truly exceptional is the linen cupboard with two hinged doors. The twelve hinge points, three to the side and three in the middle of each door, are painted over with a small red rectangle. The screws that attach the beadboards to the framework are clearly visible. The top is crowned by a slightly overhanging ledge, while the substructure of the cupboard also protrudes minimally, so that it stands, as it were, on a low table. Thanks to the use of oak and the expert construction, the octagonal table and the tall cupboard are fine examples of living-room furniture. The 'beadboard' linen cupboard, as Rietveld called it because of the cheap material used, is hardly deserving of such a label.

While working at the Begeer workshop, Rietveld had met Erich Wichmann (1890–1929) and Jan W.

Eisenlöffel (1876–1957). Wichmann dabbled as an artist, but was a flamboyant personality first and foremost, anti-bourgeois and socially and culturally active in many domains. Eisenlöffel was the leading Dutch silversmith of the early twentieth century. His work belongs to the so-called Nieuwe Kunst (New Art) school, a pared-down, geometrical variant of Art Nouveau. Like many other innovators, he was convinced that industrialization would bring well-designed utilitarian objects within everyone's reach. Thanks to these two striking artists, Rietveld came to the realization that designing furniture and other objects for the interior presented opportunities for innovation as well.[8] He decided to return to the trade of cabinetmaker. That is possibly why he moved to Ooftstraat 23 in 1913, a corner property owned by his father with a shop-cum-workspace on the ground floor. His father's furniture-making workshop was just a stone's throw away. Rietveld had become an adult, with enough work to support himself and his family as well as time for his own experiments.

Rietveld and Utrecht

The city of Utrecht grew rapidly during the second half of the nineteenth century. The laying of various railways and the digging of the Merwede Canal – an improved link between the Rhine and the port of Amsterdam – transformed the city into an important transport node that served the whole province and beyond. Better accessibility attracted new industry and tertiary services, creating employment opportunities and resulting in a tripling of the population. Urban development expanded beyond the city's moats.[9] Utrecht University's professors, the engineers of the Dutch Railways (Nederlandse Spoorwegen), the result of the merger of two railway companies in 1917, and directors from other business sectors constituted a cultural élite that was enthusiastically interested in the new. People made each other's acquaintance at the various cultural associations and societies in the city. Some of them emerged as Maecenases and hosted salons, such as *jonkheer* M. R. Radermacher Schorer, a minor aristocrat and director of the Brand-Waarborg-Maatschappij, a fire insurance company.[10] Although Utrecht had a fairly insular and hierarchic social structure, in these circles the artists and art lovers treated each other as equals. The contradistinctions were adhered to less rigidly than in a city like Amsterdam, where differences of political and cultural opinion led to uncompromising standpoints. This still pertains as a remarkable feature of social relations in Utrecht.

Rietveld garnered a certain reputation among the progressive cultural élite in this booming city. J. N. Verloop, who had ordered the 'Wright furniture' from Rietveld, was not the only one who came knocking on the door of Rietveld's father for 'modern furniture', in the knowledge that they would be referred to his son, who had an interest in and talent for the innovative. A suite of furniture and a sideboard designed by Klaarhamer in 1915 are known to have been produced by Gerrit Rietveld.[11] Rietveld also produced furniture to designs by Sybold van Ravesteyn, an architect for the Dutch Railways who in his later work developed an idiosyncratic, more baroque style.[12] Others purchased Rietveld's experimental furniture from early on. The engineer J. H. Maronier, who also worked for the railways, owned three small tables that were probably produced around 1915.[13] The engineer H. G. J. Schelling occupied a special place among this company of progressive, culture-loving railway employees.[14] He was a close colleague of Van Ravesteyn and in the 1920s served as chief of the Dutch Railways' architecture department for the southeast region. He and Rietveld became close friends. They designed furniture together and talked about architecture, politics and philosophy – in sum, about life.

Thanks to Klaarhamer, Rietveld was able to keep abreast of the latest developments. In addition, almost all the important books and periodicals were available to him in the library of the 'Love of Art' ('Kunstliefde') society.[15] However, to truly understand such material it was essential for Rietveld, whose education was limited to six years of elementary school and a few years of vocational training, to discuss this subject matter with others. Schelling was Rietveld's 'sparring partner' when it came to the assimilation of these new insights in actual designs. The close bond between them during these years was so important to Rietveld that he displayed a cupboard designed by Schelling in Gallery II of his 1958 retrospective exhibition in Utrecht with the caption '"First attempts at innovation" ±1908 – ±1915'.[16] The furniture that Rietveld produced for himself and

Drawing table for J. H. Maronier, c.1915–22

Child's cot (top left and right) and playpen (bottom) for H. G. J. Schelling, 1918

Convertible child's chair, 1922. In 1918 Rietveld designed this chair for H. G. J. Schelling, coloured light green with a red cushion. This was the first piece of Rietveld's furniture to be published in *De Stijl*. Four years later he made another one for W. G. Witteveen in red, blue, yellow and black.

for the Schelling family between 1911 and 1918 is a somewhat motley collection and cannot always be dated precisely. Schelling married in 1916 and asked Rietveld to make a cupboard, a sideboard, a table, a frame for posters, a hat stand and an umbrella stand. The cupboard is almost an exact copy of Rietveld's linen cupboard from five years earlier. The birth of Schelling's eldest daughter, Johanna Karin, on 19 May 1918, led to a new series of furniture: a cot, a commode, a baby's chair and a playpen. Bep, Rietveld's eldest daughter, was convinced that her father made the cot for her birth in 1913 and gave it to the Schelling family later on. The style of this fairly massive piece of furniture, which is comprised of a box standing on a base with four stylized female figures at its corners, favours the earlier dating. A text is carved out around the lower part of the sides of the box: 'two lives made one and visible as one / O love thou art a child / you were hidden in my heart as its desire / Tagore.' Schelling was a devotee of the author of these lines, the Indian sage Tagore, and owned all his volumes of poetry, but the first collection in English translation was not published until 1913, so it seems plausible that the cot was indeed made for the birth of Schelling's daughter in 1918. It is conceivable that Schelling played a major part in the design of the cot, as well as in the design of the commode with a walnut veneer, which are both unusually lavish for a Rietveld design.

The influence of clients might also explain Rietveld's graphic work from this period and the figures for the facade of the jewellery shop overlooking the Oudkerkhof square in Utrecht that he designed for Cornelis Begeer (1883–1948), the brother of his former employer Carel. The style of the latter is in keeping with the Symbolism of the highly popular painter Jan Toorop (1858–1928) and the ornamentation inspired by the Orient, as was employed by the architect K. P. C. de Bazel (1869–1923). By 1917 this type of decoration could hardly be termed progressive.

Truly innovative was the baby's high-chair that Rietveld made for Schelling. A baby's chair is a complicated piece of furniture because of the combination of functions: a toddler must be able to sit, play, eat and spend a penny in it comfortably, without hurting him or herself or falling out. In his explanation of the design,

Birth announcement, 1918 (top); logo, 1917 (bottom). Rietveld designed this logo for himself, using relatively old-fashioned lettering influenced by Jugendstil, probably on moving to his own workshop on Adriaen van Ostadelaan in 1917; he used a similar lettering style on a birth announcement for Johanna Karin Schelling, the daughter of H. G. J. Schelling, in 1918.

Rietveld also mentioned the criteria of adjustability, being washable, and being strong but not overly heavy.[17] It took him some effort to reconcile all these requirements in a clear-cut three-dimensional form. The panels of the upper section are attached to the frame by slender leather straps. Little pegs were used to fix these straps into the holes in the plank-like boards. This 'soft' lattice-work closed up the gaps through which a child might fall; it was an ingenious but elaborate flash of inspiration and therefore not wholly satisfactory. For the chassis, which is a small playpen when folded out, he employed a peg-and-hole construction method with dowels – small cylindrical pegs inserted into holes drilled into adjacent parts. Moreover, such holes can be drilled at any chosen point and, according to Rietveld, the dowel joint allowed greater freedom than the standard mortise-and-tenon when positioning the component parts, as well as making possible a clearly defined form, because both the posts and the rails can extend beyond the point of junction. This prevents a rail and a post forming a right angle at the joint, which then acts as the boundary of a plane, an effect that Rietveld was keen to avoid. Such a dowel joint was also simple to make, according to Rietveld, and therefore better suited to modern production methods.

The first argument is especially important, not only distinguishing the baby's chair from Rietveld's earlier designs but also from the work of his great predecessors, such as Charles Rennie Mackintosh (1868–1928), Frank Lloyd Wright and H. P. Berlage. The back of the baby's high-chair is reminiscent of the Ladderback Chair by Mackintosh, but Rietveld was focused on something completely different. The linear, decorative form of the Mackintosh chair is aimed at integrating the item of furniture into the overall design of the interior like an ornament: a simple but extremely elegant variation on Art Nouveau principles. Rietveld, by contrast, had found a method that made it possible for him to break open the closed form of an item of furniture and create a spatial structure. It was, as he sensed with instinctive acuity, the dawn of something utterly new. It was a complete departure from, for example, the modern furniture by Klaarhamer, which Rietveld had actually fabricated. He commented on these designs by Klaarhamer more than forty years later:

Though I admired these chairs greatly I found them overly rounded-off in form rather than seeing a future in them. I saw it more as an end period… [T]his was, of course, Berlage's influence as well, and he perfected it in such manner that you could not take it any further and I noticed fairly quickly that it was impossible.[18]

Schelling's children were ideal guinea pigs. The baby's high-chair and a playpen, which was also constructed using dowel joints, were followed by a baby's high-chair to a different design, a child's washstand and a low child's chair, all dating from circa 1921.[19]

The Red-Blue Chair

Rietveld was able to concentrate on these experiments because he had opened his own workshop at Adriaen van Ostadelaan 93 in 1917. The freedom of being his own master meant that his professional development gained momentum. In 1918, a year that was a turning point, Rietveld also produced the first version of the Red-Blue Chair, then still unpainted and perhaps better described as the 'slat armchair', the key to his oeuvre, the manifesto of his ideas. In 1919 he described the essence of the design as follows:

With this chair an attempt has been made to allow each component simply to be what it is, and that in the most elementary form according to function and material, in the form that is the most responsive, through proportionality, to attaining harmony with the whole. The construction helps to interconnect the parts without mutilating them, to ensure that no part dominates or is subordinate to the others, in order that above all the whole stands free and clear in space and the form wins from the material. This wood construction makes it possible to construct a large chair like this with rails of 2.5 × 2.6 cm.[20]

He made the components into visually distinct elements and subsequently assembled them into a spatial composition that is not dictated by constructive joints. By allowing the slanting back and seat to continue beyond the frame at the same angle he detached the parts that support the body from the structural frame.

This is a logical elaboration of Berlage's analysis of the archetype, the Egyptian chair, in his book *Over Stijl in Bouw- En Meubelkunst* (On Style in Architecture and Furniture).[21] Rietveld had undoubtedly read this book, which was published in 1908 and reprinted in 1917, and he would also have seen diverse applications of this principle in chair designs by Berlage, Klaarhamer, Wright and Mackintosh, whether in actuality or as illustrations. The distinction between the seat and the frame as realized by Berlage in imitation of the German architect and architectural theorist Gottfried Semper (1803–79) was, however, of no interest to Rietveld. His approach stood closer to developments in the visual arts: he dissects the shape of the furniture, simplifies the components to the most elementary geometrical form and strips the material of its texture. What remains are visually defined elements that are assembled into a three-dimensional composition. The method resembles the process of abstraction and reduction, the *doorbeelding* or 'through-imaging' that the artist Bart van der Leck devised in 1918, simplifying figurative subjects into geometric planes in primary colours, separated from each other by a white background left visible.

In 1919 Van der Leck presented a solo exhibition at the Voor de Kunst (For Art) society in Utrecht, of which Rietveld was a member. Rietveld must have been familiar with this work, all the more so because he had already met Van der Leck many years earlier at Klaarhamer's studio.[22] Rietveld's receptiveness towards this kind of visual art enabled him to go a step further than Berlage and Klaarhamer. Rietveld may well have modestly stated in 1963 that when he made that chair he had never thought that it would be so important for himself and possibly also for others, but at the same time he knew very well what he was doing, because in one and the same breath he added, 'And when I got the chance to make a house based on the same principles as that chair, I seized it eagerly.'[23]

Rietveld, c.1924

3. The cabinetmaker of De Stijl

I would have liked to have seen whether my small items of furniture – in which I also always try to avoid enclosing the space, really would … allow the space here to continue.[1]
– Rietveld 1920

Rietveld could hardly have wished for a better moment to make his debut among the international avant-garde than July 1919. World War I had officially ended on 11 November 1918. Now that frontiers had been reopened, the contact between artists from across Europe flourished once more. People were eager to travel, and for those who could not afford to the many avant-garde publications provided a wealth of information from abroad. The war had not passed unnoticed even in the neutral Netherlands: mobilization, a million refugees primarily from Belgium, and the limited supply of basic foodstuffs had stirred up plenty of social unrest. Nevertheless, in many respects life had continued as normal and the country's enforced isolation had also presented new opportunities.

During the war years Theo van Doesburg established contacts with many artists, some of whom were more or less forced to spend the war period in the Netherlands.[2] In the first half of 1917 he hatched the plan to start a journal and the first issue of *De Stijl* was published that October.[3] The intellectual triumvirate formed by Van Doesburg together with Piet Mondrian and J. J. P. Oud would in a short time garner high regard for the journal. In the July 1919 edition of *De Stijl*, Van Doesburg published the baby's chair that Rietveld had made for Schelling and two months later he published an illustration of the first, unpainted version of the slat armchair.[4] Van Doesburg waxed lyrical about Rietveld's designs. He describes the slat armchair as 'a slender spatial animal … [an] unintentional but unmerciful treatment of open spaces', and likens it to a painting by Giorgio de Chirico.[5]

Before 1918 Rietveld must have felt somewhat isolated, despite his contacts with Schelling and others. It is, for example, surprising that he apparently had not met Van Doesburg, who had been billeted in Utrecht from September 1915 to February 1916. Besides his military duties, Van Doesburg gave lectures for Utrecht's art-loving public and mixed with the same artists as Rietveld, such as Erich Wichmann and Bart van der Leck. That Rietveld for many years hid his work out of timidity, as he is alleged to have told Bibeb in a 1958 interview, seems somewhat far-fetched, though broadly speaking the tenor of this statement was correct.[6] Until 1919 Rietveld had shied away from the limelight.

The publication of Rietveld's work in *De Stijl* gave his career and life in general a considerable boost. It created a market for his work, both one-off purchases and fabrication on commission. His buyers were art lovers who purchased the occasional item for themselves, or architects and artists who wanted to furnish interiors they had designed with suitable furniture. On a few occasions Rietveld was commissioned to supply a whole suite of furniture. He also submitted his work to exhibitions in the Netherlands and abroad, often receiving favourable reviews. This did not generate floods of orders, but it spread his name and reputation and encouraged him to continue with his experiments. In actual assignments he could, moreover, demonstrate where all this was actually leading. Was he able to give other types of furniture

Sideboard, 1919 (left); upright chair, 1918 (right). These were two of Rietveld's pieces used in model housing by J. J. P. Oud in the Spangen district of Rotterdam in 1920 (bottom). Other items included an an armchair, a table, and a frame over the mantel. Variants on this furniture were produced and used in various settings, including the home of Bart de Ligt and of P. J. Elling. The original sideboard of Elling was destroyed by fire, but a reconstruction was made by Rietveld in the 1950s.

Left: Drawing for a white table with blue, yellow and red armchairs, c.1925

Right: Child's chair, 1919, as published in *De Stijl* in 1923

Bottom: Red-Blue Chair, c.1923

Side table, 1923

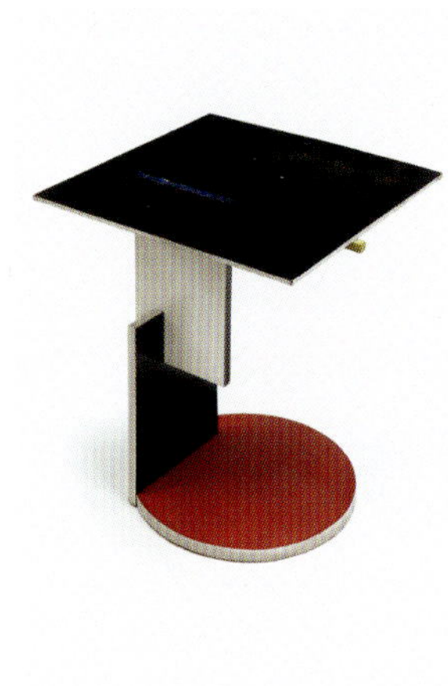

Military Chair, designed for the Catholic Military Home, Utrecht, 1923

'Space-Colour-Composition', in collaboration with Vilmos Huszár, 1923, as published in *l'Architecture Vivante* (1924)

Berlin Chair, 1923. Designed for the 'Space-Colour-Composition'

the same spatial quality as the slat armchair and what was the effect when these pieces stood together in a single space? 'I would have liked to have seen whether my little items of furniture – in which I also always try not to enclose space, would really … leave the space here uninterrupted,' he wrote to Van Doesburg on 28 February 1920. He had made a table and two chairs for a room painted to a colour scheme by Van Doesburg at the home of the clergyman Bart de Ligt in Katwijk aan Zee. However, when Rietveld visited, the furniture was yet to arrive.[7]

Rietveld was at that time working on a suite of furniture for Oud's residential blocks (1918–19) for the new working-class estate of Spangen in Rotterdam, for which Van Doesburg designed the colour schemes for the interiors.[8] The model home was furnished with a sideboard, a table, an armchair and two upright chairs, along with a mirror over the mantelpiece. The correspondence also mentions a cot, bedsteads, a linen cupboard and a child's chair. There is no evidence that Rietveld ever realized the bedsteads or linen cupboard, but a child's chair that matches this furniture series was published in *De Stijl* in 1923.[9]

Rietveld strove constantly to take things a step further, through thick and thin. 'You ought to know that I have always had a hectic, turbulent life with all its practical wretchedness,' he wrote to Oud on 23 January 1920, before he began work on the furniture for Spangen. 'I never want to dissociate myself from this, because I know that I need it, but sometimes I allow myself to be overly absorbed and then one of you comes and grabs me by my blue smock. It is splendid how you are persevering with those pieces of furniture.'[10]

After 1920 Rietveld simplified the 1918 slat armchair even further by omitting the side panels; in 1919 he had already modified it by painting the crosscut end-grains of the legs, laths and armrests in a contrasting colour. Inexpensive items of furniture were often painted in colour to protect the wood and augment their visual appeal, and Rietveld did likewise. The linen cupboard was painted white with red rectangles over the hinges, and the baby's chair for Schelling was also realized in colour: green with pale green dowels and a red leather cushion.[11] In 1921 Rietveld presented a sledge held together by nothing but nails and painted red, blue and black at an exhibition of applied art staged at a pavilion in Zwolle. The crosscut ends of the sledge's timber components were painted white to reveal what a reviewer described as 'the naked truth', the logical outcome of a theory that he respected for its 'honesty' though he failed to understand the need for it.[12]

Rietveld's application of colour around 1920 and the reasons why he used it in this way are remarkable. Rietveld wanted first and foremost to produce a lucid three-dimensional form. In the red and blue variant of the slat armchair, which was produced around 1923, he at last managed to achieve his goal perfectly. By applying colour to the crosscut ends of the slats he gave these components their own starting and end points along a line that in principle extends into infinity, an endless space that can be perceived thanks to this articulation. The backrest and seat of the slat armchair are also distinct elements, because each has been given its own colour. In this version he has achieved the objective he had stated as his ambition in 1919, namely that 'the whole stands free and clear in space and the form wins from the material'.[13]

The enclosed nature of furniture for storage presented Rietveld with a new challenge:

Here you can see a little cupboard that is composed of a frame of, let's say, little sticks, we'll call them laths, all the same size … But seeing as I didn't want to close that cupboard with a flat door I closed it with an assembly of planes that are set spatially in the three dimensions of space in the same way as the frame itself, and you can therefore see the unusual form of that little door here. The small drawer, which is also assembled from little planks and laths, all of the same sort, has that same quality. You see I would have very much liked to make this sideboard asymmetrical, because I felt that even this symmetry was actually too closely tied to the mass and I would have preferred to set it freely in space, but that was still too difficult at the time. I was already pleased that I could take it this far, so I just made it the same on either side.[14]

Rietveld stated this in retrospect in 1959, when he also commented that he did not really know how to describe things in words back in the 1920s, but it is highly likely that he already 'sensed', somehow unconsciously realized, what was bothering him. His next step was indeed to design furniture with an asymmetrical form.

In 1923 Rietveld designed the 'Space-Colour-Composition' ('Ruimte-Kleur-Compositie') together with another member of De Stijl, the painter Vilmos Huszár, for the Juryfreie Kunstschau (Non-juried Art Exhibition) in Berlin. The design never progressed beyond a scale model, but it became known thanks to its being published in, for example, *L'Architecture Vivante*. The walls, colour panels and two items of furniture – a chair and a table – would have compelled visitors to follow a peremptory route.[15] Which aspects can be attributed to Huszár and which to Rietveld is not clearly indicated in the publication, but Huszár was certainly responsible for the geometrical planes of colour on the walls, which overlap in places or continue around a corner. This flew in the face of the spatial structure, which consisted of upright walls with a floor and a ceiling. Besides designing the furniture, Rietveld probably designed the form of the space as well. He had gained some experience in guiding the path of the visitor through his remodelling of the shop for the Gold- and Silversmiths Company on the Kalverstraat in Amsterdam two years earlier. The chair in the design was the only item of furniture to be realized as an autonomous object and has come to be known as the 'Berlin Chair'.[16]

An asymmetrical side table, the asymmetrical sewing cupboard that Rietveld made for his wife and the design for an almost identical music cabinet all probably date from this same period. Rietveld supplied the side table to various clients, including the author Til Brugman, for her music/living room designed by Vilmos Huszár, in this instance together with a white version of the slat armchair.[17] The asymmetrical form and the use of rectangular or square boards are essential to these designs. It is not for nothing that the Berlin Chair was called the 'plank chair' (*planken stoel*) in the catalogue for the Rietveld retrospective at Utrecht's Centraal Museum in 1958. The distinction between the frame and the parts that support the body – seat and backrest – has disappeared. In the Berlin Chair and the asymmetrical side table all the sides are visually equal. The sewing cupboard's storage space was created by setting the painted panels – apparently unattached – against one another.

In these items of furniture Rietveld added another important procedure to his method of working: the coat of paint camouflages the texture of the timber and a board becomes a field of colour in a three-dimensional composition. That is also the strength of the renowned red and blue variant of the slat armchair. The colour combination predominates over the material and structure, alllowing, in Rietveld's own words, 'the form to win from the material'. For Rietveld these colours were not sacrosanct; he also supplied the slat armchair in plain black, white, grey or bright red. The intended effect is, however, strongest in the red and blue version.

Architecture

Cornelis Begeer, an elder brother of the silversmith Carel, commissioned Rietveld to remodel his jewellery shop overlooking the Oudkerkhof in Utrecht in 1919. The facade was realized in fair-faced concrete. The display windows and the entrance were flanked by Oriental figures – the Middle East was a popular source of inspiration for ornamentation at the time. The Utrecht members of the Architectura et Amicitia (Architecture and Friendship) Society were so impressed by the design that they awarded Rietveld a bronze medal for it, but the facade bore no semblance to the innovative architecture that Van Doesburg and the De Stijl architects – Van 't Hoff, Oud and Wils – had in mind, so it was not featured in *De Stijl*. This accolade was reserved for the second shop remodelled by Rietveld.

Once again this commission came Rietveld's way via Cornelis Begeer, who asked him to transform the Goud en Zilversmid's Compagnie (Gold- and Silversmiths Company) jewellery shop on the Kalverstraat in Amsterdam into a tasteful showcase that would stand out among the 'gaudy row of colourful and alluring shops'.[18] The shop interior was an elongated space set obliquely to the building line; the exterior was a narrow shopfront. The new street-level facade was dominated by a large, rectangular display window that was set back slightly from the building line. Above this, recessed slightly further, stood a second glazed rectangle. The display window's transom light extended above the

Cupboard (top) and design for a music cupboard (centre), both 1923

Bottom: Storefront, Cornelis Begeer jewellery store, Utrecht, 1919

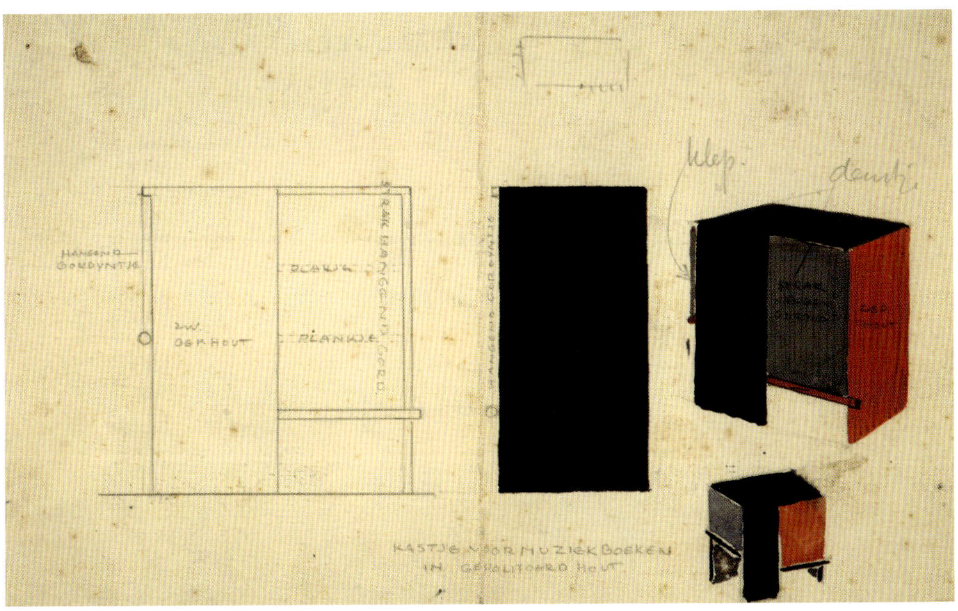

front door of the upstairs apartment and the entrance to the shop stood perpendicular to this front door to the side of the display window. This organization of the entrance as a three-dimensional composition of rectangular volumes was similar to the architecture of, for example, Wright and Oud. With Rietveld this stacking of volumes was extremely functional: attracted by the display of sparkling products the customer would walk into this 'hole' in the street elevation. This effects a gradual transition from the public space of the street to the commercial private domain, an ingenious spatial solution. Rietveld employed this principle in almost all of his subsequent shop conversions.

In the interior Rietveld also opted for a solution that would become typical of his work: he transformed the space into a unified whole by applying planes of colour to the walls and ceiling that matched the furniture and carpet. Using sophisticated proportions and a fine balance between daylight and artificial light he transformed an oblique, narrow room into a congenial space. Rietveld did not receive a medal for his design this time, but in 1923 the shop was featured in the De Stijl exhibition in Paris and, besides being published in *De Stijl*, it was illustrated and discussed in the *Bouwkundig Weekblad*, the *Schweizerische Bauzeitung* and *L'Architecture Vivante*.[19]

The project had far-reaching consequences for Rietveld in another respect. Cornelis Begeer invited his lawyer, Frits Schröder, to see the scale model of the shop, and Frits took along his wife, Truus Schröder-Schräder.[20] She was so enthusiastic about the design that in the same year, 1921, she asked Rietveld to furnish a small room for her in the imposing townhouse on the Biltstraat in Utrecht where the couple lived. Rietveld's approach was the same as for the interior of the Gold- and Silversmiths Company. He screened off the top section of the high windows and had a composition of rectangular planes painted in different shades of grey onto the walls and doors, which had the effect of making the ceiling seem lower and gave the room the proportions that Truus Schröder found agreeable. The painted plaster 'wainscoting' extended no higher than the windows and the door. The height of the door panel was also broken by painting dark, horizontal bands at the top and bottom of the door, with on either side two vertical

Gold- and Silversmiths Company shop, Amsterdam, 1921. This photograph dates from 1921, before the black and white facade was repainted in blue, yellow, red, grey and white at Rietveld's suggestion.

The interior of the Gold- and Silversmiths Company store, as published in *De Stijl 5* (1922)

Room for Truus Schröder-Schräder, Utrecht, 1921

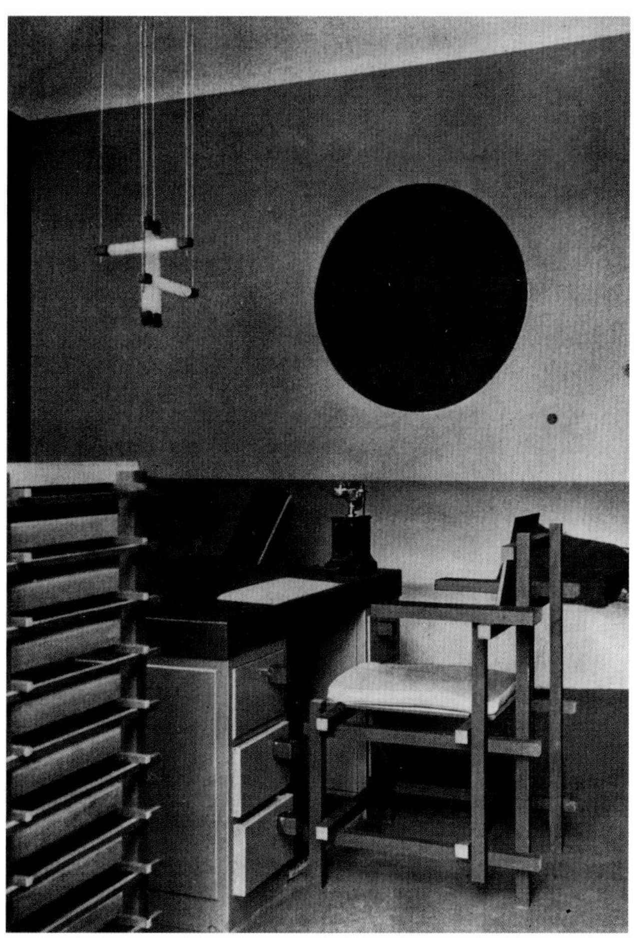

Surgery for A. M. Hartog, Maarssen, 1922, as published in *De Stijl* 6 (1923). Rietveld supplied both upright chairs and armchairs for this room, as well as designing the desk, chest of drawers, a bookcase and a lamp. In this room, the floor and ceiling had an L-shaped pattern of black and white planes, the walls were grey, and the switches and areas around the door handles were highlighted with primary colours.

strips in a lighter grey that stood out against these bands and the central panel. The floor covering was also realized in various shades of grey. The divan bed with a rectangular cupboard at its head and the small, built-in settee between the hearth and the window formed a transition from wall to floor in this spatial composition. Rietveld wanted to place a couple of his own furniture designs in the room, but at the time Truus Schröder found his chairs 'quite a problem'. Even with her own furniture this 'little room with the beautiful greys', as she described it, looked very modern.[21] Rietveld showed it to several colleagues, including Piet Elling (1897–1962), Bruno Taut and Sybold van Ravesteyn.

Rietveld and Truus Schröder came into contact on other occasions. For example, in 1923 Truus hosted a special guest at Rietveld's request: Kurt Schwitters. With Theo and Nelly van Doesburg's assistance, Schwitters had organized a Dada evening at the Gebouw voor Kunsten en Wetenschappen (Building for Arts and Sciences) at the Mariaplaats in Utrecht on 29 January 1923.[22] Schwitters declaimed his sound poems, Van Doesburg delivered a speech and Nelly played piano. The performance was disrupted by members of Utrecht University's student union, to Schwitters' delight and to Van Doesburg's chagrin. Schwitters then wanted to give a solo performance for some friends and acquaintances and had asked Rietveld to organize this. Truus Schröder placed her house on the Biltstraat at their disposal and it turned out to be a splendid evening with the Maarssen-based artist Willem van Leusden (1886–1974) and Sybold van Ravesteyn among those present.[23]

In 1923 Rietveld received two major commissions via the businessman P. van der Pluijm: the interior design of Utrecht's Katholiek Militair Tehuis (Catholic Military Home) and the remodelling of the E. Wessels en Zoon (E. Wessels and Son) leatherware shop at the Janskerkhof, also in Utrecht.[24] For the hospice Rietveld designed a table, a chair, a stool and sliding walls.[25] These were robust pieces of furniture, similar in design to the slat furniture but sturdier and more practical. The components were held together by chunky bolts and the rails protrude less, reducing the risk of damage to the chairs or to someone's limbs.

The new facade of E. Wessels and Son is similar in

form to that of the Gold- and Silversmiths Company. The large display window seems to stand almost detached from the facade, because of the recessed transom light that continues across the shopfront and extends above the door to the dwelling upstairs. The facade of the upper floors is supported in the middle by a steel cantilever beam that is hemmed in by the remnants of the structural party-wall of the two original properties. Rietveld accentuated the facade's load-bearing structure, by extending this beam 50 cm (20 in) beyond the building line and by highlighting it in his colour scheme: the bright blue frame of the display window stands out conspicuously against the white plaster wall and the beam itself is painted in a contrasting colour, specified as red in the design drawings. Rietveld also designed the shopfront lettering, a task he took upon himself often from then on, though he paid more attention to the division of the planar surface than to the form and spacing of the letters.

Besides these remodelling projects and his participation in various exhibitions, including the 'Space-Colour-Composition' project with Huszár in Berlin, Rietveld had many smaller commissions, such as the child's wheelbarrow for Oud's little son, the furniture for the Nathans family and the child's beach buggy that he supplied to various clients. In just a few years he established a successful furniture-making workshop with clientele from Utrecht and beyond, he was in contact with national and local artistic talents, and artists and architects from the Netherlands and beyond went out of their way to visit him. In letters and postcards he repeatedly complained that he could hardly find time for his own work because of other obligations.

From postcards Rietveld wrote to Cornelis van Eesteren (1897–1988), it appears that a lack of time was also one of the reasons for him ultimately making no significant contribution to one of the most ambitious undertakings of the De Stijl group: the new projects for an architecture exhibition in Paris in autumn 1923. Theo van Doesburg had assembled the team that would create these designs: Van Eesteren for the plans and exhibition structures, Rietveld for the interiors and the realization of the scale models, and Van Doesburg himself for the colour scheme. In the end Rietveld withdrew, having produced just one scale model. He probably preferred to busy himself with concrete tasks and a short time later he was presented with a unique opportunity to do this, but not via his friends in De Stijl.[26]

E. Wessels and Son shopfront, Utrecht, 1924. Photograph of the completed shop (top) and design drawing (bottom)

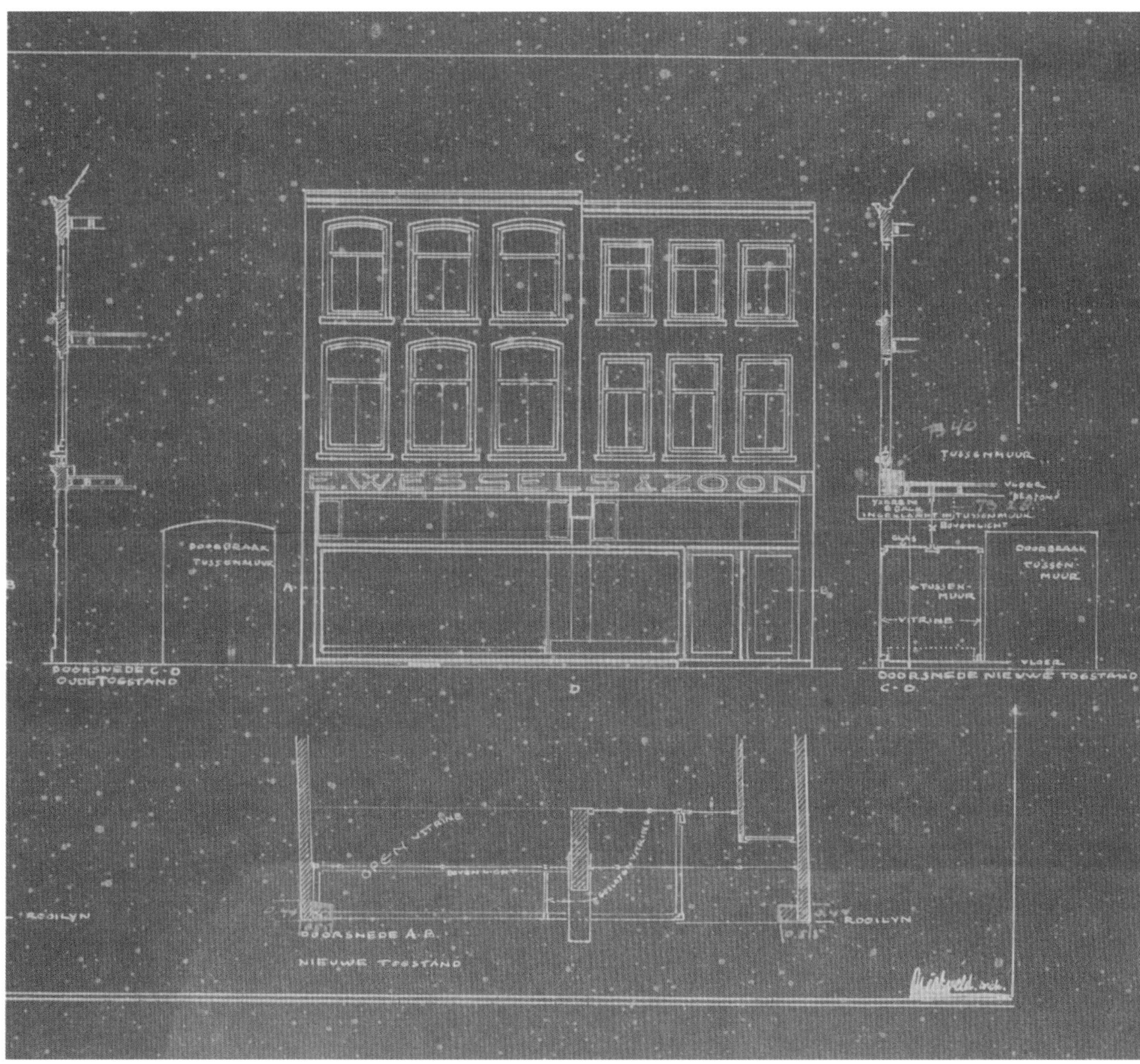

Price list for Rietveld's furniture, c.1923

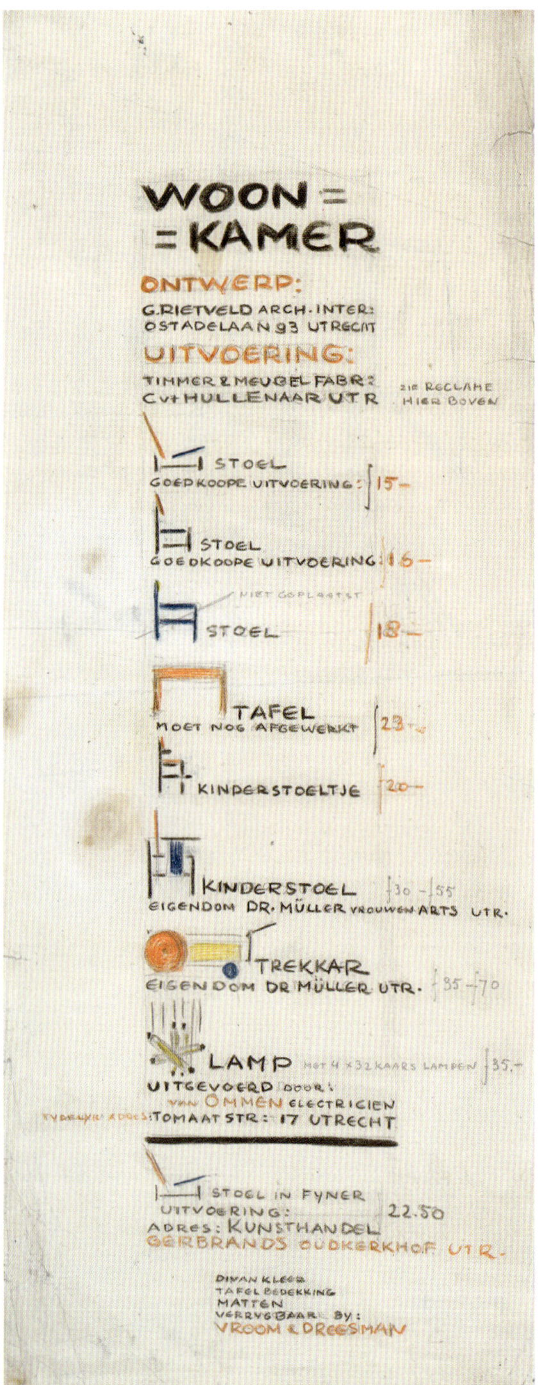

WOON=
=KAMER

ONTWERP:
G.RIETVELD ARCH. INTER:
OSTADELAAN 93 UTRECHT

UITVOERING:
TIMMER & MEUBEL FABR:
C v/d HULLENAAR UTR

ZIE RECLAME
HIER BOVEN

STOEL
GOEDKOOPE UITVOERING: ƒ 15–

STOEL
GOEDKOOPE UITVOERING: ƒ 16–

STOEL ƒ 18–

TAFEL
MOET NOG AFGEWERKT ƒ 23–

KINDERSTOELTJE ƒ 20–

KINDERSTOEL ƒ 30 – ƒ 55
EIGENDOM DR. MÜLLER VROUWEN ARTS UTR.

TREKKAR
EIGENDOM DR MÜLLER UTR. ƒ 35 – ƒ 70

LAMP MET 4 × 32 KAARS LAMPEN ƒ 35.–
UITGEVOERD DOOR:
VAN OMMEN ELECTRICIEN
TOMAAT STR: 17 UTRECHT

STOEL IN FYNER
UITVOERING: 22.50
ADRES: KUNSTHANDEL
GERBRANDS OUDKERKHOF UTR.

DIVAN KLEED
TAFEL BEDEKKING
MATTEN
VERKRYGBAAR BY:
VROOM & DREESMAN

Child's wheelbarrow, 1923

Child's high-chair, 1923

Child's beach buggy, 1922–3 (top and centre), advertising image (bottom left), sketch showing construction (bottom right)

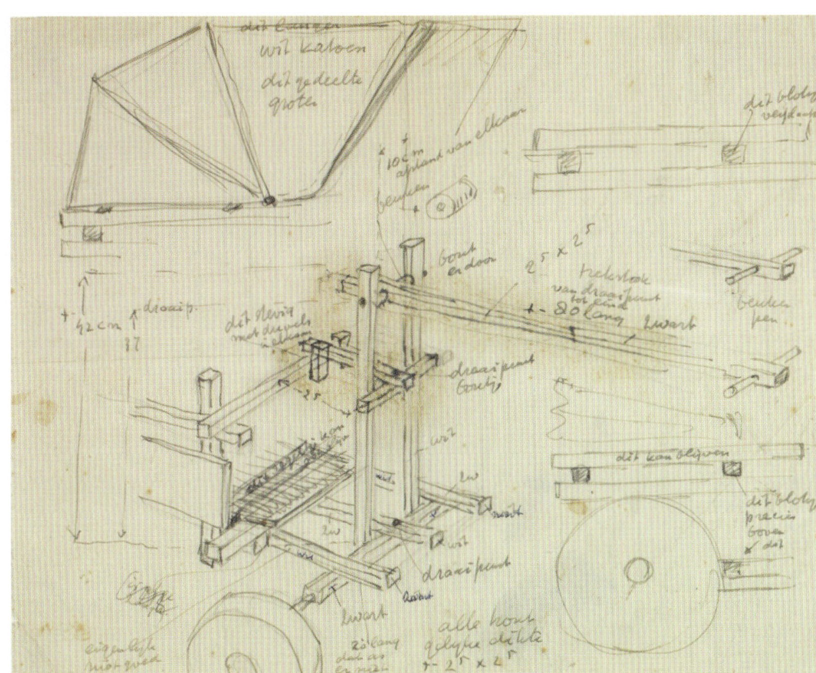

Rietveld (middle) with Mart Stam (left) and El Lissitzky (right), 1926

4. The Schröder House

I think that in this house Rietveld isn't so completely 'Rietveld'. I think he adapted himself somewhat to what I wanted. And I believe I loved this house more than Rietveld did. There's so much of myself here, I respond to the whole atmosphere of the place.[1]
– Truus Schröder, 1982

Gerrit Rietveld called Truus Schröder 'a small miracle' in the book he gave her as a present on her seventieth birthday.[2] The house he had built with her some thirty-five years earlier is also a small miracle and marked the start of their enduring collaboration and love.

The house still surprises and moves all the passers-by who pause near the viaduct over the Prins Hendriklaan and allow their gaze to travel along the facades. The house at number 50 stands out clearly and cheerfully against the other houses of drab masonry in the street. Seen from here, the top right-hand corner of the building is a horizontal band of continuous glazing; the transparent view into the interior is an inviting foretaste. A second surprise awaits those who accept the invitation and cross the threshold. Behind the front door lies a small hall that leads via three steps up to a half-landing, which gives access to the spiral staircase leading to the first floor. On climbing the stairs, as soon as visitors are at eye-level with the upper floor they see a space that is bathed in light that floods in from all sides. This is space in the literal, pure sense of the word.

The house has three levels: the cellar; the ground floor with the compact hall, a kitchen/diner, an office, a room for the domestic help and a studio; and the first floor with the open-plan living space. Nowadays the house lies almost hidden between the motorway viaduct, which was raised in 1963 and later provided with a noise barrier against the speeding traffic, and the row of houses that it abuts. The situation in 1924 was quite different: it was the last house on the edge of the city, where the Prins Hendriklaan crosses the Laan van Minsweerd and continues as the road to Bunnik. On the southeast side of Utrecht lay an extensive area where development was forbidden, because it formed part of the New Holland Waterline (Nieuwe Hollandse Waterlinie), a nineteenth-century military defence line. In case of an attack from the south or east this low-lying land would be inundated and defended from the forts built at regular intervals along the defence line. In the urban development plan by H. P. Berlage and L. N. Holsboer dating from 1920, the Laan van Minsweerd was to be extended towards the northeast: the Schröder House was built on the small parcel of land remaining.

Truus Schröder

Truus Schräder was born on 28 August 1889 in Deventer. Her mother died when she was four years old. Two years later her father remarried and moved to Amsterdam with his new wife and two small daughters, Truus and her sister, An, who was two years her senior. After primary school the girls were sent to boarding school. Truus attended the Pensionnat des Soeurs de Notre-Dame in Amersfoort, a reputable establishment for Catholic girls where it was obligatory to speak French outside lessons. On completing school Truus went to Arnhem to train as a pharmacist's assistant. To round off her education she spent half a year in London and a few months in Hanover, where she attended lectures at the university. At the age of twenty-

The south corner of the Schröder House, 1924

At night, the multiple planes of the facades read even more strongly.

The east corner

The southwest facade on Prins Hendriklaan

The heart of the house is the airy, light-filled main living space of the first floor.

In 1924 the site for the Schröder House was at the very edge of the city of Utrecht, adjacent to a large area where development was forbidden for military reasons.

The Schröder House as seen from the east in 1925

Truus Schröder, around the age of twenty-five

two, having returned to the Netherlands, she married the lawyer Frits Schröder, who was eleven years her senior. They agreed that the marriage would remain childless so that Truus could go and study.[3] But things turned out differently and she became pregnant with a son, Binnert, who was followed by two daughters, Marjan and Han. The difference in character and views between the couple soon became obvious and led to painful conflicts, especially with regard to the children's upbringing. After the death of her father, Truus officially left the Roman Catholic Church and withdrew the children from their Catholic school, sending them to a Montessori school instead. This was beyond the comprehension of her husband's family and his circle of acquaintances, in contrast to the reaction of her sister An, who was married to the paediatrician Rein Harrenstein. This couple lived on the Weteringschans in Amsterdam and maintained an extensive circle of acquaintances, primarily of left-leaning intellectuals and artists. An co-founded the feminist periodical *De Werkende Vrouw* (The Working Woman) and later became its editor-in-chief. The awkward relationship between An and her brother-in-law Frits Schröder was, however, an obstacle to contact between Truus and her sister.

Truus was unhappy in her marriage and walked out a couple of times, but she always returned for the sake of the children. The 'room with the beautiful greys' designed by Rietveld was an attempt to keep the situation bearable, a solution true to the best traditions of the upper echelons of society. The death of Truus's husband on 5 October 1923, after a protracted illness, was a huge relief for Truus Schröder, though out of reverence for her children she never expressed it in these terms. Some seventy years later, still with a certain wistfulness and irony in her voice, she described him as follows: 'A very handsome man. Extremely cordial and extremely difficult to live with. Only I didn't know that then, you see. But really extremely charming and I fell for that, and I still understand why. He was very handsome, very tall and broad. Yes.'[4]

The design process

Rietveld was too busy to apply himself to the De Stijl exhibition in the way that Van Doesburg demanded of his comrades, who were expected to be available day and night. Rietveld had to support his family and took on all manner of assignments small and large, whether a little chair or an alteration. Truus Schröder's request to find and remodel a rented house for herself and her three children belonged to the latter category. After the death of her husband she found their house on the Biltstraat too large. Truus was very fond of her room remodelled by Rietveld. They had occasionally been in contact over the preceding years, notably when Rietveld had wanted to show the room to colleagues. He seemed to be the obvious person to assist her.

Finding a suitable rental property proved to be difficult and Rietveld broached the idea of building a house. They went in search of a plot independently, but were both drawn to the very same 'really filthy bit of land', as Truus later described it, set on the Prins Hendriklaan, right on the edge of Utrecht.[5] From then on things moved swiftly, even though Truus rejected the first design, which Rietveld produced the very next day.

This almost impromptu and casual approach typified the whole design and construction process. They each had their own ideas, some of them clear-cut, others still vague or subconscious. They simply began and did not consider in advance whether something was feasible. They were not hampered by too much expertise, but in a broader perspective knew very well what they wanted. 'Once I baby-sat for a friend of mine who lived in a large, empty attic space. I sat there that evening and imagined what it would be like to live somewhere like that. I think that for me this was the beginning of thinking about this sort of lifestyle,' Truus Schröder explained in 1982.[6] Rietveld saw it as an ideal opportunity to realize a house 'based on the same principles as that chair', meaning the Red-Blue Chair.[7] This statement seems more like a conclusion that evolved over time, but it makes clear how Rietveld was keen to build a house as a progression from what he had done thus far.

The tracing paper with the caption 'SCHETS-ONTWERP 1/100' ZYDE PRINS HENDRIKLAAN' – 'SKETCH PLAN 1/100, PRINS HENDRIKLAAN SIDE' – is probably the design rejected by Truus. The house has the form of a box that is almost square, with balconies to the south and east. The sketches show the plan of the ground floor, the three elevations, of which one is accentuated in ink, and an extra variant of the east elevation. The front door is set on the Prins Hendriklaan, the kitchen to the left of it against the wall of the adjoining property, while to the right of the front door there is a lavatory and a bathroom. The living/dining room is situated in the northeast corner on the ground floor, accessible via a door next to the stairs in the little hallway. Adjacent to this room and the kitchen lies a sitting room/bedroom. A staircase leads from the hallway to the upper storey. The floor-plan of this level is not included in the drawing, but from the elevations it is possible to deduce that the upper floor had two different ceiling heights: slightly less than 3 m (9 ft 11 in) on the northwest side but almost 4 m (13 ft 1½ in) on the southeast side. The probable plan was to set a living room in that corner, with a horizontal band of fenestration continuing around the southeast and northeast elevations. An additional rectangular window was planned in the northeast elevation. At the southeast corner the living room has an extension 'like scaffolding with glass'. In the bottom right-hand corner of the sheet there are two little sketches of three circles with the midpoints connected by lines, possibly representing the sightlines from the interior. The house stood on a sloping site bordered by a ditch.[8]

The scaffolding with glass is clearly a translation of the three-dimensional openness of the slat furniture as the bay window of a house. Later on Truus commented that she barely glanced at this design. 'It was a very nice little house, but it wasn't my kind of thing at all. In fact I think it was more attractive than I realized ... I clearly must have had something completely different in mind.'[9] It is not difficult to guess what was preoccupying Truus Schröder: she at last had the chance to turn her dream into reality and to organize her life spatially according to her personal insights. She primarily needed someone who could translate her ideas into reality.

They started afresh, this time beginning with the plan for the upper storey. They first determined the most beautiful view and where the sun rose. That, according to Truus, is how the house gradually took shape.[10] For Rietveld the main point was that they were no longer working with volumetric massing but with the space within the

First model. Made of a block of wood, this model shows the house as a solid that is carved into and painted on. A later model, which has been lost, was made from cardboard, glass and matchsticks and, according to Truus Schröder, the change of material contributed to the evolution of the facades into a composition of planes.

First sketch. This design was rejected by Truus almost immediately.

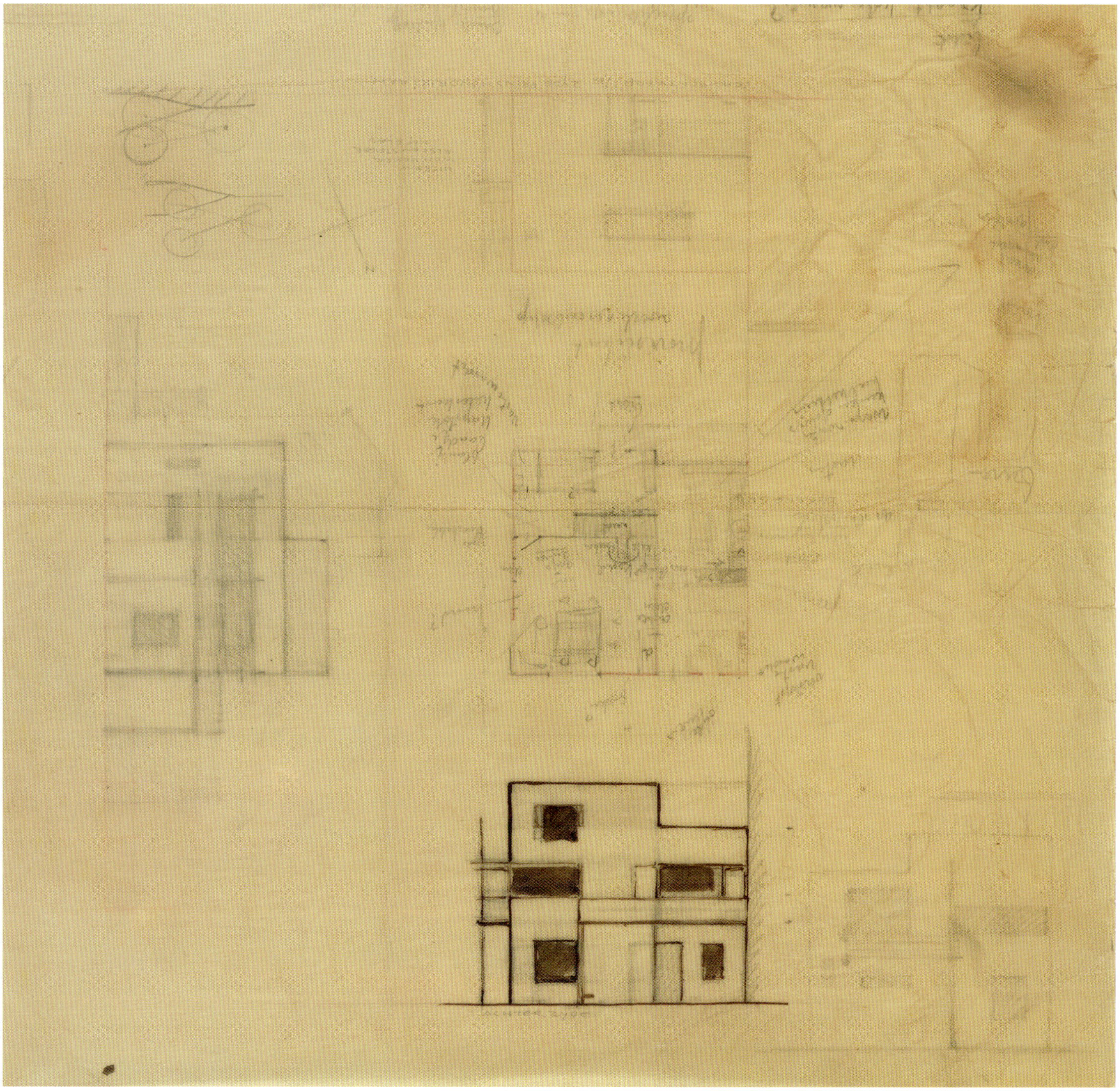

Perspective sketches (left and bottom). Drawings made between the first model and the final construction show the alteration of the initial form through the use of linear and planar elements, including balconies, railings and overhangs, as well as the evolution of the colour scheme.

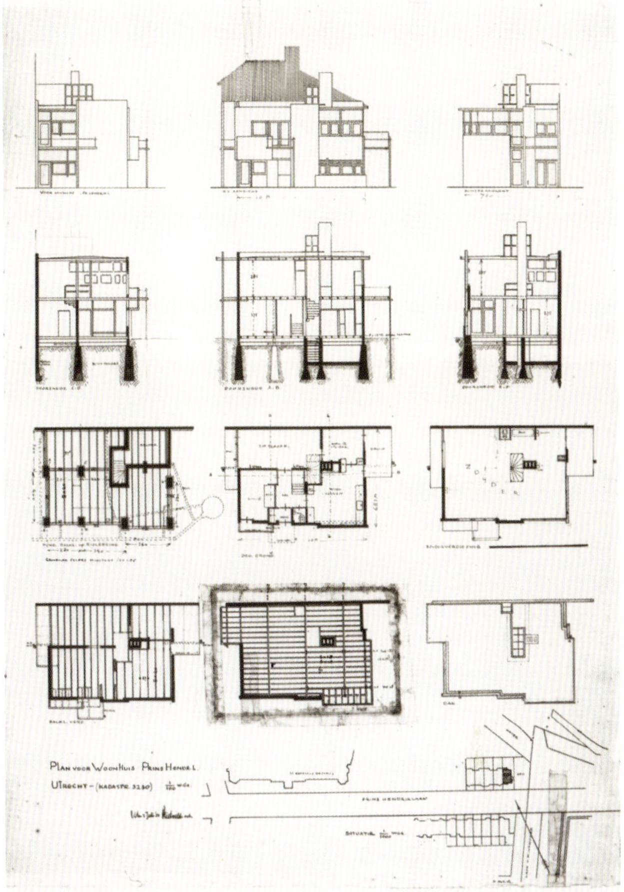

Permit drawing. This drawing, the culmination of only a few weeks' work, was submitted to the city by Rietveld in July 1924 to get permission to build. The entirety of the upper floor is labelled 'attic', in order to ensure that the unconventional main living space did not cause the application to be rejected.

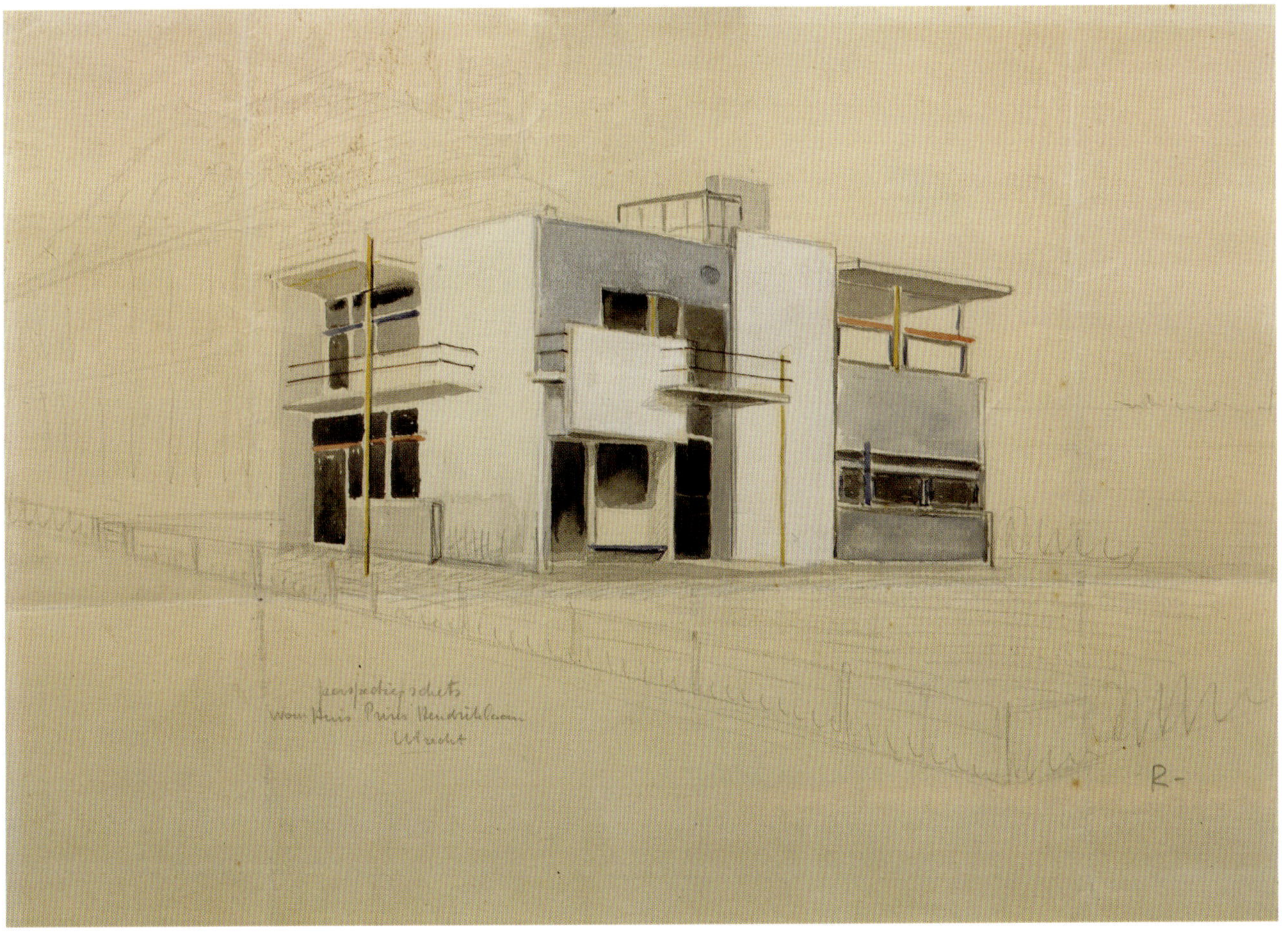

Isometric drawing of the first floor. The importance of the built-in furniture is particularly evident.

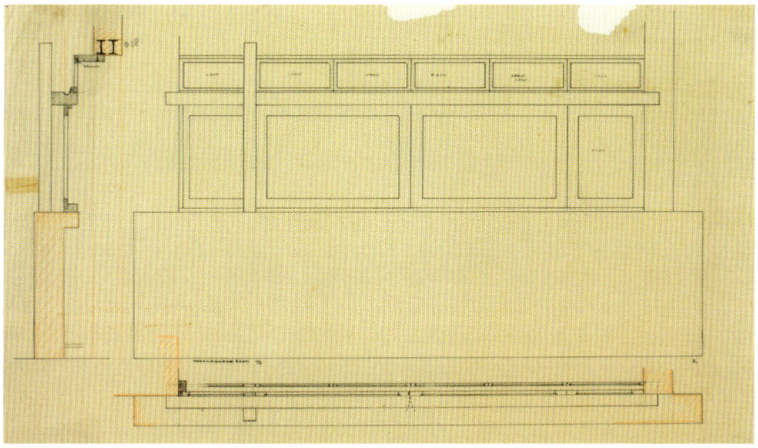

Detail drawing of the kitchen windows

building and its continuation beyond the shell. The first floor was completely open, with no fixed walls, which they labelled as attic space. On the ground floor, however, Rietveld and Schröder opted to present a standard subdivision that would satisfy the building code, because they did not expect planning permission to be granted for the open-plan upstairs living space they had in mind.

It was very difficult to prevent that lower part being too massive compared to the upper part, because then it would have been two things, different ideas. That is how it started out and then the concept gradually became clear. But initially it of course became a massive thing when seen from the outside, because it is incredibly difficult to shake off a specific idea, to let something go.[10]

The 'massive thing' is probably the small-scale model known as the 'Eerste model' – 'First model'.

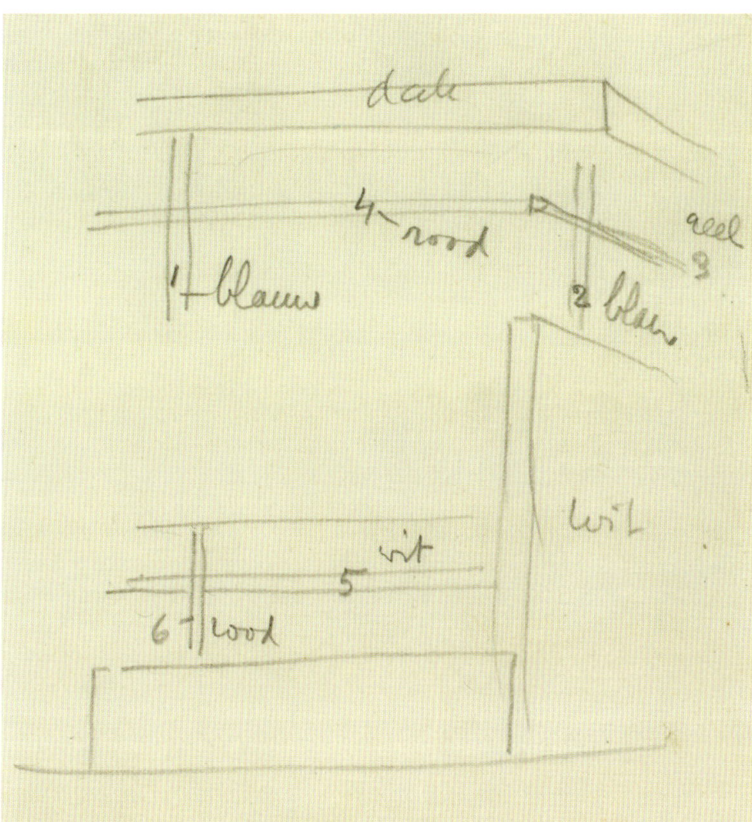

Sketch. Rietveld continued to develop the design during the construction process in sketches like this, which indicates the colour of various elements.

The division of the elevations suggests that at this stage the outline plan for the house was fixed, with the exception of the internal garage that is accessible from the Prins Hendriklaan via two folding doors. The front door is set in the east elevation, the side of the house where the Laan van Minsweerd extension was constructed later on. The difference with the final design, as Rietveld himself pointed out, is the bulkiness. The model was, after all, literally fashioned from a block of wood. The room next to the front door, probably also the kitchen in this sketch model, has three windows at the front and a door and a vertical window at the rear. Above the front door is a rectangular fanlight, to the right of it a small opening for ventilation, and close to the corner there is a tall, narrow window, suggesting a bathroom. There is a horizontal window on the first-floor level above the front door and likewise in the elevation facing the Prins Hendriklaan, while the northeast corner has a large, horizontal band of fenestration that continues around the corner. The roof above these living quarters is also partially glazed and there is no chimney.[12] All in all, at this stage the house was a long way from its spectacular definitive form. Truus was not yet satisfied either: she wanted to have balconies on all sides, but this house would have just one to the north. Rietveld then probably produced a model of cardboard,

The Schröder House as seen from the northeast (top) and south (bottom) in 1925

Truus and her youngest daughter Hanneke, c.1925

The first floor, looking towards seating area and wrap-around windows of the east corner

Bottom left: The house contains many pieces of built-in furniture, including a coat rack in the entrance hallway with two levels, one for children and one for adults.

Bottom right: The sleeping area of Truus's daughters, located in the west corner of the house glass and matchsticks. Truus Schröder commented later that the use of these materials was essential to the design's evolution. According to her, when the scale models were produced with materials other than the customary plaster or clay it affected the design and manner of construction.[13] This model is no longer extant, but the drawing with the legend '1e schets exterieur' – '1st sketch, exterior' – possibly dates from this phase. The facades are divided into white planes, black lines, black rectangles for the windows and blank sections of wall that have retained the brown of the cardboard. The design was now practically complete.

A second perspective sketch of the exterior shows the colour scheme of the realized design in broad outline, though Rietveld introduced various changes during construction and thereafter as well.[14] For example, the chimney-breast was over the years painted yellow, lavender and ultramarine, and a yellow band in Truus's bedroom was painted over later on.[15] The house also diverges from the design submitted in the application for planning permission: the windows and doors do not match exactly and the junction of the elevations and the floor-plans is depicted incorrectly. To what extent this was carelessness or an attempt to mislead the 'Architecture Police' (*Bouwpolitie*), as the municipal body responsible for granting building permits was called, is unclear. The designation *'zolder'* (attic) on the plan of the upper floor was chosen deliberately, because there was a possibility that the planning application would be rejected if this open area was designated as living space.

Even though Rietveld found it 'incredibly difficult to shake off a specific idea', together with Truus Schröder he succeeded in this project remarkably well in a relatively short time. The contract of sale for the land is dated 18 June 1924 and the drawing for the planning application was signed and dated by Rietveld on 2 July 1924. Five days later the price agreement with the contractor was signed, so the entire design process took no longer than a few weeks. 'I am busy with a little house, here in Utrecht,' Rietveld wrote to Oud on 3 August 1924. 'As soon as I have drawn it on a slightly better scale I will show it [to you]. It has to be realized soon. If I have the permit next week we begin.'[16]

Construction

Construction proceeded less smoothly. The installation of the radiators proved to be complicated and expensive, while the decorating and finishing took many months. It all became too much for Truus Schröder, who had moved into the house shortly after the new year. She went on vacation to Switzerland and hoped that the floor would be ready on her return, which it was, but not to her satisfaction, because she found the composition very restless; Rietveld changed it later.

Truus Schröder's finances meant that the house could not be overly expensive. The land cost 5,400 guilders, the construction costs were 9,271 guilders, the estimate for the heating system 1,623 guilders with a supplement for other technical components of 410 guilders, and Rietveld was to receive a fee of 900 guilders, amounting to about 17,500 guilders (approximately $6,700 or £1,500) in total.[17] The heating was relatively expensive, because Rietveld and Schröder thought that the standard domestic radiators with vertical ribs and decorations were ugly and had chosen an industrial type.

The total cost was probably driven up further because what at first glance seems to be a straightforward design actually includes all kinds of unusual details.[18] For example, the doors and frames had to be flush and everything finished square without mouldings. The flat roof had to be angled slightly with wedges for rainwater drainage and it had to be covered 'with mastic cement, asphalt or rubber(roid), everything executed well, so that a ten-year written guarantee can be issued for it… The casings [set] simply in the masonry (no laths or frames – no plinth).'[19] Rietveld must have explained or tested out many aspects while work was under way, given that there are only twenty-three detail drawings extant, seven of them with supplementary instructions. The construction was probably completed by the end of summer 1925, including the layout and planting of the garden with two quince trees for the southern elevation and a flowerbed on the boundary with the garden of the neighbours. A low fence with two small gates was raised along the Prins Hendriklaan. The terrain just opposite the front door falls away quite steeply towards the ditch, so steps were cut into the incline.[20]

A background for life

Han Schröder, Truus Schröder's youngest daughter, emigrated to the USA in 1963 and from 1979 taught interior architecture at Virginia Commonwealth University at Richmond. From afar she kept a watchful eye on the future of the Schröder House and with regard to restorations she had a decisive say. More than anyone else she underscored how the house was the expression of a conviction. Without some knowledge of Truus's beliefs, her way of life and the small details of her everyday routine, the house is but an empty shell and the architecture impossible to understand.[21] That awareness is important, all the more because almost a century later it is hard to appreciate how radical Truus Schröder's choices were or to ascertain to what extent her ideas as the client contributed to the architectural result. In a notebook in which Truus Schröder jotted down notes about the house in later years, she wrote, 'Was Rietveld actually ready to build a house?'[22] To others she put this more diplomatically: 'We did it together. It is like a child. Then you don't really know what it has inherited from the mother and what from the father.'[23] The message is clear: her contribution was of equal weight.

For Rietveld it was the first time he had built a house, and until then he had probably given barely any thought to the layout of a house. In any case he allowed Truus Schröder, who had a clear-cut programme of requirements, to take the lead. She wanted to live on the upper floor and, quite remarkably, to sleep with her three children in close proximity. This meant that other functions were accommodated on the ground floor: a large kitchen/diner, a room for the domestic help, a small reception room to receive visitors who did not belong to their circle of personal acquaintances, and a garage. In practice this created a fairly traditional division into a ground floor intended for more public, work-oriented or external relations and private quarters above.

The function of the ground-floor rooms was already modified during the design process or shortly after construction began. The garage became a studio space for Rietveld. The small reception room became a study for the children or anyone who wished to withdraw to somewhere quiet. The room for the live-in domestic servant became a sitting room for the domestic help, who was only in attendance during the day. The core of the design was the first-floor living space, which was and is exceptional in every respect. Rietveld had initially sketched out separate bedrooms in the floor-plan, which prompted Truus to ask, 'Can those walls go too?' To which he responded, 'With pleasure, away with those walls!' The result was one large, open space, so open that Truus was keen to have the option of dividing it up after all and sliding partition walls were installed, against Rietveld's wishes.[24] In the specifications these walls are described as 'sliding and pivoting partitions of one-inch planks strengthened with T- or V-irons, with cork panelling nailed on and covered in stretched fabric (light-coloured screens up to 2 metres, glass directly above)'. This gives the impression that Rietveld wanted the upper section of these partitions to be transparent. It is still an amazing solution for an unusual situation: a small, private house where individual freedom was painstakingly guarded. On the ground floor each room has its own outside door and a water and gas supply that make it possible to prepare something to eat or drink. Upstairs, however, is one big space, where a mother lives, sleeps and eats close by her growing son and two daughters. The children do their homework at the plank-like shelves beneath the windows next to the dining table, the house's main sitting area. It is a small, intimate house with many large windows that allow the world to enter from every side. According to Rietveld and Schröder the house was nothing more than a 'movable background to life',[25] but it was certainly a new way of life that clearly broke with the conventional hierarchy of the bourgeois family. Schröder's ideal family life was literally rendered in Rietveld's spatial structure: a close-knit formation of autonomous parts.

Colour

Since his very first experiments it had always been Rietveld's intention to use colour to emphasize the spatial structure of his designs and suppress their material aspect. In earlier alterations, such as Truus Schröder's room and the Gold- and Silversmiths Company shop interior, Rietveld used coloured planes to mask the actual limitations of the space and thereby to influence the visual perception of the space. The

Ground-floor plan

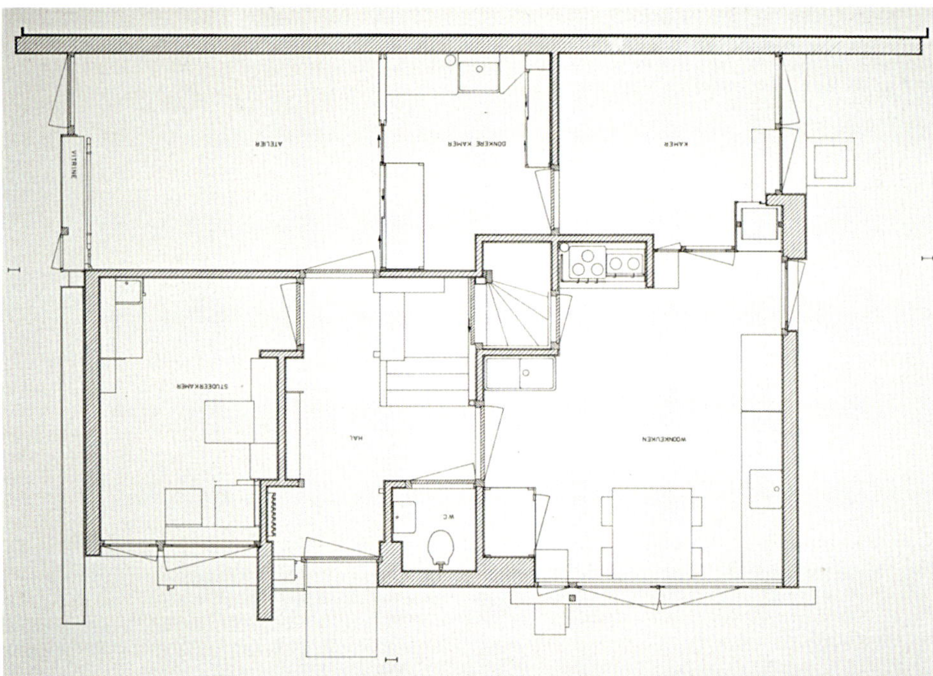

The windows and doors of the atelier, facing the Prins Hendriklaan

Top and bottom right: The front entrance of the house leads to a brightly-coloured entrance hall that acts as pivot for the house, leading to three of five rooms and the lavatory on the ground floor, and up to the main living space on the first floor.

Left and centre: In the study, the L-shaped window and door unit faces south.

Top and bottom: The kitchen, like most of the rooms on the ground floor, has both windows and a door, which leads to the garden.

The wrap-around windows in the eastern corner make this space, intended for sitting and dining, the brightest area in the house.

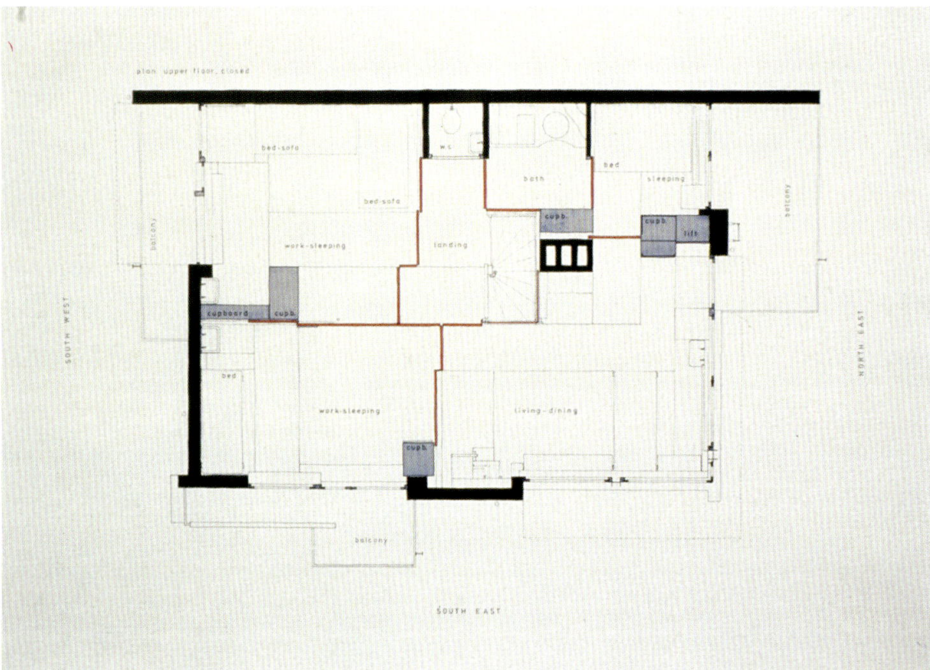

First-floor plan

The upper floor is also lit from a rooflight just above the central staircase. White window frames above the balustrade can be opened to enclose the stair or, as shown here, folded back against the blue chimney.

Near the northern corner of the house, Truus's sleeping area (bottom right), including a sink and shelves, shares the space of a cupboard (top left), which is painted half black and half white.

Bottom left: This door leads from the sleeping area for Truus's son to a balcony on the southeast side. The modular yellow cabinet to the left was part of the built-in furniture designed for the house.

Top right: Sliding partitions and graphic elemets are used to demarcate the 'rooms' on the first floor. Here, the sleeping area of Truus's son, to the southeast, has a red floor, and the sleeping area of her daughters, in the western corner, is bordered with a thick black stripe.

In the Schröder House, the partitions on the first floor can be open, closed, or set in-between to create different rooms as the need arises. On each page, the same space is shown in a variety of configurations.

interior of the Schröder House was designed in the same way. Wherever the space was most in danger of seeming poky because of the limited number of cubic metres, he managed to achieve the opposite effect with such interventions. Thanks to the natural lighting, the half-landing and the use of planes of colour on the floor and ceiling, the house's small hallway, which occupies a surface area of just two square metres, is transformed into an inviting portal for the living space upstairs.[26]

The effect of the colour scheme is not only a function of the selection of white, grey and black in combination with yellow, red and blue; at least as important is the use of a matt coating paint on almost all possible components. The house is built from brick, timber, iron and glass on concrete foundations. From the exterior there is no visible trace of these materials or the sometimes clumsy construction; various authors, including Walter Gropius, thought that it was a concrete structure.[27] This was indeed the initial plan, but it would have been prohibitively expensive. Rietveld's preference for concrete was inspired by the possibility of producing clearly defined planes in that material. He underscored the character of the elevations as compositions of autonomous planes of colour by masking the texture of the materials behind stuccowork and a coat of paint.

The house's interior is finished in a similar manner, with movable and fixed items of furniture forming an entity with the boundaries of the space because of their smooth, gloss-painted surfaces in yellow, blue, black, grey or white. The transition from exterior to interior is almost impalpable. For example, the blue-painted bench in front of the study's window and sheltered beneath the overhanging balcony is a continuation of the interior. Despite the upper floor's multitude of functions and the sometimes complex articulation of its shell, the uniformity in colour and finish ensures that the spatial experience remains central. This was a huge leap from the 'honesty of construction' and 'truth to materials' advocated so strongly in the first two decades of the twentieth century by, for example, Berlage.

Form

In 1925 it was already abundantly clear to Jean Badovici, editor-in-chief of *L'Architecture Vivante*, that the Schröder House was a practical application of the freshest ideas of the De Stijl group: 'There one finds, brought to their pinnacle of perfection and realized materially, the ideas that the group's founder, Theo van Doesburg, developed in his article on "L'Evolution de l'Architecture moderne en Hollande".'[28] Van Doesburg readily endorsed this in the anniversary edition of *De Stijl* two years later, writing that the 'spirit' of the architectural designs that were presented in the 1923 De Stijl exhibition at the Galerie de l'Effort Moderne run by Léonce Rosenberg (1879–1947) had been materialized in Rietveld's house on the Prins Hendriklaan in Utrecht.[29] Rietveld always implicitly refuted this claim, which was in fact nothing more than an assertion, by emphasizing the similarities between the house and his furniture designs. He never mentioned the colour scheme, which he probably considered to be the least successful aspect of the house.[30]

The interrelationship of the Schröder House, Rietveld's earlier work and the work of others – including that of architects and artists who were briefly or extensively involved with De Stijl – is complex. A paucity of factual information leads to interpretations that are often informed by a hidden agenda or personal beliefs.[31] It is impossible to determine the influences that were significant for the design of the Schröder House with precision. It seems self-evident to search for the key in the architectural designs produced by Theo van Doesburg and Cornelis van Eesteren for the De Stijl exhibition at Rosenberg's gallery: the Maison Rosenberg, Maison d'Artiste and Maison Particulière.[32] Rietveld produced the model of the Maison Rosenberg and was undoubtedly familiar with the two other designs by Van Doesburg and Van Eesteren from their publication in *De Stijl*.

The Maison Rosenberg is a spectacular design, composed of well-defined rectangular volumes of varying height, flat roofs, horizontal bands of fenestration and a deep porch.[33] With a little effort it is possible to discern a relationship between this work and Rietveld's initial design for the Schröder House, which was rejected by Truus, but the difference in scale makes such a comparison fairly futile. The small houses that Walter Gropius (1883–1969) presented at the Bauhaus exhibition in Weimar in 1923 are in that respect more likely candidates.[34] We cannot be sure how the designs by Van Eesteren and Van Doesburg would have looked had they actually been realized, but it is interesting to compare Van Doesburg's approach to the way in which Rietveld tackled the Schröder House.[35] Van Doesburg made a three-dimensional composition of blue, yellow and red rectangular planes shaded in white, grey and black. In the model these become rectangular volumes that project from the core asymmetrically: a stacking of volumes that are joined to the centre in an ingenious way and seem to hold each other in equilibrium.

The Schröder House is much simpler. The plan is a plain rectangle with the ground-floor rooms arrayed around the little hallway, while upstairs an orderly rectilinear space is retained. Rietveld breaks through the building's mass by dissolving the facades into a three-dimensional composition of seemingly autonomous, free-standing planes. The large wall surfaces are painted white, light grey or dark grey, in order to demarcate each plane individually and clearly indicate their interrelationships. From the outside, the windows, bordered by black casings, are transparent or appear as a black surface in the composition. The '1e schets exterieur' – '1st sketch, exterior' – demonstrates that Rietveld was aware of this. He introduces accents using the colours red, blue and yellow. In the Schröder House the interior and exterior are not sharply divided by a massive wall; an imperceptible transition between indoor and outdoor space is achieved by building the facades from separate elements into a three-dimensional structure. When the corner windows on the upper floor are open, the corner stile disappears and the outer shell dissolves, the interior becoming one with the exterior space.

By contrast, in Van Doesburg's design for the Maison d'Artiste the relationship between interior and exterior is sculpturally defined. This is much more in line with the way that Rietveld remodelled the facades of the Gold- and Silversmiths Company shop in Amsterdam and the Wessels and Son leatherware shop in Utrecht with glazed, apparently free-standing rectangular volumes, in Amsterdam even stacking up four apparently dissimilar blocks. Such stacking is also a feature of architectural models by Willem van Leusden (1886–1974) from the years 1922 to 1924. Van Doesburg presented work by Van Leusden in the exhibition at Rosenberg's Galerie de l'Effort Moderne in Paris, even though he was not affiliated with the De Stijl group.[36] Rietveld may have been the catalyst for this, given that he knew Van Leusden well and had possibly worked with him on the surgery for Dr A. M. Hartog.[37] Van Leusden executed his models in red, yellow and blue with black, grey and white. In 1923, two years after the initial remodelling, Rietveld had the frames of the shopfront of the Gold- and Silversmiths Company painted blue, yellow and black and the interior walls white and grey, while for Wessels and Son he chose red for the projecting console. Yet all these spatial compositions are fundamentally dissimilar to the Schröder House.

It is also conceivable that the work and ideas of Bruno Taut influenced Rietveld and Truus Schröder.[38] In 1923, during a tour through the Netherlands, Taut gave several lectures and gathered material for *Die neue Wohnung. Die Frau als Schöpferin* (The new dwelling. The woman as creator), a book which appeared a year later. At Rietveld's invitation he also visited Utrecht, and according to Taut their meeting was highly instructive. 'He is such a worthy character that the whole Bauhaus would be rendered obsolete by just one such fellow,' Taut wrote to Oud. 'I would very much like to fetch him to Magdeburg, and he would also like to come, but it is by no means certain that I will succeed in this.' The meeting between Rietveld and Taut took place when Rietveld was working on the scale model for the Maison Rosenberg. On that occasion Taut also made a visit to Truus Schröder, 'to see the little room with the beautiful greys'. The grandiloquent texts penned by Van Doesburg are always somewhat difficult to translate into reality, but Taut's booklet deals extensively with the practical aspects of the dwelling. He writes about form and colour, but also about the layout of kitchens, about flexible partition walls and built-in cupboards, and the possibility of each family member being able to withdraw and find seclusion. In Taut's opinion, colour on the walls lends structure to the space and serves as a substitute for paintings and other decoration.

It is not only the functional similarities between the Schröder House and Taut's ideal dwelling that are striking; Taut also makes a clear link between the house and the mental disposition of the inhabitant: 'Wer frei in die Welt blickt, hat auch den Mut, sein Haus so hinzustellen' (Whoever looks at the world freely also possesses the courage to arrange his house in this way).[39] Truus Schröder owned a copy of the third reprint of Taut's booklet, first published in 1924, and made myriad annotations in it. To what extent she and Rietveld were familiar with its contents prior to the construction of the Schröder House is impossible to determine, though they undoubtedly discussed the ideal form and layout for the house.[40]

In 1963, when Rietveld said that he had realized the house on the basis of the same principles as 'that chair', meaning the Red-Blue Chair, he could just as well, if not more appropriately, have mentioned the Berlin Chair, which was less well-known at the time, or the sideboard from 1919 which he considered less of a success. In all three designs he tried to replace mass with space. With the sideboard he did not want to enclose the storage space, but to delineate it using individual little panels in order to dissolve the object's sheer mass. When working on the sideboard he was still at a loss with regard to the best way to handle symmetry in his furniture, but with the Berlin Chair and the asymmetrical cabinet he discovered a means to conjoin the various planes as autonomous elements. He did the same thing with the elevations of the Schröder House.

Was the Schröder House really a practical translation of the architectural tenets of De Stijl? In 1924 Theo van Doesburg published his ideas about architecture in *De Stijl* in the form of sixteen propositions.[41] This manifesto, 'Tot een beeldende architectuur' ('Towards a plastic architecture'), seems to be a conceptual blueprint for the Schröder House, but there are also obvious differences. In point 10, Van Doesburg introduces the concept of the unity of space and time that 'gives the appearance of architecture a new and completely plastic aspect'. He expands upon this plasticity in point 11:

The new architecture … throws the functional space … out from the centre of the cube, so that height, breadth and depth plus time become a completely new plastic expression in open spaces. In this way … architecture acquires a more or less floating aspect which, so to speak, runs counter to the natural force of gravity.

Here Van Doesburg is in effect providing a description of the Maison d'Artiste, which stems from an idea diametrically opposed to that for the Schröder House, which is essentially a cube with three spatially disposed walls.

There is, moreover, nothing to indicate that Rietveld and Van Doesburg had much contact after the rather unsuccessful initial phase of the Rosenberg project. Van Doesburg sent Rietveld a postcard that conveys his disappointment regarding the lack of contact or collaboration with his De Stijl confrères:

I hear from various quarters that you're hard at work. And I haven't heard from you myself for a long time. Apparently you've got an ideal commission … is that so? Send me some news! As soon as you have some photographs, send me a few! I suppose you'll do the COLOUR yourself. I haven't heard anything from you on that score![42]

Perhaps the extent to which the Schröder House is the materialization of De Stijl ideas is irrelevant. As André Gide stated in 1900, 'L'influence ne crée rien; elle éveille' (Influence creates nothing; it rouses).[43] Stimulated and inspired by all these different influences, in 1924 Rietveld created a backdrop for Truus Schröder's life and that was more than enough.

The east corner of the Schröder House

Rietveld at the first meeting of CIAM in 1928, in La Sarraz in Switzerland. From left to right, seated: A. G. Mercadal, unknown; first row: unknown, P. Chareau, P. Jeanneret, Rietveld, A. Sartoris, G. Guevrékian, H. Häring, unknown, Le Corbusier, H. Mandrot, unknown, A. Lurçat, H. R. von der Mühl, unknown, H. Hoste, S. Giedion, W. M. Moser, J. Frank; second row: unknown, V. Bourgeois, M. E. Haefeli, R. Steiger, E. May, H. Schmidt, unknown

5. Architect in heart and soul

By searching for the correct materialization of the necessary things, the architect also fixes the essence of the age.[1]
– Rietveld, 1926

Rietveld's affiliation with De Stijl had steered his life in a totally different direction, and the year 1925, when he deliberately changed tack and decided to become a full-time architect, marked another watershed. Ownership of the furniture workshop was transferred to Gerard van de Groenekan (1904–94), who had worked for him since 1917.[2] Rietveld established his architectural practice in the brand-new studio at Prins Hendriklaan 50 in Utrecht, in the very house that had been depicted and discussed in all kinds of national and international journals and was therefore also his showpiece. He was bristling with new ideas, but he was little more than a novice in terms of professional experience in the promised land of 'architecture'. Truus Schröder's support and encouragement probably gave Rietveld the decisive prod. No longer simply a client-collaborator, she had become his official business associate and lover. For Truus, her long-cherished dream of working as an interior architect came to fruition.[3]

The commissions for the Schröder and Rietveld office came in by dribs and drabs but were scarcely enough to support Rietveld's family, so Truus Schröder sometimes had to come to their aid financially.[4] As the Schröder House neared completion, Rietveld was already busy designing a property with two apartments in Wassenaar for Marie Lommen, but thereafter demand flagged.[5] A small temporary house in Nieuwersluis for Miss J. A. van der Veen was never realized, while work on a house in Bergen was halted before completion.[6] Rietveld had found it difficult to comply with all the wishes of the commissioner of the latter property, as he explained in a letter to Oud:

And to top it all she even wanted it so that when she saw the house standing like that at the chosen spot then it had to extend a friendly invitation, perhaps even a smile – it was not ill-intended, but at the time I couldn't stand it and I botched it up – Right now I'm suddenly without [work], but I would rather make chairs at this time.[7]

And chairs he made, but not to earn his living; he had burnt that bridge when he transferred the furniture workshop to Van de Groenekan. For Rietveld, the chair and other items of furniture presented an excellent training ground for trying out new ideas, materials and techniques. A fine example is the radio cabinet that Rietveld designed for M. R. Radermacher Schorer in 1925. The cabinet is composed of hinged plates of glass and stands on casters, so that the marvellous technology can be spun around and admired from every side. Like many designs from the 1920s, the radio cabinet is jointly credited to Schröder and Rietveld, while the small lamp on top of the cabinet, which was also produced as a free-standing table lamp, is attributed to Rietveld alone. Rietveld said that he drew inspiration for this design from the tall lampposts at Utrecht's main railway station, which on a misty evening emanated a cone of soft light.[8] Nothing more than a light bulb, a fitting, three lengths of hollow metal tubing in various diameters and an electric cable were needed to produce it, yet only a few were made. Truus Schröder also encouraged Rietveld to write short texts and undertake other initiatives. In the 1920s

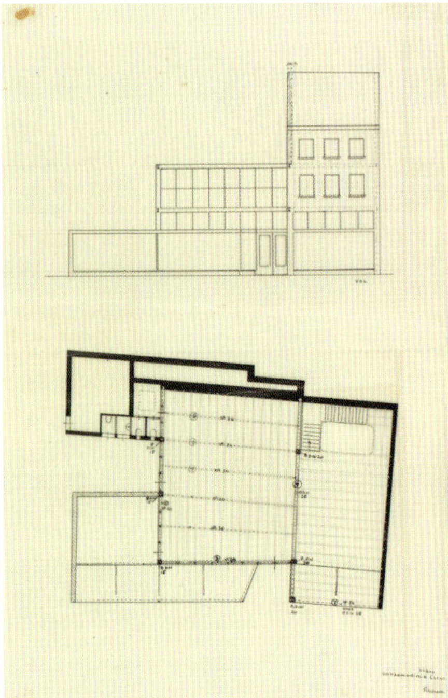

Gonsenheimer shop, Kleve, Germany, 1929 (top left and right); Record shop, Utrecht, 1927 (bottom). In many of his shopfronts, including those shown here, Rietveld created a glass cube within an inset ground floor, sometimes at an oblique angle to the facade. Because these cubes are part of the display both outside and inside the shop, the client is led from looking at them on the street directly into the shop. For these projects, Rietveld also designed the lettering and placed it in such a way that it gives a three-dimensional articulation to the facade, drawing additional attention to the shop.

Mildenberg shop Kleve, Germany, 1929 (left); Zaudy shop, Wesel, Germany (right), 1928. In the Zaudy shop, Rietveld was able to vertically extend the corner of the cube up the facade of the three-storey building as a window setback.

Collage of an isometric drawing and photograph of a now-demolished child's room for M. J. Muller, Utrecht, c.1924 (top); Modular bookshelf, 1925 (bottom left); Living room for the Birza family, 1927–8 (bottom right). These projects, like many others from the late 1920s and early 1930s, were jointly credited to Truus Schröder and Rietveld. In the photograph of the Birza living room, Rietveld is visible in the mirror.

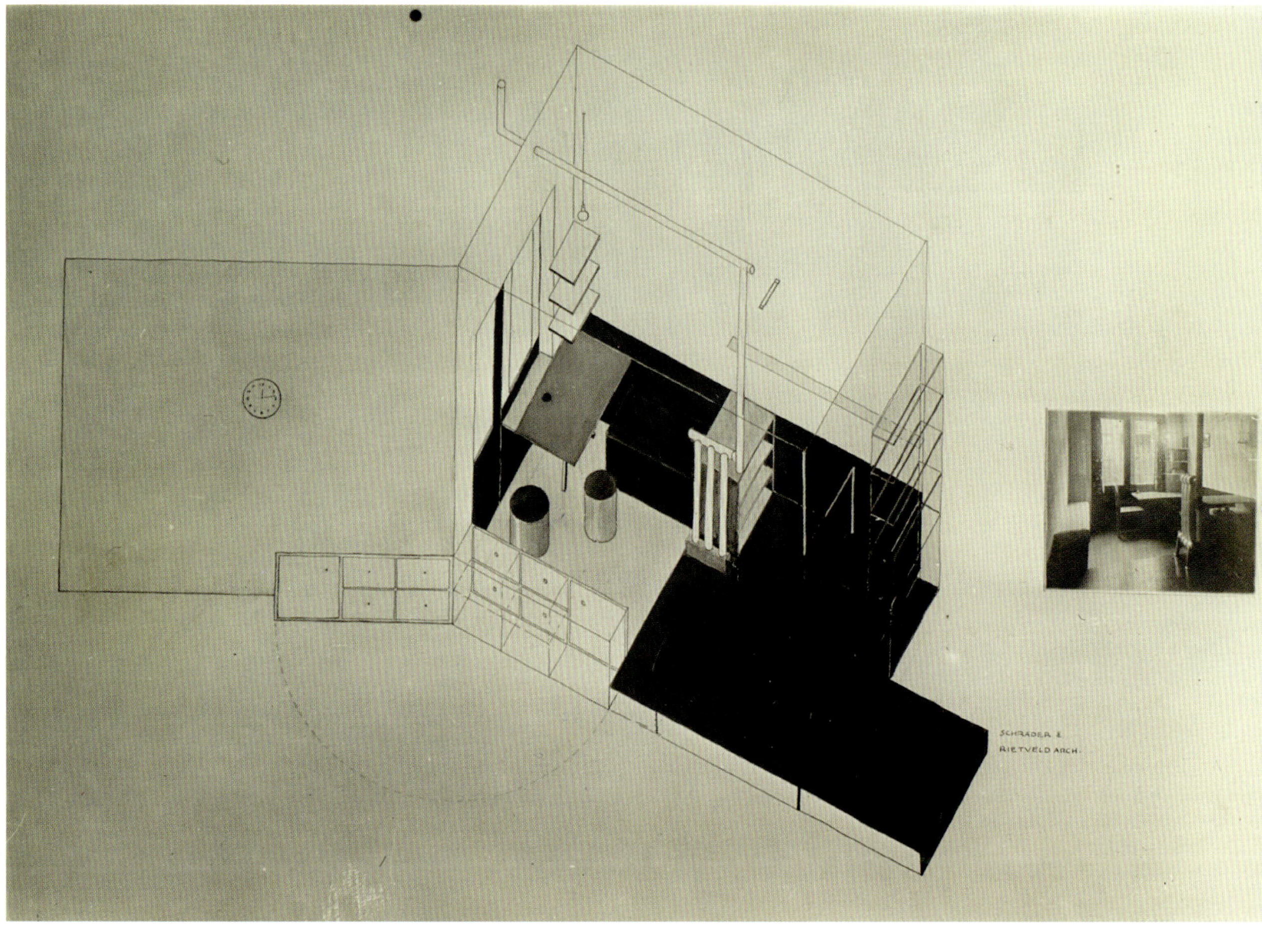

Rental property, Wassenaar, 1925. This building for Marie Lommen contains apartments with almost identical layouts.

Chairs, 1925 (left) and 1924 (right). In the late 1920s, Rietveld produced many variations on his earlier chairs, including this black chair, based on the Red-Blue Chair, and this red chair, based on the Military Chair.

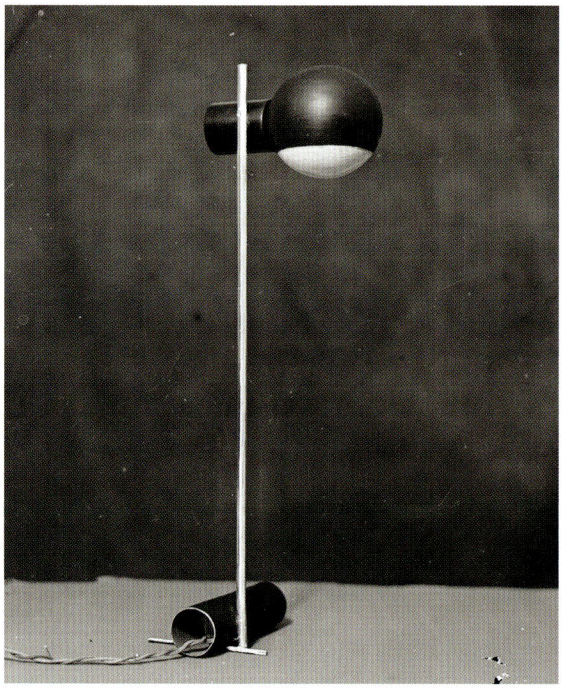

Table lamp, 1925

Rietveld played an increasingly prominent role on the local and national cultural stage, and after building the Schröder House he actively participated in the international architectural debate. He contributed two articles to *i10*, a recently established journal. The first, published in 1927, was titled 'Nut, constructie: (schoonheid: kunst)' – 'Utility, construction: (beauty: art)' – and the second, from 1928, bore the title 'Inzicht' – 'Insight'. Both texts are general in nature and difficult to follow.[9] A postcard that Rietveld sent to Oud concerning the draft of the first text seems to indicate that Oud did not understand it. Rietveld proposed a revision, but then he asked for the return of the whole package of article and drawings, stating that he would resubmit it in a week's time.[10] The articles were accompanied by designs for affordable housing: the 'Ontwerpen voor Normaal-woningen' (Designs for Standard Houses) with the credit 'Schröder-Rietveld' dates from 1927, while the 'Ontwerp kleine woningen te Utrecht' (Design for small dwellings in Utrecht) bears only Rietveld's name and is dated 1928.

A while later, Rietveld asked Oud to publish a questionnaire in *i10* in order to make an inventory of the domestic wishes of all kinds of people. He and Truus Schröder had devised it together, intent on giving people who lacked the wherewithal to have a house built to their personal specifications some influence over their future housing conditions. Rietveld thought that Oud was the right person to approach, because in a lecture with the title 'Huisvrouwen en architecten' ('Housewives and architects') Oud had commended the housewives of Stuttgart for drawing up a programme of requirements for the home on the occasion of the Deutsche Werkbund's housing exhibition.[11] The questionnaire was never published and the various design proposals for simple dwellings failed to generate any commissions.

For the time being Rietveld had to rely on contacts in his immediate vicinity. He was a member of the Utrecht-based 'Love of Art' society (Genootschap 'Kunstliefde') and secretary of the Utrecht chapter of the Netherlands Film League (Nederlands Filmliga), and via these cultural associations he came into contact with potential clients. Truus Schröder and her circle of acquaintances continued to play a major role. Rietveld and Schröder remodelled the bedroom and living room in the house of Truus's sister and brother-in-law, An and Rein Harrenstein-Schräder, on the Weteringschans in Amsterdam.

These two rooms, both realized in 1926, reveal how Rietveld's style had rapidly evolved. The beds, cupboards and timber partitions in the bedroom were painted red, yellow, black and off-white, forming a spatial composition that is still closely related to the Schröder House. Above one of the doors Rietveld suspended a panel, so that the bulbs directly beneath the ceiling scatter an attractive, diffuse light on the dark side of the room adjacent to the hallway. The single bed was used by Rein Harrenstein, a physician who was regularly called away during the night and preferred not to disturb his wife on his return. It was not intended for the painter Jacob Bendien (1890–1933), with whom the married couple for many years formed a *ménage à trois*, a suggestion that was occasionally aired and possibly led to the rather acerbic comment by J. Jans. 'By including every functionality, a typical example of the complicated way in which the bourgeoisie go to bed, sleep and get up again, and want to appear presentable. Seems simple, but it comes at an exorbitant price,' he wrote in the booklet *Bouwkunst en cultuur* (Architecture and culture), which was published in 1934 by the socialist publisher De Arbeiderspers.[12]

The living room is totally different: a round iron stove, a Red-Blue Chair, crockery and other household utensils, books and houseplants combined with new items of furniture in glass, iron and wood lend the interior a less formal atmosphere. The long, suspended stovepipe is a defining visual element. This horizontal accent is reiterated in the other items of furniture, including the long glass display case and two long bands – probably of leather – that were possibly intended as a backrest for the settee beneath them.

The Harrensteins commissioned Rietveld and Truus Schröder as a team, for obvious reasons. With other designs from the period 1925 to 1933 it is unclear why Truus is sometimes mentioned as an equal partner but at other times not. Perhaps it depended on the client's social mores, because the relationship

Music stand, c.1927. Originally designed for the composer Piet Ketting

Music room for Piet Ketting, 1927. Rietveld adapted the divan and table he designed for this room in order to create strong diagonal lines in the plan; around the same time, Theo van Doesburg was advocating the use of the diagonal line in painting. Rietveld received many commissions from artistic acquaintances.

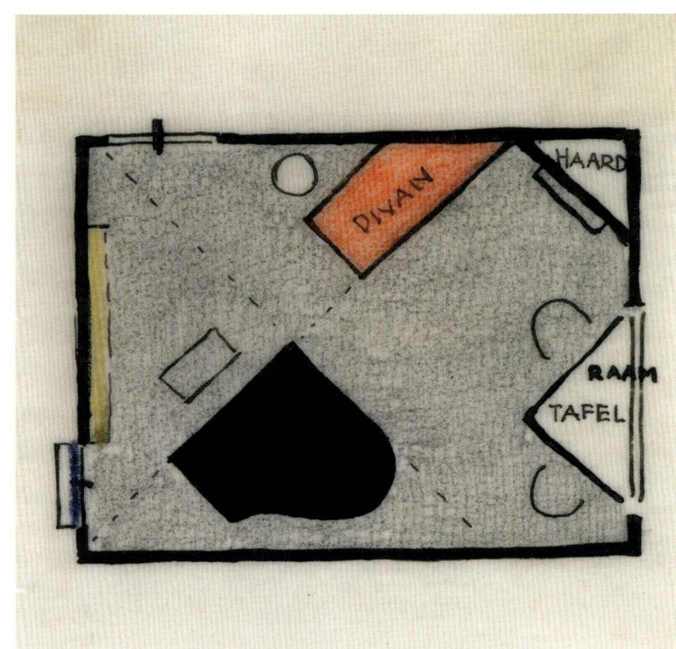

Smoking table, 1927. Rietveld used the same leg design for this table that he used for Piet Ketting's music stand.

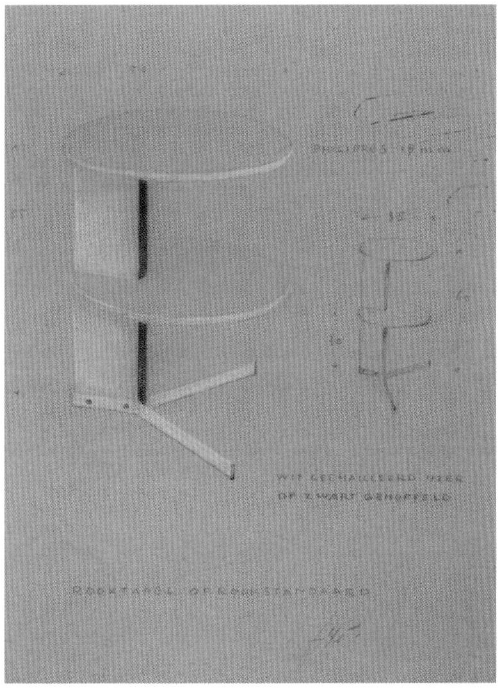

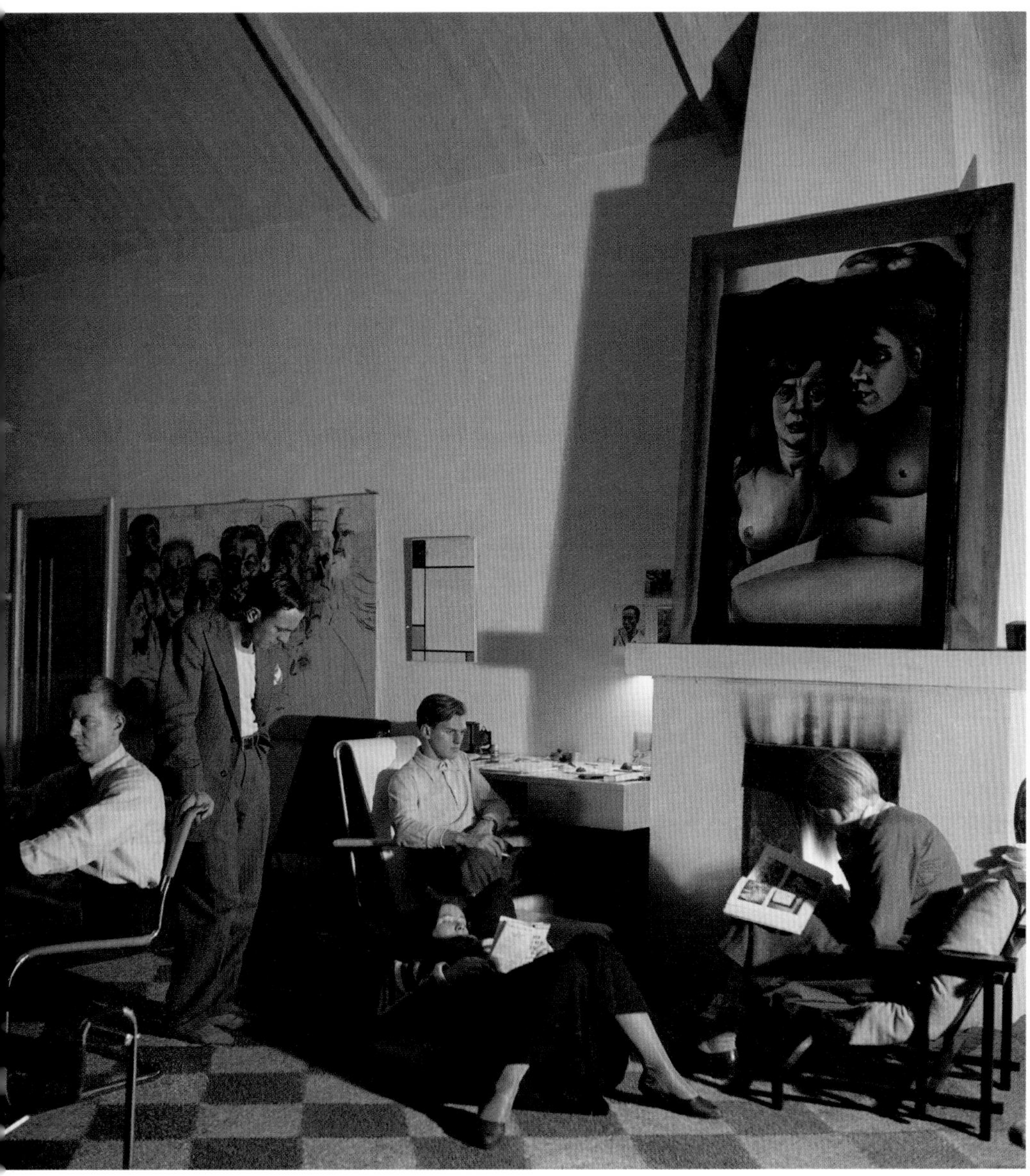

Interior for the painter Charley Toorop, Bergen, 1931. This photograph of Charley and her friends at her home was taken c.1933

Table, c.1928–30. Designed for Charley Toorop, this table was made to hold paint and brushes.

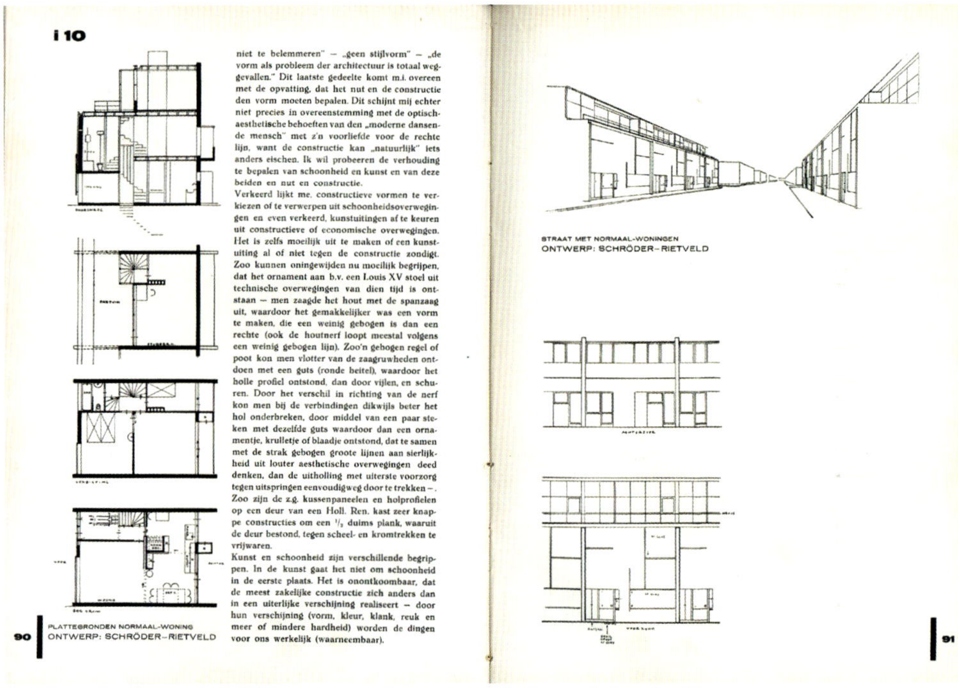

i 10

niet te belemmeren" – „geen stijlvorm" – „de vorm als probleem der architectuur is totaal weggevallen." Dit laatste gedeelte komt m.i. overeen met de opvatting, dat het nut en de constructie den vorm moeten bepalen. Dit schijnt mij echter niet precies in overeenstemming met de optisch-aesthetische behoeften van den „moderne dansende mensch" met z'n voorliefde voor de rechte lijn, want de constructie kan „natuurlijk" iets anders eischen. Ik wil probeeren de verhouding te bepalen van schoonheid en kunst en van deze beiden en nut en constructie.

Verkeerd lijkt me, constructieve vormen te verkiezen of te verwerpen uit schoonheidsoverwegingen en even verkeerd, kunstuitingen af te keuren uit constructieve of economische overwegingen. Het is zelfs moeilijk uit te maken of een kunstuiting al of niet tegen de constructie zondigt. Zoo kunnen oningewijden nu moeilijk begrijpen, dat het ornament aan b.v. een Louis XV stoel uit technische overwegingen van dien tijd is ontstaan – men zaagde het hout met de spanzaag uit, waardoor het gemakkelijker was een vorm te maken, die een weinig gebogen is dan een rechte (ook de houtnerf loopt meestal volgens een weinig gebogen lijn). Zoo'n gebogen regel of poot kon men vlotter van de zaagruwheden ontdoen met een guts (ronde beitel), waardoor het holle profiel ontstond, dan door vijlen, en schuren. Door het verschil in richting van de nerf kon men bij de verbindingen dikwijls beter het hol onderbreken, door middel van een paar steken met dezelfde guts waardoor dan een ornamentje, krulletje of blaadje ontstond, dat te samen met de strak gebogen groote lijnen aan sierlijkheid uit louter aesthetische overwegingen deed denken, dan de uitholling met uiterste voorzorg tegen uitspringen eenvoudigweg door te trekken –. Zoo zijn de z.g. kussenpaneelen en holprofielen op een deur van een Holl. Ren. kast zeer knappe constructies om een ½ duims plank, waaruit de deur bestond, tegen scheel- en kromtrekken te vrijwaren.

Kunst en schoonheid zijn verschillende begrippen. In de kunst gaat het niet om schoonheid in de eerste plaats. Het is onontkoombaar, dat de meest zakelijke constructie zich anders dan in een uiterlijke verschijning realiseert – door hun verschijning (vorm, kleur, klank, reuk en meer of mindere hardheid) worden de dingen voor ons werkelijk (waarneembaar).

90 PLATTEGRONDEN NORMAAL-WONING
ONTWERP: SCHRÖDER-RIETVELD

STRAAT MET NORMAAL-WONINGEN
ONTWERP: SCHRÖDER-RIETVELD

91

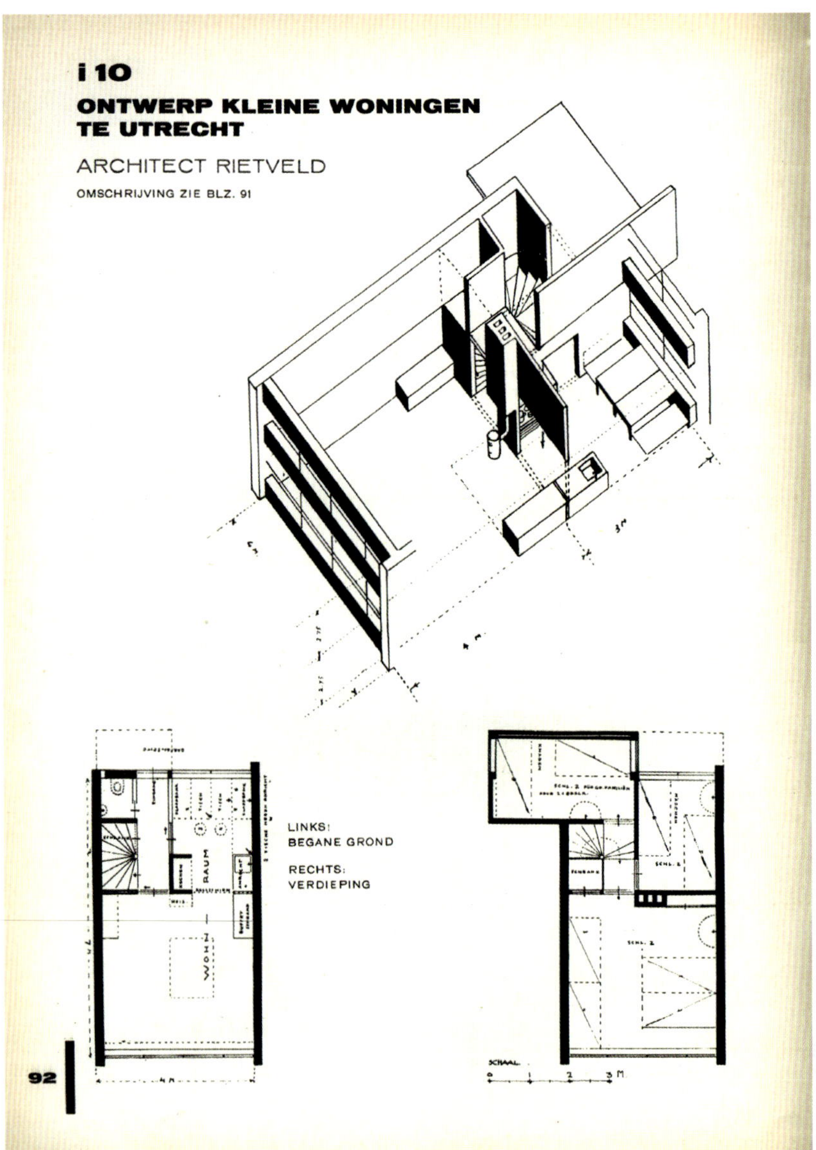

i 10

ONTWERP KLEINE WONINGEN TE UTRECHT

ARCHITECT RIETVELD

OMSCHRIJVING ZIE BLZ. 91

LINKS: BEGANE GROND

RECHTS: VERDIEPING

92

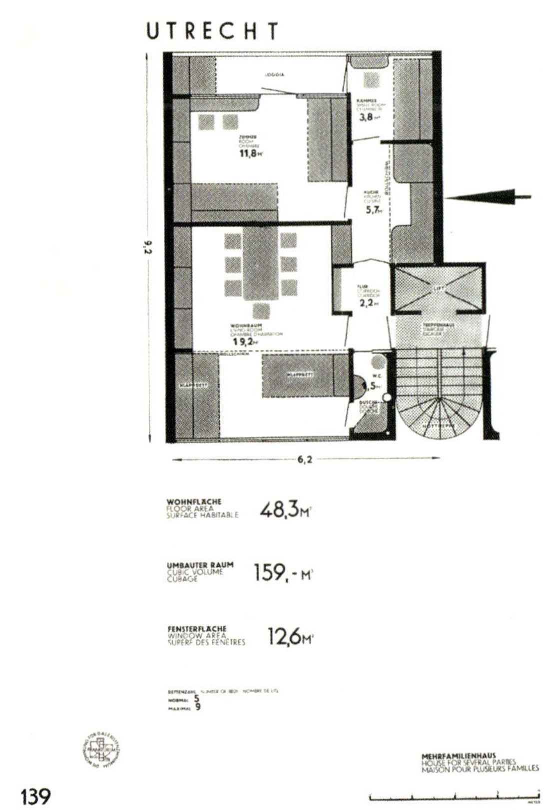

UTRECHT

WOHNFLÄCHE 48,3 M²

UMBAUTER RAUM 159,- M³

FENSTERFLÄCHE 12,6 M²

139

MEHRFAMILIENHAUS

Design for standard houses, published in *i10*, 1927 (top); design for twenty-three small houses in Utrecht, intended to replace slums, published in *i10*, 1928 (bottom left); design for a 'minimum dwelling', 1929, published in 1930 in the catalogue of the second CIAM conference, *Die Wohnung für das Existenzminimum* (bottom right). These were among the several designs for houses Rietveld published in the late 1920s that were intended for the working class, reflecting both his interest in large-scale housing and his ambition for an international reputation.

Cover design for *De Gemeenschap*, 1925 (top); cover design for *De 8 en Opbouw*, 1938 (bottom left); cover design for *Nieuw Rusland*, 1925 (bottom right). Rietveld contributed to these periodicals not only as an architect and a writer but also as a graphic designer.

between Rietveld and Truus Schröder did not meet with everyone's approval. Even H. G. J. Schelling, formerly one of Rietveld's closest friends, had great difficulty with it.[13] Be that as it may, the house for the painter Kees van Urk (1895–1976) in Blaricum (1930) and the row of houses on the Erasmuslaan in Utrecht are the only realized architectural designs apart from the Schröder House with which Schröder's name is associated. With the Erasmuslaan there was little alternative, as this residential project was her own initiative.

Living room and bedroom for An and Rein Harrenstein-Schräder, Amsterdam, 1926. Rietveld designed the open-plan living room with a kitchenette (top) and the bedroom (bottom).

The Erasmuslaan

When the construction restrictions for the polder to the southeast of the Schröder House were lifted in 1930, Truus Schröder purchased the plot of land measuring more than 1,000 sq m (10,760 sq ft) opposite the Schröder House. Given that the house's open views would be lost, a design by the Schröder and Rietveld bureau presented the best alternative. Their plan succeeded: the project is now one of the most handsome and acclaimed designs by Rietveld.
The first design for the plot consisted of a block of four dwellings and a block of three. In this unrealized design from 1930 Rietveld introduced elements that would return repeatedly in his later designs. The stairwell connects the various spaces: the cellar to the scullery; the kitchen, dining room and living room as a single through space, but set at different levels that are bridged by a few steps. On the uppermost floor the balconies to the front and rear are deep enough to serve as terraces. The basement has a separate entrance to the front. Natural light enters the stairwell via a glass roof. The broad horizontal bands of fenestration are set flush in the elevations of whitewashed stucco. Length, height and depth are based on a one-metre module. In this preliminary design the layout is indicated only in outline, but it is obvious that the *Frankfurter Küche* served as a model for the kitchen's layout. This kitchen was designed by Margarete Schütte-Lihotzky (1897–2000) in 1926 at the request of Ernst May (1886–1970), Frankfurt am Main's chief of planning for new districts, and was founded on practical and ergonomic requirements. Truus Schröder included an illustration of this kitchen's floor-plan in an article she wrote in 1930 for *De Werkende Vrouw*.[14]

Exhibition of the 'Union des Artistes Modernes', Pavillon de Marsan, Paris, 1930. Rietveld's high armchair was among the pieces exhibited by Metz & Co. The lamp and the table are also by Rietveld and the carpets are by the painter Bart van der Leck.

Interior for Charley Toorop, Bergen, 1931

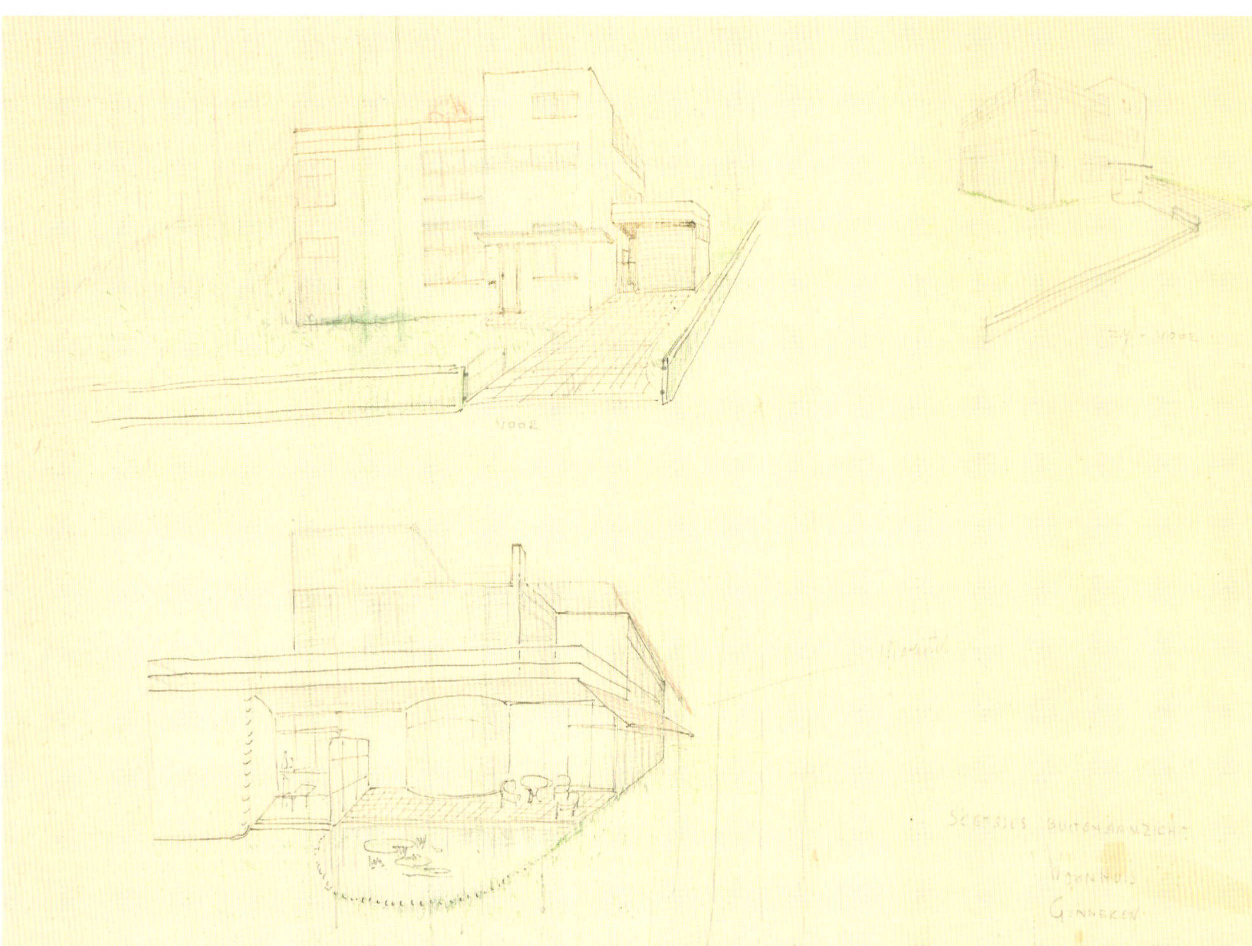

House for A. M. F. Klep, Breda, 1931–2 (top) and preliminary sketch, 1931 (bottom)

House for Kees van Urk, Blaricum, 1928–31. In this home for a painter, living space is on the ground floor with studio space and art gallery above. The graphic horizontal and vertical lines on the exterior are made through window and door details that sit flush with the facade, while the roof over the covered outdoor stair (on the left of the photograph) creates a diagonal spatial form.

Music school with two apartments, Zeist, 1931–2. The colour scheme of the interior of this school was similar to the Schröder House.

Maquette of a block of four houses for Erasmuslaan, Utrecht, 1930. Rietveld and Truus Schröder designed several schemes for this parcel of land opposite the Schröder House. This model was part of the first scheme for seven dwellings.

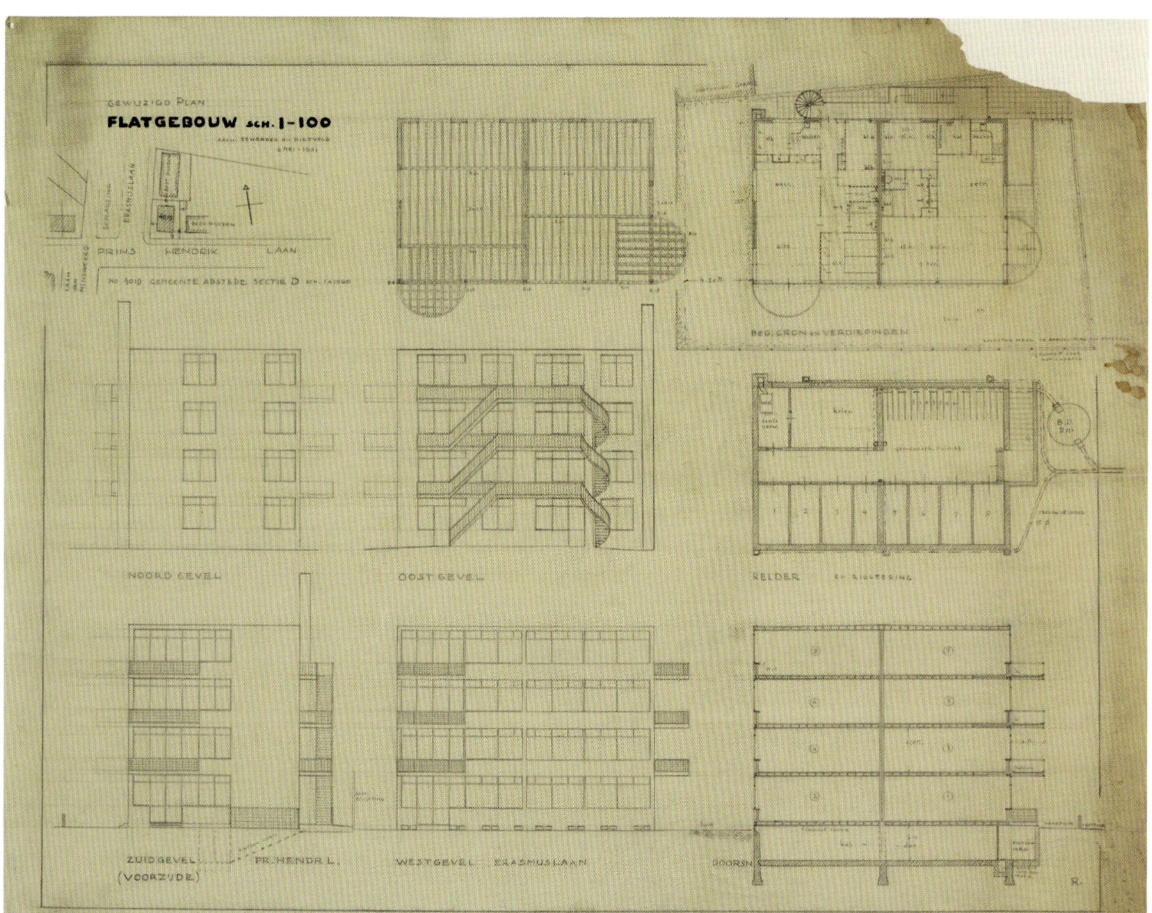

Preliminary drawing for the Erasmuslaan corner building, c.1931

Top: Two residential blocks, Erasmuslaan, Utrecht. The row of four houses on the left was completed first, in 1931, and the building on the right with five apartments in 1935.

Bottom: Ground-floor plan, Erasmuslaan building with five apartments, Utrecht, 1935

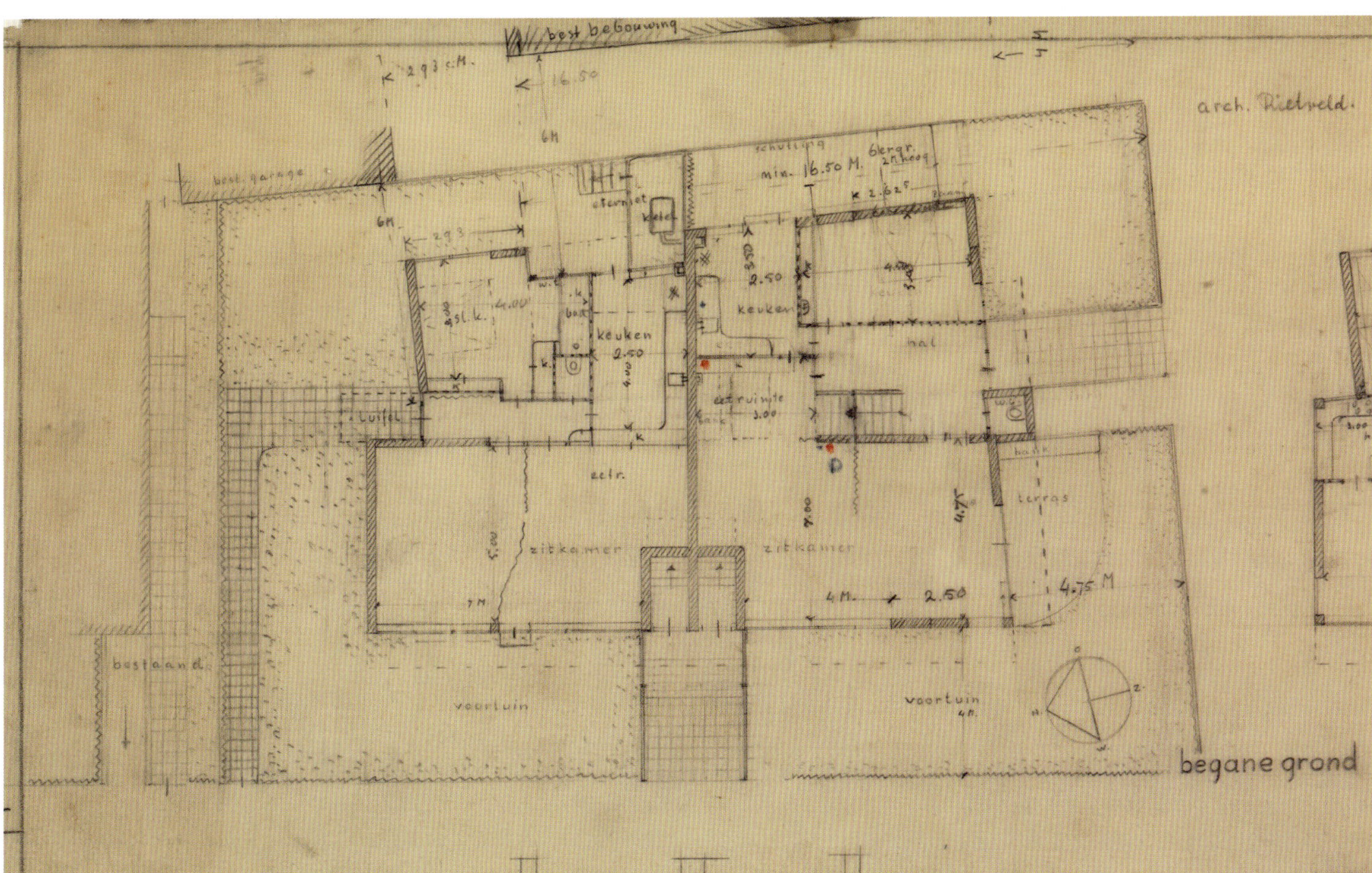

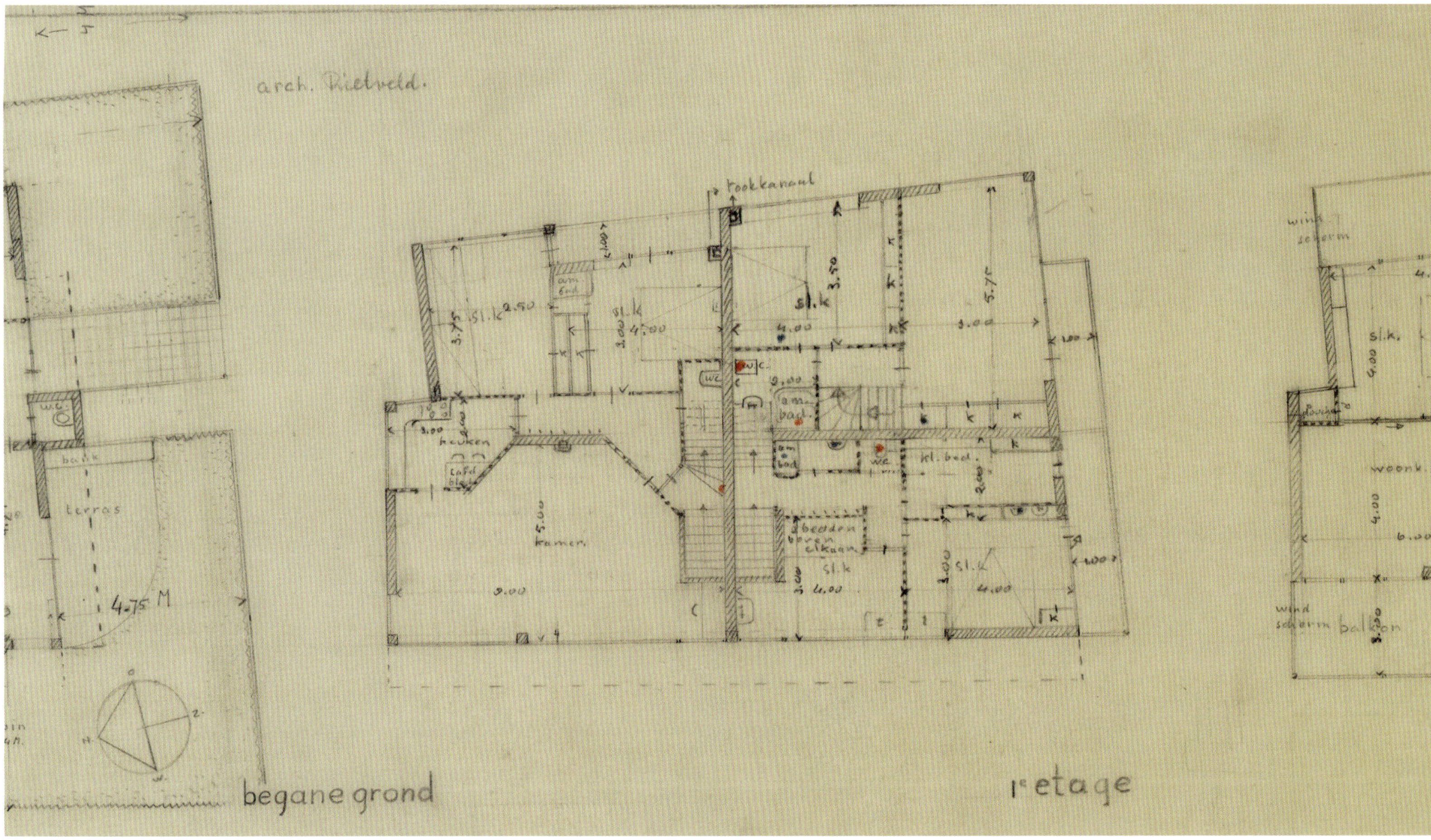
arch. Rietveld.
rookkanaal
terras
4.75 M
kamer
keuken
sl.k
wind scherm
woonk.
balkon
begane grond
1e etage

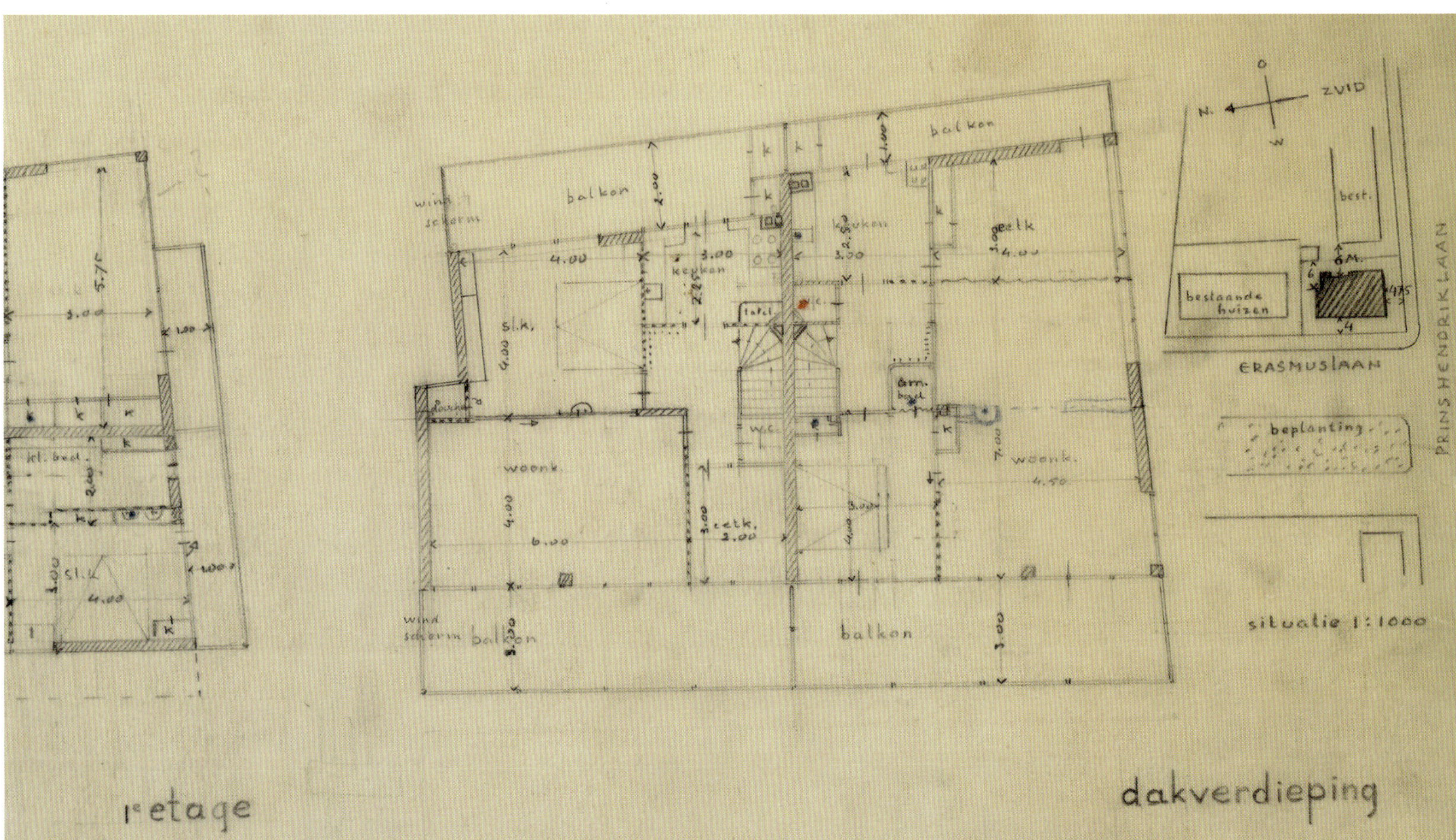
N.
ZUID
W
balkon
wind scherm
keuken
eetk
sl.k.
woonk.
kl. bed.
best.
bestaande huizen
ERASMUSLAAN
PRINSHENDRIKLAAN
beplanting
situatie 1:1000
1e etage
dakverdieping

Three of the four houses on the left-hand side of the plot were advertised for sale at 17,500 and 17,000 guilders (approximately $6,700 or £1,500 and $6,500 or £1,470, respectively). The house on the right-hand corner had already been sold, as the advertisement makes clear; the conditions of sale for the plot of land to the right, for which a block of three houses was envisaged, could be determined in consultation with the buyer.[15] Going by the semicircular protruding stairwells to the side of the block it seems that the design in the advertisement is one of the variants of the preliminary design from 1930. Truus Schröder probably failed to finalize the sale of these properties and therefore could not complete the financing of the project: she sold the land together with a new design by Rietveld for four dwellings on the northeast section of the site to Bredero's Bouwbedrijf, a local building firm. The dwellings that were eventually realized here in 1931 lack the split-level layout and the interconnection of cellar, scullery and kitchen/diner. The semicircular balconies and protruding stairwells on the side elevations are also absent. The rooms are, however, grouped around the stairwell and the spacious ground floor can be divided with concertina partitions into sections for dining, lounging and studying. For the corner property on the right, which has its entrance to the side, Rietveld designed a suspended glass ceiling above the study area at the owner's request. The opaque glass diffuses the light from the lamps affixed to the ceiling proper, making it easy on the eyes.[16]

First-floor plan, Erasmuslaan building with five apartments, Utrecht, 1935

The whitewashed plaster facades, the steel door and window frames, and the large horizontal bands of glass create the impression that the newest construction technologies were used. The text on the invitation for the public viewing of the houses was also slightly misleading: 'This exhibition aims to demonstrate the new manner of building that has so far been employed more frequently elsewhere than in our own country, not by means of new details but by replacing the heavy brick masses with space, light, air.' Some reviews actually mentioned a concrete or steel structure, but in reality this block of houses is a steel skeleton filled in with masonry. For friend and foe alike, on the completion of Erasmuslaan 5–11 it was obvious that Rietveld had wholeheartedly embraced the *Nieuwe Bouwen* – literally 'New Building' – the Dutch interpretation of the Functionalist style.

Second-floor plan, Erasmuslaan building with five apartments, Utrecht, 1935

The model home was open for public viewing from 4 to 25 October 1931, with Rietveld and Schröder in attendance to provide explanations. There was a run of interest: thousands of people visited the house and at times it was so busy that visitors had to exit via the balconies of the adjacent properties. Two houses were sold for 22,000 guilders (approximately $8,400 or £1,900) during the viewing days.[17] The layout drew plenty of attention. The walls were finished in soft pastel hues: pale green, mauve and grey.[18] The sparse furniture was fabricated in modern materials: glass and steel for cupboards, chromed tubular metal and three-ply wood for the chairs, and rubber for tabletops. The form was transparent, the colours muted. Light, air and space were lord and master in this interior.

Most of the furniture designs were from the previous five years. Metz & Co., a department store with a modern range similar to Liberty of London, produced the prototypes.[19] New was the desk, consisting of a tabletop with drawers and a storage block, which Truus Schröder and Rietveld had designed together. On the floor lay Berber rugs that were also sold by Metz & Co.

The project won admiration everywhere. On 27 October, *De Telegraaf*, a national newspaper, reported that Rietveld had stolen the hearts of a section of the public in one fell swoop, and the regional daily, *Het Utrechtsch Provinciaal* en *Stedelijk Dagblad*, proffered the headline 'Houses of Glass and Steel. A Gloria of Light.'

After the Erasmuslaan, Rietveld designed the row of houses on the Schumannstraat in Utrecht, a commission from Bredero's Bouwbedrijf that was completed in 1932, and in 1935 he designed a block of five apartments next to the row of houses on the Erasmuslaan for the same firm.[20] He produced various unrealized designs for this project as well. A design for a four-storey block of flats with eight units was rejected by the municipal building inspectorate, because 'the accumulation of eight dwellings of very limited size and of relatively low rental value at this spot would, in view of the standard of the neighbouring buildings, not be desirable.'[21] Rietveld eventually designed five apartments within a three-storey block with a total

Upright chair with an adjustable back, 1931. The chair featured in Rietveld's Erasmuslaan interior, and was sold by Metz & Co.

Model interior in one of the four Erasmuslaan houses, Utrecht, realized in collaboration with Metz & Co. in 1931

volume of about 1,320 cubic metres (46,615 cubic feet). The left-hand section contains three units and the right-hand section two, the bedrooms of the two latter apartments situated on the middle storey.

Building a reputation

These architectural projects did not lead to a true breakthrough in Rietveld's career in the 1930s, though the signs boded well initially. Rietveld had managed to build up an international network and an extensive circle of friends, but as late as 1927 he wrote to Oud that 'you are the only one who I trust'.[22] In 1928 he stood radiant in the midst of the other architects and planners invited to the founding meeting of the Congrès Internationaux d'Architecture Moderne (CIAM) in La Sarraz. In 1929 he sat alongside Le Corbusier, Josef Frank (1885–1967) and Adolph G. Sneck (1883–1971) on the jury of a furniture design competition organized by the furniture manufacturer Thonet Mundus and in that same year he attended the CIAM meeting in Frankfurt am Main with Mart Stam. His reputation even extended as far as Asia, and in 1931 the Kyoto International Architects' Association made him an honorary member, an accolade that Rietveld probably owed to Bruno Taut.[23]

The block of four houses that Rietveld built for the Wiener Werkbundsiedlung (Wiener Werkbund's housing exhibition) in 1929–1932, seemed to herald an international meteoric rise. There, under the supervision of the architect Josef Frank, a housing estate with seventy-six units was built, to designs contributed by thirty-two architects. The emphasis was on the most economical construction methods. Rietveld designed a block of four houses, each with a distinctive ground-floor layout, because his proposal with flexible sliding walls could not be realized.[24]

Rietveld felt confident enough to turn down certain commissions or ignore instructions. In 1931, in response to a rejection of his initial plans for a little summerhouse, he submitted a design with a pitched thatch roof as an example of how things ought not to be done. When the local planning committee approved this design, he wrote that on practical and aesthetic grounds he could not execute it, because 'as a Delegate to Le Congrès International ... I have a name to lose'.[25] An impeccable reputation was important to Rietveld because CIAM delegates were at that time chosen by the plenary conference. Moreover, he owed his selection to the more or less chance circumstance that Van Eesteren and Oud declined the invitation to the preparatory meeting at La Sarraz in 1928 at the last minute.[26]

After *i10* folded in 1929, Rietveld felt he was capable of producing a new publication himself.[27] The *periodiek in briefvorm* (periodical in letter form), as this little journal was called, paints an amusing picture of Rietveld and the cultural circles in which he moved. The idea was born after a new committee had taken control of the moribund 'Love of Art' society (Genootschap 'Kunstliefde'), the result of a coup staged by more progressive artists in 1930. Three new committee members, including Rietveld, proposed setting up a new periodical: 'A very simple journal without editors, e.g. with 150 contributors, of whom each week there are e.g. 3 who write down the ideas that are actually occupying them or make known their insights by means of prints of their work.'[28]

Rietveld announced the launch of this journal on 9 February 1931, at a meeting of the Dutch chapter of the CIAM where the possibility of publishing its own periodical was discussed. The list of contributor-subscribers to Rietveld's little journal included many architects from this group.[29] After just two years and six issues the periodical disappeared; the formula was probably overly reliant on the personal initiative of the members. The content of the periodical was, as one might expect, pretty chaotic and not terribly interesting, with the exception of the publication of Rietveld's own 'Idee voor een eenvoudige woning' – 'Idea for a simple dwelling' (1931), but it does offer a revealing snapshot of Rietveld in the early 1930s: self-assured, active and engaged, someone with clear-cut standpoints but opposed to any form of ideological exclusion.

Experiments for industrial production

In *Modern Times*, Charlie Chaplin's 1936 masterpiece, the worker is the main victim of the mechanization of the production process. This anti-industrial stance had exponents in architecture and design as well – in the

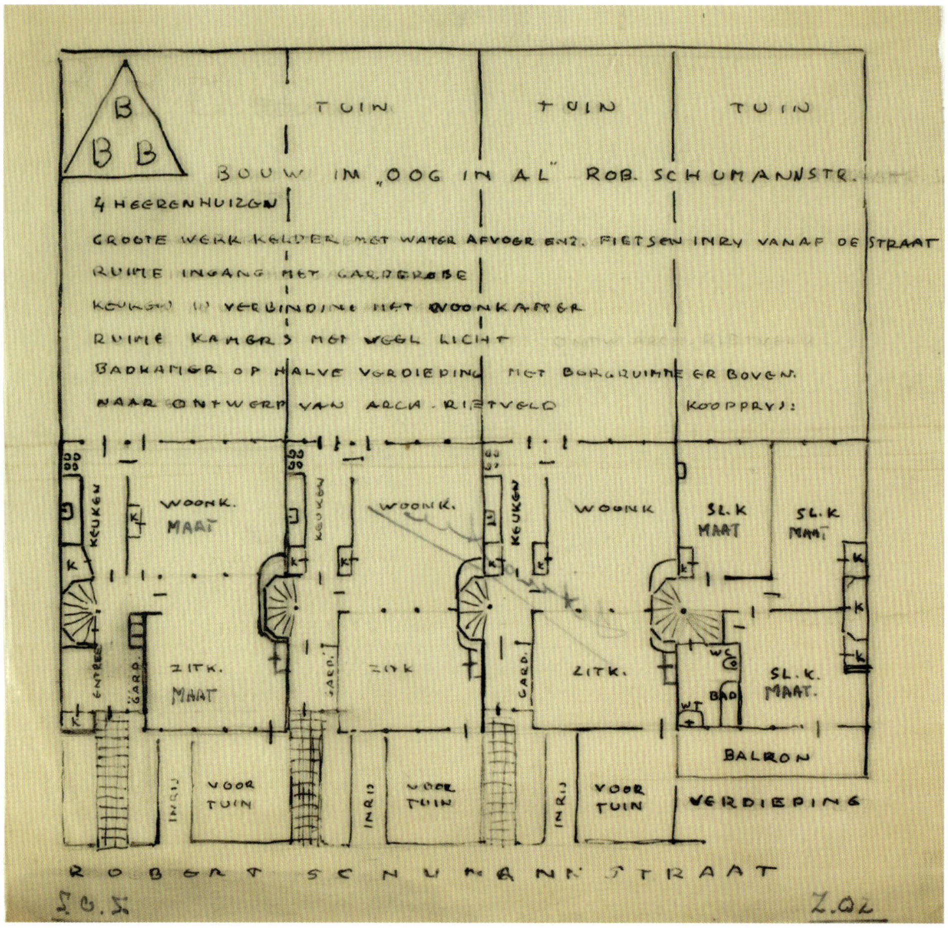

Row of four houses on the Schumannstraat, Utrecht, 1932. Preliminary drawing (top) and photograph of the completed building (bottom)

Block of four houses for the Wiener Werkbund housing exhibition, Vienna, 1929–32. Photograph of the completed building (top) and sketch with ground-floor plan variations (bottom right)

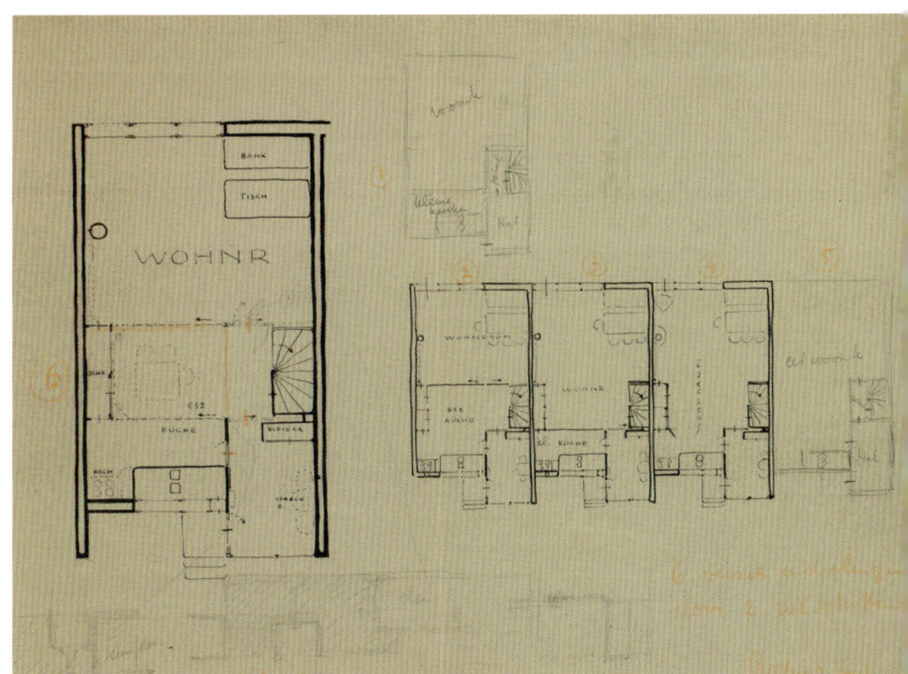

Aerial view of the Wiener Werkbund housing exhibition. Other architects who built on the site included Adolf Loos and Richard Neutra.

nineteenth-century Arts and Crafts movement led by William Morris (1834–96), for example – but such pessimism was quite alien to the European avant-garde in the early decades of the twentieth century. Rietveld firmly believed in the benefits of the industrial revolution. The pursuit of industrialization and mass production runs through Rietveld's work as a leitmotif from early on, but he did not specifically focus on these possibilities in his experiments until after the Schröder House's construction. He clearly had to shake himself free of his habits as a cabinetmaker before he could develop revolutionary ideas in this sphere. His designs from the 1920s foreshadow a more radical industrialization of the production process. Rietveld's approach in these furniture experiments was similar to his tackling of the Schröder House, which he had wanted to build using concrete. This was not feasible at the time, but for him that was no impediment to devising a form that proceeded from this idea: if he wanted something then he persevered in his quest for a means to achieve it.

Around 1925 Rietveld set aside the cabinetmaking techniques that were so familiar to him in order to experiment with other materials and methods of fabrication. He began by making variants of models from previous years: he replaced rectangular slats with round billets, made backrests and seats more comfortable by introducing a gentle curve in the wood or by using leather. The chair for Dr Hartog has a frame of gas pipes connected by T-shaped brackets.[30] The seat is a piece of leather and the back and sides are made of thin leather straps. A review in the *Nieuwe Rotterdamsche Courant* newspaper on 30 October 1924 mentions round leather seats that can be inflated with air.[31]

Rietveld's intentions are illustrated perfectly by the Birza Chair, named after Jacob Birza, owner of the only known example.[32] This one-piece fibreboard chair was illustrated together with a chair of three-ply wood in the 1929 yearbook of the Netherlands Association for Crafts and Industrial Art (Nederlandsche Vereeniging voor Ambachts-en Nijverheidskunst, or VANK) with the caption 'Machinaal vervaardigde stoelen 1927' – 'Machine-made chairs, 1927'. From the drawing and the explanatory text one can deduce that a panel of fibreboard with pre-cut incisions was soaked in water

Rietveld's *Periodical in letter form*, 1931, with an illustration of his 'idea for simple dwelling'.

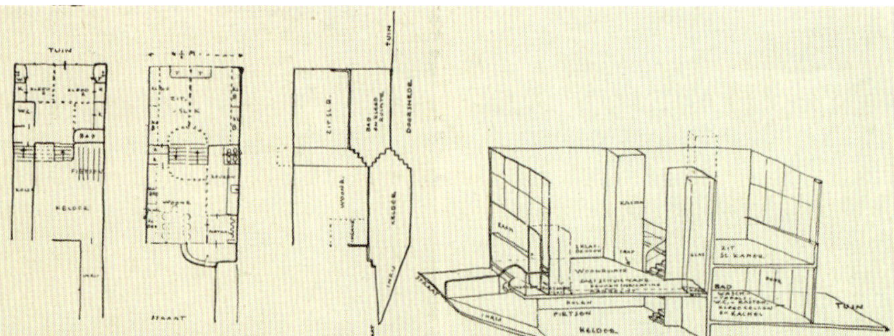

IDEE VOOR EENVOUDIGE WONING

Alles wat in architectuur meer is dan juist toereikend; elk deel dat belangrijk gemaakt wordt, hetzij uit misplaatste vakkennis, hetzij uit onkunde, belemmert een ander deel.
Weinigen overzien, dat alles wat imponeert, door b.v. afmeting, schoonheid of constructie, de in welstand verkeerende en het moeilijkst te overwinnen belemmeringen zijn.

Rietveld.

Oproep.

Kom tot bezinning en erken, dat je uitge-Hawaiand, uitge-negerd, uitge-Russischd, uitge-Amerikaanschd, uit-gedweept, en uitgeput bent, maar, dat je het desondanks niet kunt laten je ten dienste te stellen, je ondergeschikt te maken, je te wijden aan een roeping, een drang, eerzucht en ijdelheid: zijn die met z'n alle niet verbonden aan het scheppen?
Scheppen is ook voeding voor je eigen afgunst en voor den nijd bij anderen: maar zijn naijver en leedvermaak o.a. niet eenige van de schoonste vormen van geluk?
Heeft men —, heb jij geen recht op geluk? Behaal het dan; al moet het over den rug van de afgunst en van den nijd heen.
Maar, om te kunnen werken, moet je weten, waaraan je toe bent. Welnu: je bent toe aan de absoluut-vrije schepping. Geen -isme, geen enkel ander ding kan je ooit meer dwingen je in te pennen in een corset vol baleinige decreten en beginselen.
Totnutoe waren de ongeschreven romans de beste, de gedroomde verzen de verrukkelijkste, de ongebouwde paleizen en arbeiderswoningen de doelmatigste en schoonste. . . ., omdat ze niet voor de werkelijkheid behoefden te staan en zich nederig hadden te onderwerpen aan alle mogelijke en onmogelijke antieke of criant-„moderne" conventies, conventies van de vervloekte of de aangebeden massa, conventies van de middelmatigen (die maar al te lang regeeren en geregeerd hebben), — conventies van de happy few (God beter' ze), — en de eigenlijke gebreken van jezelf.
Weg met dat alles!
Weg met je eigen oude ik. Weg met iedereen, die er zoo'n pedante IK op nahoudt. En nog in ditzelfde moment begonnen met het nieuwe, het totdusverre angstvalling-onderdrukte, of hoogstens heimelijk-gekoesterde.
Voor den dag met wat je steeds maar niet durfde.
Vroeger gold bij alles: het doel.
Alles wat vroeger doel was, mag nu hoogstens middel worden.
Waag den sprong, en wees bevrijd.
Slechts de vrijen kunnen geven en gegeven worden.
Alleen bevrijden zullen bevrijden.
En het nemen? Och, stik met je „nemen"!
Kruip uit je huid; meer is niet noodig.

Jan Willem de Boer.

Noodig is: een plan tot cultureel-politieke-economische opbouw van Europa.

Een plan wil zeggen: concentratie van krachten. Een plan is: synthese èn vormgeving. Het laatste tiental jaren hebben we meer dan genoeg gehoord van: synthese. Maar alle pogingen hadden maar één resultaat: de boekbinders-synthese: het aan elkaar plakken en lijmen van heterogene gedachtencomplexen, het compileeren van los en vast. Wat ontbrak was: scheppende kracht.
Vormgeving echter veronderstelt: scheppende kracht.
Evenals de Russen een grootsch plan ontworpen hebben tot economischen opbouw van hun ineengestort land — zoo hebben wij West-Europeeërs een plan van opbouw noodig tot opbouw van onze geruïneerde samenleving. Op allerlei terrein is opbouw noodig. Onze cultuur verlangt algeheele opbouw: geen van de tot dusver aanvaarde maatstaven geldt nog. Onze staatkunde stelt denzelfden eisch. De drang naar de Vereenigde Staten van Europa wordt voortdurend sterker. Welke weg moeten wij volgen om dit doel te bereiken: welke vorm moeten we hier geven? Economisch is de wereld geheel en al ontwricht. Indien wij over moeten gaan tot een gebonden, een goed georganiseerd economisch stelsel — welk stelsel en welke uitwerking in details? Dient de gemeenschap over het individu te domineeren zooals op 't oogenblik in Rusland en Italië of dient het individu zich volkomen ongehinderd te kunnen ontplooien n'en deplaise de gemeenschap. Of dient er een evenwicht tusschen die beide machten tot stand gebracht te worden. Zoo ja, welke evenwicht? Hervorming van Hoogeschool, Middelbare school, van tooneel is allernoodzakelijkst.
Hoe zal ze er uit zien, welke vorm geven wij?
Enfin: een plan van opbouw is noodig. En een tijdschrift voor dit doel is noodig waarin door onderlinge discussie mogelijk die nieuwe vorm ontstaan kan.

E. Smedes.

„Kunst" en „Religie".

Bij de opening van een kunstzaal heeft een mijnheer van een velletje papier de schoone woorden gelezen, dat kunst (in dit geval nota bene de bouwkunst) religie was. Dat is heel erg. Het is in 1931 toch al duidelijk genoeg, dat iemand schildert om te schilderen, componeert om te componeeren en dicht om te dichten. Terwijl men nooit zal bidden omdat het bidden op zichzelf zoo prettig is om te doen, bij uitstek nutteloos als het schrijven van lyrische verzen. Wie bidt zooals hij schilderen zou (het behoorde te doen) is een pharizeeër; wie schildert zooals hij zou moeten bidden is een dilletant, een mislukt apostel van een mislukte aesthetiek.
Toch geloof ik niet, dat de openende mijnheer het zoo slecht bedoelde als hij het zei. Hij had het over de bouwkunst en bouwkunst is wel iets anders als dichten, het verschil is grooter dan het verschil in materiaal. Bouwkunst heeft sociale beteekenis, maar maak een dergelijke beteekenis toch vooral niet ethisch, religieus. Maak van een architect geen apostel; hij is iemand, die uw leven veraangenamen wil, als u hem geld geeft, zonder woorden, zonder ethica, met beton, glas, ijzer en hout. Hij zal het leven prettiger maken, geriefelijker; wat u daarna en daarmee doen wilt, is (gelukkig!) niet zijn zaak.
De menschen, die voortdurend hun mond vol hebben van de diepe achtergronden, van de religieuse beteekenis, zijn de onuitstaanbare vinders van het twijfelachtige kwartje der eeuwigheid. Wees daar verzekerd van: ze maken u met veel woorden wijs, wat zij gaarne zouden willen dat ù in hun werk zag. En zij vergeten daarbij de roeping, die ze als kunstenaar in deze ontredderde maatschappij hebben: deze maatschappij te verbeteren is het werk van predikanten of pastoors (dat is hetzelfde); haar schoon te maken, haar te bezielen door een eeuwigen, levenden vorm, dat is de taak van den kunstenaar. The rest is silence.

Gabriel Smit.

Zendt allen zoo spoedig mogelijk copie, critiek of foto's van werk en *f* 1.— voor de eerste 7 à 10 nummers! **R.**

Armchair for A. M. Hartog, 1925–7. In the late 1920s, Rietveld explored innovative methods of manufacturing in his chair designs and developed several ideas that he would continue to explore for the rest of his career.

Birza Chair, 1927. This chair (right) was the first of many pieces of 'folded furniture' designed by Rietveld to be constructed from a single sheet of material, as can be seen in the design drawing (bottom).

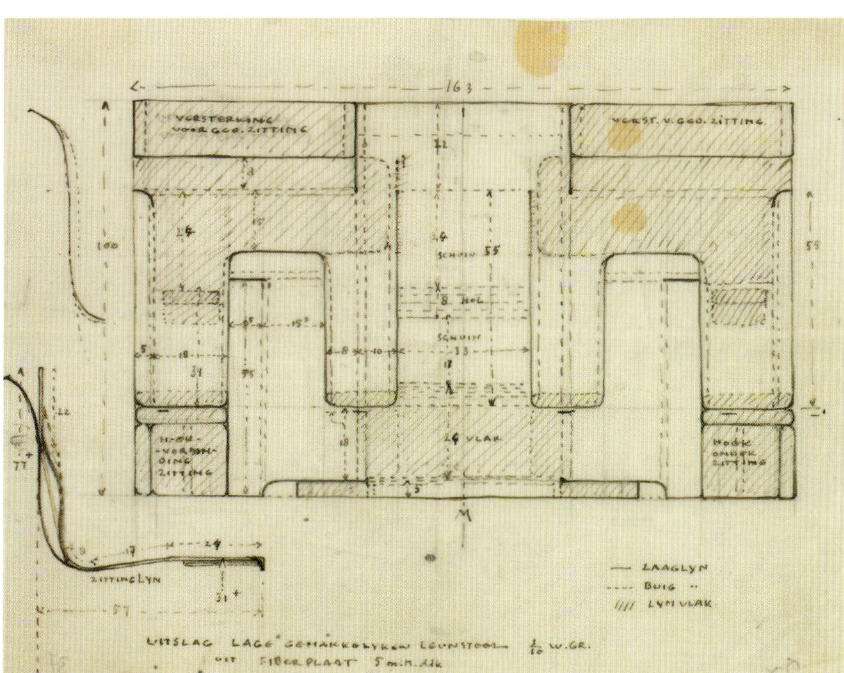

before being pressed into shape and dried.[33] It seems straightforward, but in practice it was tricky and labour-intensive. The notched pieces of organic fibreboard lay soaking in the ditch by the Schröder House for days before they were soft enough to be flexed into shape.[34] Everything was clamped in place with sturdy nuts and bolts.

Rietveld was pleased with the result: perhaps the chair was 'not very beautiful, but something was achieved nonetheless'.[35] He presented this one-piece fibreboard armchair along with the black armchair from 1924 with a frame of round wooden billets (*ronde stokkenstoel*), and a prototype tube framed chair (*beugelstoel*), at the exhibition 'Architectuur, Schilderkunst en Beeldhouwkunst (ASB)' – 'Architecture, Painting and Sculpture (ASB)' – in 1928. This group presentation was organized by the artists' initiative of the same name and was staged at the Stedelijk Museum in Amsterdam. The critic Otto van Tussenbroek (1882–1957) concurred with Rietveld that the degree of beauty or ugliness should not be the principal criterion for the assessment of a design:

These things are not, moreover, born as homework assignments, but out of the exigencies of modern mechanical fabrication. A new beauty can emerge from the reduction to an acutely concentrated utilitarian principle… Forces like R i e t v e l d are only used by life in order to attain by degrees a new formal beauty, and even if what they contribute strikes many people as strange or even laughable, one cannot (and never can) manage without such forces, even if one mistakenly thinks the opposite.[36]

The tube framed chair stands between the highback chair, which is a variant of the Red-Blue Chair, and the Birza Chair. The ongoing development of the Red-Blue Chair, in which the frame and seat are two separate entities, proceeds via the tube framed chair, in which the seat serves as a structural connection between the two supports, to the Birza Chair, in which form and construction converge. Thirty years later, at his 1958 retrospective in Utrecht, Rietveld presented an armchair of bent plywood that he labelled the 'Eerste Model' – 'First Model' – which was probably made specially for this event. It uses the same constructive principle as the tube framed chair and the form is reminiscent of the armchair from the brochure 'Meubels om zelf te maken' (Furniture to make yourself), which he and Truus Schröder worked on in 1943–4. All in all this presentation model seems more like a summary of Rietveld's thought processes during the 1920s than a prototype.[37] Theo van Doesburg had described Rietveld's initial experiments as 'slender spatial animals', but in these experiments the slender three-dimensionality recedes into the background somewhat, while the 'animal', the playfulness and autonomy of the form, has been retained. The three chairs trace out Rietveld's development.

Upright chair, 1927. This chair is made of round maple poles and a piece of plywood.

In 1930 Rietveld designed a series of modular furniture for the Metz & Co. department store. The method for the industrial production of furniture based on standardized elements was conceived and propagated in Germany.[38] Before Rietveld, the Dutch designer Willem Penaat (1875–1957) developed a series of 'combinable furniture' for Metz & Co. in 1928. The principle of Rietveld's series of modular 'plank furniture' is as simple as it is ingenious: using metal brackets and wooden planks it is possible to assemble open and closed cupboards in any size desired. The system included components and end-pieces for beds and tables as well. In his board furniture Rietveld demonstrated once again that it is pre-eminently space that defines the quality of his work. The standard module is 30 × 30 × 90 cm (1 × 1 × 3 ft), the same as for the stacked modular cupboard he designed together with Truus Schröder in 1925. This module was also employed by Rietveld for a frosted-glass ceiling lamp and glass display cabinets.[39] In 1931 he and Schröder exhibited the 'glass case-cupboards', as one reviewer called them, as part of the suite of board furniture in the model home at the Erasmuslaan. The spatial effect is also essential to the design of this forerunner of post-war collections of modular furniture.[40]

Architecture: the dwelling core and the Garage with Chauffeur's Apartment

Rietveld's complaint (in the abovementioned letter to Oud) that he would rather make chairs than design a house down to the most trifling detail for his client from Bergen was a touch melodramatic. However, he could hardly depend on making chairs as his main source of

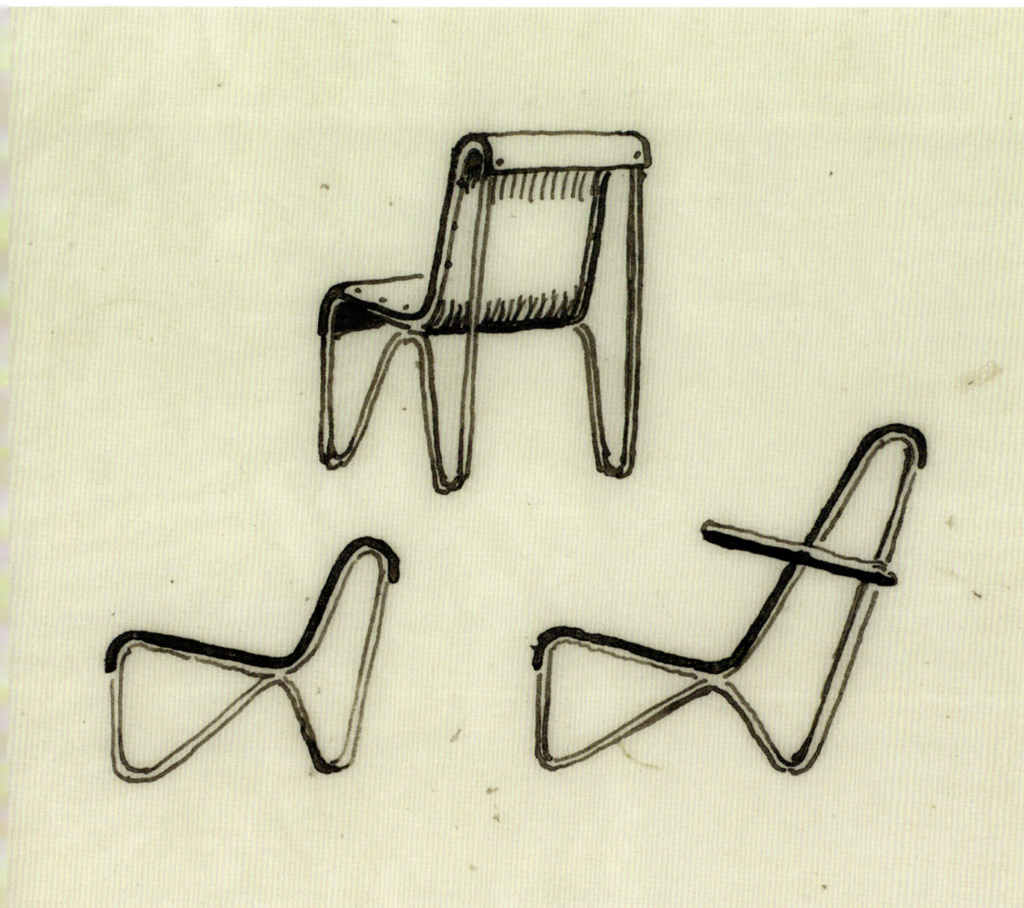

Tube framed chair, 1927. The first prototype (top right) of this chair type was made of fibreboard and iron tube; Rietveld designed other variations (top left) and other models were produced by Metz & Co. after 1927 (bottom right).

Armchair of Wouter Paap,
c.1928–30

Hopmi Chair with armrests,
1932–4

income, because he considered the experiment more important than the result and did not concern himself with commercial viability. Whether it was a house or an armchair, whether he had a client of flesh and blood or was elaborating his own concept, for Rietveld it was imperative that he made progress, took steps along the path that he had found intuitively and was often unable to describe clearly until later on. Some clients thought that was terrific, others could live with it, and a few felt they were taken for a ride. The physician H. van der Vuurst de Vries, for whom Rietveld built a Garage with Chauffeur's Apartment above it on the Waldeck Pyrmontkade in Utrecht in 1927–8, belonged to the latter group.[41] Van der Vuurst had no complaints about the alterations to the facade or the interior of his substantial house on the Julianalaan in Utrecht, which was also part of the assignment, but plenty about the Garage with Chauffeur's Apartment. The structure leaked 'like a sieve', so all kinds of urgent modifications were called for.

In 1932 Van der Vuurst placed an announcement in the *Utrechtsch Dagblad* thanking the 'fine' architects who had advised him on how best to render the property waterproof.[42] The problems were not, however, caused by Rietveld, because the flaws were largely the fault of mistakes during construction and the demands of the municipal surveyor, who did not trust the unusual structure and insisted on the bricks being set directly against the inside of the concrete slabs.[43]

Rietveld shortened the existing garage in the back garden of the main house on the Julianalaan and extended it as far as the building line on the Waldeck Pyrmontkade to the rear. Above this new section he realized an apartment with three rooms arranged around the landing. Light enters through the roof lantern, the bay window and the window in the front elevation, in a manner similar to the upper floor of the Schröder House. For its construction Rietveld used a steel skeleton of posts and girders, to which concrete panels measuring 1 × 3 m (3 ft 3 in × 10 ft) were bolted.[44] The framework was filled in with brick masonry, intended by Rietveld as a cavity wall. The black background of the concrete panels was stencilled with enamel paint in horizontal rows of two white dots, though at the top and bottom edge of the panels a strip

Armchair with a frame made of bent metal tube, c.1928–30

Drawing of an armchair for the brochure 'Do-It-Yourself Furniture', 1943–44

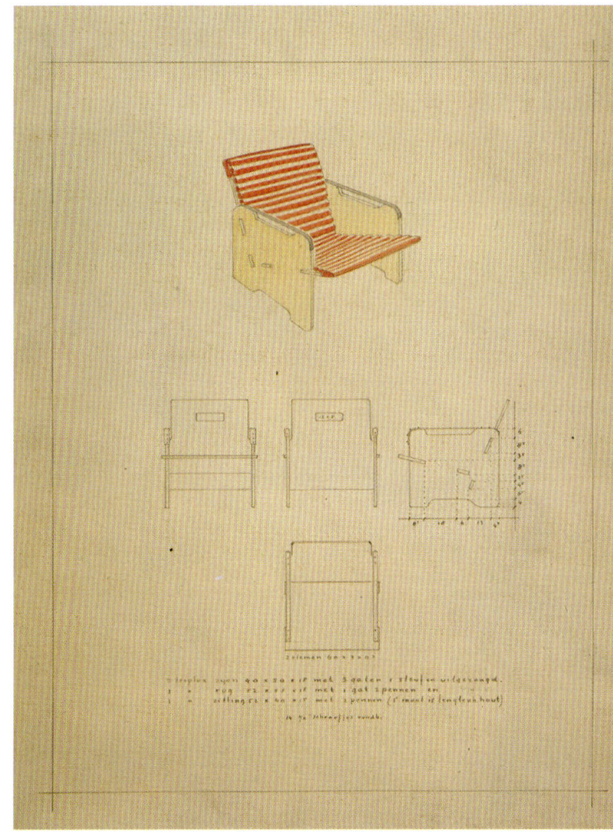

Armchair prototype, c.1958 (bottom left); Drawing of armchair, 1927 (bottom right). Some of the ideas Rietveld developed in the late 1920s would appear again and again in his designs. This plywood prototype was probably built for his retrospective in Utrecht in 1958, to show a construction method he invented in 1927, and which he also used in the 'Do-It-Yourself Furniture' armchair from c.1943.

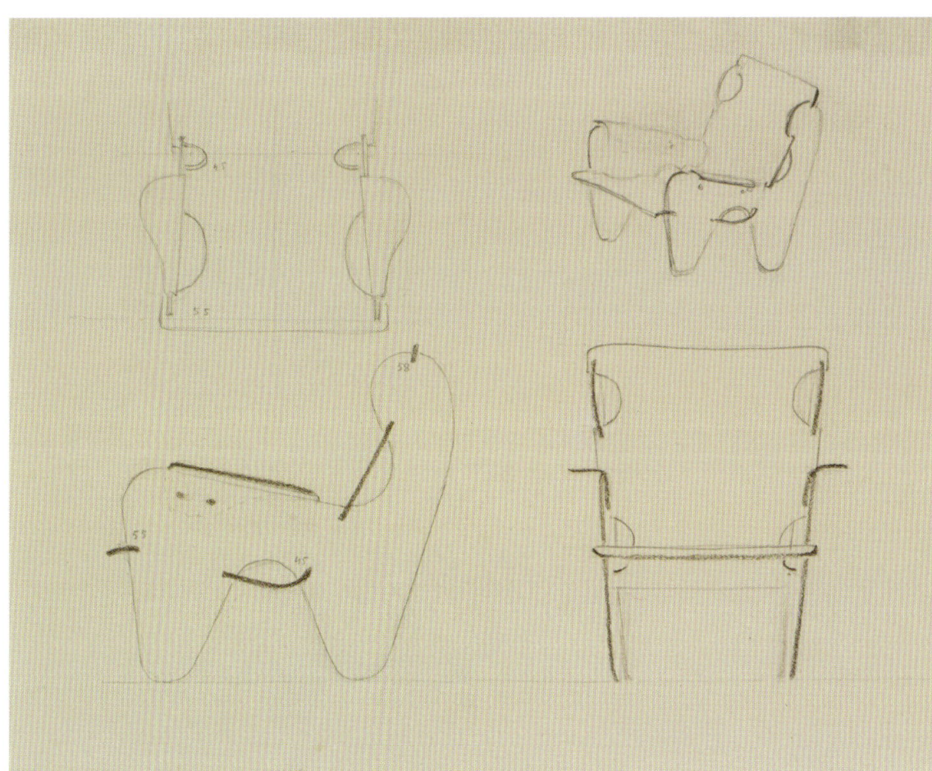

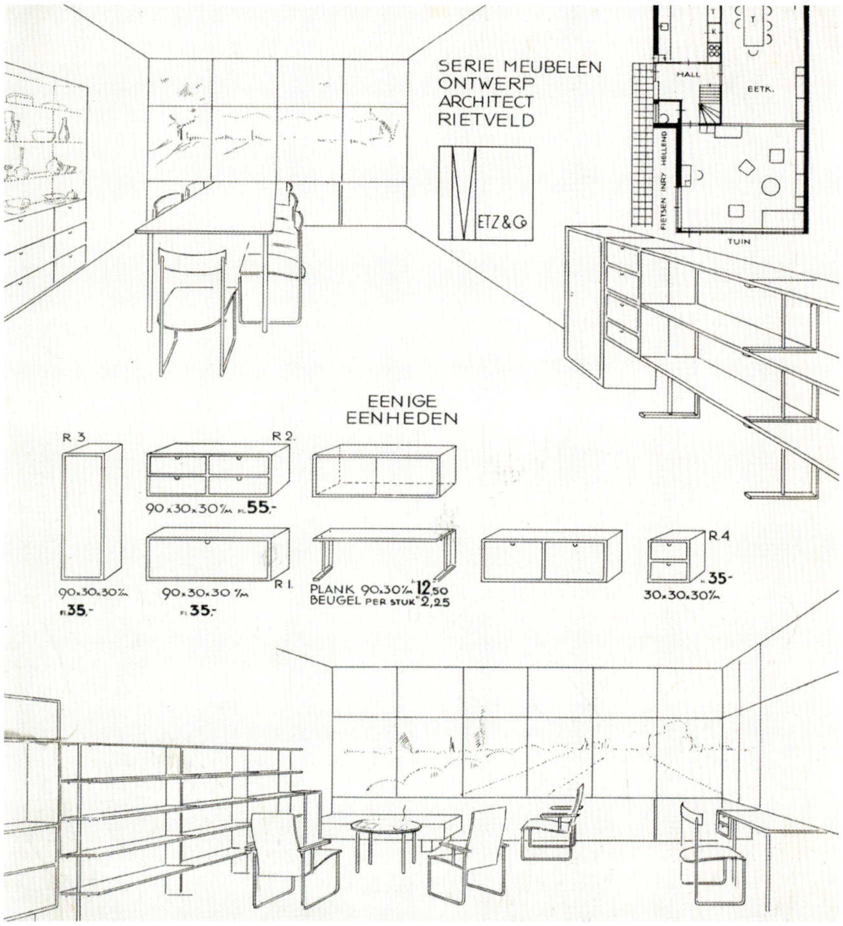

Pages from Metz & Co. brochures advertising Rietveld's modular furniture (top left), desk (top right), and tube framed chairs, (bottom left), 1930–8

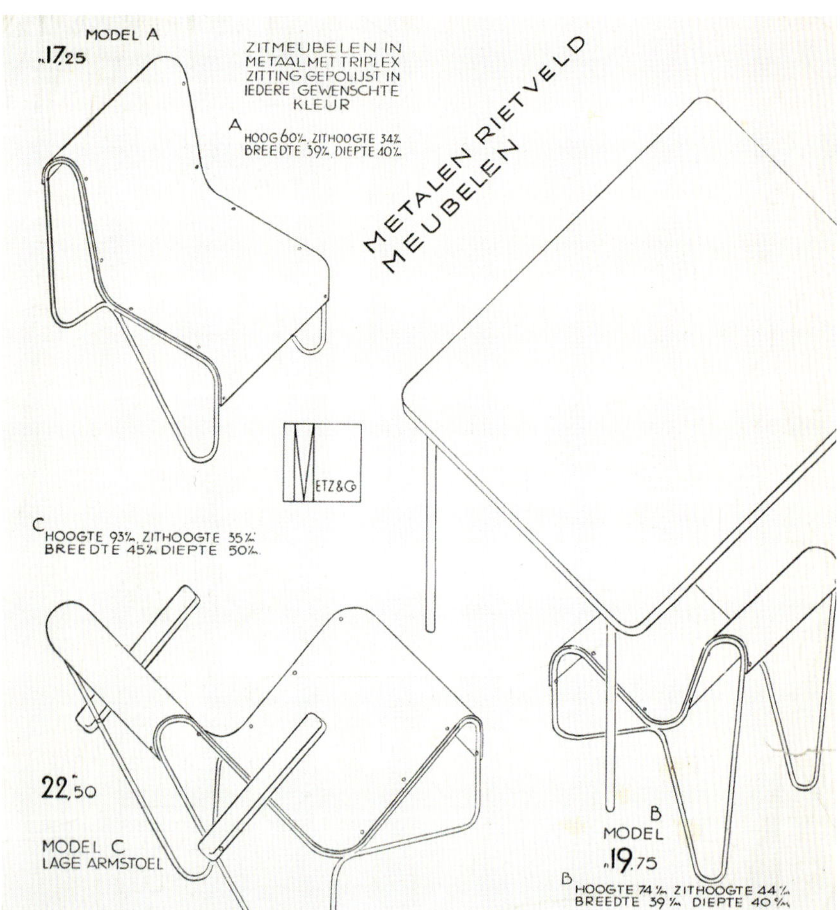

Bottom right: Metz & Co. store, The Hague, 1934, collaboration with W. Penaat and B. van der Leck

Metz & Co. rooftop pavilion, Amsterdam, 1933 (top); Metz & Co. shop, Amsterdam, 1940 (bottom). Rietveld did not only design furniture for Metz & Co.; he also designed shops for them, which frequently displayed his own designs. The steel tube framed bed shown in the 1933 pavilion was designed by Rietveld in 1931, and it was also shown as a daybed in the model interior in the Erasmuslaan.

Garage with Chauffeur's Apartment, Utrecht, 1927–8. The flat for the chauffeur was located on the first floor. The building is constructed of an iron framework filled with masonry and covered with concrete slabs, adorned with a pattern of white dots on a black background made with enamel paint.

Presentation sheet of the elevations, ground plan and details of the Garage with Chauffeur's Apartment, 1927

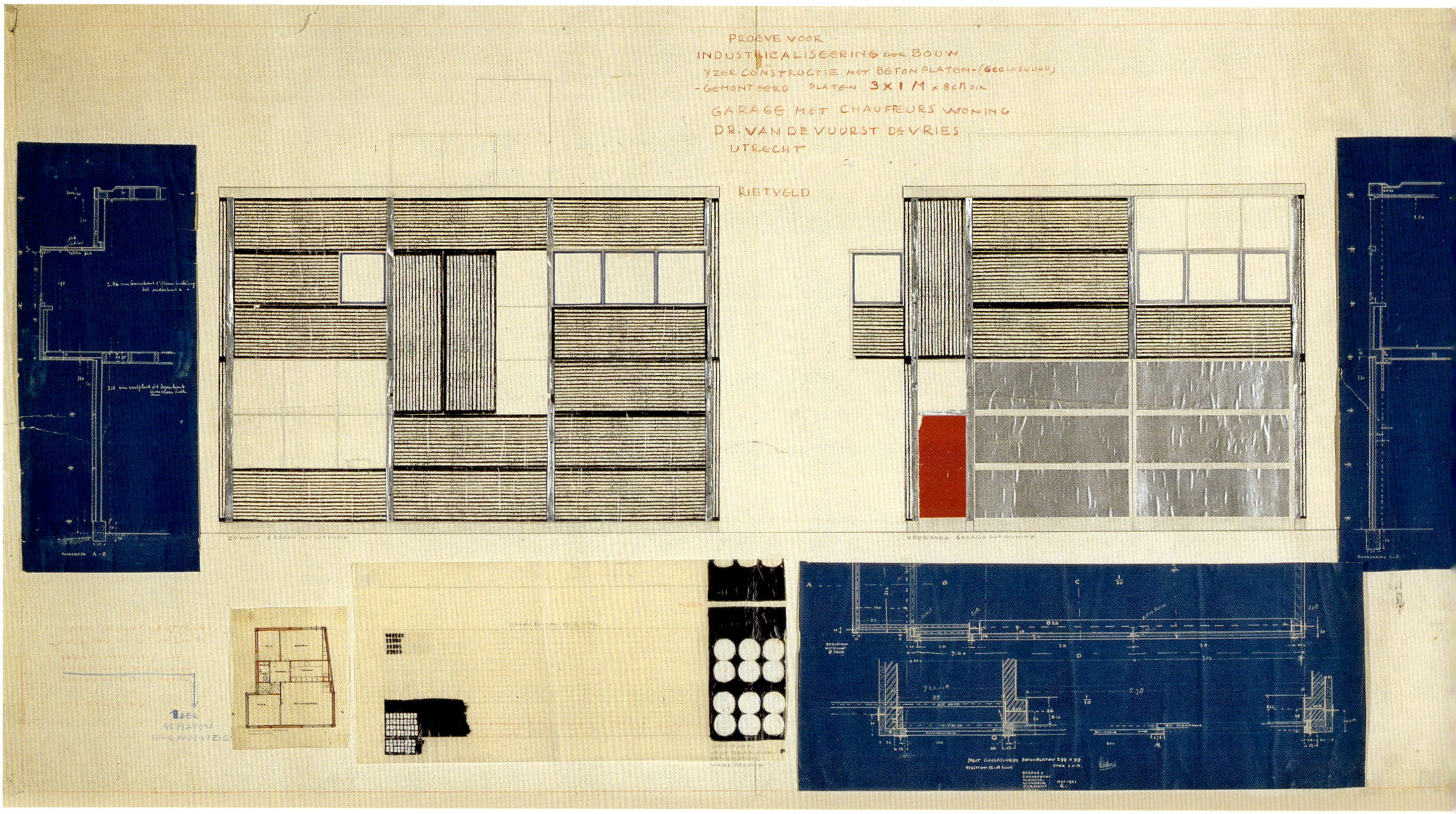

of approximately 5 cm (2 in) was left unpainted. From a distance this looks like a pattern of horizontal and vertical lines in a slightly off-white colour, approximating the visual effect of a metal grille. The front door was painted bright red and the garage doors a silver grey.

It was an important design for Rietveld. He produced a 143.2 × 76 cm (4 ft 8 in × 2 ft 6 in) presentation sheet, with drawings in colour of the front and side elevations, three blueprints for the concrete slabs, two drawings of the floor-plan and a small sketch of the dwelling's situation and its finish. This sheet bears the title 'Proeve voor industrialiseering der bouw' – 'Case study for the industrialization of building'. A second sheet presents the steel carcass with the concrete panels partially drawn in. These sheets were probably intended for the 'ASB' exhibition in 1928, where besides the abovementioned chairs Rietveld also presented the Schröder House, the Harrenstein interiors and his recent design for twenty-three small dwellings.[45]

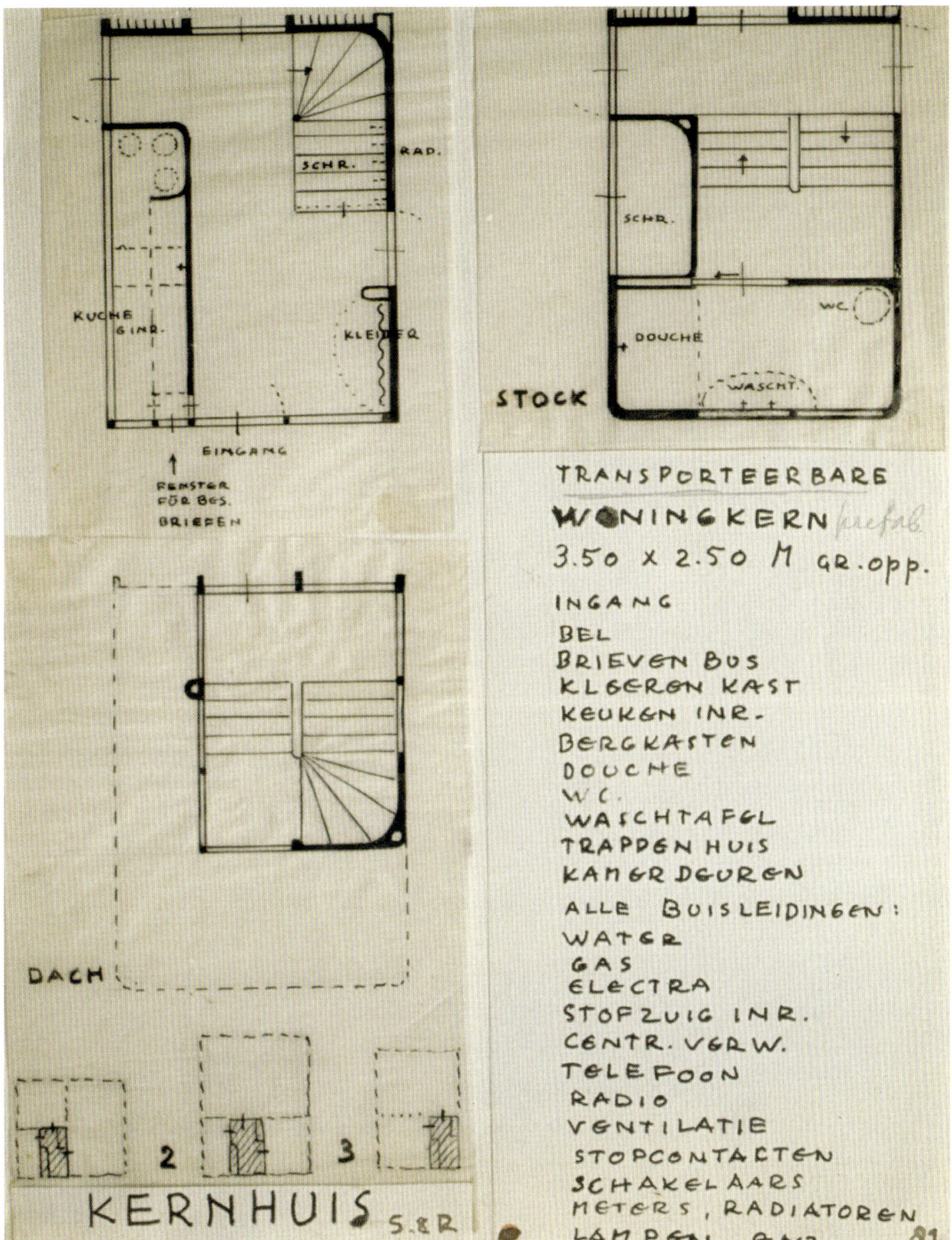

Design for a transportable house core, 1929

Mart Stam was categorical when he wrote in 1935 that a working-class home could not be a down-sized detached house or a scaled-down (and therefore cheaper) middle-class dwelling.[46] Rietveld agreed with him completely and adopted this principle in his gloss for 'Een nieuwe plattegrond voor een volkswoning' – 'A new floor-plan for a worker's dwelling'. He published this design, which was the fullest elaboration of one of his ideas from the 1920s, in 1941: the dwelling core.[47] The first opportunity for the public to become acquainted with Rietveld's dwelling core was at the 'Neues Bauen' (New Building) exhibition staged in Utrecht in 1929. The idea was to prefabricate the core of the house, comprised of a front door, stairwell and bathroom along with technical services such as water, gas and electricity. The desired number of rooms could be added to the core at the building site and the house completed.[48]

Industrial production or prefabrication for the construction sector had not been considered prior to World War II. Rather than focusing on the civil engineering aspects, Rietveld concentrated on the development of the type of dwelling in which the stairwell together with the abovementioned core functions stood in the middle, with the living spaces to

Design for a prefabricated dwelling, 1929. The exterior walls are primarily of glass. A lift gives access to the upper floors. The ground floor can be completely opened by a sliding wall.

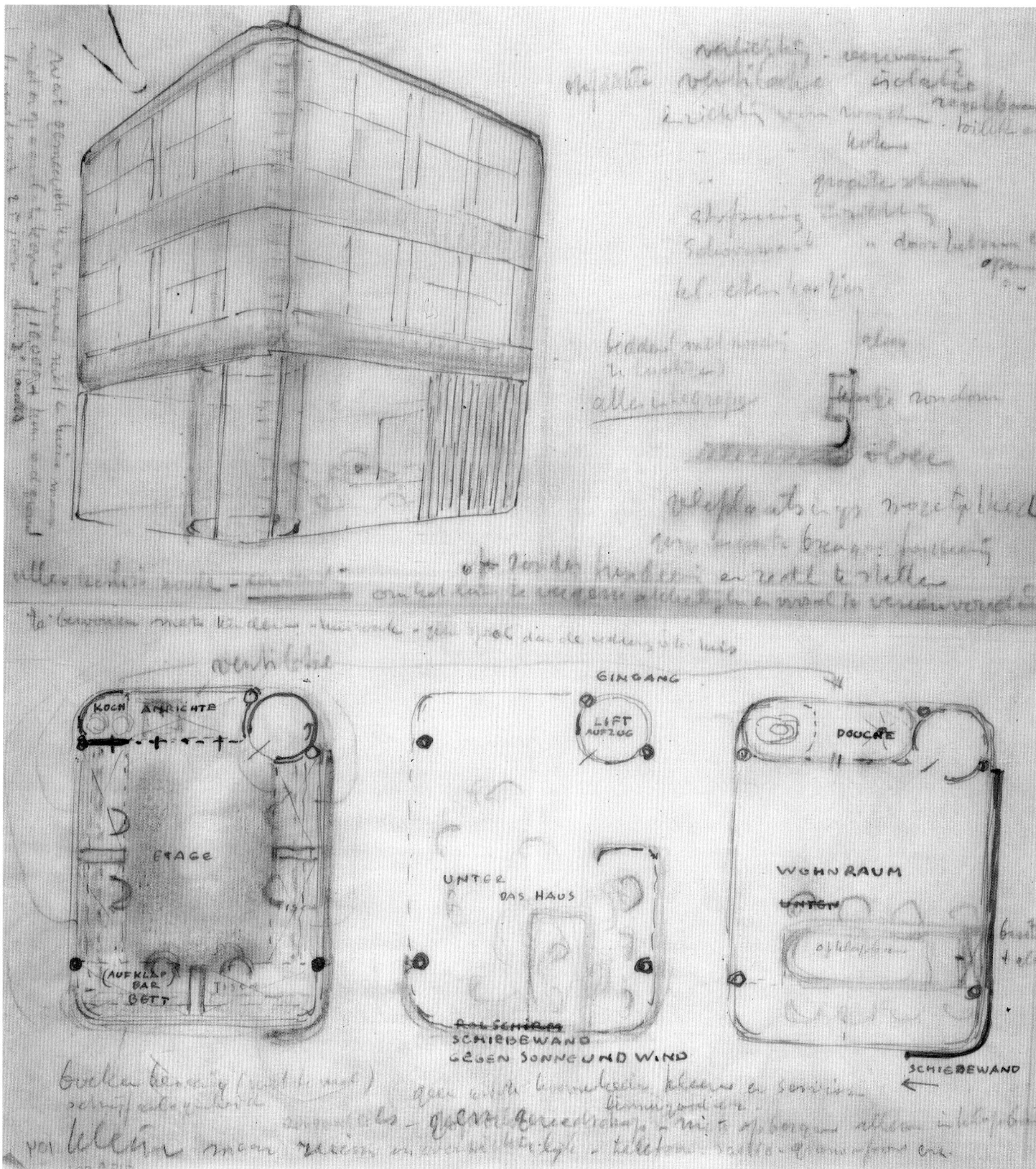

Plans for a prefabricated house core with an oval bathroom, 1929

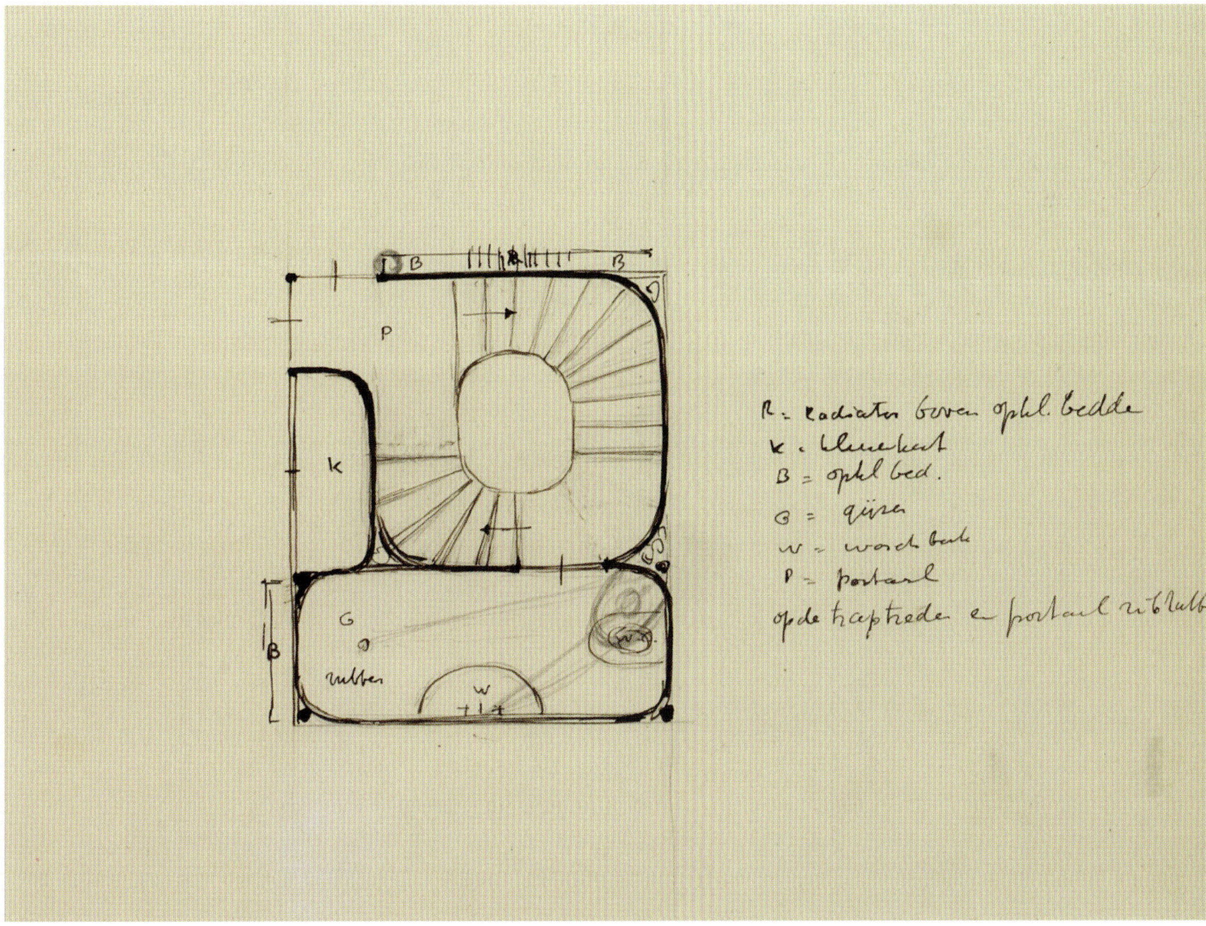

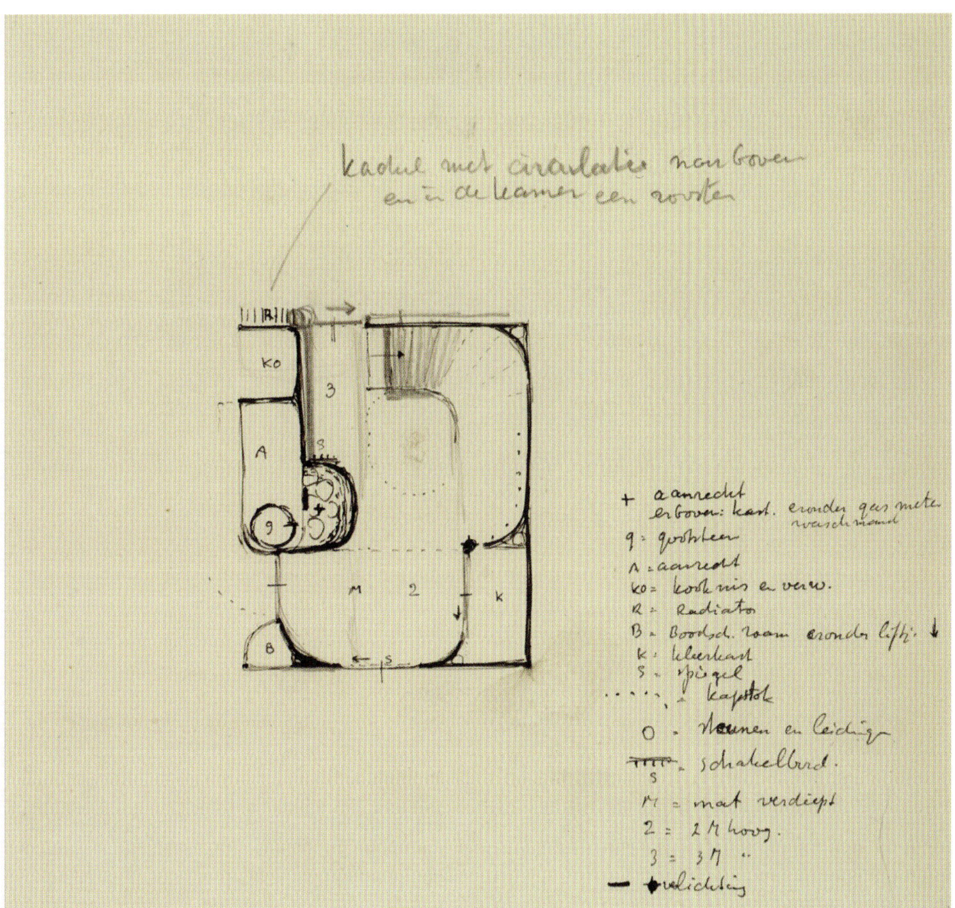

Drawing of a prefabricated bathroom and kitchen unit in several floor-plans, 1956. Rietveld continued working on his idea of a prefabricated central house core, first developed in the late 1920s, through the rest of his life.

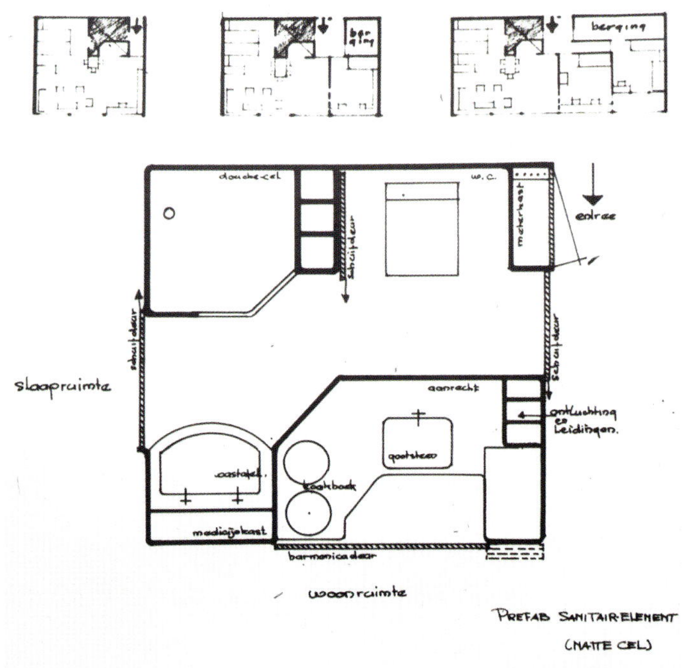

Model for a working-class dwelling with a central core, 1941

Design for a workers' residential district, Tolsteeg, Utrecht, 1941: Model (top); Site plan (bottom). Most of the houses in this design are built with a prefabricated core.

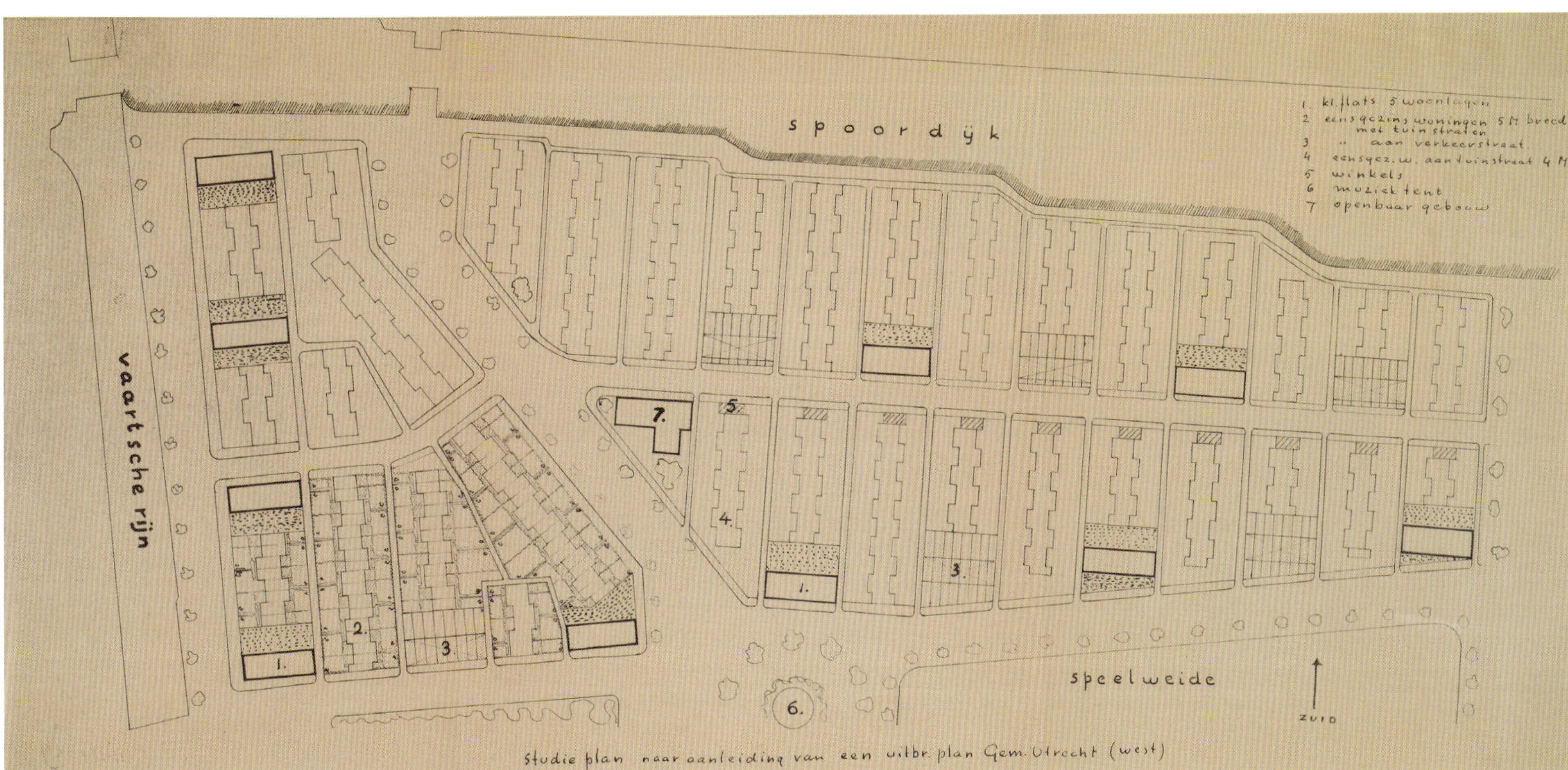

the front and rear. This idea would exercise him until the late 1950s. He drew variants of different size and designed residential districts with houses and flats that used this core.

Of the many unrealized plans, 'Een nieuwe plattegrond voor een volkswoning' – 'A new floor-plan for a worker's dwelling' – is important because it consolidates various recurring elements and Rietveld gives a detailed explanation of the design. The basic principle is a specific typology for affordable housing, a typology that is normative. The mass product could not be a cheap, smaller version of the luxury product; a detached house was to be 'at most a luxury edition' of the basic type. The architect can 'unite all the bits of space that have been lost or are used one-sidedly ... into a single practical space, a sort of reallocation of living spaces ...' One example of the amalgamation of functions is the combination of hallway, bicycle storage and utility room in a single space. This keeps the kitchen tidier and it can therefore be used as a kitchen/diner, which reduces coming and going in the living room and frees up more space there. The corkscrew staircase gives access to all the rooms, which are set at different levels. There is a small landing on each level, which makes it possible to realize more floors within the same volume and renders a hallway unnecessary. The light in the staircase enters via the partially glazed roof.

In the type with a frontage of 6 m (19 ft 8 in) there is no division between the split-level lounging and eating areas. When there are lots of visitors the steps can serve as extra seating. In the rooms the 'reallocation of space' – what we now call multifunctionality – is continued. The children's rooms have a divan and a foldaway bed with pivoting storage boxes above them, their open sides turned to the wall. The windowsills are 0.5 metre (1 ft 8 in) deep and can be used as a worktop. A washbasin is integrated into the worktop, covered by a flap with a mirror on the underside. Under the worktop is a second leaf to put away papers temporarily when using the washbasin or when the window is open.

In a model Rietveld indicated how he wanted to combine this type of housing into a residential block and a neighbourhood. He set the houses two by two, alternately oriented in opposite directions, resulting in a building line that is staggered by more than 2 m (6 ft 7 in). The advantages of this are variation, sheltered spots, bigger gardens and a safe environment for children. In combination with a few blocks of flats this layout made it possible for him to realize sufficient dwellings within a planned district.[49] This is how children could have lived in the 1950s if the construction industry had adopted Rietveld's idea for a core dwelling, but that was not to be the case.

The same fate befell the 'wet cell', a plastic unit that incorporated a kitchen, shower, WC and washbasin. He presented the prototype at the 1958 World Expo in Brussels. In a 1953 lecture, he commented about this in an untypically bitter tone, referring back to the Garage with Chauffeur's Apartment:

For example, in 1926 I already built a garage myself, with an upstairs dwelling of enamelled concrete panels measuring 3 × 1 metres on a steel frame, as a first test – with inexperienced workmen it took 3 weeks. The fact that my romantic client had a roof put on it and painted the whole thing brown and cream, because he did not find it beautiful, cannot be taken as proof that it was not good architecture, and it was certainly not uneconomical for the first implementation.[50]

Rietveld had by then drawn the conclusion that industrialization in the building trade was a question of staying the course and looking to the distant future. He thought that the construction industry had missed its chance by failing to tackle the post-war housing shortage with prefabrication and assembly techniques. The situation for the production of furniture and other appliances was more favourable, because the discipline of industrial design was at that time undergoing a tremendous development.

The realities of industrial production

In the 1950s Rietveld designed several chairs for industrial production, none of which became a commercial success. Some designs were a continuation of his experiments with the 'one-piece chair', such as the chair of bent steel wire from 1950, but they were usually prompted by an architectural commission.

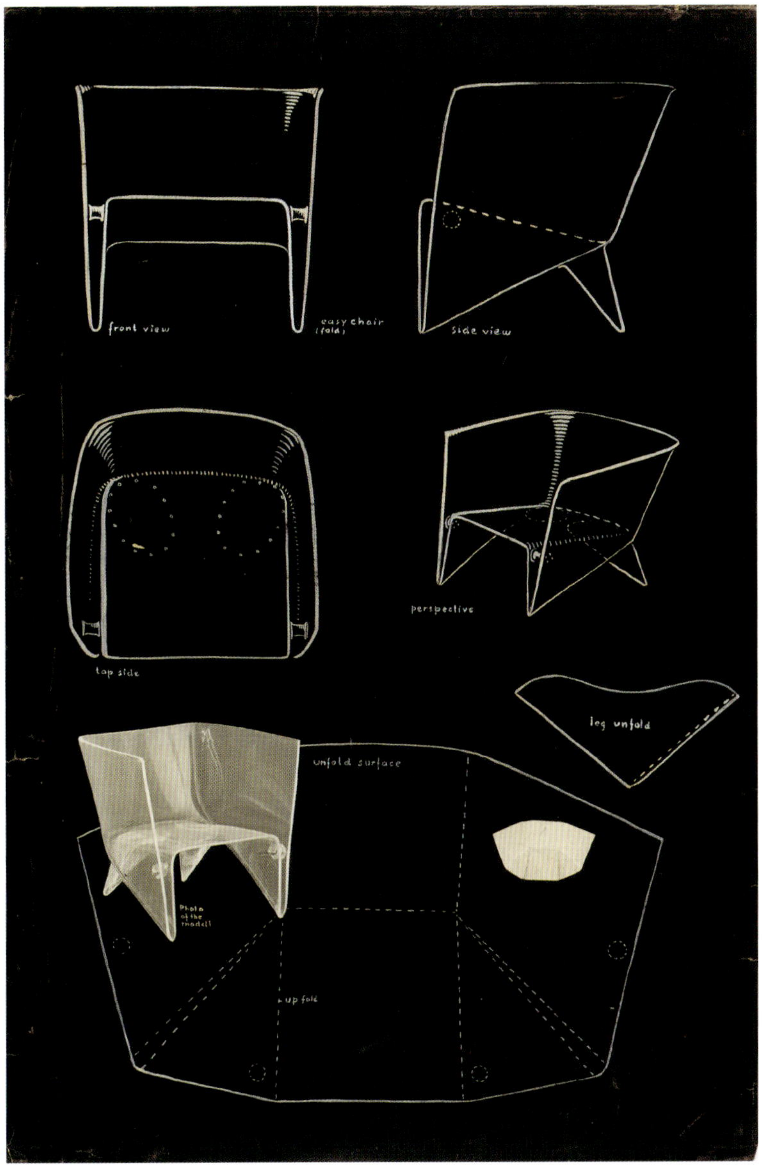

Aluminium prototype chair, 1942 (top right). Rietveld worked on his 'folded furniture' throughout the 1930s and 40s, producing many sketches and models (top left, bottom left and bottom right).

The Mondial Chair is Rietveld's most successful industrial product. It is a stackable and linkable chair with a moulded steel frame and a seat of anodized aluminium. It was designed for the 1958 World Expo in Brussels and was produced by Gispen's Fabriek voor Metaalbewerking N.V., a manufacturer of office and home furniture. Rietveld developed the model together with his son Wim, who worked at Gispen.[51] Gispen made two prototypes, one with Bakelite armrests and one without, both of which were already exhibited in 1957 as part of the Dutch entry for the XIth Triennale in Milan. The chair was awarded a gold medal.

Gispen had in that same year offered to supply the Netherlands section of the World Expo Brussels 1958 Foundation (Stichting Wereldtentoonstelling Brussel 1958, afdeling Nederland) with the Mondial Chair, using a steel frame and a polyester seat, for 35 guilders. A second letter to the Rietveld architecture bureau followed in December, stating that the price had risen to 56.50 guilders per unit. Various colour options were possible and the quote was based on an order of about one hundred pieces, but no order was placed. At Rietveld's request, Gispen provided five white polyester examples for the dining table in the 'ideal flat', a model home designed by Rietveld for the Dutch pavilion.
The bent steel and the tub-like aluminium seat give the chair a profile that is almost graphic. The decision to switch from aluminium to polyester was taken by Gispen, perhaps in reaction to commentary in the magazine *Goed Wonen*, which recommended a less heat-sapping material.[52] The graphic quality of the form was lost in the polyester version, prompting Gerrit and Wim Rietveld to protest against Gispen's intervention, but to no avail. This was why Wim Rietveld left the company.[53] At his 1958 retrospective at the Centraal Museum in Utrecht, Rietveld exhibited the polyester model nevertheless. As the conclusion to a review of the exhibition, the editors of *Goed Wonen* placed an illustration of the chair with this jubilant commentary: 'In conclusion, last year this chair of moulded sheet steel [sic] was developed ... Here the dream of 1928 has become reality. Here he has helped "to simplify life".'[54] Despite the Italian award and positive reactions in the press the chair failed to become a commercial success. Only 250 units were produced, according to a former Gispen employee. Before the remake in 2006, the Mondial Chair was actually rarer than the renowned Red-Blue Chair. It was Rietveld's last attempt to design an item of furniture for industrial production; the Steltman Chair, which is now so popular, was designed specifically for a jeweller's shop in The Hague in 1963. The original examples, upholstered in white leather, are much more components of the white-and-black shop interior than they are independent items of furniture intended for serial production.

The importance of mechanized production was for Rietveld beyond question: '[T]o the machine we ... owe the possibility of the expansion of socialism ... Humanism without the machine remains a pious wish – empty words.'[55] Yet he did not draw the conclusion that he should extensively and systematically immerse himself in the possibilities of industrial production for architecture and design. There is a striking discrepancy between his faith in the exigency and blessings of ongoing industrialization and the steps Rietveld actually took to advance it. The position he chose was crucial. He did not adopt a subservient attitude, but as a designer allowed himself the freedom of thought of an artist. In a 1953 address for students at the Secondary Technical School for Architecture and Academy of Art in The Hague he may well have said that a workshop equipped with smaller machines was important for training in order to avoid falling back on crafts methods, but he actually thought that the designer had to possess technical know-how in order to be able to counter any arguments against the feasibility of a design and to 'technically substantiate' it. In Rietveld's vision, the designer, for all the good intentions, stands opposite or above industry, and his ultimate and only objective is the spatial experience.

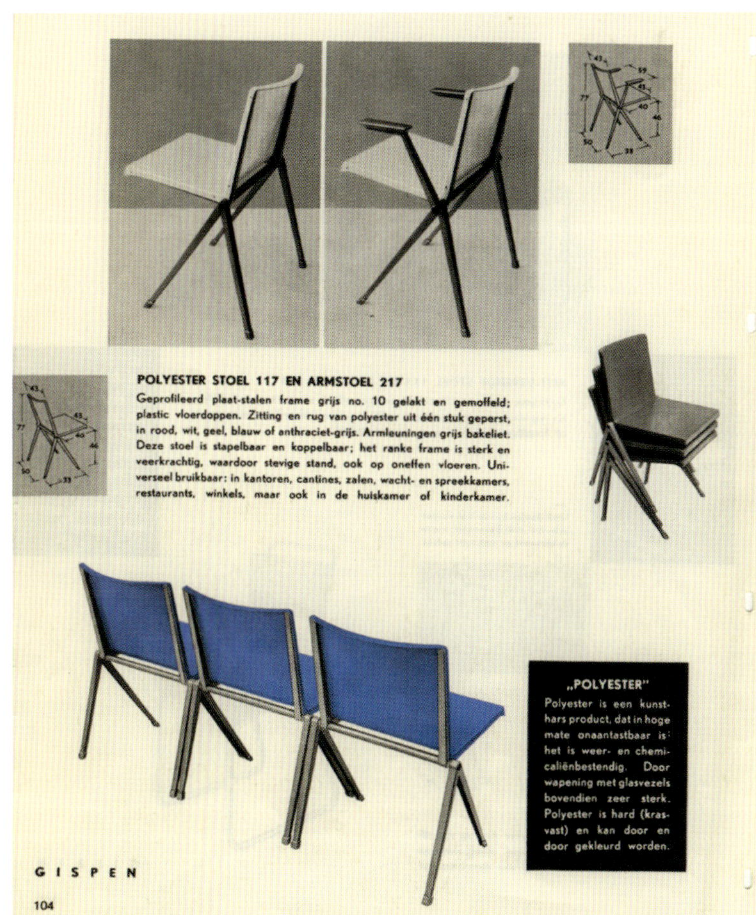

POLYESTER STOEL 117 EN ARMSTOEL 217

Geprofileerd plaat-stalen frame grijs no. 10 gelakt en gemoffeld; plastic vloerdoppen. Zitting en rug van polyester uit één stuk geperst, in rood, wit, geel, blauw of anthraciet-grijs. Armleuningen grijs bakeliet. Deze stoel is stapelbaar en koppelbaar; het ranke frame is sterk en veerkrachtig, waardoor stevige stand, ook op oneffen vloeren. Universeel bruikbaar: in kantoren, cantines, zalen, wacht- en spreekkamers, restaurants, winkels, maar ook in de huiskamer of kinderkamer.

„POLYESTER"

Polyester is een kunsthars product, dat in hoge mate onaantastbaar is: het is weer- en chemicaliënbestendig. Door wapening met glasvezels bovendien zeer sterk. Polyester is hard (krasvast) en kan door en door gekleurd worden.

GISPEN

104

Top left: Chair made of steel wire, 1950

Bottom left: Mondial Chair, 1957.

Top right: Dining chair with a wicker seat, designed for the Van Daalen House, 1956–8

Bottom right: Gispen brochure for the Mondial Chair, 1957.

Rietveld and his wife in his flat
above the Vreeburg Cinema,
Utrecht, c.1947

6. Flexible functionalism

What we do know is that the value of our mechanically fabricated work shall not be that of rarity but, in my view, much more a general humaneness. We are not yet seeing the emergence of a style in the way the Gothic, the Renaissance or the Baroque was a style. Shall our style in fact be stylelessness? What difference does it actually make to us?[1]
– Rietveld, 1937

The stock market crash of 1929 divides the inter-war period in two: the 1920s typified by high expectations and revolutionary developments, and the 1930s, which saw the germs sown with the peace of 1918 reach maturity in calamitous consequences.

The many avant-garde movements that boisterously stirred into life after World War I continued to fight for a better society unabated in the 1930s. Their utopian body of thought was, however, no proof whatsoever against the economic and political upheavals. Dramatic were the developments in Soviet Russia and Germany, where an entire generation of intellectuals and artists disappeared: they conformed, went into exile or were murdered. In European countries where they found refuge it gave a temporary stimulus to cultural life. As a committee member of the Netherlands-New Russia Society (Genootschap Nederland-Nieuw Rusland) and architecture adviser for its journal, *Nieuw Rusland* (New Russia), Rietveld must have known something about the purges under Stalin,[2] but he reserved comment about this and the rise of fascism. He did, however, side with initiatives such as the General Artists' Congress for Mental Resilience (Algemeen Kunstenaars-Congres voor Geestelijke Weerbaarheid) in 1935, a group that campaigned to mobilize artists against the 'growing might of the ideologies of violence'.[3]

The pages of the *Bouwkundig Weekblad*, *De 8 en Opbouw*, the *R. K. Bouwblad* and other architecture journals of the 1930s give the impression of lively and substantive debate and a flourishing architectural practice. The former is true; the latter only in part.[4] The unemployed dominated the streetscape: 35.2 per cent of the Dutch labour force was jobless and therefore scraped by on a paltry state benefit. Some people were unaffected by the crisis, but in the years leading up to World War II the mood was bleak. Within the circle of like-minded individuals who engaged with progressive ideas in architecture the atmosphere became harder. People sized each other up in a manner that was far from good-natured. When various architects called into question the principles of Functionalism on paper or in practice it caused a rift within the ranks, which hardly took the editors of *De 8 en Opbouw*, the mouthpiece of the Functionalist movement in the Netherlands, by surprise. 'Everyone who carries out his work with conviction shall not hesitate to withdraw and seek "his own path", if his work no longer binds him with colleagues with whom he initially felt connected,' they commented detachedly in 1938.[5]

The crisis also caused a caesura in Rietveld's working life, it seems. The construction of the Schröder House had been followed by a period of feverish creativity and dynamism: the one-piece fibreboard chair, experiments with the industrialization of construction methods and his participation in the CIAM congresses where he hobnobbed with the crème de la crème of modern architects. From the latter half of the 1920s,

Rietveld's work acquired all the stylistic features of the International Style, the term that the American critic Henry-Russell Hitchcock popularized for international Modernist architecture in the early 1930s: facades as continuous, whitewashed planes with horizontal bands of fenestration, an emphasis on the building's spatial unity in the ground plan, asymmetrical compositions that follow the functional layout, and the shunning of ornamentation. Rietveld embraced all these ideas unreservedly.[6] Le Corbusier must have made an especially profound impression on him.

The block of four houses on the Erasmuslaan had been very well received, and shortly thereafter Rietveld designed a row of houses in the Schumannstraat and a second block of apartments on the Erasmuslaan, both projects commissioned by Bredero's Bouwbedrijf. His revolutionary concept for the dwelling core was not, however, taken up and he failed to win any commissions for public housing, with the exception of the row of four houses for the Werkbundsiedlung housing exhibition in Vienna (1929–32). The jury of the design competition for 'Inexpensive Housing for Workers' organized by the City of Amsterdam in 1933 described Rietveld's entry as 'factory architecture'. He had divided the flat measuring 6 x 11 m (19 ft 8 in x 36 ft) into a living area and a sleeping area, where the 2 m (6 ft 7 in) high partitions separated the beds. The jury did not comment on this, but deemed 'the combination of living room and cooking alcove' as well as the 'rubbish chutes and delivery lift in the living rooms' to be unacceptable.[7]

Rietveld produced his best work of the 1930s for private clients who were evidently relatively unaffected by the crisis. He combined rectangular and cylindrical volumes in many of the detached houses he built between 1931 and 1936. The circular form was a fascination shared by other Dutch and foreign architects. There is, for example, a striking similarity between the Hartog Villa in The Hague, which was built by J. B. van Loghem in 1938, and the Wijburg House that Rietveld realized a year later within walking distance of this property.[8] In *Die neue Wohnung* (The New Dwelling), Bruno Taut offers a functional rationale for this preference: a round house loses less heat and the ratio of floor area to volume is optimal, making it more economical for mass production.[9] Rietveld's glazed rooftop extension for the Metz & Co. department store in Amsterdam (1933), several of the unrealized house designs and the Wooden Summerhouses (the *Houten Zomer Huis* or HZH project) from 1937 were based on a plan that is essentially circular.

Rietveld still usually chose the self-evident functional layout of an asymmetrical floor-plan, in which the ground-floor hall provides access to the living/dining room as well as to the kitchen with adjoining storage space and a lavatory. He placed the bathroom, a second lavatory and the bedrooms on the upper floor. By far the greater part of the house is taken up by the living/dining room, which is often oriented towards the southwest on the garden side of the property. The street side of the house is therefore closed off and private, unless the size of the plot makes this unnecessary. The living room often has a polygonal basic form, in which Rietveld introduces an additional articulation in the guise of a difference in floor level or a physical partition. In the Székely House (1934–5) in Bloemendaal, for example, the continuous space of kitchen, living room and music room is articulated by building up the floor-plan from segments of two concentric circles and a rectangle; the kitchen could be partitioned off from the lounge area with a curtain.

In houses based on the dwelling core Rietveld used differences in level to separate discrete functions within a space. Such a shift in level often marks the transition to another, specific use of the space in his detached houses as well. The Hillebrand House in The Hague (1934–5) has a music corner set a few steps higher and the Lels House in Doorn (1939) has a sunken hearth with a settee-like surround. Rietveld had an inspiring example for variations in floor levels and the use of circular segments close to home: in 1932 Sybold van Ravesteyn had built a house for himself on the Prins Hendriklaan with a plan in the form of a right-angled triangle with a rounded-off apex; in the living room there is a shift in level between the lounge area and the corner where the bureau stands.

The exteriors of Rietveld's houses correspond closely to the stereotype of modern European architecture of

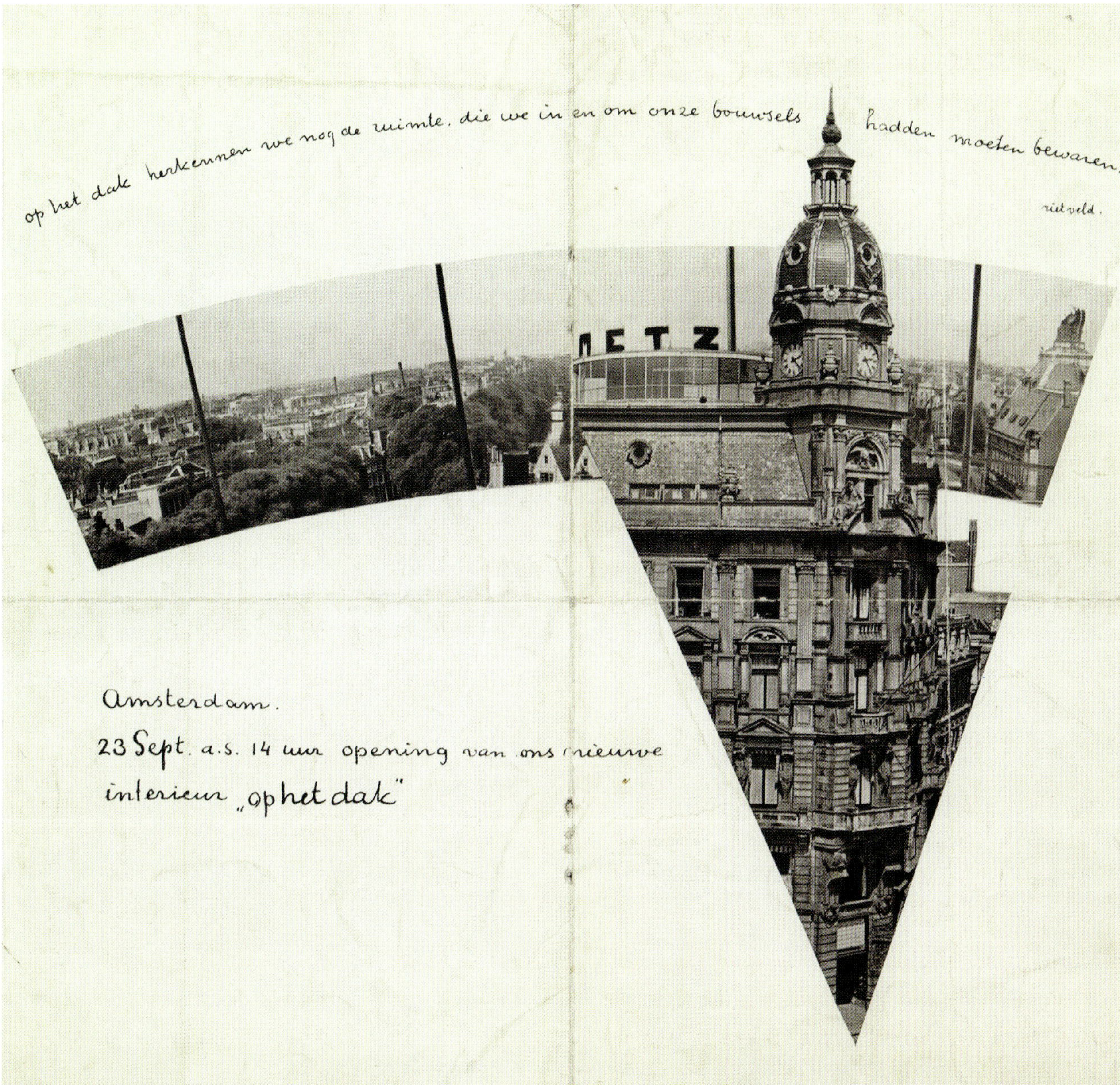

Rooftop cupola, Amsterdam, 1933. Building announcement (top), drawing (bottom left), photograph of completed pavilion (bottom right). Designed for Metz & Co., Rietveld's rooftop pavilion is a glass drum with a metal frame, incongruously built on top of a late nineteenth-century historicist store in Amsterdam. The space was used to show Metz & Co. furniture, often including pieces designed by Rietveld.

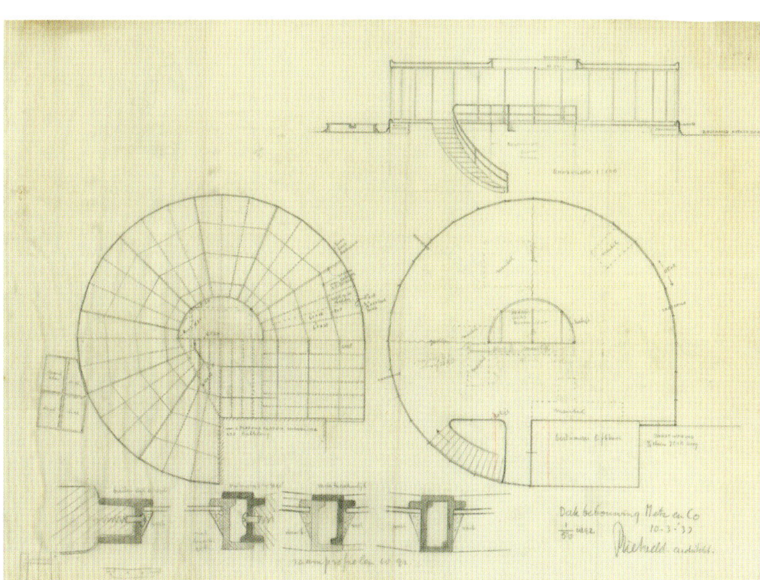

Lels House, Doorn, 1939. Interior and exterior. The Lels House is located in a patch of heathland surrounded by woods. During the summer, the eaves and balcony protect the living and sleeping areas from the sun.

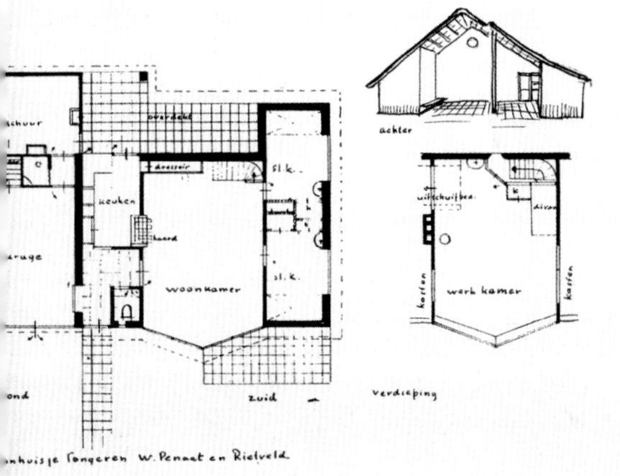

Penaat House, Epe, 1937–9. Presentation drawing and exterior. Unlike most of Rietveld's other houses from the 1930s, this home for the head of the Metz & Co. furniture department has a vernacular look, but a large glass expanse on the south facade and a movable storage facility on rails are good examples of Rietveld's ongoing concerns with light and an optimum use of space.

Wijburg House, The Hague, 1939. This house includes a striking two-storey, semicircular annex.

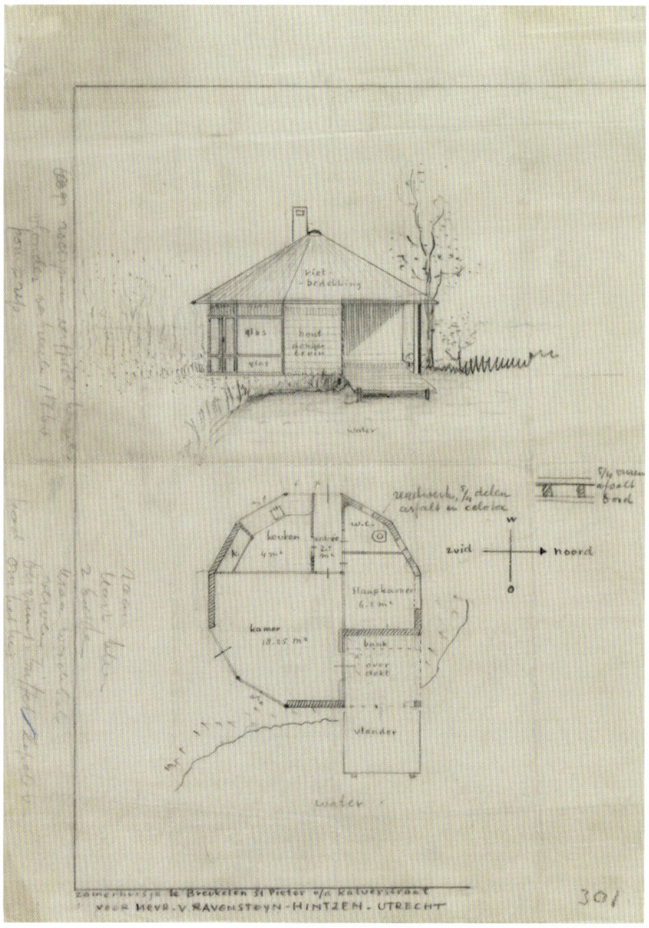

Ravesteyn Summerhouse, Breukelen St Pieters, 1934–5. Presentation drawing and exterior. Built on the Loosdrecht lakes, this wooden house has a dodecagonal plan and a thatched roof. It was built for Dora van Ravesteyn-Hintzen, the ex-wife of Rietveld's friend and fellow architect, Sybold van Ravesteyn.

Hildebrand House, Blaricum, 1935. Presentation drawing and exterior. This house was built for writer A. D. Hildebrand. As with many Rietveld villas from the 1930s, the plan is basically a square, here penetrated by semicircular and rectangular annexes, which have floor-to-ceiling glass walls that are contained in a steel frame. The brick walls are plastered white.

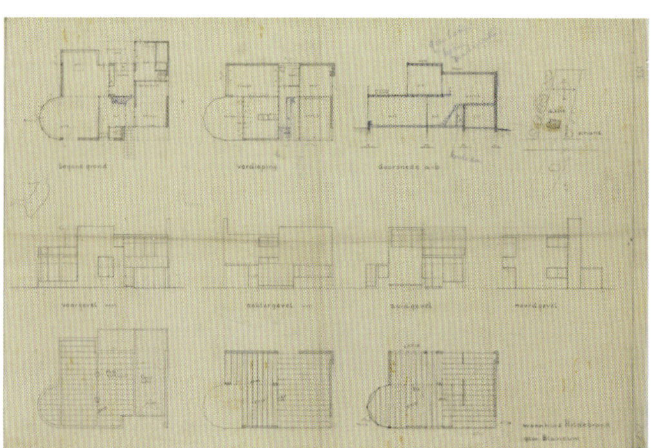

Mees House, The Hague, 1934–6. Exterior, model and interior showing the living and music room. The single-storey living and music room has a semicircular, glazed curved wall topped with a balustraded balcony. The rectangular second floor, which contains the bedrooms, is connected to this volume by an open metal ship's stair in the entrance hall. A rooflight floods the stairwell in natural light.

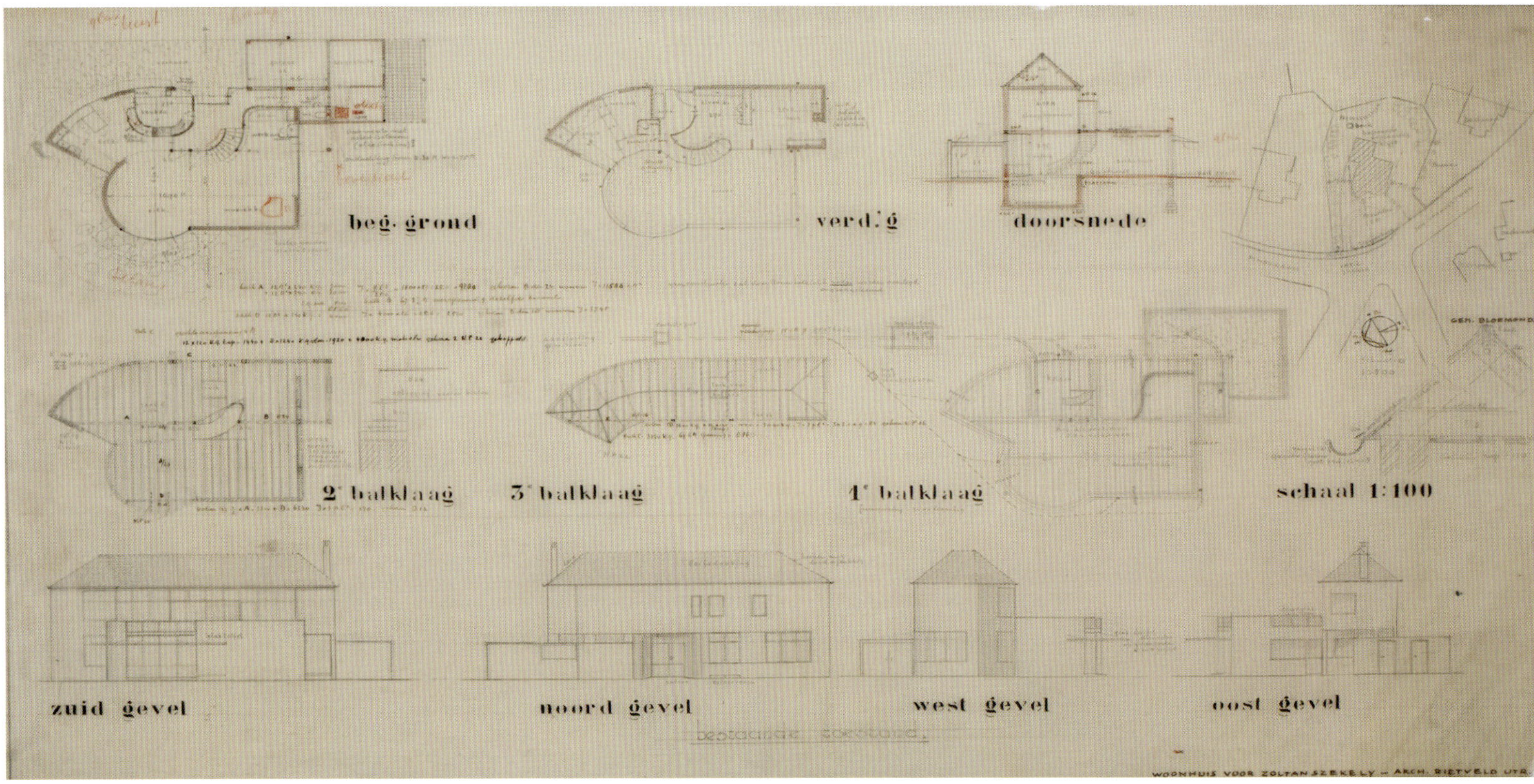

Székely House, Bloemendaal, 1934–5. Presentation drawing, exterior and interior. This house is composed of four volumes, each of which is partly curved and partly rectangular. Within Rietveld's work of this period, the house is unusual for its sharply pitched roof.

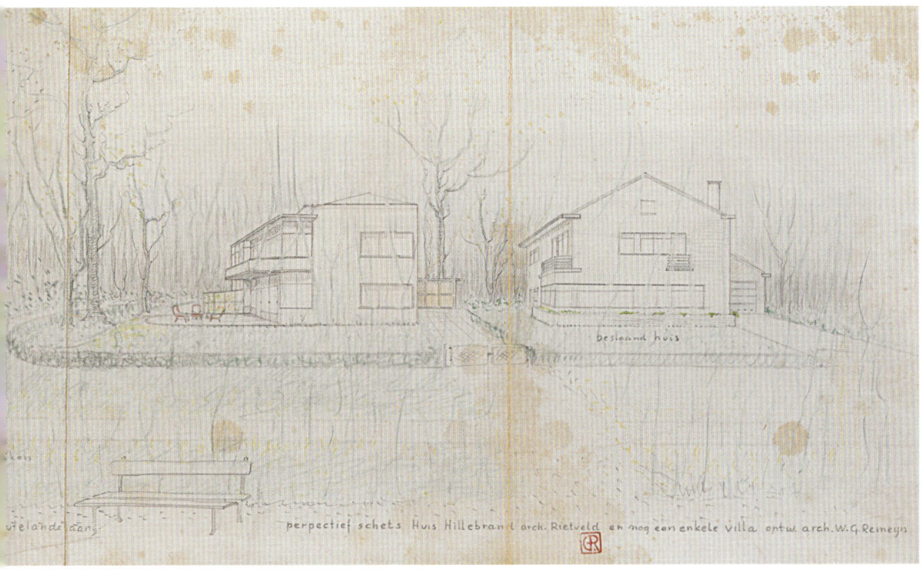

Hillebrand House, The Hague, 1934–5. Presentation drawing, exterior and interior. This white plastered house has large, steel-framed windows and a gently pitched roof designed to conform to the wishes of The Hague's local planning committee.

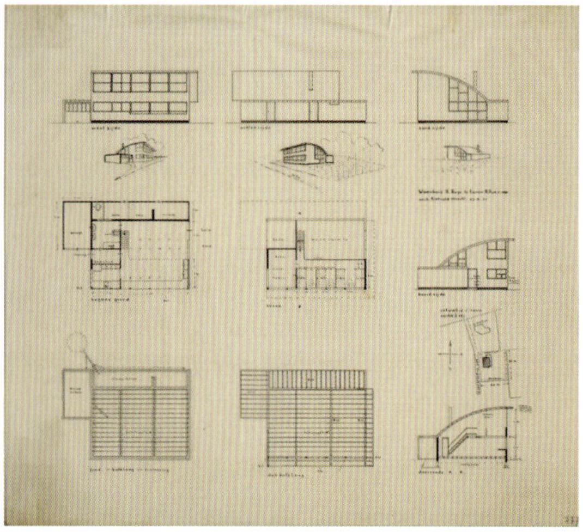

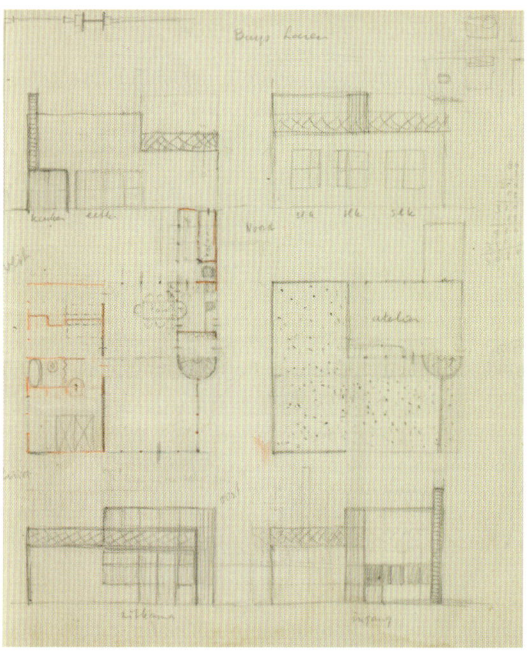

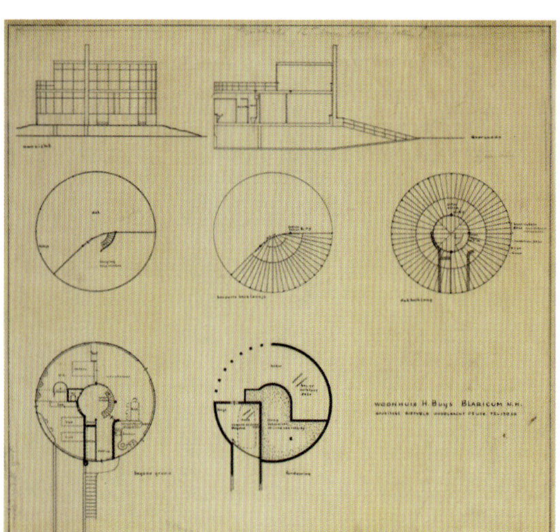

the 1930s; what distinguishes the houses is the quality of the interiors. Thanks to the flexible combination of volumes, separated by visible or merely palpable boundaries, Rietveld created a unique spatial experience in each house.[10]

'A true architect'

In 1935 Oud complimented Rietveld on the Székely House at length:

I always find your 'inventions' immensely attractive, as you are well aware, but it sometimes bothered me that they seemed so terribly like a 'model' or were so much more like sculpture than architecture. Here ... you are a true architect. We were enchanted by the beautiful, light house and by the simple way you are now going to be doing things.[11]

Rietveld had achieved his objective. In 1927 he had declined Oud's invitation to design furniture for the Weissenhofsiedlung housing exhibition in Stuttgart, explaining that if it were noticed that he was 'doing lots with interiors and furniture, it entails the risk that they pigeon-hole me'.[12] By the mid-1930s he was firmly established as an architect.

Rietveld's position was not without controversy, however. Illustrative of the stance of his Dutch colleagues and the context of Rietveld's work at that time is the debate about his designs for the house of the architecture critic H. Buys in Laren, which were rejected by the local planning committee in 1933.[13] The Functionalist architects of the Nieuwe Bouwen movement often encountered resistance from this quarter. Flat roofs, white elevations and large glazed expanses might have been acceptable in an urban setting, but in more rural areas there was a preference for a traditional style.

It was not only the members of planning committees who raised objections; landowners also tried to obstruct the construction of modern architecture because it could affect the value of adjacent plots of land and properties. The supporters of the Nieuwe Bouwen movement inveighed against this conservative stance. The debate lacked subtlety and was almost without exception moralistic in tone, which is understandable.

Designs for Buys House, Laren and Blaricum, 1933–4. Presentation drawings (opposite page), models (this page). The many variations of designs for this house for the critic H. Buys were due to its being turned down repeatedly for planning permission. Nevertheless, the range seen in the successive versions of the design show what a flexible architect Rietveld could be. There are, for example, proposals for a house with a curved roof, a cubic building and a house with a circular ground plan.

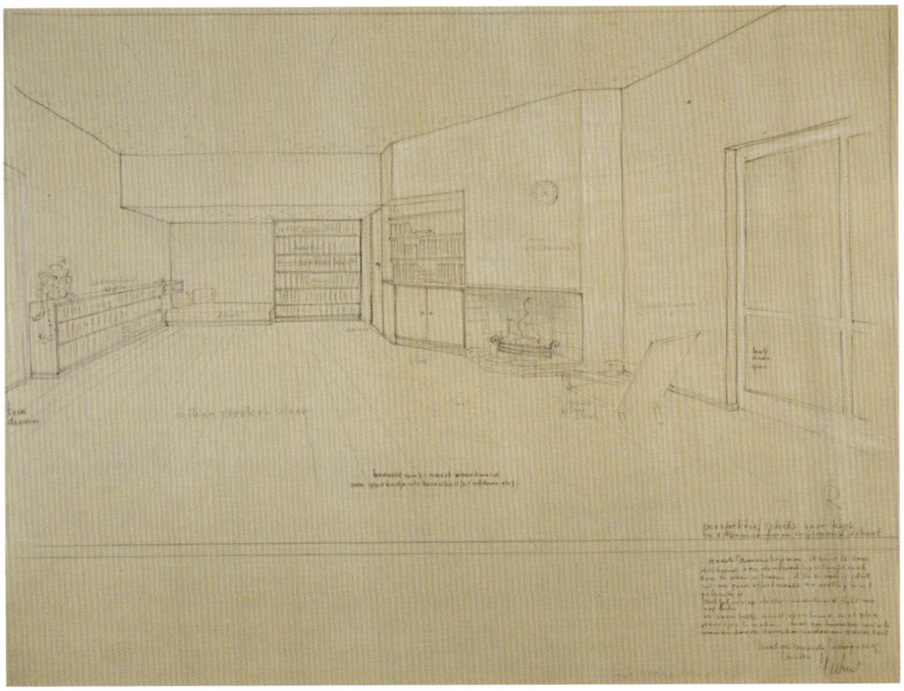

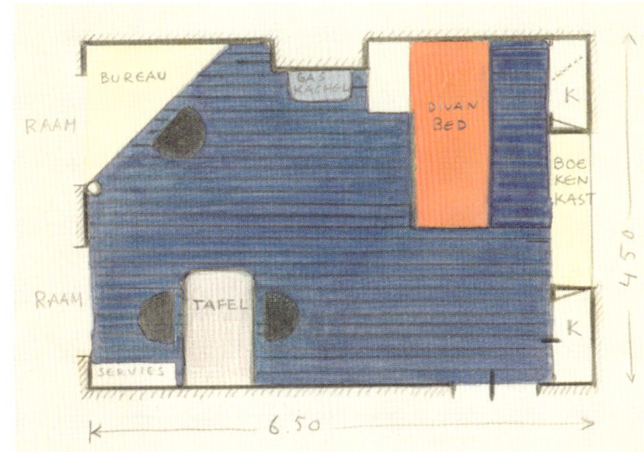

Sketch, Wijsman House, The Hague, 1938 (top left); Plan drawing, bedroom for B. Schröder, The Hague, 1930 (top right); Sketch, attic for A. D. Hamburg, Utrecht, c.1933 (bottom)

The 'new Functionalist' architects received relatively few commissions and even those declined steadily through the 1930s. In the Buys affair, however, it became clear that some colleagues did not think that all modern architecture was worth defending. The Rotterdam architect J. H. van den Broek (1898–1978) had several misgivings about the two designs for Buys and another small house by Rietveld that were published in *De 8 en Opbouw*.[14] He unerringly pinpoints the weaknesses and wonders whether the designs deserve defending.

Prompted by Rietveld's response in the next issue of *De 8 en Opbouw*, Oud wrote a private letter to Rietveld, in which he indicated that he did not consider them worthy designs either:

Perhaps you had to work in a hurry or out of financial necessity (all of which I understand and would not like to criticize), but then, in my opinion, you should not have presented them with a certain pride and ought to have quietly kept them to yourself, in the hope that you would soon be able to work under more favourable circumstances again.[15]

Rietveld's response lacked gumption: he skulked behind his client Buys, who apparently needed something to write about, and claims that he had mailed the wrong drawings, and then, apparently, someone else published a design under his name that was equally flawed. Oud thought this attitude was unprofessional and therewith the matter was closed. Someone who did enter the arena on Rietveld's behalf was Arthur Staal (1907–93), who defended Rietveld against the critique of other colleagues:

All the New Builders know that the Rietveld's name is not in the first place associated with The Indestructible Architecture, nor usually with Workable Architecture … And no matter how dubious these shortcomings would seem to us, we ought also to know that Rietveld is an indispensable fellow combatant in the struggle of Functionalist Architecture … In its onward march the New Architecture needs pioneers of every calibre, provided that they are thoroughbreds![16]

Here Staal adopted the prevailing prejudices rather too easily. Rietveld could build very soundly when the commissioner made sufficient funds available, but he had the tendency to accept each and every assignment simply in order to be able to build, and went along all too easily with the wishes of the client. This is one of the reasons why he was never completely without work, even if the results were not always to his satisfaction.[17] In such cases he had neither the desire to defend his work tooth and nail nor the will to clear up misunderstandings. To what extent this affected his reputation is difficult to say, but it was undoubtedly in a negative manner.

The Vreeburg Cinema

'One of the most flawless and most sensitive spaces in our city,' wrote a reviewer in November 1936.[18] He had already been able to take a look inside the cinema in Utrecht designed by Rietveld, which was to be officially opened on 10 December. Visiting the cinema had in a few decades been elevated from a seedy fairground attraction into a respectable cultural activity. This made the opening of the Vreeburg Cinema a special event and it was attended by representatives of a whole swathe of the city's upper echelons: bureaucrats, merchants and industrialists, academics and the judiciary, student fraternities, 'the garrison commander, the director of the military hospital, in short the "upper thousand" of Utrecht', as a journalist wrote.[19] Rietveld received the commission from the proprietor Jan Nijland, an acquaintance from the Utrecht chapter of the Dutch Film League (Nederlandse Filmliga) for whom he had already refurbished the old cinema. Rietveld was also intrigued by the technical aspects of film projection and two years later he tried to design a stereoscopic cinema. The renovation of the Vreeburg Cinema actually involved a ground-up reconstruction of the whole property and its re-equipment with the most advanced technical installations for ventilation, heating and film projection. It was a truly modern building:

All the lines move freely and run in contrasting directions. The floor ascends towards the rear and the front … to the front the ceiling slopes downwards … The offshoots of the curved balcony rise upwards towards the front … The back walls are curved convexly as with a streamlined automobile.[20]

Top: Panorama of Rietveld's apartment over the Vreeburg Cinema, Utrecht, c.1947

Opposite page: Vreeburg Cinema, 1936. Presentation drawing of the facade, 1934–6 (top) and completed facade, 1936 (bottom)

Bottom: Vreeburg Cinema interior, 1936

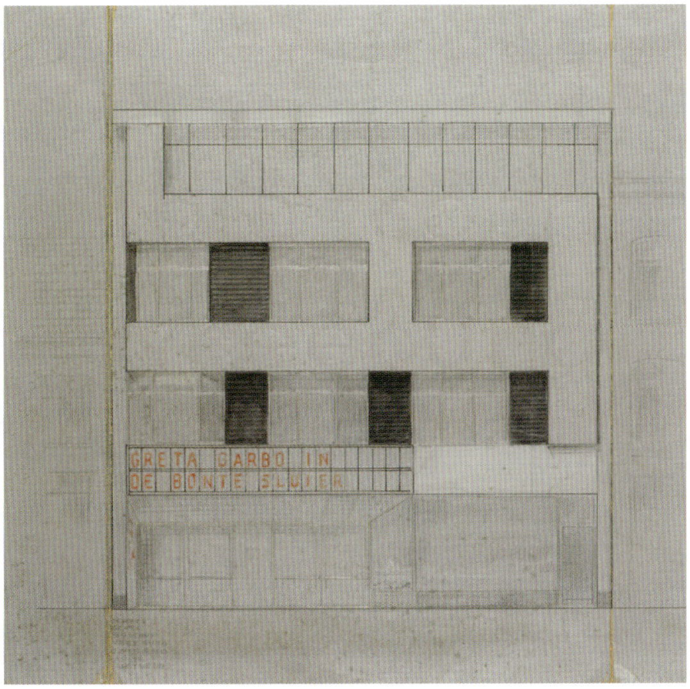

The ceiling and balcony were finished in pale green, while the side walls were painted a pale pink. This palette was continued in the mauve upholstery of the chairs and the pale green carpet. Light-coloured limba wood was used for the wainscoting and rhomboid Genemuider rush mats were worked into the ceiling and walls as insulation and to improve the acoustics. On either side of the projection screen, the painter Lambert Simon (1890–1987) created a decorative element made of figures for the walls by etching white lines in the coat of paint, which darkened from grey to black towards the screen. With its slender chrome columns and stairs and wall covering in natural stone the foyer was equally stylish.

The whole facade was clad in panes of glass: clear glass for the windows alternated with panels of opaline glass, which had light boxes mounted behind them. In the evening the name '*bioscoop vreeburg*' was illuminated in translucent letters. Rietveld proposed adding an apartment on the third floor, because he thought the edifice was too low in relation to the adjacent properties. When Nijland asked what he should do with the extra storey, Rietveld offered to rent the space himself. Rietveld never paid rent, according to Nijland's son, but nor did he submit an invoice for his architect's fee.[21] The apartment comprised a large living room, a kitchen, a lavatory and a shower, and five bedrooms that were closed off by curtains. Three of these were little more than alcoves in the living room. The friendly man standing in the doorway of the living room with a small bag over his shoulder clearly had not the faintest idea of the need for homeliness and privacy of his wife and children. Light flooded into the living space through the 9 m (29 ft 6 in) wall of glass to the front and was often so bright that his wife would sit in the Berlin Chair, her Bible and cigarettes within easy reach, wearing sunglasses.

Evidently nobody took offence at the discrepancy between the facade and the building's interior: the exterior was austere, rectangular and colourless, but from within it was a feast of curvaceous lines, plush materials and a varied palette. Rietveld made no bones about hiding the building's different functions behind the edifice either. Twenty years later, this cinema and other designs from around 1935 to 1940 were presented in the retrospective exhibition of Rietveld's work under the heading 'Soepeler vormen in het "Functionalisme"' – 'More flexible forms in "Functionalism"'. According to the catalogue this style was a continuation of *Nieuwe Zakelijkheid* – 'New Objectivity' – a term for the *Nieuwe Bouwen* style that Rietveld usually altered into *Nieuwe Noodzakelijkheid* – 'New Necessity' – but was more supple in its design and thus gave a more satisfying result. According to this explanation, the notion of 'functionality' relates not only to the function of a building or the economical use of materials and space; satisfying sensory aesthetic desires has a functional role as well. The text was not penned by Rietveld, but the choice of words makes his personal input seem likely.[22]

Furniture for the market

A more relaxed handling of material and form is also evident in Rietveld's furniture designs from the 1930s. The cooperation with the Metz & Co. department store was a guarantee for commercially attractive realizations of his designs. Metz & Co. served the consumer who was interested in modern interior and furniture design. Much of the range was imported from abroad, but Dutch designers were also given a chance; they could submit their own proposals or were asked to design specific types of furniture. Usually a few prototypes were produced for presentations at fairs and exhibitions, and if there was sufficient interest these models were put into serial production.[23]

The crucial Rietveld design from this period is the Zig-Zag Chair, which is more intriguing than that other favourite of the Modernist avant-garde, the Freischwinger (cantilever chair). The cantilever chair, which was first investigated in the mid-1920s by designers including Mart Stam and subsequently elaborated by many others, is based on a cube with one of its sides missing. The Zig-Zag Chair, by contrast, is a single line in space and therefore the ultimate symbol of Rietveld's work for many people.[24] Rietveld characterized the form as 'a little partition in space ... It is not a chair but a structural joke. I always called it the little zig-zag.'[25] A highly successful joke, even in his own eyes, because from 1933 he placed Zig-Zag Chairs around the dining table in almost all his models and drawings.[26] The design is the result of Rietveld's experiments with the one-piece fibreboard chair as well as being a form that fulfils his spatial objectives perfectly.

The German furniture designers and manufacturers, the Rasch brothers, Heinz (1902–96) and Bodo (1903–95), were first to develop a Z-shaped chair, the 'Sitzgeiststuhl' ('Spirit of Sitting Chair'). In 1927 it was shown in Mies van der Rohe's model home at the Weissenhofsiedlung and a year later the brothers published the design in their booklet *Der Stuhl*.[27] However, it was Rietveld who introduced two essential elements: the spatial form and the material experiment. Judging by the illustrations in the booklet by the Rasch brothers, the spatial effect played no part in their considerations; they were exclusively concerned with the application of wood and veneer. In the end Rietveld was also forced to restrict himself to timber, but from various sketches and prototypes it seems he was searching for a form that could be punched from the material in a single mechanical process and then folded into shape. He sketched a chair of sheet iron and produced prototypes using fibreboard, plywood with strip iron, and tubular steel. The latter was produced and presented by Metz & Co., but it proved to be structurally weak, which was also the case with the plywood variant. The execution in four planks reinforced by slats and bolts ultimately proved to be the most stable and the simplest to produce. The basic model led to endless variations, from a child's chair decorated with carving to a piano stool without a backrest. This is indicative of the lack of orthodoxy in Rietveld's approach to his work.

The many variants of the Zig-Zag Chair were possibly designed at the request of Metz & Co., but the upholstered easy chair with armrests from 1937 was almost certainly commissioned by this firm. For the first time Rietveld designed a piece of furniture that meets all the requirements of comfort. The armchair has a simple, sturdy form. The rectangular blocks of the back and seat are set at an angle of just over ninety degrees and rest on the floor to the rear. The front legs and armrests are two beams joined at right angles. The chair is generously upholstered and covered with sailcloth. The seams are decoratively finished with a half-stitch

Core House model with miniature Zig-Zag Chairs, 1947

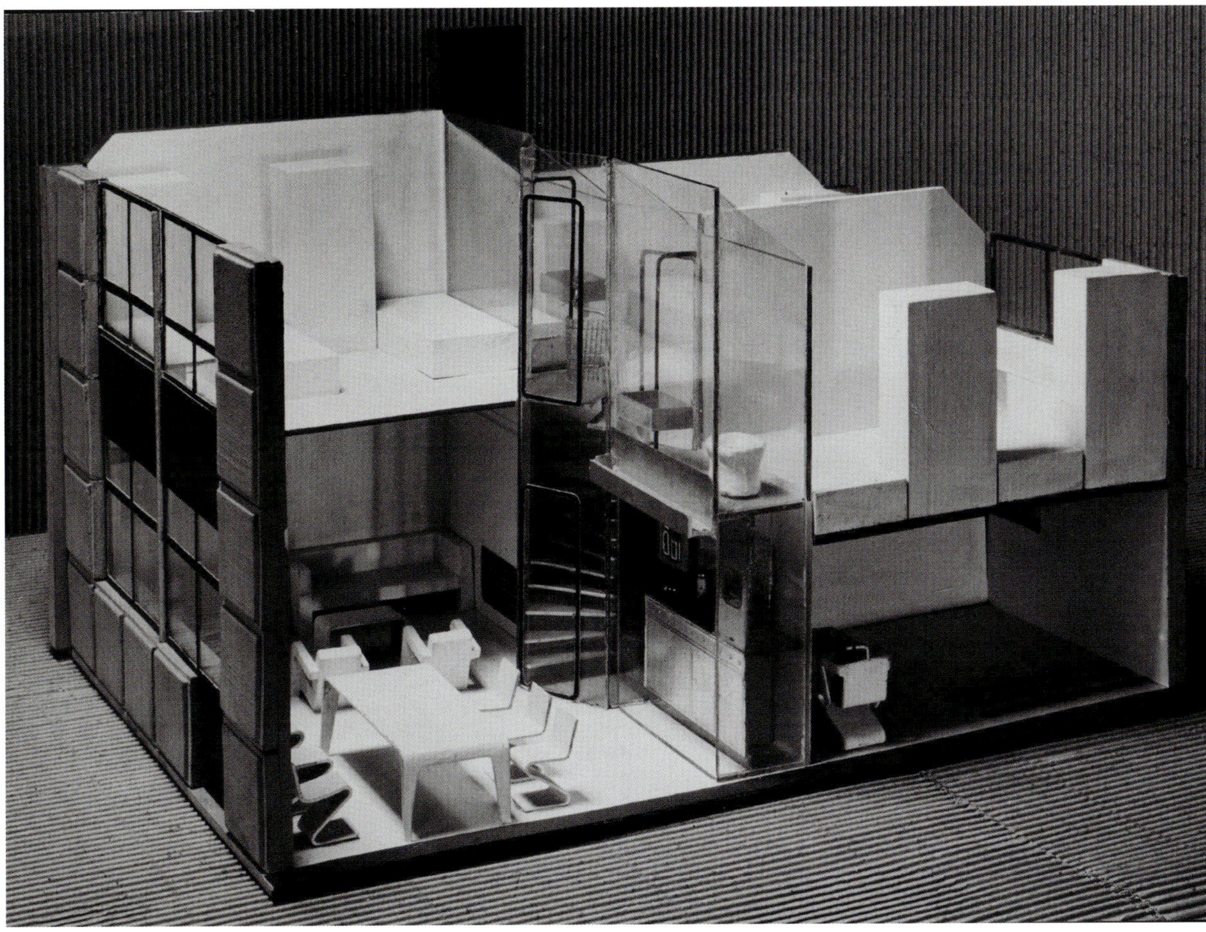

Sketch of the Zig-Zag Chair, version with tubular steel, c.1932

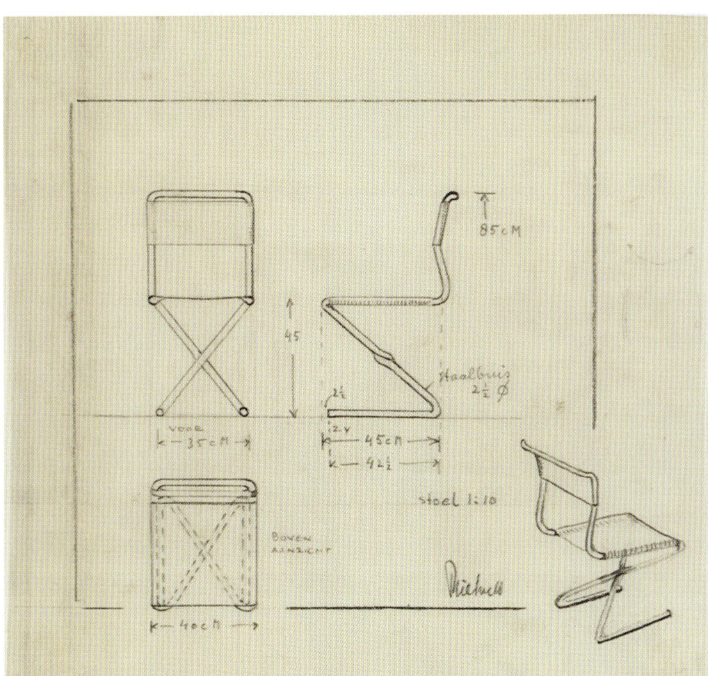

Zig-Zag Chair, version with tubular steel and plaited rubber cord, c.1932–3

Zig-Zag Chair, prototype with four planks and iron strips on the sides, c.1932–3

Drawing of a Zig-Zag Chair, version made of four cupboard planks, c.1932–3

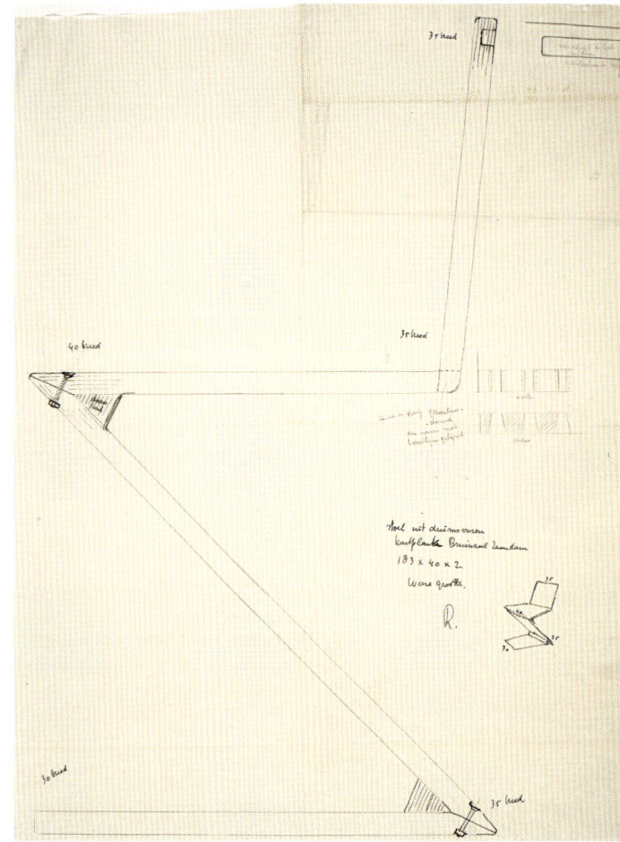

Living room/bedroom, Metz & Co. showroom, The Hague, 1937

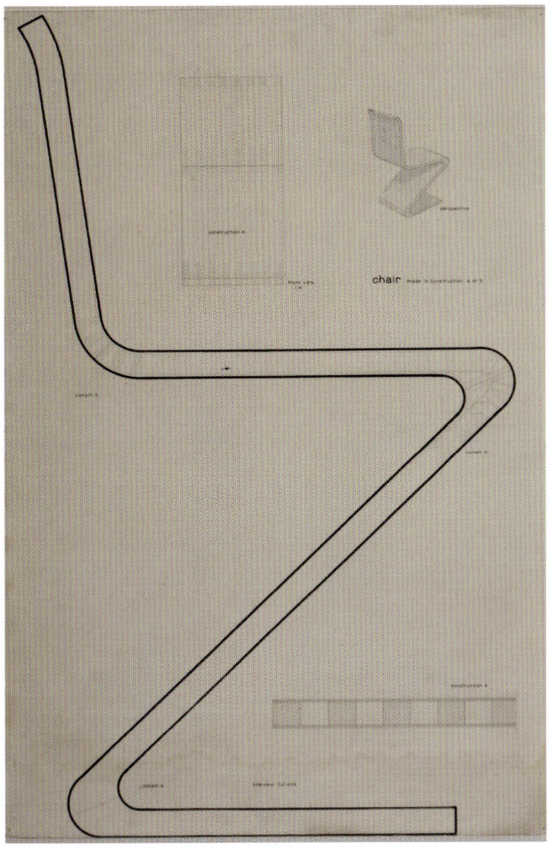

Drawing of a Zig-Zag Chair, curved plywood version, 1938

Zig-Zag Chair, curved plywood version, 1938

Living room/dining room, Metz & Co. showroom, Amsterdam, 1938

Zig-Zag Child's Chair for Jesse, 1944

Zig-Zag Chair, version with holes and short armrests, 1938

in contrasting yarn. A matching three-seat sofa was also available and customers could order the suite in different colours and fabrics if they so desired.

Rietveld had probably picked up this 'market-oriented thinking' while working on the alterations and interiors that made up a relatively large proportion of his order book in the 1930s. Such projects varied from the layout of a simple attic room to a classy cabin for the Holland-America Line's *Nieuw Amsterdam*, a luxury ocean liner. Though the client undoubtedly had a decisive say, it is evident that Rietveld's aesthetic ideas were also changing. He increasingly employed curved lines, soft pastels and natural materials for his furniture designs and interiors. Flexible Functionalism gained more and more ground via the interior.

Many interior design commissions came to Rietveld via Metz & Co. Besides building a glass extension set on the rooftop of the firm's Amsterdam store, he also designed layouts, model interiors and displays for other branches. Almost all his furniture designs could be purchased from Metz & Co., sometimes remaining in the range for decades. The 'crate furniture' (*kratmeubelen*) series from 1934 was marketed as furniture for weekend or holiday homes: a bookcase, an armchair and a low table of unpainted deal components that were simply screwed together. For a slightly higher price they could be ordered in any colour desired, while purchasers who wanted to economize could order a self-assembly pack.[28] Rietveld came up with the name 'crate furniture' because the material and construction were inspired by simple wooden crates.

This furniture of screwed-together planks with open seams was not to everyone's taste. Jan de Meijer dubbed it 'professional rot'. He was irritated by the crude finish of the painted timber, the gaps between the planks and the paint that failed to hold well on the screws. 'For my 18 guilders and 75 cents – the cost of this shoddy bookcase – I would prefer a steel bookshelf, as produced by many factories for such a price-tag,' he commented.[29] Rietveld answered him affably, but ironically and with a hint of disdain:

Do you not actually find pine beautiful? Lighter than silk. Do you not think the structure comes out beautifully

Upholstered easychair, 1936–7

Upholstered easychair as seen in interior for V. d. Reiss, Amsterdam, 1937

with mechanically planed wood? (I mean timber as it comes from Sweden.) Sawn-off ends have something picturesque. A lot of timber of the same width all together produces a calm of sorts, if the joins are clearly visible and the timber's tendency to warp is not suppressed by desperate attempts to glue it.

And to this he added that the free carpentry of a crate 'is not to blame for the worry lines of our craftsmen'. He concluded by offering to produce a really beautiful example of craftsmanship for De Meijer, should he be unable to find anyone 'who can make it sufficiently purely and flawlessly and warp-proof for your good self... and you shall see why I can permit myself the freedom to find even a crate beautiful. Rietveld, Architect.'[30] This riposte was one of the few occasions when Rietveld came out in defence of his workmanship as a cabinetmaker.

The transportable Wooden Summerhouse project was also intended for the do-it-yourself enthusiast. Rietveld developed the polygonal plan he had already proposed in several summerhouse designs into a kit for self-assembly. At the Utrecht autumn fair in 1937 he showed a dodecagonal demonstration model measuring 7.4 m (24 ft 3 in) across that provided sleeping space for six, a kitchen, washbasin, lavatory and shower. The total cost was 1,000 guilders (approximately \$550 or £110), including assembly, finishing and assistance with the planning application. The concept was held together by good intentions, which makes it rather endearing: an ideal space for an ideal price. Besides idealism, it was perhaps the economic crisis that prompted Rietveld and Schröder to market this project themselves. However, the same crisis reduced the demand for such houses appreciably. The project flopped, despite the interest and laudatory reviews in *De 8 en Opbouw* and other publications. It is symptomatic of the situation in which Rietveld found himself by the late 1930s: fewer commissions, which were often small in scale, and personal projects that had little chance of success because of the economic circumstances. Rietveld's revolutionary idea, to create self-assembly kits for furniture and for small garden houses would not be translated into successful products until after the war, and then only through the agency of other parties.

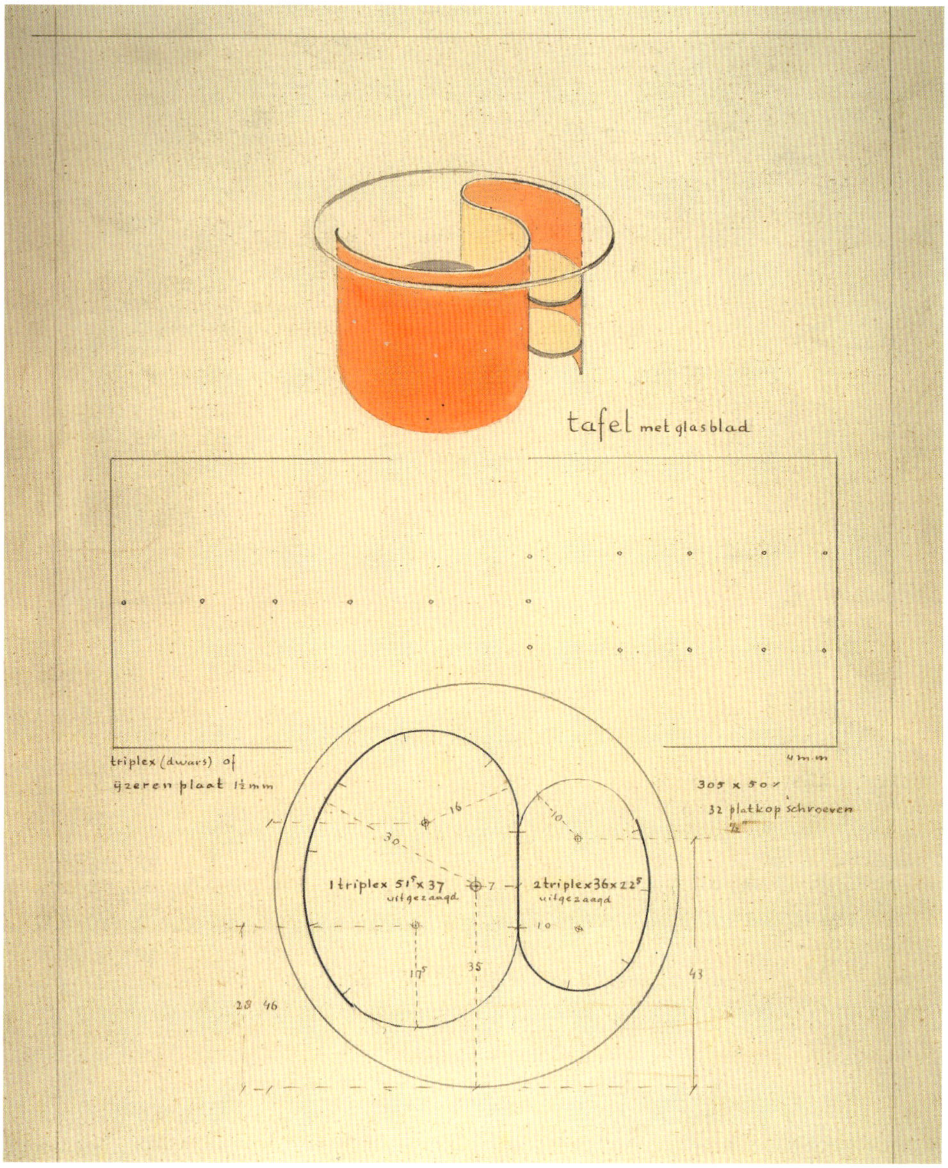

Design for a table, c.1935 (top); Sewing table, 1936 (bottom). In the 1930s some of Rietveld's furniture, like his architecture, began to include circular and curving forms. The design for a table with an S-shaped support could be made in a number of different materials, including birch and alder plywood, and with a glass top.

Design for interior and furniture of a luxury cabin in the *Nieuw Amsterdam*, a ship of the Holland America Line, 1936–8. Rietveld was one of a number of architects, including J. J. P. Oud, who were asked to participate in designing some of the interiors of this passenger liner.

Interior design for the Mortgage Credit Bank, The Hague, 1939

Crate furniture, 1935. Chair and advertising brochure. Made for Metz & Co., this relatively cheap furniture, mostly made of tongue and groove deal planks, was assembled using screws. The often unpainted final product marked a change in Rietveld's aesthetic towards a more vernacular and organic style.

Wooden Summerhouse, project advertisements, 1937

Verplaatsbaar Houten Zomerhuisje

(volgens Zomerhuis-verordening) twaalfzijdig grondvlak diameter 7.40 M buitenwerks, dubbelwandig met tocht- en vochtwerend isolatie-materiaal er tusschen, plafond houtvezel platen, dakbedekking rubberroid in ruitvorm en lood, houten-vloer op balklaag en porrings.

Afwerking: buiten ruig, gecarbolineerd, binnen blank gevernisd, vurenhouten vloeren, okerkleurig geolied, kasten van binnen geverfd.

Bevattend: woonruimte met tafel en kasten, 2 dubbele slaapplaatsen die overdag tot 2 banken met rugleuning worden neergeslagen, onder de bedden, bergruimte voor dekens; slaapkamer met 1 dubbelbed, kast, douche-ruimte, 2 waschtafels; keuken met aanrecht en gootsteen, pannenrekken en kasten met doorgeef naar eettafel, entree met garderobe en W.C.

Prijs van het zomerhuis als boven omschreven f 1000.— incl. aan- en afvoerleidingen voor het sanitair binnenshuis. Excl. stoffeering, verdere losse meubels, aansluiting op waterleiding en rioleering, eventueel gemetseld rookkanaal en fundeering waar porrings niet voldoende zijn.

Wanneer gas, waterleiding en electriciteit niet aanwezig zijn, zijn de mogelijkheden voor Koken: petroleum, persgas, ruwe olie, butagas.

Verwarmen: primusstraalkachel, kolenkachel of butagaskachel.

Verlichten: petroleum-persgas of gewoone petroleumlamp.

Watervoorziening: pomp (met reservoir in kap*).

Rioleering: put met overstort en stapelputof septictank**.

* Kosten: gemiddeld f 100 afhankellijk van plaatselijke toestand.
** „ „ f 50.- „ „ „ „

Service: hulp bij aanvrage bouwvergunning. Levering door geheel Nederland en montage en afwerking bij de prijs inbegrepen.

Verplaatsing ± f 60 + transportkosten.

Verandering in binnenindeeling is mogelijk in overleg met kooper en wordt billijk berekend.
Ook is het mogelijk een tuinhuisje te leveren met 8 zijden met diameter ± 5 Meter, inlichtingen op aanvraag.

Ingang — Opensl. deuren

Zitruimte — Kast — Keukening. — Eettafel

Entree — Zitbank 's nachts 2 Bedden — 2 Bedden onder Bewaarplaats v. dekens — Ingang Slaapk. 2 Bedden 2 Waschtafels — Kast — Keuken

Rietveld and his employees in his studio at Oudegracht 55, Utrecht, c.1958

7. War and reconstruction

Gerrit Rietveld, who was perhaps more of a genius and possessed all the simplicity of the genius, was someone who had such a direct, almost primitive approach to design that everything he touched acquired a personal charm.[1]
– Willem Sandberg, early 1970s

On 14 May 1940, German aeroplanes scattered pamphlets above Utrecht: the city would be bombarded if the Netherlands did not surrender.[2] The army capitulated that same day and Utrecht was spared the fate of Rotterdam and Warsaw.

Hitler regarded the Dutch as a cognate Aryan race that would be assimilated into his Great Germanic Empire. This was why the Nazi occupation was at first relatively bearable. The occupying forces installed a civilian rather than a military government. Dutch prisoners of war were released on condition that they promised not to resist the Germans and 'normal' life was resumed. At the start of the war the production of goods for the German army actually drove a brief economic recovery. The only signs of exceptional circumstances were the introduction of measures against Jewish citizens and the large assortment of foodstuffs subjected to rationing as early as the summer of 1940.

Verrijn Stuart Summerhouse

When Germany invaded in May 1940, Rietveld was working on two detached houses and two summerhouses. One of these, the Verrijn Stuart Summerhouse, occupies a unique place in his oeuvre. The house was built on one of the strips of land in the watery St Pieters area, between the River Vecht and the Loosdrecht lakelands near Breukelen. Peat was dredged out of the waterlogged marshland there until the beginning of the twentieth century, the clods of peat laid out to dry on strips of land just a few metres wide that extended for dozens of metres. Once the peat layer was exhausted, Mother Nature was allowed to take her course. The drying fields became strip-like islands in an extensive lakeland area, which became popular for recreation. Construction was allowed there only in accordance with strict building codes, which prescribed timber elevations and thatched roofs.

The form of the Verrijn Stuart Summerhouse is unusual for Rietveld. This was in part imposed by the planning regulations, but at the same time the design was in keeping with a stylistic shift in his work. Rietveld would hardly have been showing his true colours if he had failed to realize a wonderful space within these limiting conditions.[3] He realized the requisite floor area by building the house crossways to the strip of land and partly cantilevered over the water. The plan has the form of a truncated wedge of cake: the widest point under the thatch roof is 4.25 m (13 ft 11 in) and it extends to a length of 11 m (36 ft); in the middle it attains a height of 6 m (19 ft 9 in), sloping away to 2 m (6 ft 7 in) to the north and to 4.1 m (13 ft 6 in) to the south.

The kitchen is situated to the north and natural light from the south enters through a horizontal band of three windows set directly under the roof. Adjacent to it, but separated by a sliding partition, is the dining area with an east-facing glazed wall that rises to almost 4.5 m (14 ft 9 in). The sitting room is partly separated from the dining area by a brick wall and the curved chimney of the round open hearth. Above this lounge area there is

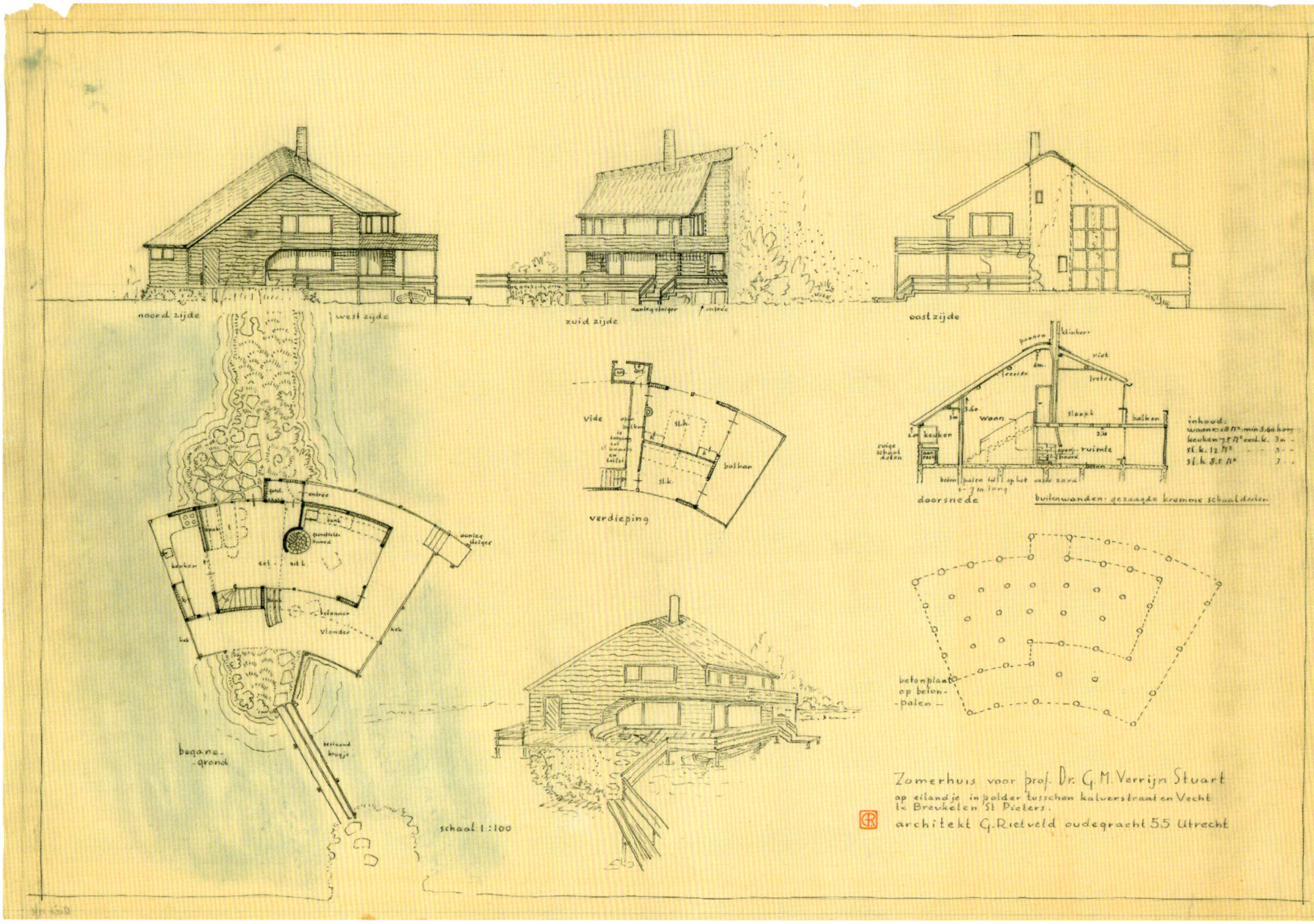

Drawings for Verrijn Stuart Summerhouse, Breukelen St Pieters, c.1940, showing the ingenious plan and the positioning of the house across two small islands

Verrijn Stuart Summerhouse, 1940–1

Dining area for the Verrijn Stuart Summerhouse, with Rietveld's Zig-Zag Chairs and table

Living room for the Verrijn Stuart Summerhouse. Behind the curtain is the dining area.

an entresol that leads to three bedrooms and a south-facing balcony, which also shelters the sitting-room terrace to the front of the house. The gentle curves of the facades are echoed in the hearth and the pattern of the floor, which has an inlay of round wooden discs.

The house is a consummate example of Rietveld's ability. By exploiting the house's setting and introducing an alternation of open and closed planes in the elevations he brought about a subtle interrelationship between the spaces in and around the house and its natural surroundings. The varied heights lend the interior an articulation that is in harmony with this, while the ever-changing Dutch light, which is so strongly influenced by the seasons, the weather and the time of day, ensures an infinite variation in the perception of the space. These aspects define the sense of space in the house much more than the form and the use of materials, which on the face of it hardly suggest Rietveld, though he had often worked with organic materials and forms over the preceding years. Rietveld's colleagues recognized his signature immediately and were full of praise. De *8 en Opbouw* published critiques by the architects J. P. Kloos (1905–2001) and J. B. Bakema (1914–81). The former praised the house's beauty, that is 'inseparably connected with all the objectives, no matter what their functional nature, whether this is material or spiritual'. Bakema waxed lyrical:

Everyone feels the longing for the simplicity of everything… and when we build then often that desire does not manage to express itself other than by setting walls vertically and laying floors horizontally… The lines of life flow freely through this work by Rietveld, and we know that this bliss, this solidarity with God-Nature, shall never be found by following the well-trodden path.[4]

After completing the Verrijn Stuart Summerhouse and realizing a detached house for J. Nijland Jr in Bilthoven, Rietveld found himself with little to keep him occupied. The Rotterdam-based architect W. van Tijen (1894–1974) invited him to contribute to several projects. One of these involved a study of housing typologies, published in 1941 as *Woonmogelijkheden in het Nieuwe Rotterdam* (Housing Possibilities in the New Rotterdam), for which Rietveld designed a middle-class

Sketches, c.1940. During his visits to Limburg, a province in the south of the Netherlands, Rietveld made sketches of castles and farms.

house. He also contributed to plans for the Rotterdam expansion districts of Tuindorp, Waalhaven and Zuidwijk. For the latter Rietveld devised a proposal with detached middle-class houses arranged along a spiral-shaped street plan. A change in the development plans meant there was no longer any room for Rietveld's proposal. A few blocks of flats that he had designed were eventually realized at the Zuidwijk housing estate in the early 1950s.[5]

Rietveld also participated in discussions about the future of Dutch architecture. In 1941 the Architectura et Amicitia Society organized two meetings in Doorn, the 'Doornse Leergangen' (Doorn Study Sessions), where representatives of diverse schools of thought debated the profession's basic principles, with the laudable ambition of cultivating understanding for each other's standpoints.[6] *De 8 en Opbouw* published comprehensive reports of the discussions. Some participants, sometimes counter to their better judgement, expressed their confidence in the future. All their attention and energy was focused on the future, in the hope that post-war society would be completely different and much better organized, but even without this optimism it was obvious to everyone that the country had to be reconstructed.

War and liberation

In the meantime the Nazi occupation became increasingly intimidating. The tentacles of the *Gleichschaltung* – the 'great alignment' aimed at Nazification of all institutions – penetrated ever deeper into civic life. The Dutch Chamber of Culture (Nederlandsche Kultuurkamer) was established on 25 November 1941 and artists were required to become members if they wanted to continue practising their profession, but Rietveld refused to register. The chief of its Legal Affairs Department, a certain D. Spanjaard, sent him a memorandum a year later:

It has come to my attention that you have received a commission from the Board of the Amsterdam Bank to design a recreation room. However, given that you have not reported to the Dutch Chamber of Culture, you are not permitted to execute the assignment… Non-compliance with this instruction will result in police measures.[7]

Prototype chair for the Amsterdam Bank, 1941–3. During the first years of the Nazi occupation Rietveld had little to do. Later on he was forbiddden to practise as an architect because he was not a member of the 'Kultuurkammer'. This chair, made from thin oak slats, was never put into production.

Nijland House, Bilthoven, 1940–2. Built for the Utrecht cinema owner J. Nijland as a wedding present for his son, the original design for this house had a flat roof and was rejected by the municipality. Rietveld made a new design with a thatched pitched roof and red tiles on the roof of the garage. Its roughly plastered walls are interspersed with green, white and black glazed brickwork, a material Rietveld regularly made use of after the war.

Plan for the Zuidwijk residential district, Rotterdam, c.1940–5. In the early 1940s, Rietveld's colleague W. van Tijen asked him to collaborate on this commission, one of several large-scale planning projects Rietveld worked on during this period.

Drawing for assembly-system houses, Gorinchem, c.1943

Rietveld was, nevertheless, granted permission to contribute to a project by Bredero's Bouwbedrijf. In 1941, with the occupier's permission, this construction company had established a factory to carry out research into new types of concrete and new construction methods. Two years later, a number of architects, including Rietveld, were invited to contribute to a study about prefabrication in concrete for housing.[8] Rietveld designed middle- and working-class housing for the town of Gorinchem, one of the locations on which Bredero's Bouwbedrijf had set its sights. The system he devised used stacked concrete panels that were joined together by hammering steel pins through precast holes, but this project remained unrealized.

Another project that dates from the war years is the design for the brochure 'Meubels om zelf te maken' (Furniture to make yourself) for the Committee for Household Information and Family Management (Commissie inzake Huishoudelijke voorlichting en gezinsleiding). There is no evidence that the brochure, which was possibly an initiative of Truus Schröder, ever reached the printing presses.

Rietveld was fifty-one years old when World War II broke out, too old to be sent to work in Germany. Forced labour was, however, a peril that his sons faced.[9] His eldest, Jan, tried to flee to England via Spain, but ended up in a concentration camp in France. His youngest son, Wim, who was still living at home, was arrested in the middle of the night and spent a year incarcerated at Camp Amersfoort, a labour and transit camp run by the German police. Rietveld travelled to The Hague repeatedly to petition the *Sicherheitspolizei* for his release and eventually succeeded. His youngest daughter, Vrouwgien, courted a member of the Nazi-friendly Dutch National Socialist Movement (Nationaal-Socialistische Beweging, or NSB) during the war, which created an awkward situation because Rietveld and his sons assisted people in hiding and were involved in the forging of identity cards.

By eight o'clock on the evening of Friday 4 May 1945, Field-Marshal Montgomery accepted the capitulation of the German armed forces that were still occupying Dutch territory to the north of the rivers Rhine and Maas. The Netherlands Forces of the Interior

(Binnenlandse Strijdkrachten) suffered a further ten fatalities while disarming German troops and NSB members at the Rosarium close by the Wilhelmina Park in Utrecht on 7 May, the same day that the Canadian First Army's troops made their triumphal entrance into Utrecht.[10]

Immediately after liberation, the solidarity and camaraderie which had grown between various political and social movements under Nazi occupation prompted a large group of christians, socialists and liberals to press for cooperation in new organizations. These 'breakthrough attempts' stalled within a few years because of the new 'Cold' War. The influence of the communists, who had enjoyed massive support immediately after the war, quickly waned when it became evident that the party was following Moscow slavishly. Party members and those suspected of communist sympathies faced rough times.[11]

This backlash also affected Rietveld in 1948, when he was nominated as director of the Institute for Education in the Applied Arts (Instituut voor Kunstnijverheidsonderwijs, or IvKNO; later the Rietveld Academy) in Amsterdam. Willem Sandberg, who had been a curator at the Stedelijk Museum in Amsterdam since 1934 and served as its director from 1945 to 1962, sat on the IvKNO's board on behalf of Amsterdam City Council and thought Rietveld was the best candidate. However, the Minister of Education, Arts and Science refused to appoint Rietveld, officially because of his 'lack of qualifications' but in reality because of his political persuasion, and a letter signed by twenty-six prominent figures was to no avail.[12]

Sandberg admired Rietveld. They had known each other since the early 1930s and often went to view Rietveld's new work together. Rietveld sat with Sandberg, Mart Stam, graphic designer Wim Brusse (1910–78), architect J. P. Kloos and art historian Hans Jaffé (1915–84) on the editorial team of the periodical *Open Oog, avantgardecahier voor visuele vormgeving* (Open Eye, avant-garde cahier for visual design), which was established immediately after the war. By choosing this title the cahier's editors wanted to indicate that their eyes were peeled to see whether the 1939–45 war would usher in a new era. Rietveld wrote a short text about industrial design and designed a cover for the journal, though the latter was not used. According to the announcement in the first issue, the cahier would appear whenever there was something to say, and in the second issue a series of ten issues was promised, but then it folded.[13] Sandberg made every effort to help find work for Rietveld: 'At that time we tried to provide him with a livelihood by giving him assignments for exhibitions … because he had not obtained sufficient architecture commissions. That improved in the 1950s. Then he no longer needed this, thank goodness.'[14]

Perhaps as a means to pass the time, in 1946 Rietveld sketched an ideal house for himself and called it the 'House for an Architect' ('Huis voor een architect'). A model of clay, a few sketches and a sheet of presentation drawings with the caption 'study for individuel [sic] building (country)' are the only extant documentation of this wonderful plan.[15] The house is situated on a gently sloping incline overlooking a river. A woodland fringe runs across the top of the hill. At the front the house is about 6 m (19 ft 8 in) high. The interior is divided in two by a glass wall: in the front section there is a studio space subdivided into terraces; in the smaller rear section there is a sunken bathroom and above it the library. Two beds are set on an east-facing entresol with a view of the rising sun; beneath this lies the kitchen with a dining area. In one of the sketches there is a sunken seating area in the middle of the main living space. It is a paradisiacal house where living and working as well as nature and culture are harmoniously combined.

Nagele: a village in the polder

The first polder reclaimed from the IJsselmeer was the Northeast Polder. Preparations began in 1936, and in 1940 the dykes around the area were sealed and drainage could begin.[16] The land reclamation process was completed in September 1942. The so-called Wieringermeer Directorate (Northeast Polder Works) was responsible for the organization and design of the new land. On 15 April 1948 the 'directorate' officially awarded the commission for an urban development plan for one village to the Amsterdam-based group of Dutch Functionalist architects known as 'De 8'.[17] This village was to provide 300 dwellings, three

Drawings, House for an Architect,
1946

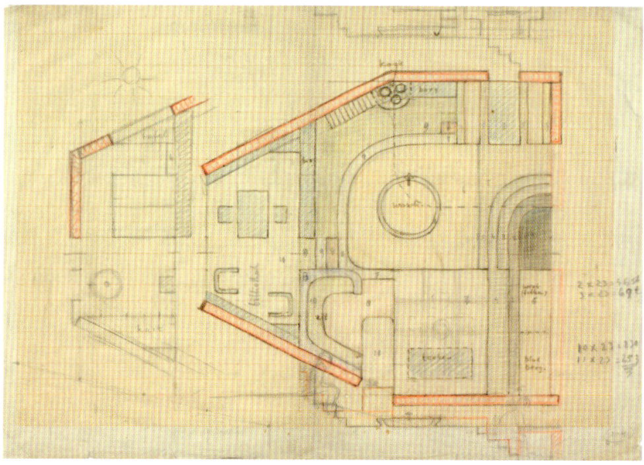

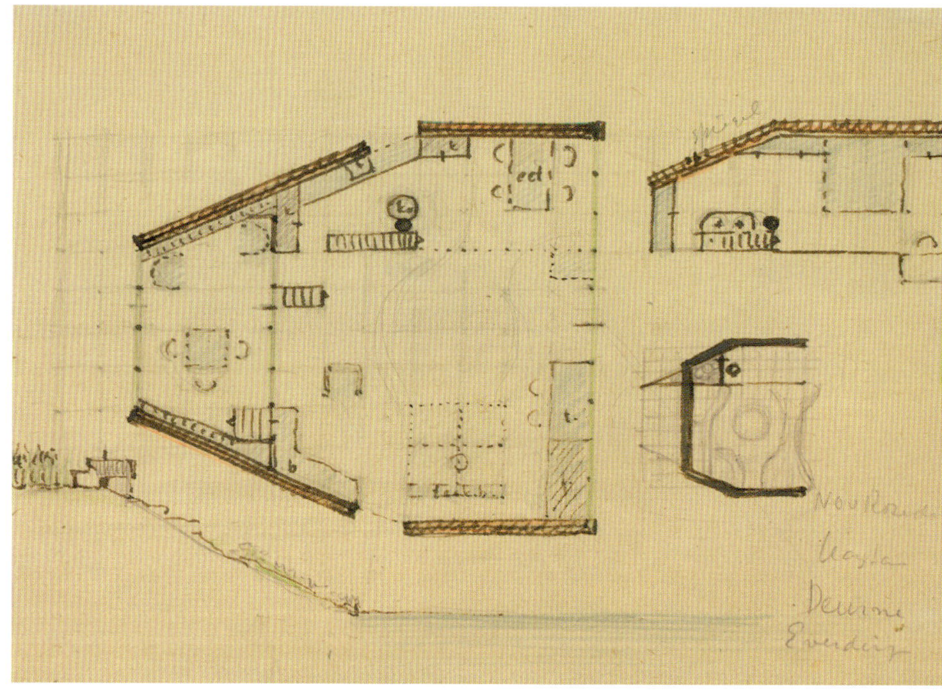

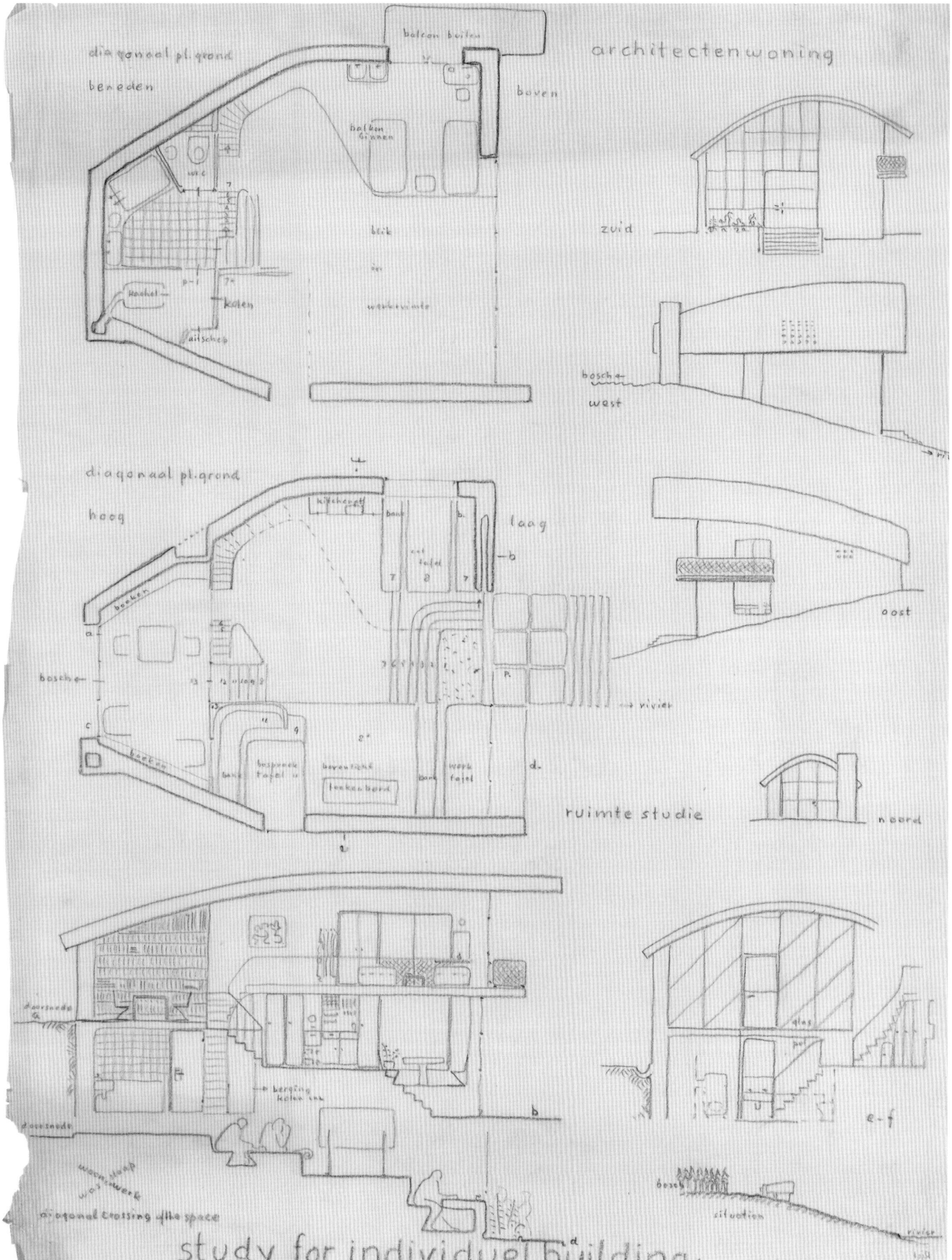
diagonaal pl.grond
beneden
balcon buiten
boven
architectenwoning
balkon binnen
wc
kachel
kolen
werkruimte
zuid
bosch
west
diagonaal pl.grond
hoog
laag
oost
bosch
rivier
boeken
bank
tafel
tekenbord
ruimte studie
noord
doorsnede
glas
berging
kolen
b
e-f
bosch
situation
rivier
diagonal crossing of the space
study for individuel building (country) 1946

Rietveld's first sketch for Nagele, a new village in the Northeast Polder, 1948

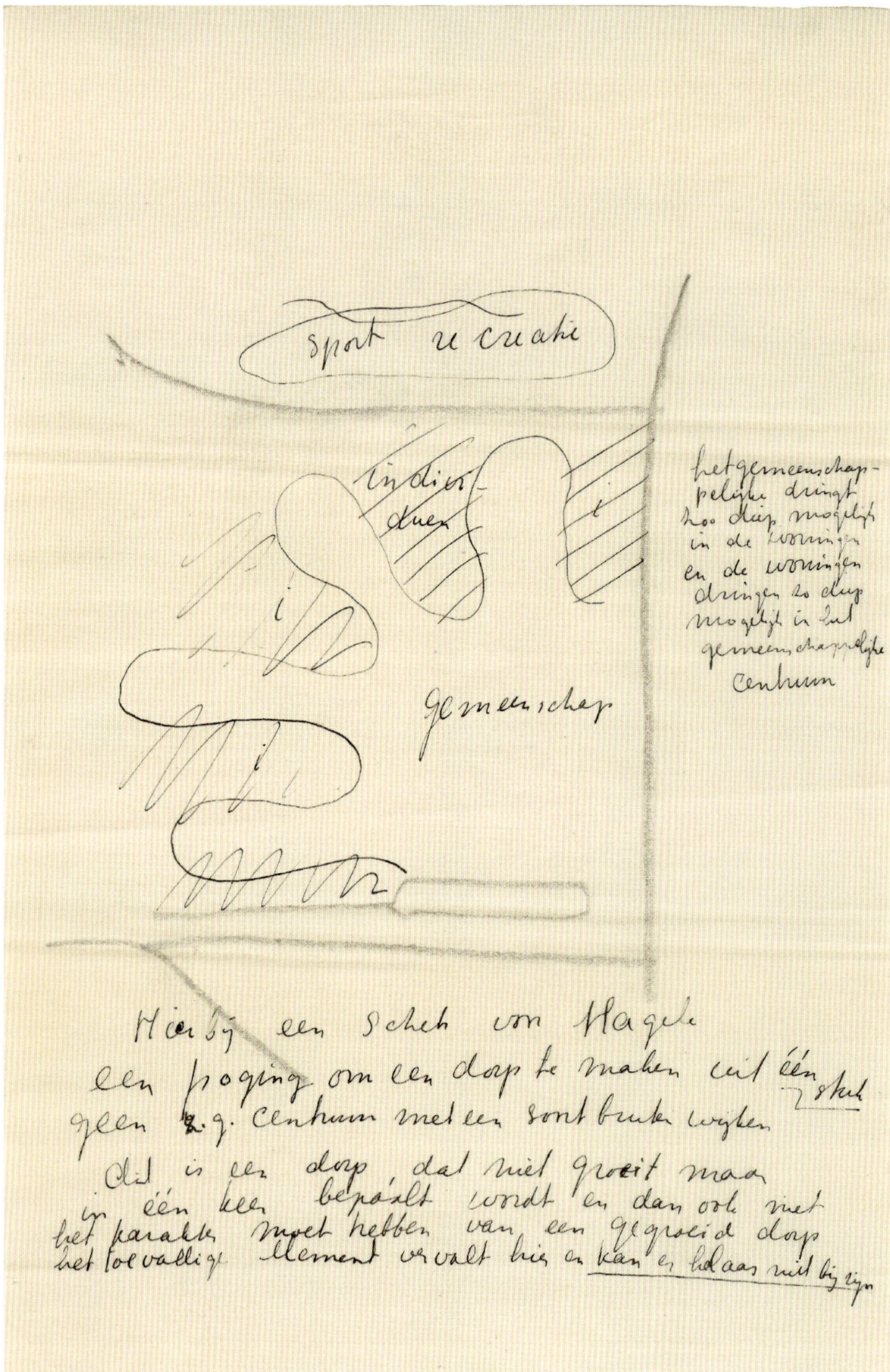

churches, three schools, a café/restaurant, a forge, some shops, an industrial zone, a couple of sports fields and a cemetery. The commissions for the design of other villages around the core of Emmeloord were awarded to architects from the traditionalist school. De 8 established a special working group for the project. Besides Rietveld it counted Aldo van Eyck (1918–99), Mart Stam and Cornelis van Eesteren among its members. The latter was also involved in the project for the polder as a whole. The commission to design Nagele dovetailed perfectly with the post-war desire to cooperate and was also wholly in keeping with the ideals of De 8: teamwork was essential to the design process. When Van Eesteren assumed the Extraordinary Chair in Town and Country Planning at Delft in 1948 he expressed this as follows: 'The possibilities that the designer, already in the process of working, at a given moment starts to see in a task, and the inspiration that he finds in the working group to which he belongs, activate his creative powers.'[18]

The various plans were all based on CIAM's most important urban planning principle: the separation of the four main urban functions of living, working, traffic and recreation. The design for Nagele was therefore introduced as a case study at the seventh CIAM meeting in Bergamo in 1949.[19] Another CIAM feature is the schematic layout with encircling woodland as the outermost shell, residential zones within this, and an open area for recreation and other communal amenities at the centre. While Van Eesteren concentrated on the village's accessibility and communications with the rest of the polder, Rietveld's design placed the emphasis on the social aspects. Alongside his first little sketch from 1948 he scribbled a note:

Herewith a sketch for Nagele, an attempt to make a one-piece village, not a so-called centre with suburbs of sorts – this is a village, which does not grow but is defined in one go and therefore should not have the character of a village that has grown – the chance element is cancelled out here. The communal penetrates as deeply as possible into the dwellings and the dwellings penetrate as deeply as possible into the communal centre.

This intention is still evident in the final village – the plan that was approved in 1949 is in part based on

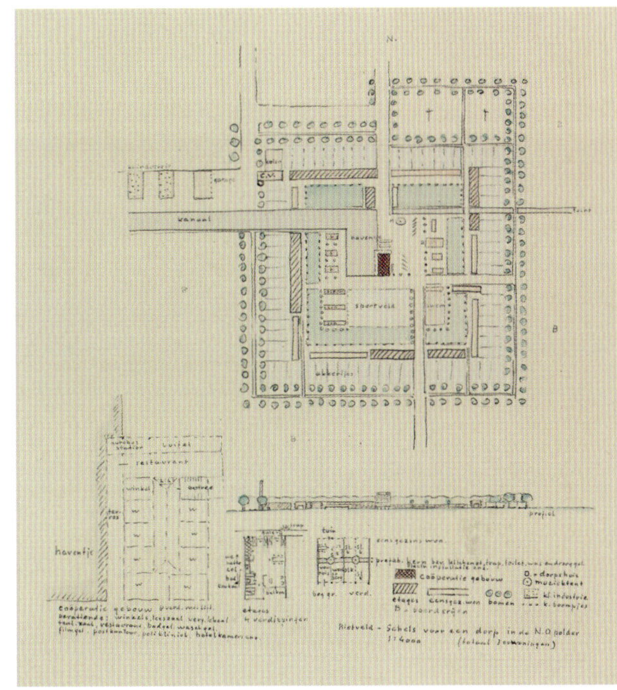

Draft site plans for Nagele, 1948. Rietveld drew several potential solutions for the Nagele urban development plan, each illustrating a different possibility.

This page and opposite page top: Draft site plans for Nagele, 1948

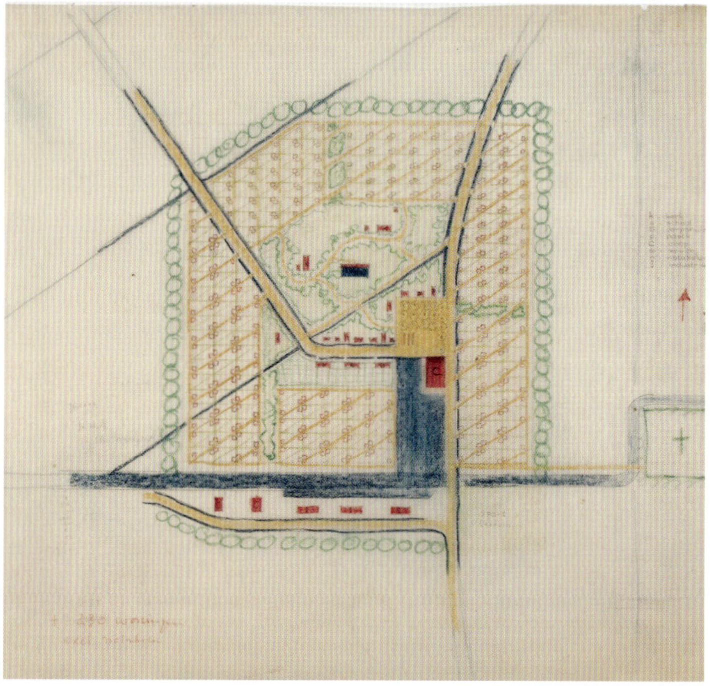

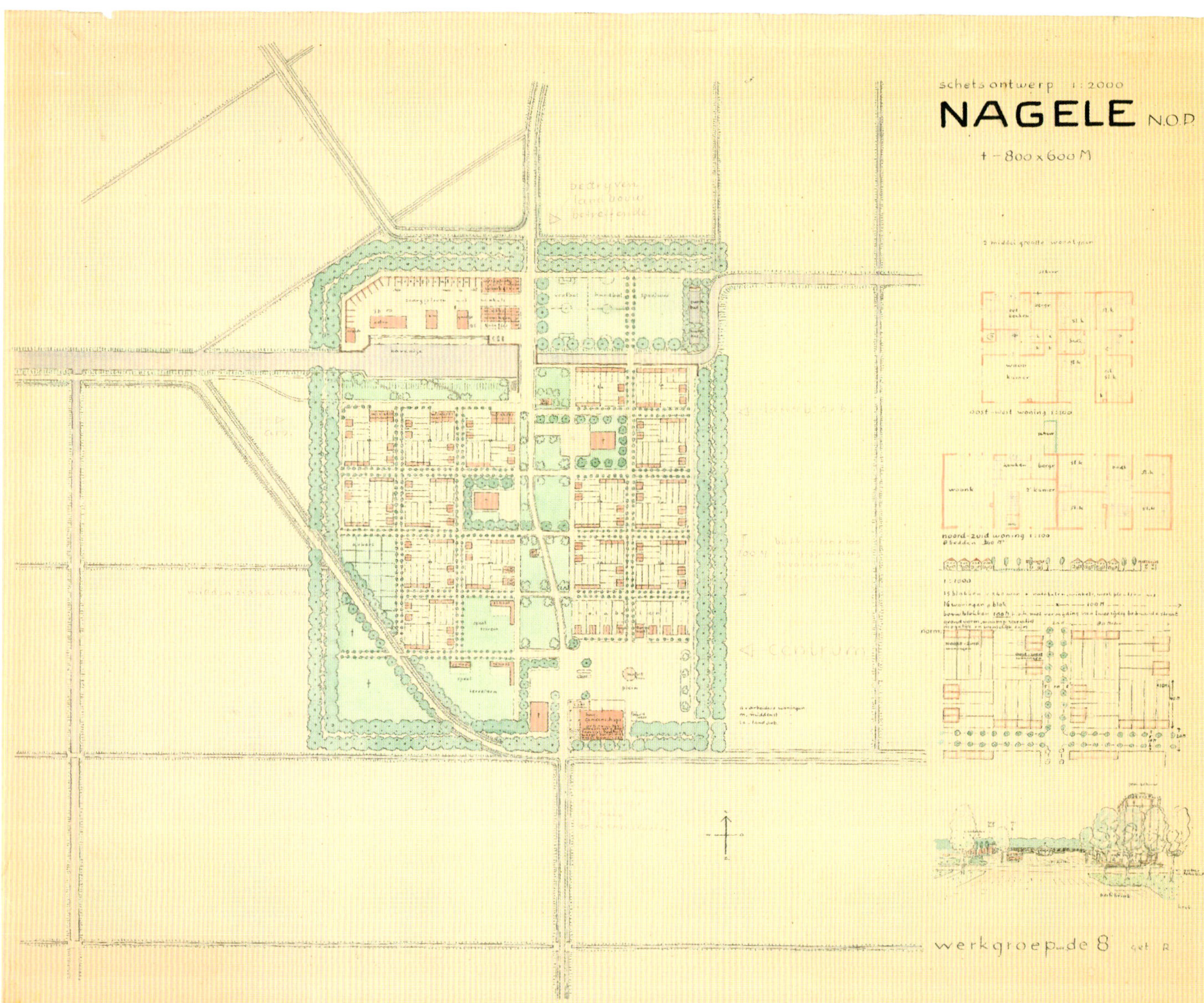

Aerial photograph of Nagele, c.1961

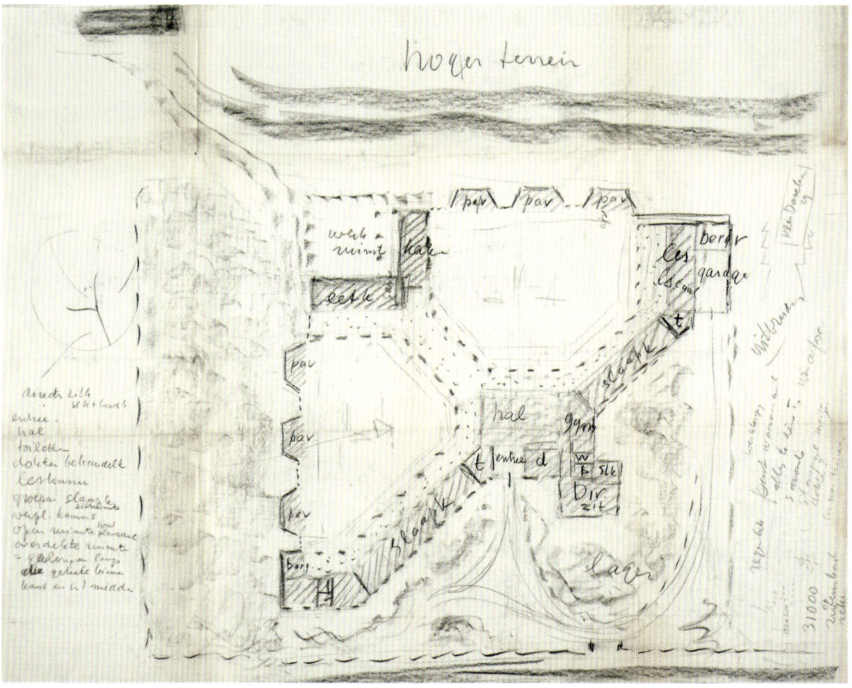
hoger terrein

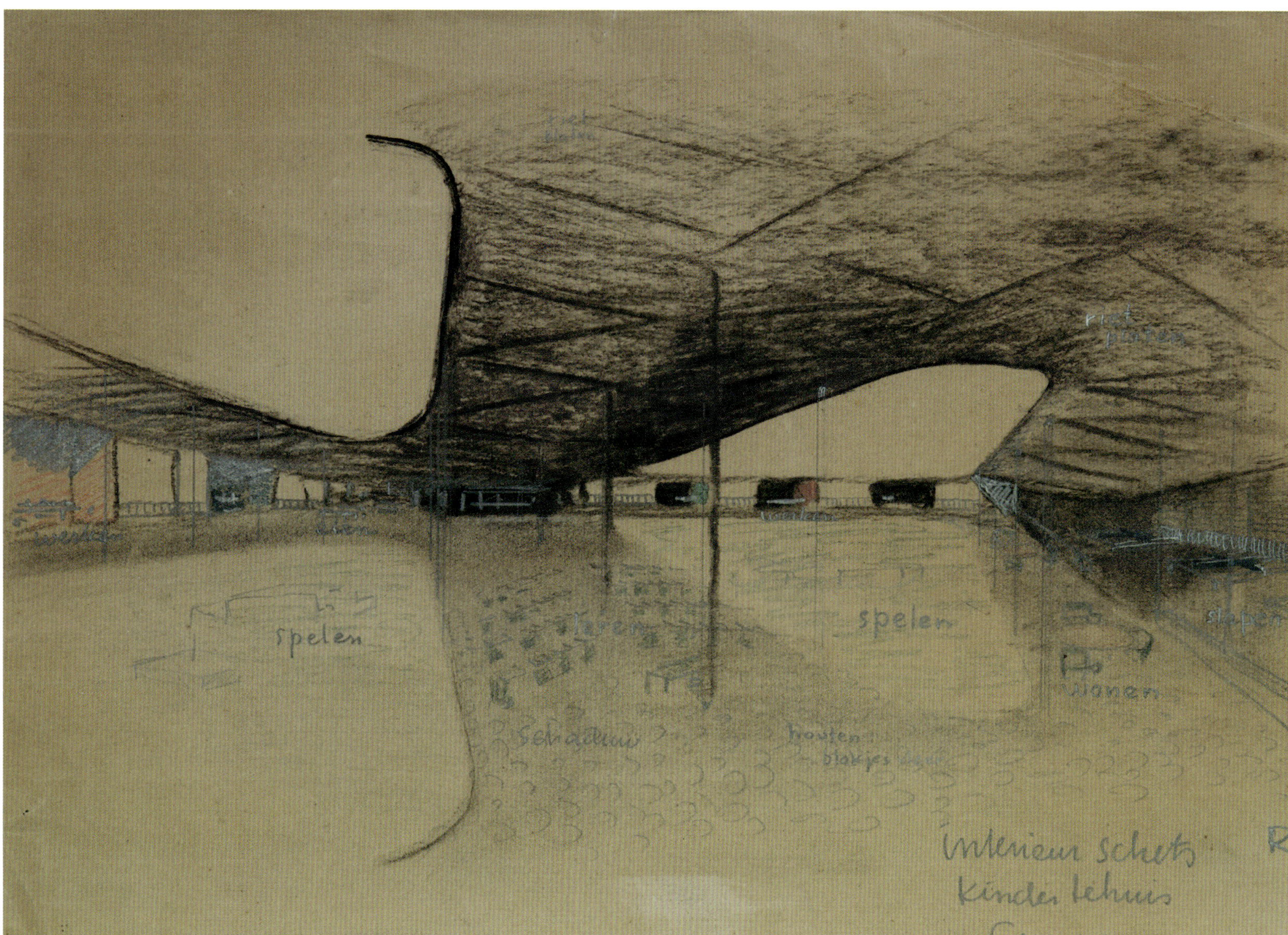
spelen
spelen
interieur schets
Kinder tehuis
Curacao
R

Home for handicapped children, Monsignor P. I. Verriet Institute, Willemstad, Curaçao, 1949–52. By 1952, when the aerial view and the photograph of the entrance were taken, the construction was complete. However, a planned wing in the middle and a row of pavilions to the east and the south were not built at that time due to lack of finances. The building is comprised of galleries with a roof made from grass-thatched mats carried on metal columns. It is an inverted pitch roof, catching rainwater in the middle.

Opposite page: The plan and perspective sketch both date from 1949; construction began that year and concluded in 1952.

the relationship between individual and community broached by Rietveld, and the interpenetration of the two realms.[20] Rietveld's involvement with the second phase of development, from 1952 to 1954, was very limited. The houses he had designed for Nagele together with his son Jan Rietveld were built under the latter's supervision.

Curaçao

In 1949 Rietveld undertook a study trip to Suriname and the Dutch Antilles. The Foundation for Cultural Cooperation between the Netherlands, Indonesia, Suriname and the Dutch Antilles (Sticusa, for short) had invited him on Sandberg's recommendation. He spent most time on the island of Curaçao, one of the Dutch Antilles, an arid lump of rock covering 44,400 hectares in the Caribbean, about 75 km (47 miles) north of the Venezuelan mainland.

During his stay on Curaçao, Rietveld lodged with the Engels family. The physician Chris Engels was, according to Rietveld, 'the man' on Curaçao. He and his wife, Lucila Boskaljon, were the linchpins of cultural life there.[21] The official purpose of the trip was to advise on the restoration of the seventeenth-century colonial country houses and the traditional architecture on the island, but the correspondence between Engels and Rietveld reveals that there was a hidden agenda: the doctor was keen to have Rietveld as his architect for a new home for disabled children, a scheme that was a complete success. Following a critical discussion of the existing plans, the White-Yellow Cross Foundation (Wit-Gele Kruis), a Catholic missionary charity, asked Rietveld to commit a concept to paper. In a letter to Truus he gave a candid account of his first impressions:

... saw lame children – it was heart-breaking for me – saw the site – quite beautiful – took measurements, had discussions with prospective foremen all day Sunday at Dr Engels's place – swam in the sea – stunning pale blue water – but you feel like a haddock in the midst of all those brown, beautiful bodies. The most wonderful thing here is driving an automobile – [Dr Engels] has his own luxurious car, drives with just one hand – other hand on the hood through the open window – wonderful arm with golden wristwatch, and only if he sees acquaintances does he briefly spread his fingers, and this drive passed through a motley collection of colourful little houses.[22]

After an 'animated meeting' Rietveld was commissioned to elaborate his plan and discuss its construction with the supervisor and building contractor before his departure for Suriname.[23] Rietveld had seen the children's temporary accommodation and had thoroughly absorbed the daily routine at the home:

It is for crippled children in Curaçao ... those mothers, they have to earn their own keep. They sometimes tie the children to a tree ... and then they have all manner of disabilities and in such a home that is brought up to standard a little. But those children ... they just lie there, but once they see the others who are slightly more advanced working away then they slowly progress towards that ... When they are a little further on then they see those little workshops that are standing round about ... It is, of course, quite an honour to get a place there and to learn a trade, and that is what it gradually progresses towards.[24]

The roof and the floor were the building's essential components, as Rietveld explained in an article:

I proposed using woodblocks as a floor, and treating the roof as a shelter for the gallery; low in the middle and ascending towards the sides – so the reverse of a saddleback roof – and bringing the columns and walls so far under the canopy that they do not reflect the sun in the middle of the day and thus do not become too hot. The whole building is comprised of such galleries, bounded to the outside, alternately by a length of wall and an opening with shutters (which lets the east wind pass through) and on the inside only columns with shutters that can be opened. The galleries are ±17 m across and are divided into a strip to the outside for sleeping and overlooking the open courtyard a strip to live (little tables and chairs) ... You can also regard the whole thing as a huge thatched roof on a great many slender round columns, into which two really big light-wells have been introduced.[25]

Because of a shortage of funds, the central wing intended as an open classroom and the side wings with

Smit House, Kinderdijk, 1947–9. Built in a village on the Lek river for the shipbuilder Leo Smit, this design dramatically changed between the first model, a two-storey building full of rounded forms, and the final building, a linear bungalow. From a large low window in the open plan dining/living room there is a wonderful view across the river to the shipbuilding yards on the other side.

Stoop House, Velp, 1950–1. This house was built for the parents of Nel Stoop, who worked in Rietveld's office. It is a bungalow, with a projecting pent. The plan is a subtle U shape with a covered space at the south forming a simple loggia. All window frames, the kitchen excluded, are floor to ceiling height.

Summerhouse, Markelo, 1951. This is one of six inexpensive, small holiday houses built together.

Slegers House, Velp, 1952–5. Built for the sculptor Piet Slegers and his family, on a tight budget, this house neighbours the slightly earlier Stoop House. It is composed of two volumes that interconnect in an L shape with a small entrance hall at the corner of the L. The larger volume houses a studio, the living area and the kitchen, and a smaller annex contains bedrooms and a bathroom. The large block has a monopitch roof, brick walls painted in a somewhat forbidding black and floor-to-ceiling windows.

workshops could not be realized in 1949–52. These were realized later under the supervision of the architect Henk Nolte (1915–2008).

The Monsignor P. I. Verriet Institute deserves a place among the masterpieces in Rietveld's oeuvre, because here he succeeded in delimiting 'a small part of… the universal, unbounded space for a specific purpose', insulating it from certain influences and reducing it to a human scale in a form that complies with the tropical climate and takes the future users into account in every respect. It is 'flexible Functionalism' at its best.[26] Later on Rietveld designed a home for senior citizens (Tehuis voor Ouden van Dagen) on Curaçao and made a few minor alterations to the house of Chris Engels.

In 1957 Rietveld sketched a dream house in the *liber amicorum* (a kind of friendship or autograph book) of the Engelses. It has an open plan with a succession of spaces for eating, sleeping and making music and is set on the coast, nestled up against the bay. It breathes the same freedom as the 'House for an Architect', and both designs would have been worthy successors to the Schröder House had Rietveld been given the opportunity to build them.

The re-evaluation of De Stijl

The tide turned for Rietveld in 1951 and he owed that to De Stijl once again. No matter how beautiful and brilliant the Verrijn Stuart Summerhouse in the midst of the Loosdrecht lakelands and the Monsignor P. I. Verriet Institute on Curaçao, these designs on the fringes of the Dutch architectural scene were of minimal significance for Rietveld's reputation. By contrast, the De Stijl exhibition staged in Amsterdam in 1951, which immediately toured to Venice and New York, made Rietveld the focus of international attention. The initiative for these exhibitions, the preparations and realization, and the reviews they received occurred in a context as polemical as the De Stijl movement itself in the period from 1917 to 1928.[27]

The Dutch government initially wanted to present an exhibition of contemporary Dutch architecture at the Museum of Modern Art (MoMA) in New York. MoMA, however, was not interested in the results of post-war reconstruction and via Philip Johnson, head of its architecture department, the museum informed the Dutch government that it was keen to organize an exhibition about De Stijl and the movement's international influence. Rietveld sat on the committee charged with preparing the presentation in Amsterdam, which set to work in 1948. There were heated discussions about various questions within this group and more broadly. Did the intellectual legacy of De Stijl still have any merit today? Was the importance and influence of architecture greater than that of painting? And was Mondrian or Van Doesburg the most important De Stijl artist?

The exhibition in Amsterdam was to be a 'pilot presentation'. Various people raised objections to a purely historical approach, including Rietveld, who was asked to design the exhibition layout. His proposals naturally reflected how he viewed De Stijl. In his first proposal he did not confine himself to the disciplines of visual art and architecture, but included experimental films and music and set aside space for theoretical texts. One intriguing component of his plans was a separate gallery where scale models of realized and unrealized architecture projects would stand in the middle on a large platform, with the plans of these buildings executed in relief hung on the walls, all of this painted in white and set against a whitewashed background. Rietveld's idea was to express how De Stijl was primarily about an endeavour, about an ideal that was by definition unattainable, but that this did not detract from its value.

The white gallery concept failed to muster support and the range of disciplines presented was slimmed down. The majority of critics and connoisseurs – including Sandberg – were not convinced of De Stijl's topical relevance. Rietveld may have been a great genius in Sandberg's eyes, but Sandberg by no means regarded him as a great thinker or theoretician.[28] Rietveld was asked to do as much justice as possible to the diverse outlooks and adjusted his layout proposals accordingly.

The ample attention devoted to Theo van Doesburg in the catalogue was largely due to the assiduous lobbying of his widow, Nelly van Doesburg, but a different picture emerges from the exhibition spaces designed by Rietveld.[29] None of the De Stijl group stood out; there was even a certain levelling out, with paintings by Mondrian and Van Doesburg treated in the same manner as photographs of Oud's architecture and watercolour renderings of the Schröder House's facades. The asymmetrical partitions and false ceilings – connected to the white rectangular platforms by slender columns – call to mind Rietveld's work from the early 1920s: his 'De Stijl furniture', such as the Red-Blue Chair, the sideboard, the hanging lamp and other designs which had become 'classics'. Rietveld's work dominated the picture, casting himself and De Stijl – perhaps unintentionally – as figures in a heroic Dutch past.

After the 'pilot presentation' in Amsterdam, the show toured to the Venice Biennale in 1952, then to New York and finally to Richmond, Virginia. In 1953–4 a selection made by Sandberg was shown at the Biennale in São Paulo, then in Montevideo, Uruguay.[30] Even as late as 1960, Rietveld was asked to design the De Stijl exhibition at the Galleria Nazionale in Rome. It was during these years that his name became inextricably linked with De Stijl.

The renewed interest in De Stijl had far-reaching consequences for Rietveld. For the first time in his life his position was undisputed. The more the canonization of De Stijl gained an international foothold, the greater the acknowledgement of his contribution to the development of twentieth-century architecture and design. Rietveld became the 'grand old man' of the pre-war Dutch avant-garde. For the Kingdom of the Netherlands he was the obvious candidate for high-profile commissions such as the design of its Biennale Pavilion in Venice, the press room for the UNESCO headquarters in Paris and – as a gift from the Netherlands to the United Nations – the base of the Foucault pendulum for the public foyer of the UN headquarters in New York.

This late recognition for Rietveld was based almost entirely on the Red-Blue Chair and the Schröder House, which were seen as 'manifestos' of De Stijl's principles. Sandberg, who knew Rietveld very well and should therefore have known better, made the following statement about the Red-Blue Chair:

That chair is actually a three-dimensional Mondrian: colourful planes – blue, red, yellow – connected by black staves. The remarkable thing is that this chair is from 1918 and Mondrian only starts using such black lines, his staves, in 1919. In 1919 he had gone to Paris and I don't know whether he ever saw that chair and was influenced by it, but in any case the black lines appeared in Mondrian's paintings a year later.[31]

Sandberg was clearly unaware or had forgotten that the slat armchair from 1918 was painted in colour only some five years later. Rietveld would not, however, have minded the 'De Stijl' label being attached to his work, so long as he could actually make and build things.

The most intriguing consequence of Rietveld's intense involvement with the post-war image and re-evaluation of De Stijl is its unmistakable influence on his late work. The supple formal idiom of the 1940s and 50s was gradually superseded by what might be described as a neo-De Stijl, that is a revival of De Stijl principles, which appealed to his clients thanks to the post-war popularity of Modernism.

Rietveld's sketch for a 'dream home' in the *liber amicorum* (a kind of friendship or autograph book) of the Curaçao doctor Chris Engels, 1957

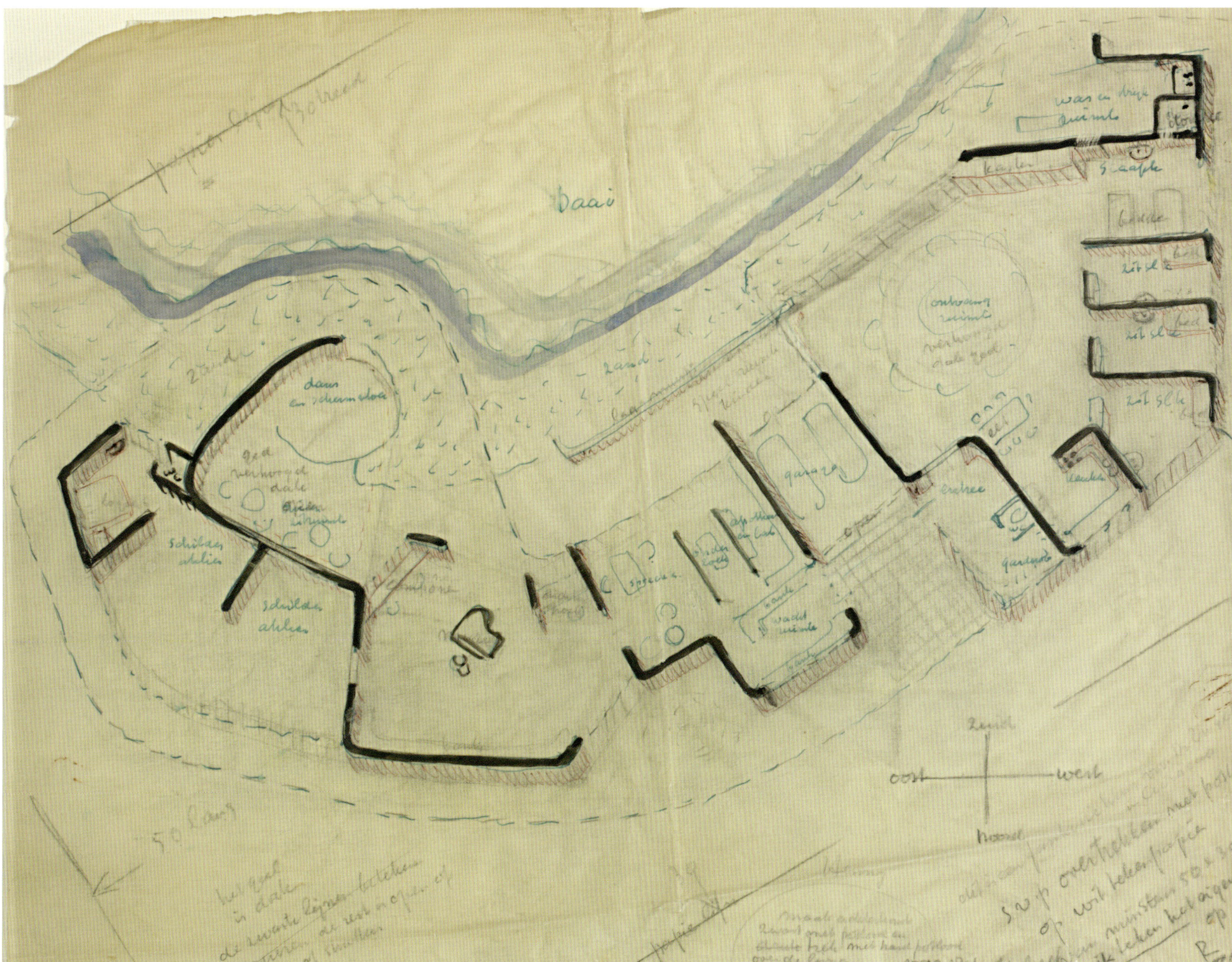

The trial presentation of the De Stijl exhibition, Stedelijk Museum, Amsterdam, 1951

The De Stijl exhibition in the Museum of Modern Art, New York, 1952

Opposite page: Rietveld's aluminium chair shown at the 'Salon des Artistes Décorateurs', Grand Palais, Paris, 1949. Exhibition design by A. Bodon and H. Salomonson (top); 'Weerbare Democratie', New Church, Amsterdam 1947 (bottom left); 'Art Décoratif Néerlandais', Liège/Ghent, 1946 (bottom right). These are some of the exhibition designs that Rietveld had carried out prior to the De Stijl exhibition.

Rietveld at the Netherlands
Pavilion for the Venice Biennale,
Venice, c.1954

8. National recognition

How am I supposed to feel? I feel crushed – a lost man who thinks he still has a very long way to go suddenly seems to be standing at a kind of terminus here.[1]
– Rietveld, 1964

Rietveld must have been uncommonly contented in the latter years of his life. Commendations of him and his work resounded from all sides. Of equal if not greater importance were the commissions that stemmed from this recognition. Although assignments for large-scale residential schemes were still not forthcoming, as the last of the De Stijl Mohicans he was selected for splendid projects: the Sonsbeek Pavilion, the De Ploeg textile factory in Bergeijk, the academies of art in Amsterdam and Arnhem, and as a coda the Van Gogh Museum in Amsterdam, for which he produced the initial designs. As ever, despite his advanced years, he worked indefatigably and with great intensity. He thought that he still had 'a very long way to go' because the number of architectural projects in hand and their scale presented him with completely new challenges, which he tried to solve by being technically innovative.

At the same time he drew inspiration from his own early work and that of other leading lights of the International Style. Rietveld was not alone in this return to the roots of Modernist architecture. Oud and Le Corbusier also harked back to older work in reaction to the dogmatic and in practice often anaemic qualities of Functionalism around that time. Postmodernism would eventually provide a much more radical response: the outright rejection of dogmas that had seemed sacrosanct for half a century. Rietveld did not live to witness this, but until his death he continued to search for the ideal realization of space within self-imposed limitations.

Monumental but fragile

The Sonsbeek Pavilion stands hidden amid the trees in the park behind the Kröller-Müller Museum in Otterlo. Rietveld needed nothing more than three free-standing walls to define a central space measuring 13.25 m (43 ft 6 in) square. These walls were constructed from B2 concrete blocks, each with three cavities to reduce their weight. Rietveld set these blocks on their sides in order to make a transparent wall and filled the cavities with a dollop of cement wherever he needed a solid plane. In two places these free-standing walls are connected from the roof to their midway point by glass panels; the roof projects through and above the walls. Around the central space there are low galleries, which continue to the edges of the plot and are partially enclosed in glass on either side. In these metres-long, man-sized display cases stand small sculptures, while the open central space is for large sculptures.

The differences in scale, the alternation of open and enclosed spaces and the varied materials of the walls – glass, steel, cement and timber – are set against a backdrop of swishing trees, rustling leaves and twittering birds, which makes an unforgettable impression: monumental but fragile. Within a year the B2 blocks would be covered with moss, the glass panels cracked and branches growing through the ceiling.

The transient character of the design was no accident. In 1955 Rietveld had received a commission from the Sonsbeek Foundation to design a temporary open-air exhibition space for sculptures at the Sonsbeek Park near Arnhem. As he headed home by train from

Sonsbeek Pavilion, Arnhem, c.1955

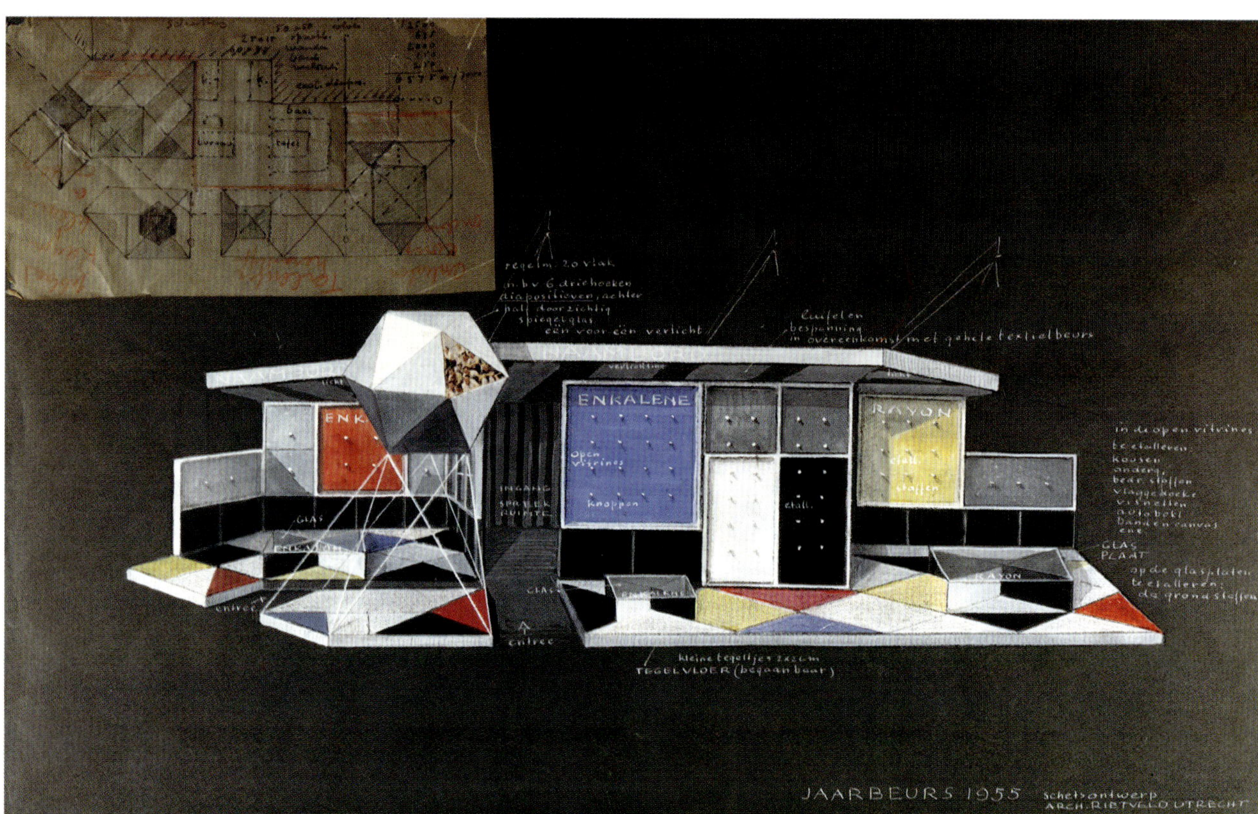

Design of the Enka stand for the Royal Trade Fair, Utrecht, 1955. In the mid-1950s, Rietveld completed a number of pavilions and temporary exhibition spaces. In this design, the emphasis is on the use of colour and pattern; the motifs used would recur in Rietveld's Press Room for the UNESCO building in Paris from 1958.

the initial meeting about the assignment he cobbled together a design from the cardboard cover of a sketch pad that he happened to have with him. The realized structure was exactly like this small model, which was no bigger than the palm of a hand. A year later it was dismantled and the materials recycled by the contractor. Ten years later the pavilion would be reconstructed at the Kröller-Müller Museum.

The Sonsbeek Pavilion resembles Rietveld's early work. The building's function and temporary character allowed him considerable latitude in form and in materials. Rietveld could freely indulge his passion for the creation of space in this design. The pavilion is a large-format Berlin Chair that visitors can walk through and around, a design that the Belgian architecture critic Geert Bekaert has described as 'a pure space-form'.[2] The Sonsbeek Pavilion is often compared with the Barcelona Pavilion from 1929 by Ludwig Mies van der Rohe. The similarities – the open floor-plan and the free-standing walls as a backdrop for sculptural art – seem so evident that the originality of Rietveld's design is at issue.

The differences are great nonetheless and so characteristic that imitation is out of the question. Both pavilions are unique interpretations of the relationship between interior and exterior, to which Modernism attached so much importance. The Sonsbeek Pavilion is high and is based on a grid of 2.65 m (8 ft 8¼ in) square. In the galleries the human scale prevails, and via the intermediate scale of the walls this is connected with the height of the surroundings trees, so that humankind's relationship with nature becomes palpable. By contrast Mies van der Rohe's pavilion is low and in the alternation of closed and open volumes is almost a sculpture in itself.

A second essential difference between the Rietveld and Mies van der Rohe pavilions is the choice of materials. The Barcelona Pavilion was also a temporary structure, but Mies van der Rohe used marble, onyx, natural stone, aluminium and steel: costly materials that defy the dusty heat of the city, emanate luxury and seem to symbolize eternity. But for Rietveld eternity did not exist: each building was an endeavour, a step in architecture's development. Rietveld chose cheap, readily available materials – B2 blocks set on their side, thatch, timber, glass and iron – that allow the Sonsbeek Pavilion to integrate easily with its natural surroundings.

The initiative for the pavilion's reconstruction in 1965 came from colleagues and friends who wanted to commemorate Rietveld, because with this structure he had 'demonstrated how architecture can have an enlightening, purifying and cheering effect upon our lives.'[3] The choice of this particular structure and this location is telling. To his colleagues Rietveld was the man who, flying in the face of all the ongoing developments, had upheld the primacy of form, the aesthetic, and the artistic in architecture. He had, moreover, adopted a stance that was self-effacing – although this was not stated in so many words – rather than that of a starry-eyed idealist, and he was neither pedantic nor admonishing towards others. He had simply done what he was good at: creating space.

Rietveld and Bergeijk

The board of the De Ploeg textile mill in Bergeijk would have liked to reconstruct the Sonsbeek Pavilion in the vicinity of their factory, but withdrew the initiative when architects W. van Tijen and S. J. van Embden (1904–2000) placed their notice in the *Bouwkundig Weekblad*, calling on their colleagues to commemorate Rietveld by reconstructing the pavilion at a location close to the Kröller-Müller Museum.[4] Rietveld had done a great deal for this idealistic enterprise in rural Brabant. Inspired by Thoreau's Walden, the socialist agricultural colony 'De Ploeg' (which means 'plough' as well as 'team') was founded in 1920 in the Kempen, an area to the southwest of Eindhoven, in southeast Brabant, with marshes, peat bogs, oak and pine woods, and drifting sands, which was all but depopulated at the start of the twentieth century. The weaving mill in Bergeijk was established three years after the colony was created.[5] The 't Spectrum furniture factory was founded as a subsidiary on 31 January 1941 to save the workers from being forced to work in Germany and to prevent the company being mothballed. Rietveld and the architects W. Jansen and F. A. Eschauzier (1889–1957) were asked to assess the designs.[6]

After the war the weaving mill and furniture factory specialized in modern, quality designs. Textiles from

De Ploeg were synonymous with high-quality, sensible design. In 1954 Rietveld proposed two designs for sofa-beds to 't Spectrum, but these were not taken into production. Two years later the board invited him to discuss the construction of a new factory. Rietveld's point of contact was Martin Visser (1922–2009), manager of the furniture department at De Bijenkorf department store in Amsterdam until 1954 and thereafter a designer for 't Spectrum.[7] In 1955 and 1956 Rietveld visited Bergeijk regularly to oversee the construction of a house for Martin Visser. Visser had initially asked Aldo van Eyck to build a home for him and his wife, Mia, but Van Eyck's complaint that yet again he was having to work for clients with limited funds did not go down well with Mia. They therefore turned to Rietveld, whom they knew from their years living in Amsterdam. In 1954 Visser had worked with Rietveld and the painter Constant (1920–2005) on the 'Kleurenplan' ('Colour Plan') exhibition at De Bijenkorf department store in Amsterdam.[8]

Schrale Beton office, Zwolle, 1957. Rietveld also designed the company's logo and various items of furniture for the office.

Bergeijk was a cultural enclave driven by ideals. To quote the director Piet Blijenburg, 'For De Ploeg the dream is to realize a pure, contemporary factory architecture, providing the people who work there with the best conditions that are possible with this industry.'[9] In its search for the ideal architect to fulfil this dream, Oud advised the board to ask Rietveld, who was cut out for the commission because of the combination of aesthetic and ethical principles. The choice was bold, even though Rietveld had demonstrated by his realization of the Juliana Hall extension (1953–6) for the Koninklijke Jaarbeurs exhibition centre in Utrecht that, in conjunction with a team of architects and advisers, he was equal to a large-scale, technically complicated project.

For the De Ploeg factory project Rietveld was assisted by the G. Beltman engineering firm. The renowned and influential Dutch garden architect Mien Ruys (1904–99) was approached to landscape the surrounding park. She had recently worked with Rietveld, designing the garden for the Van Ravesteyn-Hintzen House (1953–5) in Laren. Rietveld undertook a study tour to Italy and Switzerland with the engineer Beltman and the mill's directors in order to acquaint himself with modern factory construction. He followed the instructions given by Ruys with regard to the

Juliana Hall and entrance for the Royal Trade Fair, Utrecht, 1953–6. The Juliana Hall Royal Trade Fair building has an L-shaped plan. Its two levels are linked by two inside stairways, an outdoor stairway and the large curved ramp. Many of the walls have floor to ceiling glass; those that do not are made of layers of aluminium, steel and glass fibre.

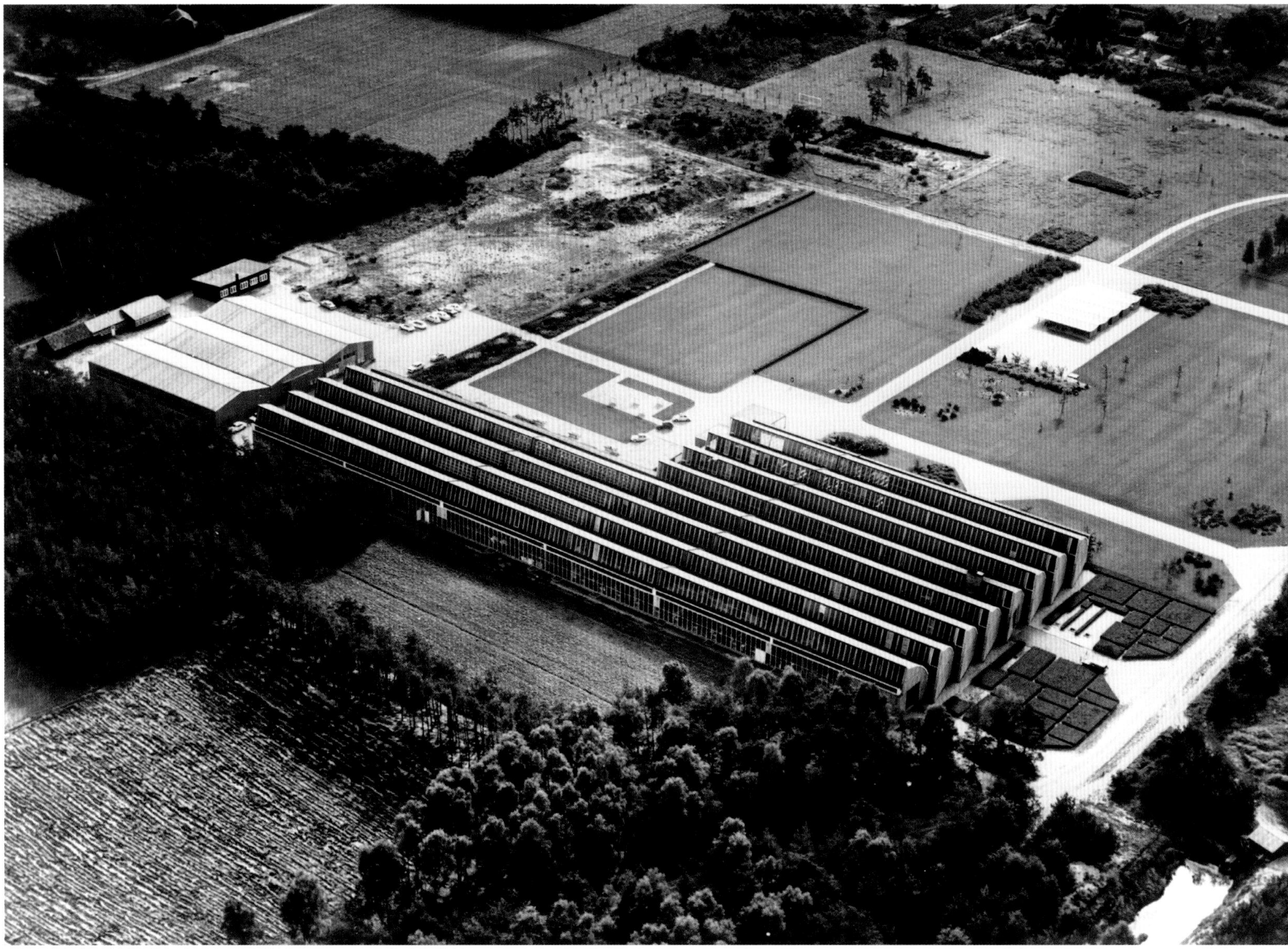

De Ploeg mill, Bergeijk, 1956–8

West facade of the De Ploeg mill

positioning of the structure.[10] The result was a stunningly beautiful, technically advanced complex in a magnificent landscaped park.

The sawtooth roof structure is the building's defining visual feature.[11] With load-bearing supports located every 24 m (80 ft), this roof spans an adaptable floor area of more than 7,300 sq m (78,580 sq ft). The air conditioning and other pipes and ducts are hidden away in the building's cellar. The north-facing elevations of insulating double glazing admit oceans of light, an important provision for a textile mill. The floors were finished with Plasnalo, a plastic poured *in situ* that made it easy to keep the spaces dust-free.[12] Besides the production halls, there are offices, conference rooms and staff facilities accommodated under this sawtooth structure. Rietveld threw himself into the layout of the interior, designing even the washbasins and soap dishes: he devoted as much attention to the aesthetic aspects as to the innovative technology.

In the western elevation the ends of the sawtooth roofing are staggered and the protruding sections enclosed from floor to ceiling with glass panels. The facade's concrete panelling is set in a slantwise pattern that follows the angle of the roof and is continued in the vividly contrasting coloured planes of the sliding door between the yarn store and the dyeworks. A low, simple awning of steel marks the entrance to the factory complex proper. The central pathway, which begins here, proceeds in a curve through an enormous garden and leads from the factory right through to the centre of the village.

Ruys had outspoken views about factory gardens and was convinced that they exercised a positive influence on the well-being of staff. 'There must be sheltered, sunny corners, where everyone can bask in the sun, for is it not delightful after standing at the machines for long hours to briefly feel the moist earth beneath you, to smell the fragrance of soil and grass?'[13] She had wanted to retain the rye fields and pine woods surrounding the De Ploeg complex, but director Piet Blijenburg preferred a garden in the English landscape style. In the end, a third of the 12 hectares of parkland around the factory was landscaped as deciduous and pine woodlands with footpaths.

The De Ploeg mill under construction

Visser House, Bergeijk, 1955. Interior and exterior. This bungalow-style dwelling was built for the furniture designer and collector of contemporary art Martin Visser. Visser worked at the 't Spectrum furniture company, a subsidiary of De Ploeg. The house contains a sleeping wing connected to the living wing at a 120 degree angle to create a sheltered and private outside space within the wide V-shaped plan. In 1968 the house was enlarged by Aldo van Eyck, who added a large circular room.

Model for three of a total of twenty-two unrealized family dwellings, Bergeijk, 1956–7

Van Daalen House, Bergeijk, 1956–8. Built for one of the directors of the De Ploeg mill, this house was the first large residential commission Rietveld received in this period. The sleeping wing has five bedrooms, each with a door to the garden.

Jansen House, Waalre, 1956–7

Cordemeyer House, Apeldoorn, 1956–7

Bláha House, Best, 1957. This house was built for O. Bláha, who had read about Rietveld in the magazine of the Dutch Railways Company. The house is composed of two volumes on separate levels meeting at a T-shaped axis. The lower block contains the living quarters (pictured on the right) and the raised block contains bedrooms and a bathroom. Rietveld's bungalow-style houses often have a sleeping wing visually separated from the living area.

Van den Doel House, Ilpendam, 1957–9. Built on marshy ground in the polder surrounded by ditches, this house was comissioned by a surgeon and his wife. It is composed of interwoven cubic volumes, each built of a differently-coloured glazed brick: white, black, blue and greyish green. Though the northeast facade (bottom), is almost totally blank, to the south (top) the house opens up with large areas of fenestration towards the ditch and the meadows. Two low walls stretch out from the house at right angles to anchor the volumes in the surrounding landscape. Due to the harmonious composition and the beautiful proportions, it is a stellar example of a house from the post-war period. Even the usually modest Rietveld described it as 'a good house'.

Theissing House, Utrecht, 1958–9. The house is composed from different types of concrete blocks. Rietveld used these large-format B2 concrete blocks for both economic and aesthetic reasons. They were labour-saving when used on a large scale, particularly when compared with bricks, and they were extremely versatile; for one of the walls they are laid on their sides and the openings are filled with glass.

Singelenberg House, Hengelo, 1961–2

Van Dantzig House, Santpoort, 1959–60. Built for one of the daughters of Mr and Mrs Mees, for whom Rietveld had built the Mees House in the mid-1930s, the house is situated on a slope so that despite having a single roof level, the building is composed of a two-storey and a single-storey structure. The two volumes are ingeniously connected by a large light-flooded hall and a metal staircase manufactured specially for the house.

Van Slobbe House, Heerlen, 1961–3. This house, built for a mining director, is the largest house Rietveld ever built, and shares with many of the houses of this period a horizontally defined composition accentuated by broad frameworks of concrete that surround the windows but also extend beyond them. The emphasis on the line as opposed to the plane visible in this house is also seen in Rietveld's last furniture design, the Steltman Chair.

Hamburger Summerhouse, Noordwijk, 1959–60. The house has a pitched roof above one section containing the living room, kitchen, two bedrooms and the entrance hall, and a flat roof above another section containing two more bedrooms. This second part of the house lies on a slightly lower level, creating clerestory lighting for the rest of the house. A large porch on the south side of the house is covered by projecting slab roofs that rest on slender stilts.

In the negotiations with Bergeijk Municipal Council, De Ploeg's directors had insisted on a portion of the building permit being set aside for housing for factory employees. The two directors, Piet Blijenburg and Roelof van Daalen, and the company's chief designer, Martin Visser, took advantage of this arrangement. All were designed by Rietveld and the Visser House was already completed in 1955, while the two other projects progressed more or less in line with the factory's construction. The house for Van Daalen was completed in the same year as the factory. The construction of the house for Blijenburg did not go ahead; Rietveld remodelled the existing house instead.[14] Nor did a plan for thirty-two single-family dwellings come to fruition; this project's commissioner is unknown, but it seems reasonable to assume that these houses were intended for De Ploeg's workers.

Housing, Hoograven, 1954–7. During these three years, Rietveld built 388 dwellings in Hoograven, with a number of different housing types spread through the development. The thin but pronounced horizontal slabs have a strong presence on the facade; in this they somewhat resemble the cubic structures of his detached houses that he was designing at the same time. Rietveld built another 194 dwellings in neighbouring Tolsteeg using the same designs in 1958.

Auditorium for a cemetery, Haarlemmermeer, 1958–67. Many of the motifs Rietveld developed in his domestic architecture of the late 1950s were also used in his non-domestic buildings of the period, like this small auditorium for a cemetery, which was begun in 1958 but only realized three years after Rietveld's death by his companions J. van Dillen and J. van Tricht.

After the factory's completion in 1958, Rietveld's activities in Bergeijk were over until the directors approached him in 1963 to carry out a few smaller commissions on the occasion of the company's fortieth anniversary. In their use of colour and geometrical forms, the street clock in the village, a few benches and the bus shelter hark back to Rietveld's De Stijl period, but they are hardly subtle in form.

The academies of art in Amsterdam and Arnhem

In the buildings for the academies of art in Amsterdam and Arnhem, Rietveld was also searching for new technical possibilities in order to realize an optimal environment for their future users, though he was not entirely clear what that involved.[15] 'I have to build an art academy,' he told Bertus Mulder, 'but how can you learn something like art?'[16] He therefore wanted to keep the buildings as open and neutral as possible, to avoid impeding future flexibility and delineating a peremptory layout.

The initial sketches for the Institute for Education in the Applied Arts (Instituut voor Kunstnijverheidsonderwijs, or IvKNO), as the predecessor of the Rietveld Academy was known, date from 1951 and were drafted for a site adjacent to Amsterdam's Amstel Station. Rietveld was the designer and the architect B. Merkelbach was charged with the technical aspects. At that point the location was still not definitive, and eventually a site alongside the Zuider-Amstel Canal in the vicinity of the Olympic Stadium was chosen. Mart Stam, who served as the IvKNO's director from 1939 to 1948, had altered the syllabus radically, among other things by recruiting new lecturers.[17] Sybren Valkema (1916–96), a lecturer in the glass department and acting director after Stam's departure, devised a new structure for the syllabus in conjunction with a few other lecturers. Following the example of the Bauhaus, the first year was for general study, followed by one of three specialized courses: spatial design, textiles or graphic design. This syllabus was to form the basis for the new academy building, but it is questionable whether Rietveld took much notice of it.

In 1955 nothing about the design had been fixed with certainty, but Rietveld already dropped hints in the academy's newspaper.[18] He had used a fixed module both vertically and horizontally to give the building calm, mathematically pure proportions and to facilitate the use of prefabricated components. The workshops and the studios were to have overhead natural light from the north. With the exception of the classrooms for theoretical lessons Rietveld strove for openness, because the visibility of the various departments would make the new building into a dynamic whole and have a stimulating effect on the international development of design.

On 10 October 1957 Rietveld sent the preliminary design to Sandberg, Amsterdam City Council's delegate on the academy's board. 'The main structure is conceived in concrete, a central structure poured on site as a backbone, with a floor-bearing structure of vibrated concrete set against it on two sides. The whole thing protected by a glass curtain wall,' he explained in an accompanying note.[19] At around the same time Rietveld produced a design for the Academy for Fine and Applied Arts in Arnhem, the present-day ArtEZ Academy of Art and Design. This plan was approved by the board on 7 October 1957. According to Rietveld it was 'a variation on the Amsterdam academy, in order to take advantage of the greater quantity of identical framework and prefabricated concrete elements.'[20]

The two academies were important projects for Rietveld, giving him the opportunity to employ industrial construction methods on a grand scale.[21] Rietveld wanted a curtain wall that was as thin and transparent as possible, for which he devised a special construction that would also be the cheapest solution.[22] A client could hardly ask for more, but the commissioners of both academies kept on raising objections. This prompted Rietveld to continue developing variants on the curtain wall, even during construction, and in Amsterdam he threatened to hand back the assignment if his proposal was rejected.[23] Fortunately that did not come to pass, because the aesthetic quality of both buildings is largely due to the crystalline, transparent look of the elevations. And despite the sometimes uncomfortable conditions – in the Amsterdam building the temperatures at the height of summer and in the middle of winter are equally unbearable – these academy buildings still inspire young people in their creative development. The spacious stairwell, the broad corridors and the display cases in the walls between the classrooms and circulation spaces are constantly being rearranged for a whole variety of purposes.[24]

'to be constructive'

After the war Rietveld taught at various academies and the new discipline of industrial design became a preoccupation for him. He articulated his views in a lecture that he gave in May 1953 for students of the Secondary Technical School for Architecture and Academy of Fine Arts in The Hague. Rietveld began with a moral reflection: when designing a new product should we not first ask ourselves whether it is really necessary? In his view, until objective criteria had been defined then listening to one's own conscience was the only means of deciding this. In addition a designer needs technical know-how; surprisingly enough, the reason that Rietveld gave for this is that the designer must be able to rebut all the arguments against the feasibility of a design. The rest of the address was fairly general in nature: form is never rational and we assess it with our intuition and our senses, in this instance the eye. Art therefore has a great deal in common with 'rational' design – the term Rietveld used for industrial design. Art sharpens and broadens our perceptions, elevates our awareness of reality.[25] It was hardly a

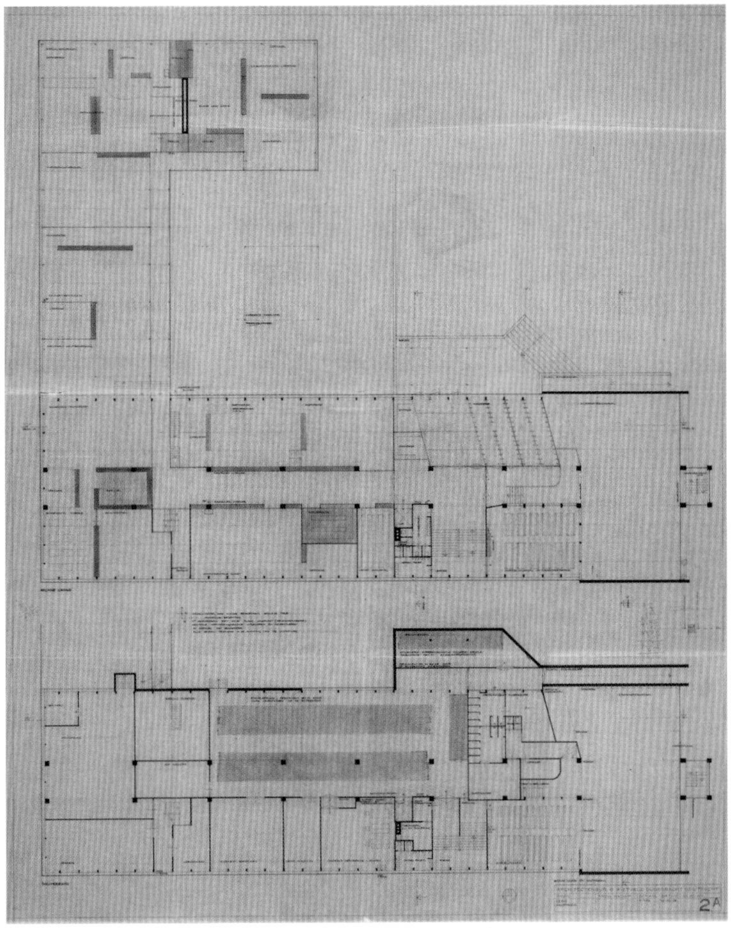

Sketches for the Institute for Education in the Applied Arts, later known as the Rietveld Academy, 1957

Rietveld Academy, Amsterdam, 1956–67. The main block of the building is seen here from the northeast, its concrete frame visible through the glass curtain wall. On the south facade a single storey L-shaped building with a jagged sawtooth roof is attached, which creates a three-sided courtyard.

Design for the Academy of Art, Arnhem, 1957

Academy of Art, Arnhem, 1957–63. Like the Rietveld Academy, this building consists of a concrete frame covered by a glass curtain wall. Both academies use the same system and a 2.1 m (6 ft 10½ in) grid module.

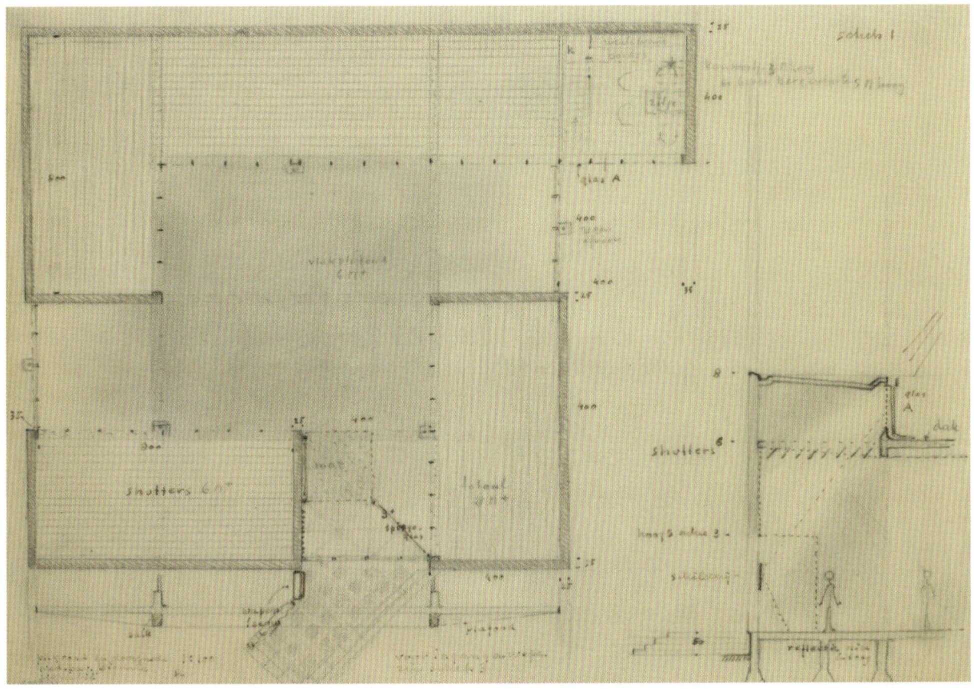

Netherlands Pavilion for the Venice Biennale, Venice, 1953–4. This exhibition building, with a 16 x 16 m (52 ft 6 in x 52 ft 6 in) ground plan, comprises three volumes; one is L-shaped and the other two are rectangular. These volumes rise 2 m (6 ft 7 in) higher than the 6 m (19 ft 8 in) exhibition space ceiling, and are fitted with clerestory lighting to illuminate the pavilion. The entrance is reached by a short flight of stairs at a 45 degree angle to the facade.

De Zonnehof Museum, Amersfoort, 1958. While built for the De Zonnehof Museum, this model actually more closely resembles the Van Gogh Museum than the actual building. The realized building has a facade made of alternating sections of fenestration and blue or white glazed brickwork. Glazed panels in the roof were inserted to top-light sculpture in the open gallery on the upper floor.

narrative on which one could base a curriculum or a building.

As the crowning accolade for his life's work thus far, on 11 January 1964 Rietveld was awarded an honorary doctorate by the Technical College in Delft, with J. H. van den Broek as his honorary supervisor. In Rietveld's word of thanks he expressed his satisfaction:

... with this official recognition, which I certainly never expected, seeing that I have for years been a kind of pirate in the building profession. With militant determination, yet systematically, I have as far as possible avoided all officially recognized forms of expression, in order to remain open to the new. It was also in my nature to do things like this. For decades I have therefore chalked up many deserved rejections, but fortunately I have never experienced spitefulness, because everything was meant – with paternal seriousness – to be constructive.[26]

Was Rietveld alluding to the problems around the academy in Amsterdam that were still to be resolved or was he thinking about the oft-heard criticism that his buildings were structurally wanting? He certainly owed a great deal, if not everything, to the people who had supported him through thick and thin, such as Sandberg, who in 1963 had helped procure yet another fantastic commission for him: designing the Van Gogh Museum in Amsterdam.[27]

Rietveld had already gained some experience with exhibition spaces thanks to his designing the Netherlands Pavilion for the Venice Biennale (1953–4) and the commissions for De Zonnehof Museum in Amersfoort (1958–9) and for an extension to the Centraal Museum in Utrecht (1960–3), though the latter remained unrealized for financial reasons. In museums and exhibition spaces the incidence of light is a critical factor. Natural light enters the Netherlands Pavilion in Venice through the band of vertical panes in the lower central section. The building therefore has a closed facade, which is opportune in a sunny climate, as well as ample wall space to hang art and an even diffusion of light. The Van Gogh Museum commission specified that light had to enter from above. The building has three levels and follows a module of 1 m (3 ft 3¼ in)

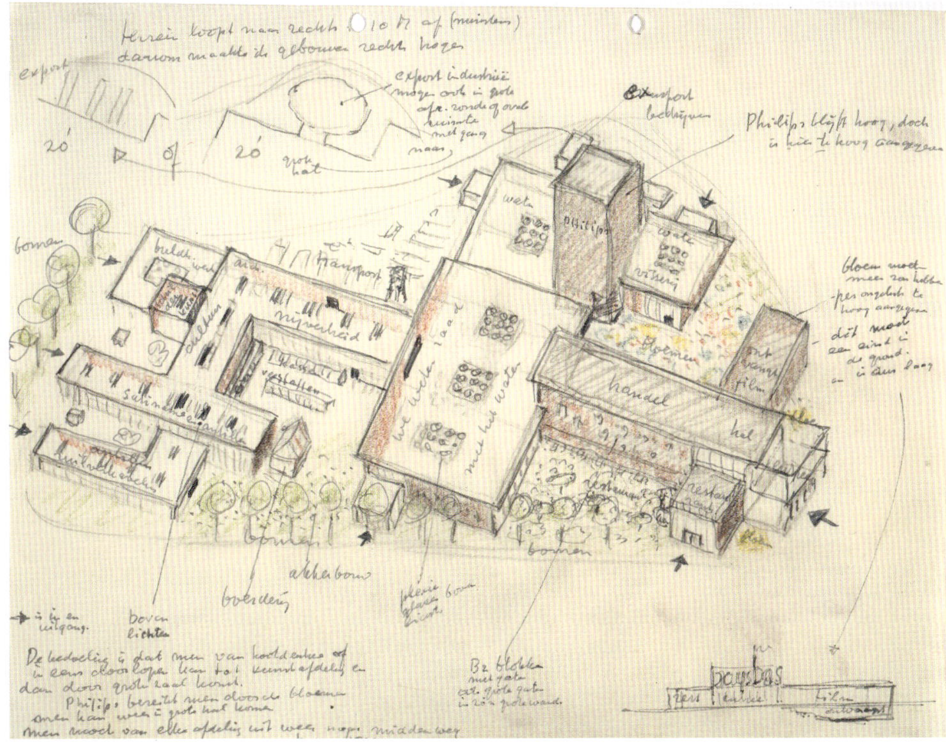

Dutch pavilion, World Expo, Brussels, 1958. Rietveld proposed a design for the pavilion, but it was not chosen (top right). However, Rietveld did participate in the Dutch pavilion by supervising the textiles section of the Dutch exhibition, and by showing both existing and new furniture in his design for an 'ideal flat' (top left and bottom).

square. The Van Gogh Museum, for which Rietveld completed only the initial design before his death, was broadly executed in accordance with this concept. It displays marked similarities with the first model for De Zonnehof Museum in Amersfoort, though in the latter case radical changes were introduced during the design process. The side elevations of this museum consist largely of glass, so the wall area available for hanging art is very limited.

On Thursday 25 June, the day after his 76th birthday, he was still working away ambitiously at his architecture bureau at Oudegracht 55 in Utrecht. He stepped into his Ford Taunus at around 3.30 p.m. and arrived at the 'Rietveld-Schröder House' on the Prins Hendriklaan a quarter of an hour later. Less than an hour later a heart attack brought the life of the architect Gerrit Rietveld to an end.

Thus began Rietveld's obituary in the *Haagse Post* weekly newspaper on 4 July 1964. Truus Schröder was shaken. 'It has all happened so suddenly that I cannot process it yet,' she said, and she was not alone. The article states that Rietveld was interred at the 'Den en Rust' (literally 'Pine and Peace') cemetery in Bilthoven amid overwhelming public interest, and in the auditorium there was insufficient room for the crowds who attended. In their letters of condolence to Truus Schröder many people mentioned how they had recently seen or spoken to Rietveld in Venice, in Arnhem, where construction of the academy had just been completed, at his acceptance of the honorary doctorate in Delft or at one of the many other professional and festive gatherings he attended. 'The tree has fallen,' read the subtitle of the article, and that was what many people felt.

Van Gogh Museum, Amsterdam, 1962–73.

Rietveld, c.1943

9. The bounding of space

Every true creation (whether it appears in the form of an invention, building, painting, dance or music) alters the insight, demands and needs of the era and collides with demands and requirements of former times that still persist. A creation must therefore conquer *the place instead of responding to the prevailing demands and the necessity.*[1]
– Rietveld, 1927

Over the almost fifty years that Rietveld was active as a cabinetmaker, designer and architect he changed his style several times. This can sometimes be attributed to external influences, but at other times it seems like an autonomous development that was the result of his personal research and experiments. Amid this stylistic variety, Rietveld's objective remained consistent: he wanted to partition off a segment of unbounded space and bring it into the human scale in order to be able to experience that space as reality.[2] That was and continued to be the essence of his work, despite all his experiments with materials and techniques, and variations in his style.

'In', 'around' and 'between'

Boundaries are necessary for the perception of space, boundaries by/through/of planes and lines. Their colour and form are, in Rietveld's view, of secondary importance; these qualities are subservient to the plane. Establishing a boundary means a separation into an inner and outer space, but an enclosed space cannot be perceived as a part of a greater whole. Rietveld was convinced that the relationship between bounded and infinite space is fundamental to a conscious experience of space. That is why he attached such importance to the transition between outside and inside, between interior and exterior, and distinguished three sorts of space: the space 'in', 'around' and 'between' things.

The 'between' is a crucial zone. By handling the 'between-space' or interstice as equal to the interior and exterior space it becomes visible and palpable that all three zones belong to infinite space. The hanging lamp from 1923 provides a fine example: its tubular lamps act like three luminous coordinates of infinite space. The lamp is at the same time an object that fits within a cube of 40 × 40 × 40 cm (1 ft 3¾ in × 1 ft 3¾ in × 1 ft 3¾ in). The boundary between the 'inner space' of the object and the infinite space of the surroundings is intentionally kept fluid, thus lending the transition, the 'between', a significance of its own.

When the essence of each building is the bounding of a segment of universal space, it seems obvious to start each design from the interior, thereby ascribing greater importance to the interior than to the exterior. The interior should not, however, be overly conspicuous; it is, as Rietveld already termed it in 1925, a 'background for life'. He later expanded upon this, stating that it 'must not infringe upon' the life of the occupant, nor 'fix anything unnecessarily'.[3]

With renovations and interior design assignments the boundary of the space is already fixed. Then Rietveld often manipulated the actual boundaries using optical means to achieve a certain effect. For example, the upper section of the high windows in the 'room with the beautiful greys' was covered over so that daylight entered the room at the required height, thus visually lowering the room's high ceilings. Where necessary

Top left: Construction detail, Red-Blue Chair, c.1924. For Rietveld, design was, at its essence, about bounding an infinite space in order to allow it to be experienced at a human scale. This is visible even in the details of his furniture and in small projects like his hanging lamp, which manage to suggest unending lines even though they have a very compact form.

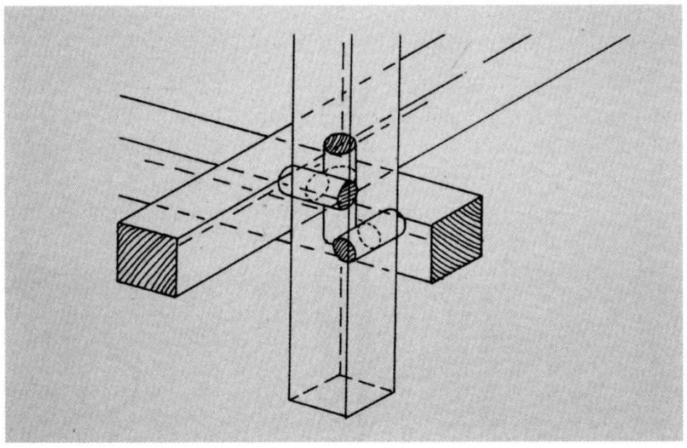

Show interior with slat furniture and Hanging Lamp, c.1923 (top right); Hanging Lamp, c.1922 (bottom left)

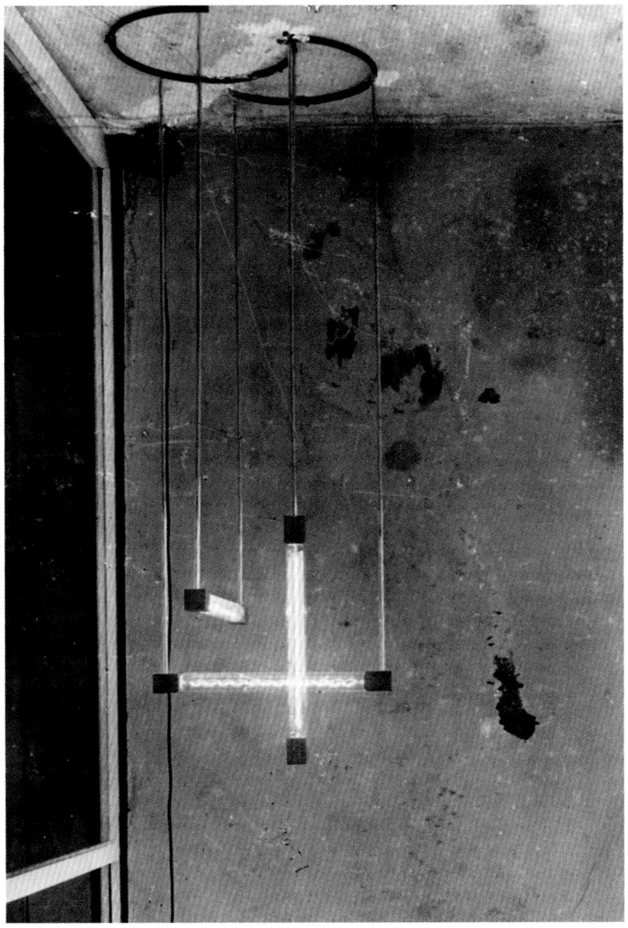

Interior for Truus Schröder, 1921. For some projects, Rietveld's ideas led to unorthodox design strategies, like blocking off the top of the windows in Truus Schröder's 'room with the beautiful greys', as she described it, in order to give the room better proportions and a softer illumination.

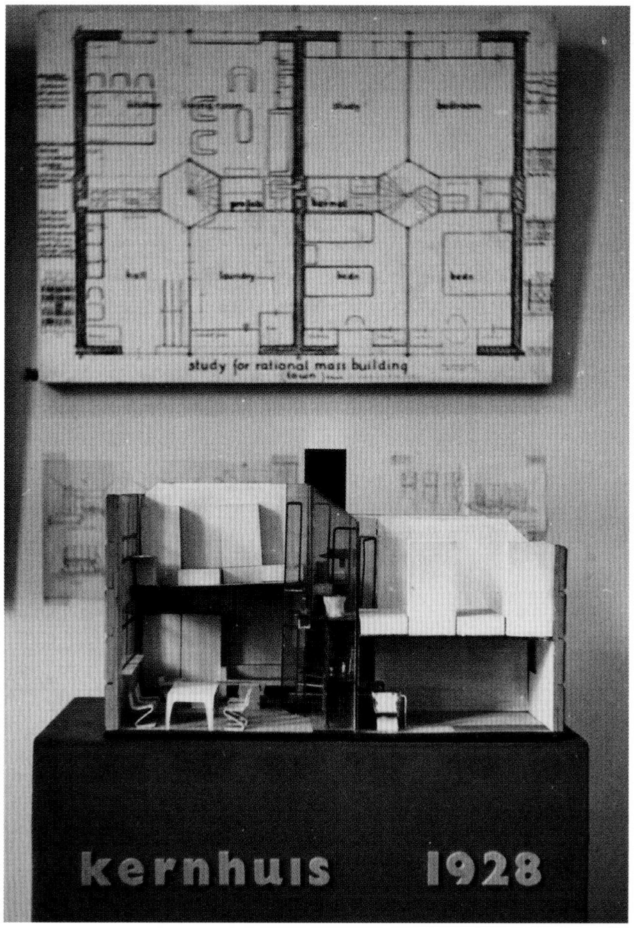

Schröder House, 1924. In this corner of the house, Rietveld's interest in the bounding of space takes the form of a game played with the transition from interior to exterior.

Core House model with Zig-Zag chairs, exhibited in Utrecht, 1958. Rietveld's furniture designs were frequently intended to complement his interiors. He saw the Zig-Zag Chair, with its minimal profile, as an object that disrupted the surrounding space as little as possible. As such, he liked to place it in drawings and models, as here, in the core house.

Steltman Chair, 1963. Rietveld's last furniture design was designed for the renovation of Steltman's jewellery store in 1963. There were in fact two chairs, each the mirror image of the other, and when placed next to each other, they form a couch that minimizes any disruption to the surrounding space. Rietveld did not live to see the realized design.

Rietveld used artificial light to proportion a space. In the Harrenstein bedroom he installed electric lighting above the suspended panel near one of the doors, which cast a diffuse light across the ceiling and gave the whole room a balanced and agreeable level of lighting. Rietveld often used a lowered glass ceiling with artificial light above it to achieve such an effect in those parts of an interior that required extra illumination.[4]

The layout is decisive for the spatial character of an interior, which is why the perception of space is central in Rietveld's furniture designs as well: a piece of furniture must at least leave the space intact and, if possible, lend structure to it. As a consequence of his architectural work Rietveld also designed chairs, cupboards, beds and matching side-tables for almost all his private clients. Usually these were simple, unobtrusive pieces of furniture that did not form massive obstacles, but 'leave the space uninterrupted', as he wrote to Van Doesburg in 1919 regarding the earliest slat armchair. The Zig-Zag Chair satisfies this criterion perfectly, because in Rietveld's words it 'is, as it were, a little partition in space'. It was not for nothing that from 1933 he very often sketched Zig-Zag Chairs in his designs and placed miniature versions in his architectural models. The Steltman Chair, Rietveld's last furniture design, also conforms to that idea and is a three-dimensional open structure of rails and posts: a space to sit on.

Fortunately Rietveld was given free rein by many of his private clients. He utilized the situation of a building, the alternation of closed and transparent facade surfaces, natural and artificial lighting, colour and to a lesser extent the materials to encourage the conscious experience of space that was in his eyes ideal.

The most famous and perhaps most beautiful example in his oeuvre is the corner window on the upper floor of the Schröder House. Here Rietveld plays a wonderful game with the transition from interior to exterior. Because of the lack of a stile at the corner, the boundary between interior and exterior space disappears when both windows are open. The outside world penetrates into the interior. When standing by the open window one has a feeling of being inside as well as outside. In Rietveld's oeuvre there are many designs where this playing with the bounding of space is the essence. It is a recurring theme in his work, with the Sonsbeek Pavilion from 1955 as one of the high points.

The module

Rietveld's buildings were often designed with the aid of a fixed modular system. In his view, a well-chosen modular unit was a prerequisite for a successful space, and determining this module was usually the first step in his design process.[5] The module was a means for Rietveld to get a grip on the design and in his view it ensured that the user's experience of the design would be clear and self-evident. It seems fairly straightforward, but as Rietveld himself stated:

It takes a lot of practice to be able to work with such a module truly productively. Working in accordance with modular units with a proper understanding and enforcing it really strictly lends a crystalline clarity to the structure... If you see a building that has been realized in strict accordance with a module then you will actually notice nothing about that building, but you experience a clarity that you find nowhere else. This must not be in the length and breadth alone, but also in the height.[6]

Rietveld probably adopted this methodology from his architecture tutor Klaarhamer, whom Rietveld considered to be one of the very few architects who was wholly convinced by Berlage's ideas about the great value of the relative proportions of space and mass in architecture. Even the smallest details in Klaarhamer's work were based on a module that was calibrated afresh for each project.[7] Rietveld worked in a similar manner, in many cases the module's size being determined by the situation.

A good example of this is the Press Room for the UNESCO building in Paris (1957–8). This was a tricky assignment because of the awkward form of the space, the irregularly positioned columns and the large quantity of furniture and equipment which had to be accommodated. The design is based on a square of 241.5 cm (7 ft 11 in), which was derived from the existing columns. By positioning all the furniture in accordance with this grid and employing the module for the dimensions of the triangular fields of colour, Rietveld managed to create unity within this space by 'juggling with colours and lines'.[8]

In Rietveld's graphic designs the grid is often dominant. Each letter is positioned in its own rectangular box. The dimensions of these sections are more important than the legibility or form of a letter, which can sometimes lead to idiosyncratic variants within a single design.

The module is, however, a means and not an end. Rietveld had a certain preference for a 'one-metre module' (3 ft 3¼ in), which he employed as it suited him. When it proved impossible to implement the chosen module strictly throughout a project, Rietveld sought a solution in which the deviation was as unnoticeable as possible: for example, by employing slightly different measurements in the corners.

The module and the dimensions are not, incidentally, decisive for the perception of the size of a space, no more than the relationship between interior and exterior is determined only by transparent or solid boundaries. A space can be perceived as smaller or larger because of the form and colour of the bounding planes or the way in which a plane meets or is connected with another, and by manipulating the lighting. An overhanging roof above a strip of fenestration has an effect quite unlike that of the same fenestration in a plain facade. There is no such thing as the 'right' size for the Red-Blue Chair and the Schröder House's dimensions seem to have been arrived at intuitively.[9]

Construction

As early as 1953 Rietveld had contended that the housing shortage would have been resolved long ago, 'had we started to build housing factories immediately after the war… Nevertheless, in the long run I can envisage mechanical production replacing the work at the building site, not only out of necessity but also because of purely architectural and professional considerations.'[10] It vexed him that the building trade and architects were so complacent and failed to explore fundamentally innovative solutions. There was good reason for Rietveld's retrospective exhibition in 1958 being given the subtitle 'Bijdrage tot de vernieuwing van de bouwkunst' – 'Contribution to the renewal of architecture' – even though architectural engineering aspects were barely touched upon in that presentation.

In 1964, when receiving his honorary doctorate, Rietveld felt compelled to voice his annoyance once more. After the splendid outpourings about his personal beliefs, he concluded his word of thanks with an unmistakable warning to his listeners: 'The construction business must still be content with structures and materials that are primitive for our time, compared with the technical means and scientific cooperation in, for example, space travel.'[11]

Yet in practice Rietveld had by no means consistently devoted enough attention to the structural engineering aspects of the discipline. He experimented a lot and often employed new techniques and materials, but he seems to have been less interested by the often lengthy process of testing that is needed in order to develop new construction technologies by trial and error. Perhaps Rietveld's lack of training in architectural engineering was at fault, but nobody is born an autodidact; Rietveld could have gained further training as an architect by working for various architecture firms, but perhaps he thought that unnecessary.[12] His experiments did, however, give him ample opportunity to elaborate his ideas.

Perhaps he was too restless or had fantasy in excess. 'With Rietveld everything was always possible,' Truus Schröder once commented.[13] She, more than anyone, was entitled to speak, given that the Schröder House is a textbook example of Rietveld's way of working. If something was technically impossible then he sought a solution that on the face of it or for the time being sufficed. He had wanted to construct the Schröder House in concrete in order to realize large, smoothly finished surfaces and for other reasons, but when that proved too difficult and thus prohibitively expensive he had the walls built in brickwork and finished with a layer of smooth plaster. He used steel girders to bridge over the large openings. The balconies are indeed made of concrete, reinforced with steel joists that were barely covered by the concrete poured *in situ*.

This poorly executed combination of steel and concrete caused considerable problems: over the years the steel was corroded by moisture and started to rust, causing cracks and leaks. The devices that Rietveld employed to make the flat roof look as thin as possible meant that

Ex libris plates, c.1919. Rietveld's use of modular systems is evident in many of his designs, from early typographic work to late building projects.

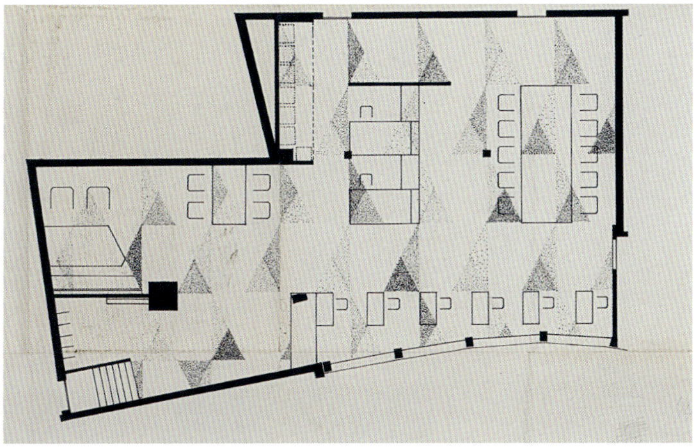

Drawings for the Press Room, UNESCO building, Paris, 1957–8

Model, probably for the Van Gogh Museum, 1964

rainwater did not drain away effectively and the house was permanently beset by leaks. That Truus Schröder put up with this, because the house 'gave her so much joy', is more than one might humanly expect of a client.[14]

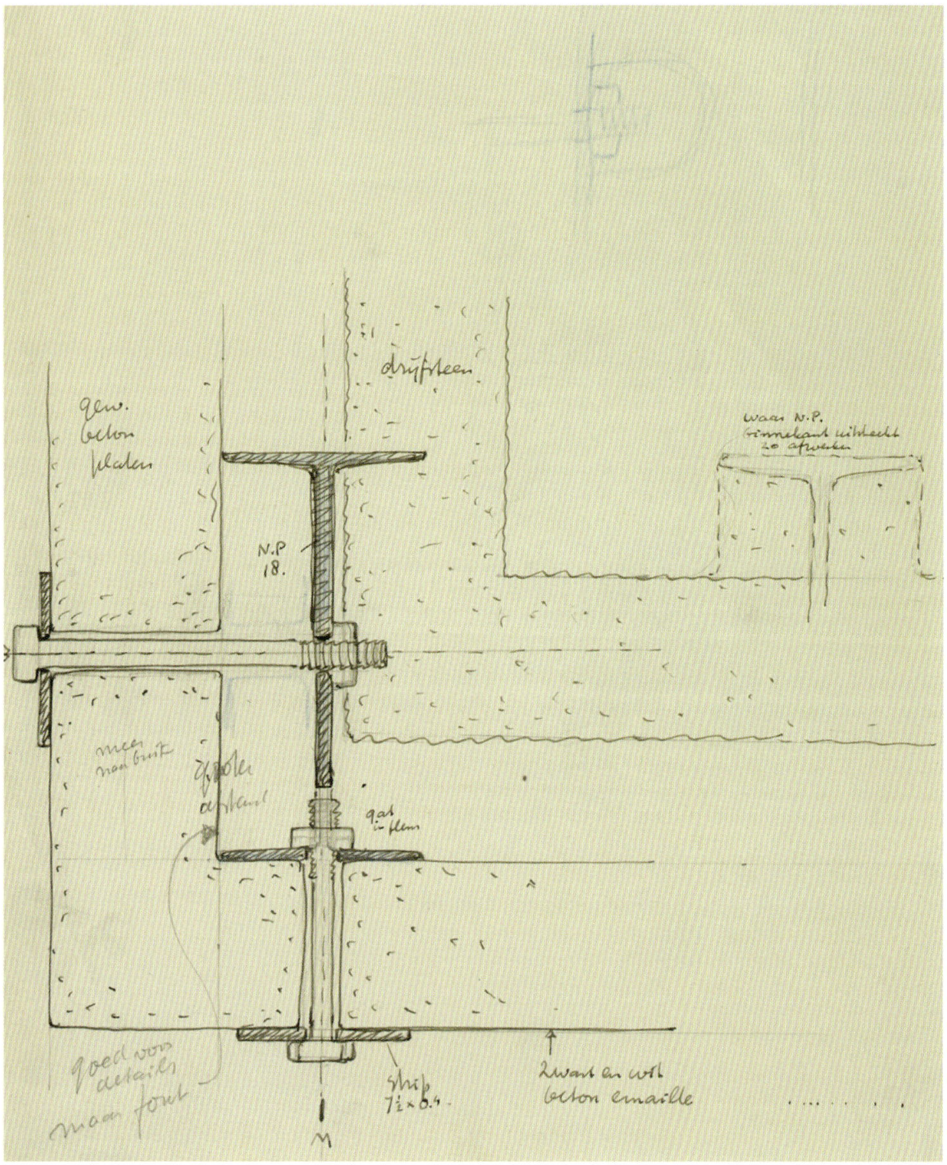

Garage with Chauffeur's Apartment, Utrecht, 1927–8. This iron structure with concrete slabs was one of the first of its kind in Europe.

Rietveld did not allow this experience to discourage him; perhaps the indulgent attitude of Truus was in fact an encouragement to continue on the chosen course. Three years later, for the Garage with Chauffeur's Apartment, he devised a structure with an iron framework on which concrete slabs were mounted. The system was unique for that time, but for various reasons this building also leaked like a sieve.[15] It is typical of Rietveld, or the circumstances under which he worked, that he did not attempt to prove he was right in subsequent projects, but simply left construction in concrete to others. It was not until World War II that, at the invitation of the Bredero construction company, he worked on a project to develop prefabrication methods in concrete for social housing.

Rietveld was evidently not inclined to enter into an alliance with third parties – builders, engineers, manufacturers or other specialists – in order at the very least to follow through an idea so that its potential would become obvious to others. In a sense he remained a craftsman who wanted to keep everything in his own hands and elaborate his ideas on a scale at which he could maintain an overview. For traditional wooden furniture it is customary to make a full-size model, which can be copied in the workshop. For industrial design, after the approval of the prototype it often requires a painstaking process to develop a mass product which can be fabricated industrially. Rietveld did not concern himself with these aspects. Many of his furniture designs never made it beyond a prototype or a few pilot models.[16] In the 1950s he had the Birza Chair from 1927 executed anew by Artifort, this time in polyester, but it was not taken into production. Nor was he ever willing or able to sell the dwelling core, the concept which he perhaps held most dear. For his architectural designs Rietveld liked to work with models, which he sometimes made with his own hands but later on had realized by his staff as well. These are little gems in glass and cardboard, from which the natural illumination, proportions and internal layout are easily read.

Chair prototype, c. 1958. In the 1950s, Rietveld explored the idea of fabricating the Birza Chair, which he had first designed in 1927, in polyester. It was in Rietveld's nature to treat his designs as ongoing experiments, continuing to work through the same ideas for decades, using different materials and techniques.

Two of many versions for a chair made from a single sheet of material, these sketch models date from 1930–40.

Danish Chair, c. 1946. Constructive techniques and forms inspired by Charles and Ray Eames are visible in other chairs Rietveld was working on around the same time, such this chair, which is made of six pieces of bent plywood.

For many years Rietveld's architecture bureau also retained the character of a small furniture workshop; he never employed many staff. Until 1933 he worked in a small studio on the ground floor of the Schröder House, then on the Oudegracht, where the bureau did indeed gradually expand but he never had more than a handful of people in his employ. It was not until the 1950s that Rietveld was compelled to increase his staff with 'real architects', because of the scale of commissions in hand. In 1961, with his seventieth birthday approaching, he entered into a partnership with Joan van Dillen and Johan van Tricht in order to guarantee continuity. These architects had worked for him since 1958 and 1959, respectively.[17] This did not mean that Rietveld's attitude to work actually changed. He sketched a design as he envisaged it and did not allow himself to be held back by a lack of know-how or experience. He tried to master a problem and find solutions as he went along. For larger projects the more technical aspects were often elaborated by others.

Materials

Rietveld chose his materials very deliberately, not from the point of view that certain materials are more useful than others, but on the basis of the visual effect he could achieve with them. For the Sonsbeek Pavilion he set cheap B2 concrete blocks on their sides, thus exploiting the incidental visual quality of their apertures rather than their constructional qualities. He knew from personal experience that furniture-making is a taxing profession and that there are but few people who can afford the costly handiwork. That is why in his early work he often used cheap materials and simple structures, which could potentially be produced mechanically. Some of the slat-built items of furniture were fabricated using different, arbitrary kinds of timber.

During the first half of the 1920s Rietveld covered all the materials with a matt coat of paint. When the texture and colour of the wood, stone or iron are hidden from view, an object, whether a chair or a house, becomes less massive. With the Red-Blue Chair he applied the black as a stain and the colours red, yellow and blue with matt paint, so here he did introduce a subtle distinction between the finish of the frame and the parts of the chair that support the body.

After this colourful period Rietveld worked with a great variety of materials, usually inexpensive, which he left in their natural colours. This was not a reversion to the 'honesty' of construction and material that was of such paramount importance to architects and designers at the dawn of the twentieth century; the simple fact was that Rietveld was interested only in the spatial possibilities of colour, material and construction, which were for him but a means to an end.

Colour

Though he had no fundamental predilection for certain forms or colours, Rietveld did assume that it would be better to work with simple shapes and primary colours, at least while the new architecture was still in its infancy.[18] For Rietveld, colour was a component of visual perception, a means to structure the bounding of space. Elementary forms and colours stimulate the active observation that makes it possible for people to become acquainted with reality. Rietveld was sustained in that conviction by the theories of Schopenhauer. According to the latter, seeing colours depended on the functioning of the eye, which is sensitive only to red, yellow and blue; other colours are the result of a combination of stimuli.[19]

Rietveld attached no deeper significance to the colours of the spectrum. His use of colour was in keeping with that of the De Stijl painters, who limited their palette to the use of the primary colours of red, blue and yellow in combination with the non-colours white, grey and black – albeit often for different reasons. Mondrian ascribed a specific psychological effect to the combination of colours in his paintings, while for Van der Leck the colour, like the form, was often a reduction of the colour of the object he had taken as his starting point.[20] Rietveld designed the boundaries of space first and only then did he select the materials and the structures to achieve what he had envisaged. The original colour and the finishing coat of the material are arbitrary and were usually not optimal for the visual three-dimensional effect. He therefore preferred to choose a grey, a neutral colour between white and black, which provided the reflection of light he desired.

Another option was to ask a painter to give the wall

planes a colour with the same luminosity as the shade of grey or 'even to alter the surface somewhat ... for my part produce a mural, so long as it is not about that mural but truly about making that space clearly visible.'[21] Of all the visual means available to the architect, Rietveld regarded colour as the least architectural, and it is therefore logical that he wondered whether or not he had been too like a painter in his approach to the Schröder House.[22] In contemporaneous publications the Schröder House was always illustrated in black and white photographs, but that did not lessen its impact whatsoever.

The colours yellow, red and blue are, nevertheless, engrained in the collective memory as essential features of Rietveld's oeuvre. Rietveld's application of the colour palette of De Stijl to his own experiments in the first half of the 1920s was a stroke of genius: the colour adds an extra dimension to these designs, a cheerfulness that appeals to a broad group of people to this very day.

Space

Rietveld was so exclusively focused on space that he did not consider other elements at all or only secondarily. His sphere of activity was generally limited to houses and furniture. In his writings he hardly touched upon urban development questions, if at all. His belief that what all people share in common ought to be the guiding principle for architect and designer meant it was easy for him to avoid becoming entangled in complex social and human relationships. Sometimes Rietveld's space seems to be restricted to what he was able or willing to comprehend, wholly blinkered to everything else that was going on. Van Tijen praised Rietveld's apartment above the Vreeburg Cinema in Utrecht in his address on the occasion of Rietveld being made an honorary member of the Royal Institute of Dutch Architects (BNA). He described it as 'that house with that splendid room with its great glass wall ... [like a] purifying abode of sheer human fellowship'.[23] It was often very convivial there, Rietveld's niece Paula van Reijn-Rietveld remembers,[24] but that notion of it emanating a purifying effect seems to be a product of Van Tijen's idolatrous admiration for Rietveld rather than reality.

These limitations do not detract from the quality of Rietveld's oeuvre. The consistency in purpose and method is its core strength, however diverse the ways that this is made manifest in form, colour and material.

Rietveld with a model of the Zig-Zag Chair, sitting on a Gothic revival chair that he made, at his retrospective exhibition at the Centraal Museum in Utrecht, 1958

10. Position and significance

When building we must also bear relativity in mind and should exercise sobriety, but however we build it will only truly become reality for us and be able to bring us joy if the visual sense of space, which we hereby give to others as a gift yet retain for ourselves, is not fragmented but complete and clear and above all unambiguous.[1]
– Rietveld 1958

On 24 June 1958 Rietveld celebrated his seventieth birthday. This anniversary gave occasion to place him in the limelight. The exhibition entitled 'Rietveld. Bijdrage tot vernieuwing der bouwkunst' ('Rietveld. Contribution to the renewal of architecture') opened at the Centraal Museum in Utrecht on Saturday 10 May 1958. Three publications appeared in which his position in and significance for Dutch and international architecture was held up to the light: an entire issue of *Forum*, the monthly magazine of the Genootschap Architectura et Amicitia (a society to which Rietveld belonged); the catalogue for the exhibition; and a dissertation by the American art historian Theodore M. Brown, 'The work of G. Rietveld, architect'. The special edition of *Forum* is predictably filled with friendly tributes to Rietveld. The catalogue is chiefly an echo of Rietveld's personal views, because everything suggests that Rietveld had a decisive say in the selection of the designs for the exhibition and in the text of the accompanying catalogue, even though the exhibition was officially curated by a working committee.[2] The book by Brown is still one of the finest studies of Rietveld's work, but it obviously goes no further than 1958. The three publications paint a much more varied picture of Rietveld's work than that which has been presented in subsequent decades.[3]

The inclusion of the Red-Blue Chair in the canon of Dutch history as the icon of De Stijl is in itself commendable, but the accompanying explanation fails to do Rietveld or De Stijl any justice. This is symptomatic of the one-sided perspective on Rietveld's work, which has now taken root in the popular media and is evidently catching on in the collective memory of the Netherlands, too. It is therefore important to shed light on Rietveld's ties with De Stijl from various angles.

The influence of De Stijl on Rietveld and vice versa

There were various aspects to Rietveld's relationship with De Stijl. Van Doesburg's publication of Rietveld's work in the group's journal altered his position radically. Via De Stijl he came into contact with the European avant-garde and soon found his place among them. As a furniture-maker he was the odd one out initially, but the interaction with other disciplines turned out to be exceptionally fruitful for his personal development. To what extent he shared the ideas and ideals of De Stijl is a question that is impossible to answer decisively. During De Stijl's heyday there was already constant wrangling about the pure De Stijl idea and who best articulated this or embodied it in his work.

Who belonged to De Stijl was largely decided by Theo van Doesburg, the pivotal figure and the journal's editor-in-chief. The group was, however, like a dovecote where kindred spirits flew in and out. Others circled around it without ever truly nestling. The perception of later generations is coloured by personal ideas and conflicts that often have little to do with Rietveld's work. Oud, for example, emphasized how his later work was not a reversion to outdated design principles but

Bart Van der Leck, Horseman, 1918

J. J. P. Oud, Factory in Purmerend, 1919

Theo van Doesburg, *Maison d'artiste* colour scheme, 1923

Opposite page: Red-Blue Chair, c.1923

a continuation of the ideas he had developed during his 'De Stijl period'. Nelly van Doesburg was more successful in defending Theo van Doesburg's pivotal position. And these were not the only people who wanted to write history from their personal perspectives.[4] On several occasions Rietveld asserted that there was a surprisingly great distance between him and the group. 'De Stijl had the intention of establishing a new style, while I was actually only pursuing my personal study, but by chance this corresponded with the principles of De Stijl,' he stated in 1959.[5]

It is understandable and also appropriate that in retrospect Rietveld placed the significance of De Stijl for his work in perspective; he had, after all, already realized the most important theme of his work – space – in a revolutionary manner in the slat armchair before he even came into contact with De Stijl. The 'Space-Colour-Composition' that he produced together with Vilmos Huszár in 1923 was the only project on which he really collaborated with another member of De Stijl, and that progressed no further than a scale model. Furthermore, in this project Huszár undermined the architectural space designed by Rietveld by overlapping the planes of colour or allowing them to continue around the corners. With the Maison Rosenberg the project did not turn out to be a true collaboration with Van Doesburg and Van Eesteren. Rietveld designed the Schröder House, which counts as the shining example of De Stijl's architectural principles, in conjunction with Truus Schröder, who would not brook any interference from other members of De Stijl.[6]

Rietveld made hardly any contribution to theoretical discussions in the *De Stijl* journal either. In 1919 Van Doesburg published two texts written by Rietveld to accompany the illustrations of the slat armchair and the baby's high-chair; Rietveld's contribution to the journal's jubilee issue in 1927 amounted to nothing more than a brief definition of what 'true creation' (*ware schepping*) is or ought to be.[7] The journal paid attention to furniture only in the context of the interior. Van Doesburg did not regard design as an autonomous discipline, a status he reserved for architecture, painting and sculpture.

Approaching design as a separate discipline did not tally with his pursuit of the *Gesamtkunstwerk*, even

though many of the De Stijl artists produced work that is considered to be applied or industrial art. Van Doesburg coined the wonderful characterization of Rietveld's slat armchair as a 'slender spatial animal', but in the same article he placed design in the context of the visual arts. 'Because of its innovative form, this item of furniture provides an answer to the question of what place sculptural art shall occupy in the new interior: Our chairs, tables, cupboards and other utilitarian objects are the (abstract-real) sculptures in our future interior.'[8]

Nevertheless, these observations provide no reason to play down De Stijl's importance to Rietveld. There is no shadow of a doubt that the work of certain members of De Stijl gave Rietveld ideas that helped him to develop his ideas. He saw how the painter Van der Leck abstracted a figurative form into a composition of red, blue and yellow fields of colour, surrounded by the space of the white background. In presentations of his work Rietveld almost always hung Van der Leck's paintings on the wall. The asymmetrical stacking of blocks in, for example, the entrance of the factory in Purmerend by Oud (1919) seems to have inspired his early shop renovations. Both Oud and Van der Leck were for that matter associated with De Stijl for only a short time; Van der Leck withdrew after just the first edition of the journal. Moreover, the work which had made such an impression on Rietveld dated from before the formation of De Stijl.[9]

It is conceivable that Mondrian's paintings from the years 1920 to 1923 with red, yellow, blue and white planes set between black lines led to the renowned red and blue version of the previously unpainted slat armchair. On 28 February 1920 Rietveld wrote in a letter to Van Doesburg that a stack of his chair frames formed such a delightful, calm interplay of lines, but that he realized, thanks to an illustration of a work by Mondrian in *De Stijl*, that a composition of planes and lines 'says something without words through its plastic quality'.[10] Other possible influences on Rietveld's thought and work were the many articles about architecture in *De Stijl*, including Van Doesburg's essay 'Der Wille zum Stil' ('The will to style') from 1922.[11] However, in interviews and lectures during the 1950s Rietveld primarily mentioned the relief that he felt when he discovered that other people were also striving after radical innovations and understood his work; he did not stand alone.

Conversely, the importance of Rietveld's work for De Stijl was greater than the minimal attention it has received might indicate. Around 1920 there were many artists and architects producing Rietveld-like furniture and the figures who were following in his footsteps were far from negligible, including Piet Mondrian, Theo van Doesburg, Willem van Leusden, his former tutor P. J. C. Klaarhamer, Sybold van Ravesteyn, Jo Uiterwaal (1897–1972), Huib Hoste (1881–1957), Felix del Marle (1898–1952), Eileen Gray (1878–1976), Marcel Breuer and Walter Gropius.[12] It would be difficult to overestimate the effect of these imitations and reinterpretations. Anyone who endeavours to capture the spatial quality of Rietveld's furniture in his own designs senses the kernel of Rietveld's work 'in the flesh'. For some designers, such as Gray and Breuer, following Rietveld's example was an important phase in their development.

Later on, Rietveld's work was essential to the growing recognition for De Stijl. It is not only paintings by Mondrian, but also the Red-Blue Chair and the Schröder House that have won international recognition for De Stijl. This was primarily thanks to a few prominent critics who formulated their ideas about De Stijl in the 1930s. In 1936, Alfred Barr, director of the Museum of Modern Art, New York, was the first person to make the connection between Rietveld's work and the visual art of De Stijl.[13] This approach to Rietveld's work culminated in the De Stijl exhibitions in Amsterdam, Venice and New York in 1951–2. In the 1958 Pelican History of Art series, Henry-Russell Hitchcock credited Rietveld with being the first person to have transformed the ideals of De Stijl into concrete architecture with his remodelling of the Gold- and Silversmiths Company shop.[14]

The Schröder House was often paraded as the architectural materialization of De Stijl ideas, even before World War II. Rietveld made no attempt to rectify this at the time, and why would he have? Van Doesburg's ideas about architecture had evolved in such a way that the Schröder House dovetailed well with them. However, Rietveld had less and less contact with Van Doesburg; he was not the type of person with whom Rietveld could get along easily. By degrees, De Stijl no longer offered Rietveld the entourage that he needed for his development. Even though he never officially withdrew from De Stijl and continued to defend Van Doesburg to outsiders, Rietveld declined to make a contribution to the journal's commemorative issue for Van Doesburg. 'When he was still here I always valued his insight highly but now it is as if everything belongs to the past, and as necessary as it was at the time … now that he is no longer there it seems to be superfluous in equal measure.'[15] For the crux of his work – the creation of space – Rietveld found insufficient resonance or support among the De Stijl group.

An international reputation

From the moment that Rietveld attended the CIAM's inaugural congress in 1927 he regarded this international group as the movement to which he belonged. For the first few years he proudly mentioned that he was a CIAM delegate in work-related correspondence. He never distanced himself from these ideas and faithfully made a contribution to CIAM conferences if asked. However, he obviously had his own interpretations and solutions, which did not always coincide with the ideas of his Dutch colleagues.[16]

There were also renowned CIAM members, including Le Corbusier, Richard J. Neutra (1892–1970), Bruno Zevi (1918–2000), Alison (1928–93) and Peter Smithson (1923–2003), Alfred Roth (1903–98), J. J. P. Oud, B. Merkelbach and Aldo van Eyck, who reciprocally held Rietveld in high regard. Each of these wrote an article in the issue of *Forum* in honour of Rietveld's seventieth birthday. They were effusive in their praise, but a certain awkwardness can sometimes to be read between the lines. Rietveld's work was impossible to capture in words; his character could not be tied down at all. Van Eyck employed a charming metaphor for this: 'Not so long ago I saw a little man running really hard after a tram, as if he was out to prove that there is no longer any gravity. People are now saying that this little man, whose legs I could hardly follow, has turned 70. But what does that matter to us?'[17]

This sketch includes three crucial elements: Rietveld does something that is actually impossible, he does not do it just once but repeatedly, and he does it with success. The rest of Van Eyck's article is no more and no less than an attack against his colleagues who have abandoned these endeavours or, worse still, are constantly proving that gravity does exist. When Rietveld's colleagues praise his imagination, describing him as honest, uncompromising and free but at the same time a voice in the wilderness, it is a reflection of this somewhat monomaniacal attitude. They know that talent is a prerequisite to achieving something, but are also aware that the obstinate will to continue down that path is just as important.

'Sometimes art escapes'

All attempts to learn more about an artist, whether this concerns facts about his life or details about his work, are often nothing more than circular movements repeated ad infinitum to avoid the only question that really matters: namely, asking where the genius of an artist lies.

So what is it that makes Rietveld's work so exceptional? Rietveld could make people aware of space. When walking around in the Sonsbeek Pavilion one breathes more freely, walks more upright, looks more perceptively; the environment has an enriching effect. Rietveld's furniture possesses a quality that is rare in design: it not only leaves the space uninterrupted, as Rietveld very much intended, but it also makes one aware of the surroundings. The Red-Blue Chair, the Zig-Zag Chair and the Steltman Chair do not stand like massive blocks that obstruct the view in a space, but are an agreeable, stimulating incentive to become conscious of the object and its surroundings.

Rietveld was a craftsman who had the eye, manual dexterity and mindset of a furniture-maker. He was so secure in his handling of materials that he could easily replace one material with another when that was more appropriate. He knew that it was not only dimensions and colour but also the texture of a surface that is decisive for the spatial effect. At the same time this craftsmanlike approach entailed a limitation, of which he was probably hardly aware: the human scale, a format that can be surveyed in a glance, suited him best. He approached larger projects as a sum of smaller ones. The city as a living room, an idea that took root within CIAM circles, probably appealed to him for that reason and not on purely theoretical grounds. He called New York City's Rockefeller Plaza 'the largest and most exciting man-made interior ... a small square of approximately 200 × 100 m surrounded by the sheer and unbroken facades of three towering buildings that together have the effect of an almost abstract bounding of space, because the height of these buildings matches the size of the square.'[18]

Rietveld was not an executive craftsman, someone who fabricates someone else's ideas; he was a craftsman in the manner of an artist who executes his own work, like sculptors, goldsmiths and painters. This meant that Rietveld was closer to attaining Van Doesburg's ideal than either of them realized: not by uniting different disciplines but by practising the discipline that gave least occasion to do this as a free art form; not by making one-off artefacts but by attaching the same spatial quality to furniture as to architecture. His stance on industrial design and mass production was entirely pervaded with the same mentality. From all his experiments, articles and lectures, educational activities and contacts with industry, it is clear that Rietveld considered industrial production desirable, even necessary, because of a moral conviction. Moreover, Rietveld regarded the industrialization of production processes as an inevitable development and, as such, he wanted to help steer this in the right direction for all of society.

In a lecture he gave for budding designers in 1953, Rietveld said that the designer must be able to give direction to the improvement of industry. He must be able 'to prove that [his designs] are technically feasible'.[19] The word 'feasible' is especially intriguing. Rietveld's criterion was the degree to which the form stimulated the awareness of space rather than the chosen material or the production method employed. The specific quality of Rietveld is the result of the combination of a craftsman's training, a clear-cut artistic standpoint and a clearly defined professional objective; all of that united in a man with an exceptional talent. And 'sometimes art escapes', Rietveld told Martin Visser when he asked whether the Crate Chair was actually art.[20]

Once Rietveld had exchanged the furniture workshop for an architecture bureau and architectural commissions became more plentiful, the quantity of furniture designs decreased. That is a shame, because among the leading lights of Modernism there were a greater number of brilliant architects than there were ingenious furniture designers. Besides, Rietveld remained a cabinetmaker in heart and soul. In scale, construction, material and function he had chairs so completely ingrained in his fingertips that he also tested out the creation of space – the medium of the architect – using this utilitarian object. Rietveld thought with his hands. He often experimented without a preconceived plan, making progress by actually doing. In architecture that is not without risks, given that an architectural prototype does not exist. The commissioner or future user hardly expects a study, as Rietveld called the Schröder House. By exception, in this case it was acceptable, but it is usually an impossibility. His background and methodology as a one-time furniture-maker, his almost obsessive preoccupation with space, his claim to an autonomous position and his experimental approach made Rietveld a maverick in the realm of architects and designers. Van Eyck was right when he wrote that they made of Rietveld 'a legend, their ingenious clown'. Van Eyck was also correct when he added that the creation of a legend is not exclusively the product of external factors.[21]

Rietveld's influence

Rietveld's position as an outsider makes it difficult to evaluate his oeuvre in relation to that of others. And the more closely Rietveld is exclusively identified with De Stijl, the less likely the chance of a more balanced and perhaps more interesting portrait of Rietveld emerges. Neither his influence on other people's work nor the converse are addressed in any depth in the literature.

Brown's 1958 dissertation is a welcome exception to this. He pinpoints Rietveld's significance for De Stijl – rather than the converse – and for the Bauhaus. He also argues that the bounding of space by planes and lines was not derived from Van Doesburg's and Van Eesteren's designs for the exhibition at Rosenberg's gallery but stemmed from Rietveld's own early furniture designs.[22] That is correct. There are indeed similarities

Marcel Breuer, Oak lath armchair, 1922

Marcel Breuer, Apartment for Erwin Piscator, Berlin, 1927

Walter Gropius, Director's room, Bauhaus, Weimar, c.1920. Gropius designed a lamp for this room that was perhaps inspired by Rietveld's early hanging lamp.

between the Schröder House and the projects for the De Stijl exhibition in Paris in 1923, but it also clearly involves a contrast in approach that cannot simply be traced back to the difference between a vision in the guise of a scale model and an actual building.

According to Brown, Rietveld continued to be a trailblazer in twentieth-century architecture and design after the realization of the Schröder House. He was the first person to investigate and test the constructive and aesthetic possibilities and qualities of the curved form. For example, his tube framed fibreboard armchair dates from 1927, which is three years earlier than Alvar Aalto's famous easy chair for the Paimio Sanatorium.[23] It was not until the 1930s that the curved form was regularly used in design and architecture. Brown concludes that for all these years Rietveld's work, in projects large and small, remained at the same high standard and that it most certainly influenced developments in twentieth-century architecture.

It is worth the effort of comparing Rietveld's whole oeuvre with that of the greatest international architects. Mutual influence can be proven by means of a painstaking analysis of individual designs and detailed research into every possible channel of information. When and where was someone's work exhibited, who spoke to whom, and when and where? Besides exploiting the work of his De Stijl colleagues to develop his ideas further, Rietveld also borrowed from others to his heart's content later on, sometimes so literally that the spectre of plagiarism is waiting in the wings, but it was almost always a case of two-way traffic.

A few examples, some of them familiar, demonstrate how productive such an investigation can be. The oak lath armchair by Marcel Breuer from 1922 serves as pre-eminent proof of Rietveld's influence at the Bauhaus. There are, however, more telling examples, such as the lamp that Walter Gropius designed for the director's room at the Bauhaus in Weimar. Just like Rietveld's hanging lamp, this lamp is composed of three tubular incandescent lamps, which are suspended in alignment with the three spatial coordinates. However, in this room the electric cables extend from wall to wall. The lamps do not form an autonomous entity in space, so in this design the subtle relationship between the object and the surrounding space – the 'in', 'around' and 'between' – is absent, and that is precisely what makes Rietveld's designs so special. It is not the dismemberment of form into component parts that is the essence, but that a massive object is prised open and transformed into a composition of planes and lines that is integral to the surrounding space yet remains an autonomous object.[24]

In 1925 Breuer designed an easy chair of tubular steel and canvas, now known as the Wassily Chair. According to Breuer the form was the outcome of a functional analysis: the combination of sitting comfortably and a simple construction.[25] Given the problems that Breuer encountered with its production this is a fine example of Functionalist rhetoric. Tubular steel furniture served an aesthetic goal, as Breuer later wrote, in keeping with the open, spatial character of the modern interior. This, in short, was what Rietveld had already envisaged and realized in 1918 with the slat armchair.[26] Rietveld's conceptualization of space laid the groundwork for tubular steel furniture.

Breuer's indebtedness to Rietveld is therefore not limited to these few chairs from the first half of the 1920s. In the widely published and highly acclaimed Berlin apartment of the theatre director Erwin Piscator dating from 1927 there is a long, horizontal display case affixed to the wall of the dining room at eye level.[27] Rietveld had already done something similar in the sitting room for the Harrensteins two years earlier. It is not improbable that Breuer was well informed about the work of his Dutch colleague.

Rietveld also drew inspiration from Breuer's work. Around 1930 he made a nest of small tables for Dr Ten Doesschate that is almost identical to Breuer's side table/stool from 1926.[28] Such plagiarism was fairly normal in that era, the design by Breuer being imitated by many people.[29] An original variant is Rietveld's side table from the early 1930s. Its frame of bent metal tubing is set on its side, so it can easily be slipped under a divan.

There was such a spurt in the production of tubular steel furniture in the 1930s and the differences between models are sometimes so minimal that it is now almost impossible to determine a design's authenticity. During the initial years of this development in the use of materials it is, however, reasonable to assert that Rietveld's seminal ideas fell on fertile soil at the Bauhaus, because there industrial design was a central concern and much energy was devoted to production and contacts with potential manufacturers. This stands in stark contrast to De Stijl, where it was artists and architects who set the tone. Rietveld would have found himself in a totally different position if an institute like the Bauhaus had been at his disposal.

In his entourage Rietveld lacked the associates – colleagues, entrepreneurs or industrialists – who might have encouraged him to translate his designs into feasible mass-market products. He was also marching too far ahead of the troops. A comparison with the famous Bauhaus table lamp designed by Wilhelm Wagenfeld (1900–90) in 1924 serves to clarify this. Wagenfeld's lamp stems from the nineteenth-century desk and office lamps with copper fittings and lampshades of green glass, a typology he translated into the Modernist aesthetic: Wagenfeld's lamp is modern. But Rietveld thought in terms of light, and his desk lamp from 1925 is more radical and more minimal, perhaps too minimal. With its simple components, Rietveld's lamp would have been much cheaper to manufacture than Wagenfeld's model, but only a few examples were made; Wagenfeld's lamp became a 'classic' design.

Dutch companies such as Gispen and the Utrechtsche Machinale Stoel- en Meubelfabriek (Utrecht Mechanical Chair and Furniture Factory) were not especially interested in radical designs, but produced and marketed an assortment of furniture that was moderately modern in style. The one-piece chair could not be put into production until after World War II, once plastics had been developed further. In 1967, after years of experimentation, Verner Panton brought the one-piece moulded S Chair onto the market. In effect this was the Zig-Zag Chair as Rietveld had always envisaged it. Other experiments did not lead to fully fledged products until the 1960s and 70s. The plank furniture was the forerunner of the suites of modular living-room furniture, while the crate furniture was supplied as a DIY pack *avant la lettre*. Rietveld was not involved in these developments, even though they were his ideas, arising from a logical elaboration of certain principles that placed the emphasis on spatiality and mass production. Rietveld's methodology was a poor match for elaborating ideas to the stage at which they could have been patented. Nor was it in his character to claim his own share; he regarded the pursuit of the new as a collective responsibility.

In architecture it is even more difficult to gauge the extent of his influence. Too little was built for his architectural oeuvre to constitute a true 'school' or a recognizable style. In the final analysis, the position he occupied in architectural discourse is rather ambivalent. For *De Vrije Bladen* he wrote an article about Nieuwe Zakelijkheid – 'New Functionalism' – in Dutch architecture, addressing all kinds of things but barely touching on actual buildings. Time and again he returns to the matters that preoccupied him: the three-dimensionality of architecture, the functioning of the senses, the relativity of what had been achieved thus far and the importance of the visual arts to prevent ossification in the fields of architecture and design.[30] A year later he designed more than seven completely different variants of the house for the critic Buys, many more than a strictly Functionalist analysis of a clear-cut programme of requirements would have generated.

This non-conformity is to be found in the work of other architects, such as Van Ravesteyn, and here lie possible interrelationships that are less evident at first glance. At around the same time, in the late 1920s, they were both combining round and rectangular forms and introducing the curved line in their work. Despite political views that were poles apart – Van Ravesteyn adopted a cooperative stance towards the German occupier – their relationship remained amicable. On 14 August 1942, Rietveld sent Van Ravesteyn a letter with fragments from a poem by P. C. Boutens. 'This poem touched me so profoundly (perhaps because it much resembles my own outlook on life) that I am taking the trouble to write to you.'[31]

There is also evidence of international reciprocity. Le Corbusier, of whom Rietveld always spoke admiringly, was probably an inspirational example. The brilliant white exterior of the row of houses on the Erasmuslaan and the pastel tones used for the interior walls are similar to the architectonic use of colour that the Frenchman developed in the latter half of the 1920s.[32] Likewise, Le Corbusier and Alvar Aalto had already prepared the way for the use of natural materials and organic forms prior to Rietveld, seemingly unexpectedly, building the Verrijn Stuart Summerhouse in the midst of Loosdrecht's lakelands in 1941.[33]

Rietveld's influence on foreign colleagues is obvious, though it sometimes surfaces much later and in unexpected places. Walter Gropius realized a house with a steel skeleton at the Weissenhofsiedlung as early as 1927. This design possibly gave Rietveld the idea of using a steel framework with concrete slabs for the Garage with Chauffeur's Apartment (1927–8). Compared with Gropius, Rietveld devoted a surprising amount of attention to the aesthetic aspects. Once affixed to the frame, the edges of the concrete panels were masked with a metal strip, accentuating the pattern of vertical and horizontal rectangles in the facade. Rietveld evidently thought it important that the technique was expressed in the form. This aspect interested Gropius less and Mies van der Rohe did not elaborate this until much later.[34]

Brown mentions two further examples: the accentuation of the corner of a building by setting back the load-bearing column slightly and the diffusion of light in an interior by introducing artificial light above a glass ceiling. Both of these Rietveld discoveries have for years belonged to the standard repertoire of modern architecture. Despite this demonstrable influence, Rietveld has not gained the same status as Le Corbusier, Mies van der Rohe or Frank Lloyd Wright. There are all kinds of possible explanations for this, but one of them is undoubtedly that the Red-Blue Chair and the Schröder House have overshadowed his other work.

Complete, clear and unambiguous

The Red-Blue Chair is without parallel. In Western European art there is no item of furniture with a comparable iconic status, and with good reason. Rietveld's design is a break with the past, the start of a completely new development in design. The Schröder House has the same magical aura, but shares a place alongside other architectural highlights of the early twentieth century.[35] The exceptional quality of these two designs cannot, however, be a reason to discount the rest of Rietveld's oeuvre. It includes wonderful designs – buildings, interiors and furniture – that look much less like the iconic Rietveld but are just as effective. Everyone has a personal list of favourites, but what these designs share in common is their spatial quality. At the cutting edge of art and architecture, Rietveld the furniture-maker experimented with the limitation of infinite space. He did that in the European humanistic tradition. I shall leave the final word to him:

When building we must also bear relativity in mind and should exercise sobriety, but however we build it will only truly become reality for us and be able to bring us joy if the visual sense of space, which we hereby give to others as a gift yet retain for ourselves, is not fragmented but complete and clear and above all unambiguous.[36]

Notes

Please note the following abbreviations appear throughout the notes:

Netherlands Architecture Institute (NAI)
NAI, J. J. P. Oud Archive (OUDJ)
NAI, Rietveld Archive (RIET)
Rietveld Schröder Archive (RSA)

Chapter 1

1
G. Rietveld, 'Korte rede van G. Th. Rietveld bij gelegenheid van het verlenen van het eredoctoraat in de technische wetenschappen door de senaat van de Technische Hogeschool te Delft op 11-1-1964'. Later published in Frits Bless, *Rietveld. 1888–1964. Een biografie* (Amsterdam/Baarn, 1982), 246–8.

2
Some five per cent of Utrecht's population belonged to the Netherlands Reformed Church, of which a relatively high proportion were artisans and tradespeople.
See T. H. G. Verhoeven, 'Stedelijk leven in een stroomversnelling (1851–1917)', in R. E. de Bruin et al., *Een paradijs vol weelde. Geschiedenis van de stad Utrecht* (Utrecht, 2000), 415–16.

3
Lecture for the Collaborating Institutes for Art Education (Samenwerkende Instituten voor Kunstonderwijs) in Amsterdam in 1958. Published as Gerrit Thomas Rietveld, 'Architectuur', *De Nieuwe Stem* 14, no. 8/9 (1959), 560–72/'Architecture' in *Gerrit Th. Rietveld: The Complete Works, 1888–1964* (Utrecht, 1992), 51–5.

4
G. Rietveld, 'In Memoriam architect P. J. Klaarhamer', *Bouwkundig Weekblad* 72, no. 13/14 (1954), 101.

5
Bless 1982, 14. Wim Rietveld earned his living as a teacher at various schools. My thanks to Paula van Reijn-Rietveld, one of his daughters, for relaying this to me in a conversation in September 2009. On Bolland's influence among artists, see C. Blotkamp, 'Theo van Doesburg', in *De Stijl: the formative years, 1917–1922*, trans. C. I. and A. L. Loeb (Cambridge, MA/London, 1986), 9.

6
B. Mulder, *Gerrit Thomas Rietveld. Schets can zijn leven, denken, werken* (Nijmegen, 1994), 21/ *Gerrit Thomas Rietveld. Life, thoughts, work*, trans. P. K. de Jonge (Amsterdam, 2010).

7
H. Ibelings, *Nederlandse architectuur van de 20ste eeuw* (Rotterdam, 1995), 42–3/*20th century architecture in the Netherlands*, trans. M. O'Loughlin (Rotterdam, 1996), 42–3.

8
Anon., 'Prof. Granpré Molière en dr. Rietveld erelid B.N.A.', *Bouw* 19, no. 13 (1964), 448.

9
De Stijl 2, no. 1 (1918), 4.

10
Jan Wils wrote to the painter Chris Beekman on 7 May 1919: 'For me there are no two ways about it: today or tomorrow Communism will also make its entry into our country. Allow me, however, to add immediately that I am a communist in heart and soul.' See G. Harmsen, 'De Stijl en de Russische revolutie', in M. Friedman, ed., *De Stijl. 1917–1931* (Amsterdam, 1982), 45. On Mondrian's ideas at this time, see E. Hoek, 'Piet Mondrian', in C. Blotkamp, ed., *De Stijl: the formative years* (Cambridge, MA/ London, 1982), 48–9.

11
Bibeb, 'Wij maken maar een achtergrond. Gesprek met architect Rietveld', *Vrij Nederland*, 19 April 1958, 3. Bibeb was an interviewer renowned for her portraits for the Dutch social-democrat weekly, *Vrij Nederland*, and famous for her ability to coax highly personal revelations from her interviewees. In this interview Rietveld revealed a more emotional side to his personality, which may have been as a result of Bibeb's acuity, though it is also possible that she doctored his statements somewhat. They should certainly not be taken too literally, because the facts are not always correct or cannot be verified, such as the correspondence between Rietveld and Mondrian referred to in the article.

12
M. Kuper, 'Gerrit Rietveld', in C. Blotkamp, ed., *De vervolgjaren van De Stijl 1922–1932* (Amsterdam/ Antwerp, 1996), 195–240, esp. 239.

13
See C. Linssen, H. Schoots and T. Gunning, *Het gaat om de film! Een nieuwe geschiedenis van de Nederlandse Filmliga 1927–1933* (Amsterdam, 1999).

14
This impression is reinforced by the fact that Oud's extensive correspondence has been preserved in such a complete form. Now in OUDJ.

15
OUDJ, inv. nos. B3 and B4.

16
Rietveld 1954, 101.

17
Quoted in H. Blotkamp et al., *S. van Ravesteyn* (Amsterdam/ Utrecht, 1977), 78.

18
G. Rietveld, 'Verbouwing van den schouwburg "Kunstmin te Dordrecht"', *De 8 en Opbouw*, 12, no. 5 (1941), 61–5.

19
Postcard to Oud, 10 February 1927 (OUDJ, inv. no. B37). Published in Kuper, 'Gerrit Rietveld', 233.

20
RIET, inv. nos. 295 and 296.

21
Manuscript, RSA, GR 210. Quoted in Mulder, 1994, 64.

22
Bless 1982, 247–8. The words 'however' (*echter*) and 'the duty' (*de plicht*) are missing in the printed version of the speech, but are to be found in the handwritten draft (RSA, GR 170).

23
I. van Zijl, curator, 'Truus Schröder: tentoonstelling per post' (Truus Schröder: exhibition by post), (Utrecht, 1998–9). This was a project that began in 1998 with a basic book. On its completion

in 1999 it included five postal submissions as inserts.
24
These were the designations used by Rietveld's niece, Paula van Reijn-Rietveld. Personal communication, September 2009.
25
Rietveld's youngest daughter, Tutti, was convinced that all the stories about the affair between Truus Schröder and her father were pure scandal-mongering. Personal communication, 1992.
26
G. Rietveld, Guided tour of his retrospective at the Stedelijk Museum Amsterdam, 6 March 1959 (Stedelijk Museum Amsterdam, sound archive of the audiovisual department, no. 1999-006, 41′ 52″).
27
B. Kroon, 'De geboorte van het Rietveld Schröder Huis', *De Tijd*, 29 November 1974, 24–6.
28
Mulder 1994, 18–19.
29
Ibid., 86.
30
G. Rietveld, 'Inzicht', *i10* 2, no. 17/18 (1928), 89–90.
31
Rietveld wrote: 'When we perceive a colour the retina must be tightly stretched; three sorts of nerve endings are then active: the 1st sort experiences red, the 2nd sort experiences blue, the 3rd sort experiences yellow; together they experience white. If the nerve endings that are sensitive to red are working on their own then we experience red intensively, if the others are also partially contributing then we experience pale red =
white with so much red, if the endings sensitive to red are working more strongly than the other.' See Rietveld 1928, 89. These lines of reasoning are a summary, sometimes faulty, of several discoveries and ideas, some more scientific than others. Rietveld stated that his ideas about colour were based on Schopenhauer, but his interpretations of philosophical texts are rather free. Georg Stahl has conducted a probing study into the relationship between Rietveld's ideas about colour and Schopenhauer's theories. See G. Stahl, trans. and intro., *On vision and colors by Arthur Schopenhauer and color sphere by Philipp Otto Runge* (New York, 2010).
32
For an excellent overview of the concept of space in architecture see Adrian Forty, 'Space', *Words and buildings. A vocabulary of modern architecture* (London, 2000), 256–75.
33
Ibid., 257. The text that Forty refers to was published as H. P. Berlage, *Gedanken über Stil in der Baukunst* (Leipzig, 1905). This lecture was held on 22 and 23 January 1904 for the Museumsverein in Krefeld and appeared in a Dutch translation
in the periodical *De beweging* that same year.
34
See Mulder 1994 and Stahl 2010.
35
Stahl 2010, 31 and 150.
36
Manuscript (RSA, GR 254).
37
Manuscript (RSA, GR 203), published in H. van Rens, *Gerrit Rietveld Teksten* (Utrecht, 1979) and in Mulder 1994, 88.
38
G. Rietveld, 'Nieuwe zakelijkheid in de Nederlandse architectuur', *De Vrije Bladen* 9, no. 7 (1932), 1–27, esp. 9 (quote). Reprinted in M. Kuper and I. van Zijl, *Gerrit Th. Rietveld. Het volledige werk 1888–1964* (Utrecht, 1992), 34/'New functionalism in Dutch architecture', in *Gerrit Th. Rietveld. The complete works, 1888–1964* (Utrecht, 1992), 34.
39
Letter to a certain Mr de Jong, in reaction to an article in the journal of the Humanistische Verbond (Humanist Alliance), 27 October 1954 (RIET inv. no. 763).
40
G. Rietveld, 'Over architect Oud', *Forum* 6, no. 5/6 (1951), 132–4.

Chapter 2

1
G. Rietveld, 'De stoel', *De Werkende Vrouw* 1, no. 9 (1930), 244. Also published in M. Kuper and I. van Zijl, *Gerrit Th. Rietveld 1888–1964. Het volledige werk* (Utrecht, 1992), 27;
Eng. trans. as 'Chairs' in *Gerrit Th. Rietveld. The complete works, 1888–1964* (Utrecht, 1992), 27 (translation modified).
2
Bibeb, 'Wij maken maar een achtergrond. Gesprek met architect Rietveld', *Vrij Nederland*, 19 April 1958, 3. See Chapter 1, n. 11.
3
J. N. van der Meulen, 'Museum en school van Kunstnijverheid te Utrecht', *Oud-Utrecht*, 66 (1993), 96.
4
The bank acquired the property on the Drift in 1906 and restored it over subsequent years. The conference room is still in use.
5
G. Rietveld, Guided tour of his retrospective at the Stedelijk Museum Amsterdam, 6 March 1959 (Stedelijk Museum Amsterdam, sound archive of the audiovisual department, no. 1999-006, 41′ 52″).
6
The title is a quotation from Bach's *Saint Matthew Passion*, a work that is still hugely popular in the Netherlands. The painting is fairly gruesome to behold, typical of the somewhat dour Dutch Calvinism. In the 1990s it was discovered in three pieces in one of Truus Schröder's desk drawers.
7
G. Rietveld, 'In Memoriam architect P. J. Klaarhamer', *Bouwkundig Weekblad* 72, no. 13/14 [1954], 101.
8
G. Rietveld, Guided tour, 1959.
9
T. H. G. Verhoeven, 'Stedelijk leven in een stroomversnelling (1851–1917)', in *Een paradijs vol weelde. Geschiedenis van de stad Utrecht*, R. E. de Bruin et al. (Utrecht, 2000), 433.
10
Radermacher Schorer was at one point a member of twenty-four committees and associations. See T. de Boer et al., *M. R. Radermacher Schorer 1888–1956. Minnaar van het 'schoone' boek* (Amsterdam, 1998), 5.
11
T. M. Brown, *The work of G. Rietveld, architect* (Utrecht, 1958) 14 and 17, figs 4–6.
12
H. Blotkamp et al., S. *van Ravesteyn* (Amsterdam/Utrecht, 1977), 16.
13
J. H. Maronier's daughter thinks that contact between Rietveld and the family was established after 1922. Gerard van de Groenekan is convinced that these pieces of furniture were produced before he entered into Rietveld's employ in 1918. On stylistic grounds I am inclined to date the furniture c.1915 rather than c.1922.
14
H. Blotkamp et al. (Amsterdam/Utrecht, 1977), 82.
15
M. Kuper, 'Gerrit Rietveld', in C. Blotkamp et al., *De Beginjaren van De Stijl 1917–1922* (Utrecht, 1982), 263–84, esp. 267; Eng. trans. as *De Stijl: the formative years, 1917–1922* trans. C. I. and A. L. Loeb (Cambridge, MA, 1986), 259–79, esp. 261.
16
J. B. Bakema et al., *Rietveld-tentoonstelling. Bijdrage tot de vernieuwing der bouwkunst* (Utrecht, 1958), 3.
17
G. Rietveld, 'Aanteekening bij kinderstoel', *De Stijl* 2, no. 9 (1919), appendix XVIII.
18

G. Rietveld, Guided tour, 1959.
19
Almost all these items have been lost, except for the cot and a rail from the playpen. Based on the black and white photographs, it could be cautiously inferred that Rietveld experimented with colour and various combinations of wood and leather.
20
Th. v[an] D[oesburg], 'Aanteekeningen bij een leunstoel van Rietveld', *De Stijl* 2, no. 11 (1919), appendix XXII; Eng. trans. in Brown (Utrecht, 1958), 21 (translation modified).
21
See T. Eliëns, *H. P. Berlage. Ontwerpen voor het interieur* (Zwolle, 1998), 14. Here Berlage is himself elaborating on Gottfried Semper's ideas in *Der Stil in den technischen und tektonischen Kunsten* (Munich, 1860–3), which probably influenced Frank Lloyd Wright's furniture designs as well.
22
G. Rietveld, Guided tour, 1959.
23
L. Büller and F. den Oudsten, 'Interview with Truus Schröder', in P. Overy et al., *The Rietveld Schröder House* (Houten, 1988), 60 n. 18.

Chapter 3

1
M. Kuper, 'Gerrit Rietveld', in C. Blotkamp et al., *De beginjaren van De Stijl 1917–1922* (Utrecht, 1982), 273; Eng. trans. as *De Stijl: the formative years, 1917–1922* trans. C. I. and A. L. Loeb (Cambridge, MA, 1986), 267 (translation modified). Also quoted in E. Hoek, ed., *Theo van Doesburg oeuvrecatalogus* (Utrecht/Otterlo/Bussum, 2000), 261; Eng. trans. as *Theo van Doesburg. Oeuvre catalogue* (Utrecht/Otterlo/Bussum, 2000), 261.
2
Piet Mondrian, on a short trip to the Netherlands from Paris in July 1914, was unable to return to France because of the outbreak of war. See E. Hoek, 'Piet Mondriaan', in C. Blotkamp et al. (Utrecht, 1982), 47–82, esp. 58/'Piet Mondrian', in C. Blotkamp et al. (Cambridge, MA, 1982), 39–76, esp. 48.
3
C. Blotkamp, 'Theo van Doesburg' in *ibid.*, 14–46, esp. 28–9/Eng. trans.,'Theo van Doesburg', in *ibid.*, 3–37, esp. 18.
4
De Stijl 2, no. 9 (1919), 102, appendix XVIII; *De Stijl* 2, no. 11 (1919), 439.
5
De Stijl 3, no. 5 (1920), 46.
6
Bibeb, 'Wij maken maar een achtergrond. Gesprek met architect Rietveld', *Vrij Nederland*, 19 April 1958. This dark side of Rietveld's younger years was never actually aired in public, and in light of the facts seems to have been embroidered upon somewhat. See Chapter 1, note 11.
7
Kuper (Utrecht, 1982), 273/ (Cambridge, MA., 1986), 276. Also mentioned in Hoek (Bussum, 2000), 261.
8
H. Esser, 'J. J. P. Oud', in C. Blotkamp et al. (Utrecht, 1982)/ (Cambridge, MA, 1986), 133–6.
9
The child's chair stood in the model interior by Rietveld for the 'tent. huisvrouwen' ('ideal home exhibition') held in 1923. The price list for the living-room furniture mentions that the child's chair is owned by Dr Müller, a gynaecologist based in Utrecht, and cost between 30 and 55 guilders ($11.50 or £2.60 and $21.00 or £4.75).
10
OUDJ, inv. no. B4.
11
G. Rietveld, 'Aanteekening bij kinderstoel', *De Stijl* 2, no. 9 (1919), 102, appendix XVIII. Along with several other authors, I previously assumed that Rietveld painted furniture for children in colour first and applied this to furniture for adults only later. This is probably incorrect. Some of the later pieces of children's furniture for Schelling are unpainted, while in Dr Hartog's consulting room dating from 1922 the furniture is fully as well as partially painted.
12
M. Kuper, *Rietveld als meubelmaker. Wonen met experimenten 1900–1924* (Utrecht, 1983), 16–17.
13
T. van Doesburg, *De Stijl* 2, no. 11 (1919), appendix XXII.
14
G. Rietveld, Guided tour of his retrospective at the Stedelijk Museum Amsterdam, 6 March 1959 (Stedelijk Museum Amsterdam, sound archive of the audiovisual department, no. 1999-006, 41' 52").
15
S. Ex and E. Hoek, *Vilmos Huszár (Huszar) schilder en ontwerper 1884–1960* (Utrecht, 1985), 78.
16
Many authors, including Troy, assume that Rietveld designed only the furniture. See, for example, N. J. Troy, *The De Stijl environment* (Cambridge, MA, 1983), 129–34. Huszár, however, always stated that the form was Rietveld's idea. See Ex and Hoek (Utrecht, 1985), 77, 117 and 170.
17
Til Brugman wrote the novel *Spanningen* (Tensions) (Amsterdam/Antwerp, 1953). The novel is set in the days around the Liberation in 1945. The architect Dirck Belders, inspired by Rietveld, is portrayed as an opportunistic whoremonger, who at the end of the novel undertakes a fairly pointless act of heroism and loses both his legs as a result.
18
Letter from Rietveld to Oud, n.p., 18 March 1922. Though its whereabouts are unknown there is a photograph of this letter in the RSA. It is quoted in Kuper and Van Zijl (Utrecht, 1992), 83.
19
A. Boeken, 'Eenige opmerkingen over de winkelverbouwing Kalverstraat 107 te Amsterdam. Arch. G. Rietveld', *Bouwkundig Weekblad* 43, no. 49 (1922), 476; A. Boeken, 'De winkelverbouwing Kalverstraat 107 te Amsterdam. Arch. G. Rietveld', *Bouwkundig Weekblad* 44, no. 45 (1923), 455; Anon., 'Holland und die Baukunst unserer Zeit', *Schweizerische Bauzeitung* 82 (1923) 18, 225–9; Anon., 'Boutiques 1921', *L'Architecture Vivante*, autumn/winter 1925, fig. 6; Anon., 'Architekt G. Rietveld. Pui N. V. Goud en Zilversmids Compagnie Amsterdam'; Anon., 'Architekt G. Rietveld. Intérieur N. V. Goud en Zilversmids Compagnie Amsterdam', *De Stijl* 5, no. 2 (1922), with the illustrations facing page 25.
20
L. Büller and F. den Oudsten, 'Interview with Truus Schröder', in P. Overy et al., *The Rietveld Schröder House* (Houten, 1988), 44. This chapter is an edited transcript of an interview recorded in 1982, the tapes of which are preserved in the RSA. Hereafter, where the tapes provide information not included in the edited transcript, this audio source is referred to as 'Den Oudsten 1982'.
21
Ibid., 44.
22
H. Buiter, 'De moderne stad 1907–2000', in Renger E. de Bruin et al. (eds), *Een paradijs vol weelde. Geschiedenis van de stad Utrecht* (Utrecht, 2000), 458.
23
L. Büller and F. den Oudsten (Houten, 1988), 48; K. Orchard and I. Schulz, *Kurt Schwitters en de avant-garde* (Cologne, 2006), 69. This is the Dutch translation of the exhibition catalogue *Merzgebiete. Kurt Schwitters und seine Freunde* (Cologne, 2006).
24
Kuper, 'Gerrit Rietveld', in C. Blotkamp, ed., *De vervolgjaren van De Stijl 1922–1932* (Amsterdam/Antwerp, 1996), 212.

25
Den Oudsten 1982.
26
E. van Straaten, 'Theo van Doesburg', in C. Blotkamp, ed., *De vervolgjaren van De Stijl 1922–1932* (Amsterdam/ Antwerp, 1996), 27.

Chapter 4

1
L. Büller and F. den Oudsten, 'Interview with Truus Schröder', in P. Overy et al., *The Rietveld Schröder House* (Houten, 1988), 84. This chapter is an edited transcript of an interview recorded in 1982, the tapes of which are preserved in the RSA. Hereafter, where the tapes provide information not included in the edited transcript, this audio source is referred to as 'Den Oudsten 1982'.
2
See C. Nagtegaal, *Truus Schröder-Schräder. Bewoonster van het Rietveld Schröderhuis* (Utrecht, 1987), 38. Truus Schröder's biographical details are drawn from this publication.
3
Büller and Den Oudsten 1988, 47 (translation modified).
4
Ibid., 47.
5
Ibid., 52.
6
Ibid., 52 (translation modified).
7
Ibid., 63.
8
Kuper hypothesizes that the circles might represent a schematic arrangement of the house, assuming that the front section of the house would be built on the lower-lying section of the plot. This scheme cannot, however, be reconciled with the depicted elevations, as noted by Kuper herself. See M. Kuper, 'Gerrit Rietveld', in C. Blotkamp, ed., *De vervolgjaren van De Stijl 1922–1932* (Amsterdam/Antwerp, 1996), 215.
9
Büller and Den Oudsten 1988, 52 (translation modified); I. van Zijl and B. Mulder, *Het Rietveld Schröderhuis* (Utrecht, 2009), 29.
10
Büller and Den Oudsten 1988, 56.
11
G. Rietveld, Guided tour of his retrospective at the Stedelijk Museum Amsterdam, 6 March 1959 (Stedelijk Museum Amsterdam, sound archive of the audiovisual department, no. 1999-006, 41′ 52″).
12
See Kuper 1996, 217.
13
Den Oudsten 1982; T. M. Brown, *The work of G. Rietveld, architect* (Utrecht, 1958), 39.
14
For a detailed description of the restoration see the first-hand account by architect B. Mulder, 'The restoration of the Rietveld Schröder House', in Overy 1988, 104–23. There is a more recent account in Dutch in Van Zijl and Mulder 2009, 68–93.
15
Den Oudsten 1982. This yellow band can be seen on the axonometric projection of the Schröder House. The date of this coloured-in collotype is unknown.
16
Postcard from Rietveld to Oud, 3 August 1924 (OUDJ, inv. no. B18). Quoted in Kuper 1996, 215.
17
The property that the Schröder House abuts dates from 1922 and cost 8,000 guilders (approx. $3,055 or £690). My thanks to Jaap Oosterhoff for providing this information (December 2009).
18
According to Truus Schröder, the building contractor probably got a raw deal because he had underestimated the work involved (Den Oudsten 1982).
19
Documents concerning the Schröder House in the RSA.
20
The photographs from the 1920s were taken before Rietveld laid the concrete paths.
21
In her curriculum vitae, Han Schröder writes: 'The house was organized and designed for a new way of living and family development. To make this possible … her new house should be based on and express freedom, openness, and flexibility … It has to be understood that the program she laid down was in essence springing from new philosophies pertaining to the education of her children, family structure, as well as life and task of the mother as head of the family and as an otherwise involved woman in her own right.' Located in the Han Schröder Papers, 1950–92, Ms 1987–064, box 5, folder 17, Special Collections, Virginia Polytechnic Institute and State University, Blacksburg, VA.
22
Documents concerning the Schröder House in the RSA.
23
Den Oudsten 1982.
24
Overy 1988, 56–7. Sliding walls were not in themselves unusual. Many Dutch houses had an *en suite* room that could be divided in two with sliding doors. In 1922 J. W. Janzen had won the Komend Wonen (Future Living) design competition with a terrace of houses, in which the ground floor could be subdivided in six different ways using sliding partitions. The design was published by Bruno Taut in *Die neue Wohnung* (Leipzig, 1924). See Kuper 1996, 221.
25
Letter from Rietveld to P. van Meurs, c. May 1926 (RSA). See M. White, *De Stijl and Dutch Modernism* (Manchester/New York, 2003), 1–2 and 10 n. 2.
26
Wim Quist provides a wonderful analysis of the structure of this space. See 'Honrado, amable e inflexible/Honest, gentle and uncompromising', in M. Kuper et al., 'Gerrit Th. Rietveld. Casas/ Houses', *2G Revista Internacional de arquitectura/International architectural review*, no. 39/40 (2006), 23–4.
27
W. Gropius, *Internationale Architektur* (Munich, 1925), 76–7 [Bauhausbücher 1].
28
J. Badovici, 'Entretiens sur l'architecture vivante. Maison à Utrecht (Pays-Bas) par T. Schräder et G. Rietveld', *L'Architecture Vivante*, autumn/winter 1925, 28–9, figs. 31–3. Schräder was Truus Schröder's maiden name.
29
Theo van Doesburg, 'Data en Feiten (betreffende de invloedsontwikkeling van "De Stijl" in het Buitenland) die voor zich spreken', *De Stijl* 7, nos 79/84 (1926–27), 53–71. See also Van Zijl and Mulder 2009, 59.
30
According to Truus Schröder, Rietveld sometimes wondered whether he had taken the use of colour too far. See Büller and Den Oudsten 1988, 73.
31
On the contemporaneous reception of the Schröder House, see Kuper 1996, 223–4, and I. van Zijl and B. Mulder, *Het Rietveld Schröderhuis* (Utrecht, 2009), 59–64.
32
In almost every book, the simularity between the architectural designs for the De Stijl Exhibition and the Schröder House is mentioned. See the section of the bibliography titled 'Schröder House'.
33
See M. Bock, 'Cornelis van Eesteren', in *De vervolgjaren van De Stijl 1922–1932*, ed. C. Blotkamp (Amsterdam/ Antwerp, 1996), 259.
34
There is a photograph in the Bauhausbilderarchiv (Bauhaus Image Archives) held by the Hochschule für Architektur und Bauwesen in Weimar. See Blotkamp 1996, 109.
35
For a detailed analysis of the Paris

models see Bock 1996, 226–68.
36
On the De Stijl exhibition see, for example, Y.-A. Bois and B. Reichlin, *De Stijl et l'architecture en France* (Brussels, 1985), and C. Blotkamp 1996, *passim*. Blotkamp hypothesizes that Van Leusden's models were inspired by Rietveld's furniture. See C. Blotkamp, 'Mondriaan – architectuur', *Wonen/TABK* 4, no. 5 (1982), 12–51, esp. 42.
37
Adelaar bases his argument on a letter from Rietveld to Oud, 10 November 1922. See D. Adelaar et al., *Willem van Leusden. Essays over een verhard romanticus* (Utrecht, 1990), 85. However, the letter only mentions a cupboard by Rietveld that was 'coloured' by Van Leusden (OUDJ, inv. no. B9). Kuper suggests that it may have been Van Leusden who introduced Hartog and Rietveld (Kuper 1982, 275–7).
38
Kuper 1996, 221.
39
M. Speidel, *Bruno Taut, Natur und Fantasie 1880–1938* (Berlin, 1995), 210–11. Speidel assumes that Dutch as well as Japanese houses served as examples for Taut. Perhaps the Japanese traits that many people discern in the Schröder House crept in via Taut. In a 1932 interview, Rietveld said that it 'was somewhat reminiscent of Japanese art'. See I. Bill, 'Lebensgestalter. Ein Gespräch in der Wiener Werkbundsiedlung', [periodical unknown, 1932], 17 (cutting in the RSA).
40
The letter from Taut to Oud is dated 30 September 1923 (NAI, OUDJ, inv. no. B13). Also published in Kuper 1996, 221, n. 41.
41
Th. van Doesburg, 'Tot een beeldende architectuur', *De Stijl* 6, no. 6/7 (1924), 78–83; Eng. trans. as 'Towards a plastic architecture', in Hans L. C. Jaffé, *De Stijl*, trans. R. R. Symonds (London, 1960), 186–7.
42
Postcard from Van Doesburg to Rietveld, 24 March [1925] (RSA). The text is more easily legible in B. Mulder and G. J. de Rook (eds), *Rietveld Schröder Huis 1925–1975* (Utrecht/Antwerp, 1975), 12. See also Overy 1988, 65, n. 26.
43
André Gide, 'De l'influence en littérature', in S. Dresden, *De structuur van de biografie* (The Hague/Antwerp, 1956); repr. as *Over de biografie* (Amsterdam, 2002.), 102. Gide delivered this oration in Brussels in 1900.

Chapter 5

1
Typescript, December 1926 (RSA, GR 5).
2
On 5 May 1924 Rietveld moved his furniture workshop from the Adriaen van Ostadelaan to the Bachstraat and half a year later relocated it to Oude Kamp 3a. Van de Groenekan continued the furniture business, later located on the main road to Soesterberg in Utrecht, for the rest of his life. He executed almost all the wooden furniture designed by Rietveld, designs prior to as well as after 1924.
3
On the collaboration between Rietveld and Truus Schröder, see M. Kuper, 'Rietveld at work: recollections of colleagues, pupils and clients', in Kaya Oku, *The architecture of Gerrit Rietveld* (Tokyo, 2009), 220–7, esp. 221–2.
4
B. Mulder, *Gerrit Thomas Rietveld. Schets can zijn leven, denken, werken* (Nijmegen, 1994), 34.
5
Marie Lommen was an estate agent in The Hague. The property was probably divided into two apartments and it is likely she had it built to sell at a profit or to lease out. See G. H. Rodijk, *De huizen van Rietveld* (Zwolle, 1991), 18, and M. Kuper, 'Gerrit Rietveld', in C. Blotkamp, ed., *De vervolgjaren van De Stijl 1922–1932* (Amsterdam/Antwerp, 1996), 224–6.
6
Kuper 1996, 226–7.
7
Letter from Rietveld to Oud [1927?] (OUDJ, inv. no. B48).
8
Letters from J. J. Fraenkel to Truus Schröder, 26 February 1967 and 25 November 1973 (RSA). The first letter is published in Kuper 1996, 199.
9
'Nut, constructie: (schoonheid: kunst)', *i10* 1, no. 3 (1927), 89–92; 'Inzicht', *i10* 2, no. 17/18 (1928), 89–90. The former is translated as 'Utility, construction; (beauty, art)', in T. & C. Benton with D. Sharp, *Form and function: a source book for the history of architecture and design, 1890–1939* (London, 1975), 162–3; the latter is translated as 'Insight' in T. M. Brown, *The work of G. Rietveld, architect* (Utrecht, 1958), 160–1. The same themes and turns of phrase recur constantly in Rietveld's later texts. Someone who has read plenty of Rietveld's writing can grasp what he means, but these early texts are fairly enigmatic for readers unfamiliar with Rietveld's idiom.
10
Oud made his own revisions as well. Postcards from Rietveld to Oud dated 9, 10 and 24 February 1927 (OUDJ, inv. no. B37).
11
Postcard, 9 February 1927 (OUDJ, inv. no. B37). Published in Kuper 1996, 233.
12
J. Jans, *Bouwkunst en cultuur* (Amsterdam, 1934), 80. On the ideas of J. Jans see B. Rebel, *Het Nieuwe Bouwen. Het functionalisme in Nederland 1918–1945* (Assen, 1983), 292–3.
13
Mulder 1994, 23; F. den Oudsten, Interview with Truus Schröder, 1982 (RSA). Published in edited form as L. Büller and F. den Oudsten, 'Interview with Truus Schröder', in P. Overy et al., *The Rietveld Schröder House* (Houten, 1988).
14
T. Schröder, 'Wat men door normalisatie in den woningbouw te Frankfort a/d Main heeft bereikt', *De Werkende Vrouw* 1, nos. 1–2 (1930), 12–14.
15
Newspaper cutting with no indication of the date or the publication's name (RSA).
16
Rietveld had already employed this type of ceiling in 1929 in the interior for the Drijver-de Leer family home in Hilversum. See Kuper 1996, 207.
17
M. Kuper, 'Rietveld's houses', in 'Gerrit Th. Rietveld. Casas/Houses', *2G. Revista internacional de arquitectura*, no. 39/40 (2006), 88.
18
These colours are mentioned in a review. See Anon., 'Huizen van glas en staal', *Het Utrechtsch Provinciaal en Stedelijk Dagblad*, 5 October 1931.
19
Some models were included in the Metz & Co. range, while others never made it beyond a prototype or demonstration model, even though they were regularly exhibited in showrooms and at fairs. See P. Timmer, *Metz & Co. De creatieve jaren* (Rotterdam, 1995), though her research did not focus on the company's production methods. Rietveld wanted to have the folding bed in the bedroom produced by d3, a division of De Eerste Nederlandsche Mechanische Apparatenfabriek Ph. Dekker. See T. M. Eliëns and M. Halbertsma (eds), *Volmaakt verchroomd: d3 en het avant-garde meubel in Nederland* (Rotterdam, 2007), 16–17. Rietveld also had contact with the Utrecht-based manufacturer Hopmi concerning the production of a steel tube

framed chair.
20
B. van Santen, 'Bredero's Bouwbedrijf, 1921–1947', in *Bredero's Bouwbedrijf. Familiebedrijf – mondiaal bouwconcern – ontvlechting*, ed. W. M. J. Bekkers et al. (Amsterdam, 2005).
21
RSA.
22
Letter from Rietveld to Oud [1927?] (OUDJ, inv. no. B48).
23
Rietveld is mentioned as an honorary member in the Japanese periodical *Arkitekturo Internacia* 2, no. 6 (1930). Kaya Oku kindly donated copies of this journal to the RSA.
24
J. Frank, 'Die internationale Werkbundsiedlung Wien 1932', in *Neues Bauen in der Welt*, vol. 6 (Vienna, 1932).
25
Kuper and Van Zijl 1992, 136.
26
In the S. Giedion archive there is a telegram in French dated 20 June 1928: 'Accepterai volontiers votre invitation, Rietveld' (Shall gladly accept your invitation, Rietveld). The invitation to Rietveld was evidently sent after Oud and Van Eesteren had cancelled at the last minute. They did not propose Rietveld as an alternative and he was possibly invited on Mart Stam's recommendation (ETH Zürich, Giedion Archive, 42-K-1928-Rietveld).
27
A. van Beusekom, 'Gerrit Rietveld en zijn "periodiek in briefvorm" 1931–1932', *jong Holland*, 1 (1991), 33–51.
28
Ibid., 34.
29
Ibid., 35 n. 12.
30
Kuper argues convincingly that the chair must date from before 1927. See Kuper 1996, 203.
31
See Kuper 1996, 200.
32
It is possible that two prototypes were realized. See Kuper 1988, 192–8.
33
The book has photos of both chairs, but for the chair of three-ply wood it looks as if a drawing or a small paper model was used. There is no known example of a plywood model. See W. F. Gouwe (ed.), *Ruimte. Jaarboek van de Nederlandsche Ambachts- & Nijverheidskunst 1929* (Rotterdam, 1929), 172, 187 and 188; see also Kuper 1996, 200.
34
My thanks to Han Schröder for providing this information.
35
Kuper 1996, 200, where she quotes a letter from Rietveld to Oud dated 27 September 1927 (OUDJ, inv. no. B44).
36
Otto van Tussenbroek describes this 'highback armchair' (*stokkenstoel*) with its frame of round billets as a variant of the Red-Blue Chair.
See Otto van Tussenbroek, 'Drie stoelen van G. Rietveld', *Binnenhuis*, 1 March 1928, 71. The armchair, which in its red-blue variant has entered the canon of Dutch history as the iconic emblem of De Stijl, was illustrated in *Das neue Frankfurt* with other industrially produced chairs that were shown at the exhibition 'Der Stuhl' in Frankfurt am Main, 20 April–20 May 1929. See A. Behne, 'Luxus oder Komfort', *Das neue Frankfurt* 3, no. 2 (1929), 26.
37
The chair was examined in 2006 by the furniture restorer Jurjen Creman, who confirmed my suspicion that this item of furniture was probably realized after the war as an exhibition model. Personal communication, December 2009.
38
C. Wilk, 'Sitting on air', in C. Wilk, ed., *Modernism: designing a new world, 1914–1939* (London, 2006), 230.
39
Binnert Schröder, Truus Schröder's son, told me that his mother designed this cabinet independently, which is probably correct, given that she alone is mentioned on a drawing of ten stackable cabinets.
40
Anon., 'Heerenhuizen te Utrecht. Rietveld heeft met één slag een deel van het publiek gewonnen', *De Telegraaf*, evening edition, 27 October 1931, 9.
41
Rietveld worked on the Garage with Chauffeur's Apartment and the fibreboard chair simultaneously. Not long before this he had produced a design for the competition for the headquarters of the League of Nations, which he did not deem suitable for publication on its own, according to a postcard to Oud dated 27 September 1927 (OUDJ, inv. no. B44).
42
Kuper 1996, 228 n. 66.
43
For a detailed description of the structure, see Kuper 1996, 227–8. See also I. van Zijl, *Rietveld in Utrecht* (Utrecht, 2001), no. 9.
44
Rietveld referred to 'enamelled concrete'. He possibly had a waterproof 'fortolite' finish for the concrete in mind.
45
Anon., *Architectuur, Schilderkunst en Beeldhouwkunst* (Amsterdam, 1928), 5–6.
46
M. Stam, 'Het vraagstuk der arbeiderswoning in verband met de steeds veranderende grootte der gezinnen', in F. Ottenhof, ed., *Goedkope arbeiderswoningen* (Rotterdam, 1936), 17–25. This publication provides an illustrated account of the entries for a competition organized by Amsterdam City Council in 1933 for designs for inexpensive housing for workers.
47
G. Rietveld, 'Een nieuwe plattegrond voor een volkswoning', *Bouwkundig Weekblad* 62, no. 27 (1941), 226–8. Also published as 'Een nieuwe volkswoning', *De 8 en Opbouw* 12, no. 9 (1941), 122–7.
48
See W. J. de Gruyter, 'Bouwkundige tentoonstelling van den Utr. Kunstkring', *Utrechtsch Provinciaal en Stedelijk Dagblad*, 22, 23 and 24 October 1929. The review also indicates that this travelling exhibition, curated by the Deutsches Werkbund, included work by the Utrecht-based architects
W. Maas, H. F. Mertens, P. J. C. Klaarhamer, K. Kuiler and S. van Ravesteyn. The work by G. Rietveld was produced in association with T. Schröder.
49
Rietveld had sent a similar plan to Breda City Council in 1938 and in 1941 he submitted these plans for a new working-class neighbourhood on the Laan van Soestbergen in Utrecht.
50
G. Rietveld, 'Rationele vormgeving. Lezing gehouden bij gelegenheid van de leerjaarbeëindiging der Haagsche Academie en MTS te Den Haag, mei 1953'; Eng. trans. as 'Rational design', in Kuper and Van Zijl 1992, 31 (translation modified).
51
P. Wever and S. van Schaik, 'De Mondial – Rietveld stoel voor de wereld'. This typescript is published in a modified form in J. Venneman and M. de Kroon, eds, *De Mondial. Rietvelds stoel voor de wereld* (Culemborg, 2006).
52
E. van Hinte, *Wim Rietveld: industrieel ontwerper* (Rotterdam, 1996), 28.
53
Mulder 1994, 101.
54
Anon., 'G. Th. Rietveld geb. 1888', *Goed Wonen* 11, no. 6 (1958), 134.
55
Letter to Mr de Jong dated 27 October 1954, in response to an article in the journal of the

Humanist Alliance (Humanistisch Verbond) located in RIET, inv. no. 763.

Chapter 6

1
G. Rietveld, 'Over de vorm van het meubel', *De 8 en Opbouw* 8, no. 21 (1937), 198–9.
2
From the trial issue in December 1928 through to September 1934, the last issue to list the names of committee members, Rietveld is mentioned as a member of the board and as architectural adviser. In 1934 he was also a member of the exhibitions committee. My thanks to Roman Koot for drawing this to my attention.
3
Jan Gielkens brought this campaign group to my attention. In the RSA there is a copy of this pamphlet from the collection of the Amsterdam-based International Institute of Social History (Internationaal Instituut voor Sociale Geschiedenis, or IISG).
4
See B. Rebel, *Het Nieuwe Bouwen. Het functionalisme in Nederland 1918–1945* (Assen, 1983), 117–21.
5
De 8 en Opbouw 9, no. 26 (1938), 249. Eight architects terminated their membership. On relations between the other *Nieuwe Bouwen* architects see Rebel 1983.
6
H.-R. Hitchcock and P. Johnson, *The International Style* (3rd edn, London/New York, 1995). In the foreword to the second edition of 1966, Hitchcock wrote, 'Hindsight suggests that Holland might have been better – or also – represented by Rietveld than Oud, who withdrew from production in 1930 for some years because of illness.'
7
F. Ottenhof, ed., *Goedkope arbeiderswoningen* (Rotterdam, 1936), 70–1 and 107. See also Rebel 1983, 200.
8
Willem de Wagt, *J. B. van Loghem 1881–1940. Landhuizen, stadswoonhuizen en wonigbouwprojecten* (Haarlem, 1995), 344; M. Kuper and I. van Zijl, *Rietveld Schröder Archief* (Utrecht, 1988), 195.
9
B. Taut, *Die neue Wohnung* (Leipzig, 1924), 80–1.
10
Brown notes the difference in quality between the interiors and exteriors of Rietveld's designs and adds that Rietveld usually began by designing the interior. See T. M. Brown, *The work of G. Rietveld, architect* (Utrecht, 1958), 110.
11
Letter from Oud to Rietveld, 29 January 1935 (RSA). Published in Kuper and Van Zijl 1988, 154.
12
Postcard from Rietveld to Oud, 24 April 1927 (OUDJ, inv. no. B39). Published in E. Reinhartz-Tergau, *J. J. P. Oud. Architect/ Architekt. Meubelontwerpen en interieurs/Möbelentwürfe und Inneneinrichtungen* (Rotterdam, 1990), 56.
13
All information and quotes about the Buys affair are drawn from M. Kuper, 'Rietveld en de Gooise schoonheidscommissies', in Kuper and Van Zijl 1988, 71–93.
14
J. H. van den Broek, 'Vragen aan Rietveld', *De 8 en Opbouw* 4, no. 22 (1933), 191–2.
15
Letter from Oud to Rietveld, 11 March 1934 (OUDJ, inv. no. B72).
16
A. Staal, 'Vragen over de "vragen van Rietveld"', *De 8 en Opbouw* 5, no. 1 (1934), 8. See also Kuper and Van Zijl 1988, 83.
17
My thanks to Bertus Mulder for providing me with this information. Personal communication, 2009.
18
Anon., 'Nieuwe bioscoop in aanbouw' [*Utrechtsch Dagblad*, ? November 1936]. Newspaper cutting in the RSA.
19
Anon., 'Vreeburgbioscoop heropend' [*Utrechtsch Dagblad*, 11 December 1936]. Newspaper cutting in the RSA.
20
See note 16.
21
B. Mulder, *Vier x Rietveld* (Amersfoort, 1991), 10.
22
J. B. Bakema et al., *Rietveld-tentoonstelling. Bijdrage tot de vernieuwing der Bouwkunst* (Utrecht, 1958), 4.
23
See P. Timmer, *Metz & Co. De creatieve jaren* (Rotterdam, 1995).
24
There is a photograph of Rietveld taken in 1958 on the occasion of his retrospective exhibition in Utrecht. He is portrayed in one of the galleries, sitting on his Gothic Chair from c.1906 with a model of the Zig-Zag Chair in his hand, and in 1959, when the Stedelijk Museum asked four designers to devise a poster for its staging of this touring Rietveld exhibition, Jan Bons used the Zig-Zag Chair.
25
M. Kuper and I. van Zijl, *Gerrit Th. Rietveld 1888–1964. Het volledige werk* (Utrecht, 1992) 145; Eng. trans. as 'Chairs' in *Gerrit Th. Rietveld. The complete works, 1888–1964* (Utrecht, 1992), 145 (translation modified).
26
M. Kuper and M. van Schijndel, 'Der Sitzgeist', *jongHolland* 3, no. 2 (1987), 4–11.
27
H. and B. Rasch, *Der Stuhl* (Stuttgart, [1928]). Truus Schröder had this booklet in her library.
28
'And because back then I had many acquaintances who had no money, but nevertheless wanted to make a modern piece of furniture, I thought that with deal being cheap at the moment I'll buy so many little planks and screw them together like that.' G. Rietveld, Guided tour of his retrospective at the Stedelijk Museum Amsterdam, 6 March 1959 (Stedelijk Museum Amsterdam, sound archive of the audiovisual department, no. 1999-006, 41' 52").
29
J. de Meijer, 'Vakverrotting', *Bouwkundig Weekblad*, 56, no. 44 (1935), 463.
30
G. Rietveld, '"Vakverrotting"', *Bouwkundig Weekblad*, 56, no. 47 (1935), 489.

Chapter 7

1
A. Leeuw Marcar, *Willem Sandberg. Portret van een kunstenaar* (rev. edn, Amsterdam, 2004), 268. Originally published in 1982, this volume draws from interviews conducted by Paul Aletrino in 1970–1 and 1981, complemented by text fragments for a 1972 television documentary and extracts from the biography by A. Petersen and P. Brattinga, *Sandberg. Een documentaire/A documentary* (Amsterdam, 1975).
2
'I hereby command that the Commander of Utrecht abandon the pointless struggle and surrender the city,' the pamphlet states, 'to spare the city itself and its inhabitants the fate of Warsaw.' (Collection of the Centraal Museum, Utrecht, inv. no. 13097).
3
Kuper asserts that Rietveld drew inspiration from a house built by A. Eibink and J. A. Snellebrand on the other side of the Loosdrecht lakelands in 1921. However, this architectural style is fairly common throughout the area and is prescribed by the local building codes. See M. Kuper, 'Casa Verrijn Stuart, Breukelen/ Verrijn Stuart House, Breukelen', in *Gerrit Th. Rietveld Casas/ Houses, 2G Revista Internacional de arquitectura/International architectural review*, no. 39/40 (2006), 152.
4
J. P. Kloos, 'Zomerhuisje aan de Loosdrechtsche plassen, Architect

G. Rietveld', *De 8 en Opbouw* 12, no. 8 (1941), 103-5; J. B. Bakema, 'De vrije vorm', *De 8 en Opbouw* 12, no. 8 (1941), 105–7.
5
T. Idsinga and J. Schilt, *Architect W. van Tijen 1894–1974* (The Hague,1987), 80–2, 314–20 and 337–44.
6
These gatherings were subsequently banned by the Germans, but the 'young people's study weekend', to which Rietveld was also invited, still went ahead on 6 and 7 June 1942. See *ibid.*, 96–7. See also N. de Vreeze, *Woningbouw, inspiratie & ambitie. Kwalitatieve grondslagen van de sociale woningbouw in Nederland* (Almere, 1993), 245–8, and H. Ibelings, *20th century architecture in the Netherlands*, trans. M. O'Loughlin (Rotterdam, 1995), 83.
7
According to documents in the RSA the fine was 3,000 guilders, but a prison sentence could also be imposed. In the NAI archives there is a drawing of a fixed bench and a table intended for this project (RIET, inv. no. 583). In 1988 a few chairs that belonged to the contractor for this project, C. Moolenbeek, were auctioned in the 'Raoul' II sale at Christie's Amsterdam, 7 June 1988 (lot nos. 402 and 403). It is possible that these were prototypes for the Amsterdamsche Bank project that Moolenbeek had kept. Later on Rietveld published a drawing of the chairs in *Goed Wonen*. See G. Rietveld, 'Ontwerp van stoel Rietveld', *Goed Wonen* 3, no. 11 (1950), 162–3.
8
B. van Santen, 'Bredero's Bouwbedrijf, 1921–1947', in W. M. J. Bekkers et al., eds., *Bredero's Bouwbedrijf. Familiebedrijf – mondiaal bouwconcern – ontvlechting* (Amsterdam, 2005),15–58. The Germans may have ordered a building freeze in July 1941 but the continued production of concrete and certain construction activities were important for their own purposes.
9
The details here are drawn from B. Mulder, *Vier x Rietveld* (Amersfoort, 1991).
10
T. Spaans-van der Bijl, *Utrecht in verzet 1940–1945* (Utrecht, 1995), 384.
11
See G. Verrips, *Dwars, duivels en dromend. De geschiedenis van de CPN 1938–1991* (Amsterdam 1995), 258–9. *Jonkheer* W. J. H. B. Sandberg was one of the few who escaped lightly, possibly due to a combination of his being a minor aristocrat and his heroic deeds as a member of the Dutch resistance during the war. See A. Petersen and P. Brattinga, *Sandberg. Een documentaire/ A documentary* (Amsterdam, 1975), 20, 30–1 and 42.
12
E. Slothouber, 'Opdracht en Ontwerp/Commission and Design', in E. Slothouber, ed., *De Kunstnijverheidsscholen van Gerrit Rietveld/The art schools of Gerrit Rietveld* (Amsterdam, 1997), 19–20.
13
Petersen and Brattinga 1975, 49–50; F. Huygen, *Designkritiek in Nederland. Een essay* (Rotterdam, 1996), 28.
14
Leeuw Marcar 2004, 274–5.
15
Rietveld mentioned this in the interview with Bibeb: 'I worked on it now and again. I had come across such a beautiful tract of land at the time, a sloping site, overlooking the river and close by woodland … I never bought that piece of land, of course. Building was not allowed there, and such a house for me alone is also unjustified, though I do make them for my clients.' See Bibeb 1958. The sketch model saved from a fire was left in a sorry state.
16
See Z. Hemel and V. van Rossem, *Nagele. Een collectief ontwerp 1947–1957* (Amsterdam, 1984); M. Kuipers (ed.), *Toonbeelden van de wederopbouw. Architectuur, stedenbouw en landinrichting van herrijzend Nederland* (Zwolle, 2002), 55. See also B. Rebel, *Het Nieuwe Bouwen. Het functionalisme in Nederland 1918–1945* (Assen, 1983), 323. For an English-language history of Nagele, see W. Oosterbaan, *Nagele Revisited: A Modernistic Village in the Polder*, trans. P. Mason (Rotterdam, 2006).
17
'De 8' was founded in 1927 by several young architects, primarily from Amsterdam, who were vehemently opposed to the Expressionist architecture of the Amsterdam School.
18
Hemel and Van Rossem, 8.
19
A. van der Woud, *Het Nieuwe Bouwen Internationaal/ International. CIAM Volkshuisvesting/Housing Stedebouw/Town Planning* (Delft, 1983), 86. See also Rebel 1983, 321 n. 21.
20
Hemel and Van Rossem, 12–20 and 43.
21
Besides his medical practice, Chris Engels served as director and curator of the Curaçao Museum, which he co-founded in 1946. He also composed music and wrote poetry, and both he and his wife painted. The couple had become friends with Willem Sandberg when he visited the Caribbean. See C. Roodenburg-Schadd, *Expressie en ordening. Het verzamelbeleid van Willem Sandberg voor het Stedelijk Museum 1945–1962* (Rotterdam, 2004), 374 n. 81.
22
Letter from Rietveld to Truus Schröder, 12 October 1949. See I. van Zijl, ed., 'Truus Schröder: tentoonstelling per post' (Truus Schröder: exhibition by post) (Utrecht, 1998–9).
23
Rietveld donated half the fee to the disabled children and shared the remaining 5,000 guilders with Henk Nolte, who supervised the home's construction. See Kuper 1988, 128–30, and R. Gill, 'De sporen van Rietveld op Curaçao – 45 jaar later', in *De Horen en zijn echo. Verzameling essays [voor] Henny E. Coomans* (Amsterdam, 1994), 141–4, esp. 141.
24
G. Rietveld, Guided tour of his retrospective at the Stedelijk Museum Amsterdam, 6 March 1959 (Stedelijk Museum Amsterdam, sound archive of the audiovisual department, no. 1999-006, 41′ 52″).
25
G. Rietveld, 'Curaçao', *Katholieke Gezondheidszorg* 20, no. 5 (1951), 198–9.
26
See Mulder 1994, 82, where he quotes from a handwritten note by Rietveld (RSA, GR 84).
27
See D. Broekhuizen, *De Stijl toen/J. J. P. Oud nu* (Rotterdam, 2000), 285–91; Roodenburg-Schadd 2004, 493–8.
28
Sandberg's admiration for Rietveld was more in the vein of his adulation of the primitive and natural in the artist, such as the authenticity that he encountered in Haiti on his tour of the Americas, which fed his later interest in CoBrA and other Expressionist movements. See Roodenburg-Schadd 2004, 137.
29
Ibid., 495–6.
30
Ibid., 499.
31
Leeuw Marcar 2004, 268.

Chapter 8

1
[G. Rietveld], 'Korte rede van G. Th. Rietveld bij gelegenheid van het verlenen van het eredoctoraat in de technische wetenschappen door de senaat

van de Technische Hogeschool te Delft op 11-1-1964.' Published in F. Bless, *Rietveld. 1888–1964. Een biografie* (Amsterdam/Baarn, 1982), 246–8.

2
G. Bekaert, 'G. T. Rietveld leeft voort', *Streven* 17, no. 11/12 (1964), 1104.

3
This text is inscribed on the commemorative plaque at the reconstructed pavilion.

4
The cost of reconstruction was estimated at 40,000 to 50,000 guilders (approx. $11,000–13,700 or £4,000–4,900). The appeal to all Dutch architects was published in the *Bouwkundig Weekblad* 82, no. 7 (1964), 7. B. W. A. den Bakker, director of the Eerste Nederlandse Coöperatieve Kunstmestfabriek (First Dutch Cooperative Fertilizer Factory), proposed rebuilding it in Vlaardingen.

5
J. Clarijs, *'t Spectrum. Moderne meubelvormgeving en naoorlogse idealisme* (Rotterdam, 2002), 9. In 1898 the author and psychiatrist Frederik van Eeden founded the Walden colony, the most famous example of Henry David Thoreau's influence in the Netherlands.

6
Ibid., 24.

7
E. van Onna and N. van Onna, *Gerrit Rietveld en Mien Ruys in Bergeijk* (Veldhoven, 2008), 143. Director P. Blijenburg informed Boterenbrood that Oud had advised him to engage Rietveld. See
H. Boterenbrood, *Weverij de Ploeg 1923–1957* (Rotterdam, 1989), 28.

8
A circular extension was added to the Visser House in 1968 and another small expansion was added in 1974, both designed by Aldo van Eyck.

9
H. Boterenbrood 1989, 28.

10
Onna and Onna 2008, 81.

11
M. Kuipers, ed., *Toonbeelden van de wederopbouw. Architectuur, stedenbouw en landinrichting van herrijzend Nederland* (Zwolle, 2002), 106–7.

12
The textile factory was recently closed down and another use for the building is being sought.

13
M. Ruys, J. Ruys and Th. Ruys, *Het vaste plantenboek* (Amsterdam, 1950; 3rd repr. 1953), *passim.* See also Onna and Onna 2008, 81–2.

14
Onna and Onna 2008, 129.

15
E. Slothouber, ed., *De Kunstnijverheidsscholen van Gerrit Rietveld/The art schools of Gerrit Rietveld* (Amsterdam, 1997). The commission for the academy in Amsterdam was granted first but owing to these circumstances it was completed later than the academy in Arnhem.

16
My thanks to Bertus Mulder for sharing this information with me in 2009. The architect Bertus Mulder (b. 1929) worked for Rietveld for a while and knew him well. He restored the Schröder House and other buildings by Rietveld and has published many articles and books about Rietveld and his work.

17
On the pedagogical changes introduced by Mart Stam at the IvKNO, see C. Boot, 'Mart Stam. Kunstnijverheidsonderwijs als aanzet voor een menselijke omgeving. Dessau-Amsterdam', *Wonen/TABK*, 11 June 1982, 10–21.

18
G. Rietveld, 'De nieuwe school', *De Zomerkrant*, Instituut voor Kunstnijverheidsonderwijs, 1955, 3–4. This article is also published in J. van Brummelen and E. Slothouber, *De Rietveld academie. Een akademiegebouw als model* (Hilversum, 1984), 8.

19
E. Slothouber, 'Opdracht en ontwerp/Commission and design', in E. Slothouber, ed., *De Kunstnijverheidsscholen van Gerrit Rietveld/The art schools of Gerrit Rietveld* (Amsterdam, 1997), 42 (translation modified).

20
Ibid., 43 (translation modified).

21
Ibid., 64.

22
This came to light during a conversation about these buildings with H.-J. Henket and B. Mulder in March 2009.

23
Slothouber, 59.

24
In 2009 there were plans afoot to transfer the Rietveld Academy to another building, because Rietveld's creation no longer satisfied modern requirements, but it sparked such vehement protests, from current and former students and teachers as well as from culture-lovers, that the plan was shelved.

25
Rietveld 1953. See also 'Rational design', in M. Kuper and I. van Zijl, *Gerrit Th. Rietveld. The complete works, 1888–1964* (Utrecht, 1992), 28–31.

26
See note 1.

27
The Kingdom of the Netherlands, the official commissioner, had initially awarded the contract to M. F. Duintjer, but on the insistence of the Van Gogh Foundation, which included Vincent Willem van Gogh (1890–1978), son of Vincent's brother, Theo, and Willem Sandberg among its board members, the commission was withdrawn and awarded to Rietveld. Duintjer's comment was that for Rietveld he was prepared to step aside. See M. van Bijleveld et al., *M. F. Duintjer. Strak, helder, open – architectuur als drager van een nieuwe samenleving 1908–1983* (Rotterdam, 2007), 158.

Chapter 9

1
G. Rietveld, [no title], *De Stijl* 7, nos. 79/84 (1927), 46.

2
Manuscript (RSA, GR 84). Published in B. Mulder, *Gerrit Thomas Rietveld. Schets can zijn leven, denken, werken* (Nijmegen, 1994), 82.

3
G. Rietveld, 'Het interieur', published in two parts in *Bouwkundig Weekblad* 66, no. 25 (1948), 188–201, and no. 26 (1948), 206–9, esp. 206 (quote). Based on a lecture he gave in 1947, these texts are also published in an adapted form as 'Interiors', in M. Kuper and I. van Zijl, *Gerrit Th. Rietveld. The complete works, 1888–1964* (Utrecht, 1992), 40–7, esp. 45 (quote, translation modified).

4
M. Kuper, 'Gerrit Rietveld', in C. Blotkamp, ed., *De vervolgjaren van De Stijl 1922–1932* (Amsterdam/Antwerp, 1996), 207.

5
G. Oorthuys, 'Een denkbeeldig geraamte van lijnen/An imaginary skeleton of lines', in E. Slothouber, ed., *De Kunstnijverheidsscholen van Gerrit Rietveld/The art schools of Gerrit Rietveld* (Amsterdam, 1997), 105–16. Truus and Han Schröder also mention this as an important feature of Rietveld's designs.

6
G. Rietveld, 'Tweede min of meer herhaalde lezing tijdens de architectuur-tentoonstelling in het Centraal Museum te Utrecht, 1958'. Also published in F. Bless, *Rietveld. 1888–1964. Een biografie* (Amsterdam/Baarn 1982), 220–39, esp. 223–4.

7
G. Rietveld, 'In Memoriam architect P. J. Klaarhamer', *Bouwkundig Weekblad* 72, no. 13/14 (1954), 101.

8
G. Rietveld, Lecture for the Collaborating Institutes for Art Education (Samenwerkende Instituten voor Kunstonderwijs) in Amsterdam in 1958. Published as Gerrit Thomas Rietveld,

'Architectuur', *De Nieuwe Stem* 14, no. 8/9 (1959), 560–72. See also 'Architecture' in Kuper and Van Zijl 1992, 51–5.

9
During his research for the house's restoration, Bertus Mulder did not discover any module in the house's design or its eventual execution. Personal communication, October 2009.

10
G. Rietveld, 'Rationele vormgeving. Lezing gehouden bij gelegenheid van de leerjaarbeëindiging der Haagsche Academie en MTS te Den Haag, mei 1953'; Eng. trans. as 'Rational design', in Kuper and Van Zijl 1992, 31 (translation modified).Kuper

11
G. Rietveld, 'Korte rede van G. Th. Rietveld bij gelegenheid van het verlenen van het eredoctoraat in de technische wetenschappen door de senaat van de Technische Hogeschool te Delft op 11-1-1964', in Bless 1982, 248.

12
For example, on completing his training as a furniture designer at the Bauhaus, Marcel Breuer took a job at an architecture firm in Paris. See C. Wilk, *Marcel Breuer. Furniture and interiors* (New York, 1981), 37.

13
F. den Oudsten, Interview with Truus Schröder, 1982 (RSA). Published in edited form as L. Büller and F. den Oudsten, 'Interview with Truus Schröder', in P. Overy et al., *The Rietveld Schröder House* (Houten, 1988).

14
For a description of the restoration see the first-hand account by architect B. Mulder, 'The restoration of the Rietveld Schröder House', in P. Overy et al., *The Rietveld Schröder House* (Houten, 1998), 104–23. There is a more recent and more comprehensive account in Dutch in I. van Zijl and B. Mulder, *Het Rietveld Schröderhuis* (Utrecht, 2009), 68–93.

15
Rietveld's unrealized design for the Palace of the League of Nations (1927) was presumably intended as another concrete structure. In the RSA there is a typed description in French that is very probably about this design, but it is too brief to envisage how it might have actually looked.

16
See I. van Zijl, 'De Mondial in Rietvelds oeuvre/The Mondial in Rietveld's oeuvre', in J. Venneman and M. de Kroon, eds., *Mondial: Gispen & Gerrit Th. Rietveld* (Culemborg, 2006), 26–36.

17
M. Kuper, 'Rietveld at work: recollections of colleagues, pupils and clients', in Kaya Oku, *Rietveld: the architecture of Gerrit Th. Rietveld* (Tokyo, 2009), 225.

18
G. Rietveld, 'Nieuwe zakelijkheid in de Nederlandse architectuur', *De Vrije Bladen* 9, no. 7 (1932). Also published as 'New Functionalism in Dutch architecture', in M. Kuper and I. van Zijl, *Gerrit Th. Rietveld. The complete works, 1888–1964* (Utrecht, 1992), 32–9.

19
See G. Stahl, trans. and intro., *On vision and colors by Arthur Schopenhauer and color sphere by Philipp Otto Runge* (New York, 2010), *passim*.

20
E. Hoek, 'Piet Mondrian', in C. Blotkamp et al., *De Stijl: the formative years, 1917–1922*, trans. C. I. and A. L. Loeb (Cambridge, MA/London, 1986), 67–9, and C. Hilhorst, 'Bart van der Leck' in *idem*, 160–1.

21
Bless 1982, 231.

22
L. Büller and F. den Oudsten, 'Interview with Truus Schröder', in Overy 1988, p. 73.

23
B. Mulder, *Gerrit Thomas Rietveld. Schets can zijn leven, denken, werken* (Nijmegen, 1994), 27.

24
Personal communication, September 2009. See also T. Idsinga and J. Schilt, *Architect W. van Tijen 1894–1974* (The Hague, 1987).

Chapter 10

1
The final sentence of Rietveld's 'Tweede min of meer herhaalde lezing tijdens de architectuur tentoonstelling in het Centraal Museum', 1958. Published in F. Bless, *Rietveld, 1888–1964. Een biografie* (Amsterdam, 1982), 220–39.

2
The members of the working committee were J. B. Bakema, R. Blijstra, T. M. Brown, J. G. van Gelder, M. Elisabeth Houtzager, S. H. Levie, G. Th. Rietveld, T. Schröder-Schräder and H. Schröder. See J. B. Bakema, *Rietveld-tentoonstelling. Bijdrage tot de vernieuwing der bouwkunst* (Utrecht, 1958). Mr S. H. Levie confirms that the exhibition was planned together with Rietveld, who busied himself with every aspect. Personal communication, November 2009.

3
A more balanced and wider-ranging perspective on Rietveld's oeuvre is to be found in scholarly publications by Marijke Kuper, Paul Overy, Peter Vöge and others.

4
Much of the literature about De Stijl devotes ample attention to the passive and active image-building and perception of the movement. See, for example, M. White, *De Stijl and Dutch Modernism* (Manchester and New York, 2003), 136–64; on Oud, see D. Broekhuizen, *De Stijl toen/J. J. P. Oud nu* (Rotterdam, 2000), and on Theo van Doesburg, see W. van Moorsel, *Nelly van Doesburg 1899–1975* (Nijmegen, 2000).

5
G. Rietveld, Guided tour of his retrospective at the Stedelijk Museum Amsterdam, 6 March 1959 (Stedelijk Museum Amsterdam, sound archive of the audiovisual department, no. 1999-006, 41′ 52″).

6
L. Büller and F. den Oudsten, 'Interview with Truus Schröder', in P. Overy et al., *The Rietveld Schröder House* (Houten, 1988), 64.

7
The explanatory text for the baby's high-chair is signed 'G. Rietveld 1919', while the note accompanying the slat armchair was a modified quote by Van Doesburg taken from a letter from Rietveld. See Th. v[an] D[oesburg], 'Aanteekeningen bij een leunstoel van Rietveld', *De Stijl* 2, no. 11 (1919), appendix XXII; Eng. trans. in T. M. Brown, *The work of G. Rietveld, architect* (Utrecht, 1958), 21. The definition of 'true creation' (*ware schepping*) is to be found in *De Stijl* 7, nos. 79–84 (1927), 46.

8
Th. v[an] D[oesburg], 'Schilderkunst van Giorgio de Chirico en een stoel van Rietveld', *De Stijl* 3, no. 5 (1920), 46.

9
C. Blotkamp and C. Hilhorst, 'De dissidente kunstenaars: Bart van der Leck, Vilmos Huszár en Georges van Tongerloo', in C. Blotkamp, ed., *De vervolgjaren van De Stijl 1922–1932* (Amsterdam/Antwerp, 1996), 311–62, esp. 313–14. In this chapter the authors state that the difference in age and artistic development between Rietveld and Van der Leck was so great when they first met at Klaarhamer's studio that 'it is doubtful whether there was a fruitful exchange of ideas'. However, it is not improbable that they met again later, when Van der Leck was exhibiting work in Utrecht, for example. There was certainly contact between them in the years that Van der Leck's work was displayed in the 'gallery window' of the studio at the Schröder House.

10
M. Kuper, [untitled], in Marc Visser and Sabine Labesque, *Het beeld van Rietveld* (Rotterdam, 1993), 12–18, esp. 13 (quote).

It is impossible to demonstrate a direct link between Mondrian's paintings from 1920 to 1923 with their red, yellow, blue and white planes framed by black lines and the renowned red-blue version of the slat armchair, as Sandberg hypothesized. See A. Leeuw Marcar, *Willem Sandberg. Portret van een kunstenaar* (1982; rev. edn, Amsterdam, 2004), 268.

11
Th. van Doesburg, 'Der Wille zum Stil', *De Stijl* 5, no. 2 (1922), 23–32.

12
Kuper also points out Rietveld's influence on others and specifically mentions Breuer's furniture from 1922–3 and 1925. See Kuper 1996, 209.

13
A. Barr, *Cubism and abstract art* (1936; repr. New York, 1974), 144. Barr discerns the influence of Georges Vantongerloo's sculptures in the Schröder House and sees the furniture in the house as evidence that the De Stijl architects drew inspiration from paintings by Van Doesburg.

14
H.-R. Hitchcock, *Architecture: nineteenth and twentieth centuries* (1958; 10th repr., Kingsport, Tennessee, 1985), 492.

15
Letter from Rietveld to Oud, 27 April 1931 (OUDJ, inv. no. B66). Quoted in M. Kuper, 'Gerrit Rietveld' in C. Blotkamp, ed., *De vervolgjaren van De Stijl 1922–1932* (Amsterdam/Antwerp 1996), 197.

16
For example, on 29 May 1947 Rietveld sent a letter to Sigfried Giedion with his responses to the sixth CIAM congress. In the opening lines he wrote, 'The proposal of the 8 looks like a form of tax; is useful for rebuilding of the Netherlands, but I cannot see it as a wide subject of the congress. Now I am trying to answer the questions myself…I am convinced that some questions have to be answered with more attention. I have done my best.' (GTA ETH Zürich, Giedion Archive, inv. no. 43-K-1947-05-29).

17
A. van Eyck, 'De bal kaatst terug', *Forum* 13, no. 3 (1958), 104–11, esp. 104 (quote).

18
G. Rietveld, 'Het interieur', *Bouwkundig Weekblad* 60, nos. 25 and 26 (1948), 188–201 and 206–9. The text is based on a lecture for students at the Academie voor Beeldende Kunsten (Academy of Fine Arts) in Rotterdam, in March 1948. The typescript is also published as 'Interiors', in M. Kuper and I. van Zijl, *Gerrit Th. Rietveld. The complete works, 1888–1964* (Utrecht, 1992), 40–7, esp. 40 (quote, translation modified).

19
G. Rietveld, 'Rationele vormgeving', lecture on the occasion of the close of the academic year at the Secondary Technical School for Architecture and Academy of Fine Arts in The Hague, May 1953. Also published as 'Rational design', in Kuper and Van Zijl (Utrecht, 1992), 28–31, esp. 29 (quote).

20
The anecdote is repeated often, but is formulated most eloquently in F. Huygen, *Martin Visser. Oeuvreprijs 1998 vormgeving/ Oeuvre Award 1998: Design* (Amsterdam, n.d.).

21
A. van Eyck, 'De bal kaatst terug', *Forum* 13, no. 3 (1958), 104–11, esp. 107.

22
Nevertheless, Brown devotes so many pages to Van Doesburg's theories and differences with the work of Mondrian that the relationship between Rietveld's work and De Stijl inevitably draws the attention once again. My thanks to Rob Dettingmeijer for highlighting this discrepancy. See Brown 1958, *passim*.

23
Brown 1958, 147–9.

24
Mácel calls this the De Stijl aesthetic. See O. Mácel, 'Marcel Breuer – "inventor of bent tubular steel furniture"', in A. von Vegesack and M. Remmele, eds, *Marcel Breuer: design and architecture* (Weil am Rhein, 2003), 52–115, esp. 56.

25
M. Droste, *Bauhaus 1919–1933*, Dutch trans. (Groningen, 1990), 82. [German orig., *Bauhaus 1919–1933* (Cologne, 1990)]. In the note she cites M. Breuer, 'Die Möbelabteilung des Staatliches Bauhauses in Weimar', *Fachblat für Holzarbeiter*, no. 20 (1925), 18.

26
M. Breuer, 'Metallmöbel und moderne Räumlichkeit', *Das neue Frankfurt* 2, no. 1 (1928), 11. See also C. Wilk, 'Sitting on air', in C. Wilk, ed., *Modernism: designing a new world, 1914–1939* (London, 2006), 229.

27
A. Von Vegesack and M. Remmele 2003, 75. Breuer frequently employed such horizontal elements in his interiors.

28
This nest of three side tables is included in Kuper and Van Zijl (Utrecht, 1992), but was never previously presented or published as a design by Rietveld.

29
Von Vegesack and Remmele (Weil am Rhein, 2003), 66.

30
G. Rietveld, 'Nieuwe zakelijkheid in de Nederlandse architectuur', *De Vrije Bladen* 9, no. 7 (1932). Also published as 'New Functionalism in Dutch Architecture', in M. Kuper and I. van Zijl, *Gerrit Th. Rietveld. The complete works, 1888–1964* (Utrecht, 1992), 32–9.

31
NAi, Van Ravesteyn Archive (RAVE), inv. no. 152.

32
In this regard Le Corbusier's development was stimulated by the De Stijl exhibition in Paris in 1923. See J. de Heer, *The architectonic colour. Polychromy in the Purist architecture of Le Corbusier*, trans. G. Hall (Rotterdam, 2009), 71–86.

33
See T. Benton, 'Modernism and nature', in Wilk 2006, 310–39.

34
Brown describes the Garage with Chauffeur's Apartment as 'decades ahead of its time'. The design reminds him of later work by Mies van der Rohe, such as the IIT campus buildings in Chicago (1942–3). He also draws a comparison with Gropius's house for the Weissenhofsiedlung: 'The basic difference between the two solutions is that, where Gropius stopped after the satisfaction of the engineering requirements, Rietveld carried the engineering of the garage into a visual expression which is still alive today.' See Brown 1958, 88–9.

35
H. Ibelings, 'La fama de Rietveld/ Rietveld's fame', in 'Gerrit Th. Rietveld. Casas/Houses', *2G Revista Internacional de arquitectura / International architectural review*, no. 39/40 (2006), 30–3.

36
G. Rietveld 1958, 239. See note 1.

General notes

Dates and other information about Rietveld and his work are based on M. Kuper and I. van Zijl, *Gerrit Th. Rietveld 1888-1964: The Complete Works* (Utrecht, 1992)

Dates and other information about the Schröder House are based on the following sources: F. den Oudsten and L. Büller's interviews with Truus Schröder, 1982, which are kept as tapes at the RSA; P. Overy, *The Schröder House*, (Houten, 1988); M. Kuper, 'Gerrit Rietveld', in: C. Blotkamp (ed.), *De vervolgjaren van De Stijl 1922–1932*, (Amsterdam/Antwerp, 1996), 195–240; I. van Zijl and B. Mulder, *The Rietveld Schröder House* (Utrecht, 2009)

Chronology

1888
24 June: birth of Gerrit Rietveld, Ooftstraat 14, Utrecht

1900
Leaves primary school and goes to work with his father in the furniture workshop at Poortstraat 98, Utrecht

1904–8
Takes an evening course at the art and industry educational society of the Utrecht Museum of Arts and Crafts; during the day Rietveld works at the goldsmith workshop of the jeweller C. J. A. Begeer

1908
Upright armchair

1906
Takes an evening course with the architect P. J.C. Klaarhamer, Heerenstraat 19, Utrecht

1911
28 September: marries Vrouwgien Hadders (born Assen, 1883)

1917
1 May: moves to Adriaen van Ostadelaan 25 (later 93), Utrecht, where he would later start his furniture workshop

1918
Convertible child's chair in green and red

Unpainted Slat Armchair

1919
First meets Theo van Doesburg and J. J. P. Oud

1921

Room for Truus Schröder-Schräder, Biltstraat 135, Utrecht

1922

Surgery for Dr A. M. Hartog, Emmaweg 1, Maarssen

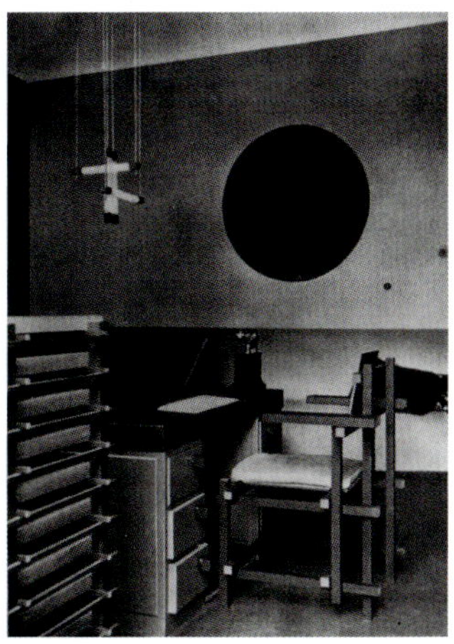

1921–3

Gold- and Silversmiths Company shopfront and interior, Kalverstraat 107, Amsterdam

1923

'Colour-Space-Composition', Berlin

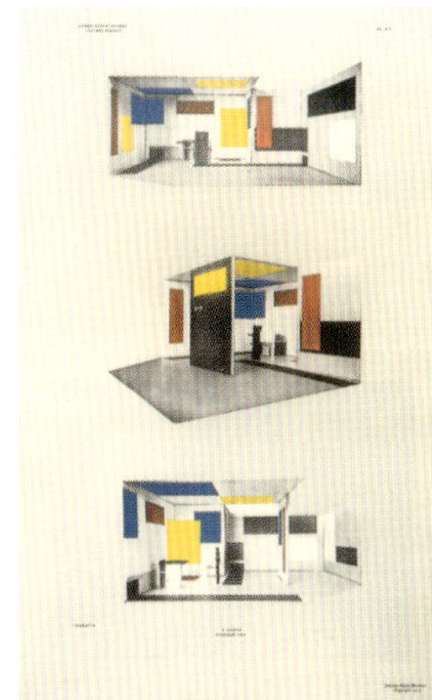

First meets El Lissitzky, Bruno Taut (who is giving a lecture in Utrecht) and Kurt Schwitters (who comes to Utrecht on a Dada tour)

1924

E. Wessels and Son leatherware shopfront, Oudkerkhof 15, Utrecht

Rietveld Schröder House, Prins Hendriklaan 50, Utrecht

5 May: moves to Bachstraat 11, Utrecht

1925

Radio cabinet

Rental property for Marie Lommen, Klein Persijnlaan 39, Wassenaar

Established as architect in the Rietveld Schröder House, Prins Hendriklaan 50, Utrecht

1926

Interior for An and Rein Harrenstein-Schräder, Weteringschans 141, Amsterdam

1925–7

Armchair for A.M. Hertog

Birza chair

Design for a 'standard home'

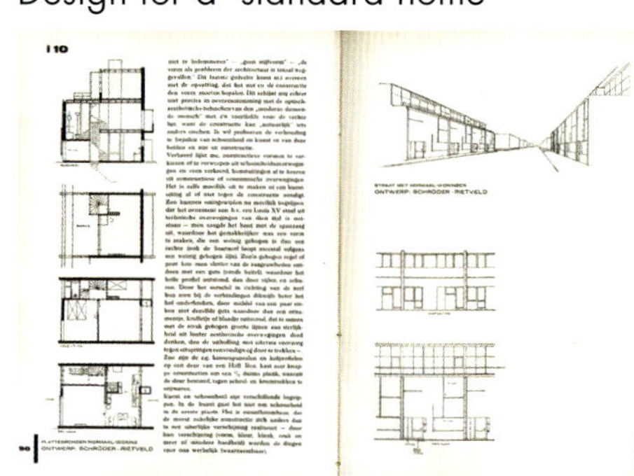

Tube framed chair

Renovation, Van der Vuurst de Vries house, Julianalaan 10, Utrecht

1927–8

Garage with Chauffeur's Apartment, Waldeck Pyrmontkade 20, Utrecht

1928

Zaudy shop, Brückstrasse, Wesel, Germany

Design for twenty-three small dwellings, Utrecht

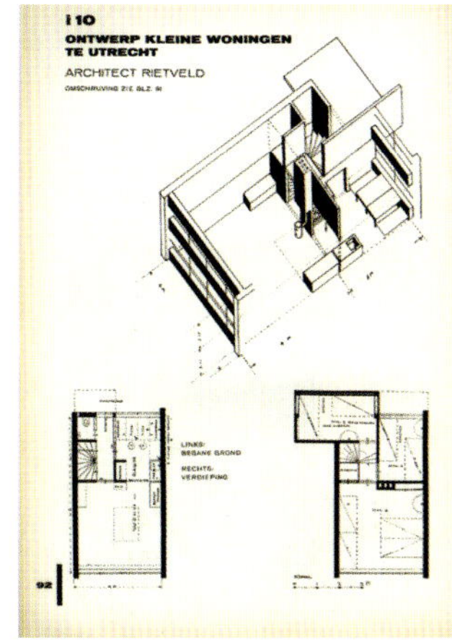

Takes part in the preliminary congress for the Congrès Internationaux d'Architecture Moderne (CIAM) in La Sarraz (Switzerland). Other Dutch representatives include H. P. Berlage and Mart Stam

1929

Design for a movable house core

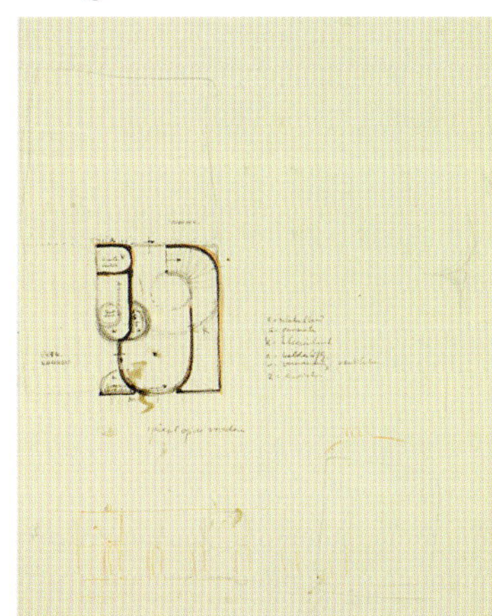

With Mart Stam, Dutch delegate to the CIAM conference *Die Wohnung für das Existenzminimum* (The Minimum Dwelling), Frankfurt am Main

1927–30

Serves as a member of the board of the Utrecht branch of the Dutch Film League

1930
Design of seven houses, Erasmuslaan, Utrecht

1931
Row of four houses, Erasmuslaan 5–11, Utrecht

Model interior, Erasmuslaan 9, Utrecht

1929–32
Row of four houses for the Wiener Werkbundsiedlung, Woinovichgasse 14–20, Vienna

1931–2
Klep House, Montenspark 8, Breda

1932
Travels to Vienna on the occasion of the opening of the Wiener Werkbundsiedlung

1932–3
Zig-Zag Chair

1933
The Rietveld architectural office moves to Oudegracht 55, Utrecht

1933–4
Székely House, Johannes Verhulstweg 70, Santpoort

1934
Crate furniture

1930–5
Four houses, Prins Hendriklaan 64, Erasmuslaan 1–3, Utrecht

1934–5
Hillebrand House, Van Soutelandelaan 42, The Hague

1934–6
Renovation and addition of two apartments, Vreeburg Cinema, Vredenburg 8, Utrecht

1936–7
Upholstered easychair

1937
Dodecagonal wooden summerhouses

Moves to Vredenburg 8 bis, Utrecht, but is registered at the address of the architectural office: Oudegracht 55, Utrecht.

1937–8
Conversion of a villa to fifteen flats for women and a caretaker's flat, Ekawo, Kenaupark 4, Haarlem

1940–1
Verrijn Stuart Summerhouse, Breukelen St Pieters

1941
Design for a worker's residential district (including designs for various dwellings), Tolsteeg, Laan van Soestbergen, Utrecht

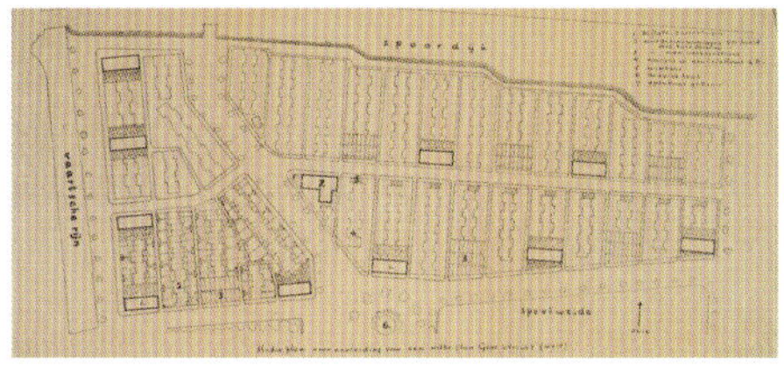

1942
Aluminium prototype chair

1943–4
Design for assembly-system houses, Gorinchem

1946
House for an Architect

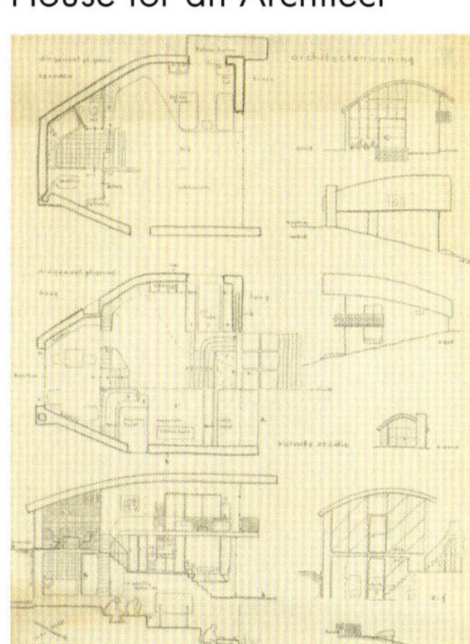

20 March: officially registers at the address Vredenburg 8 bis, Utrecht

1943–8
Plan for the Zuidwijk residential district (with houses, flats above shops, and a nursery school), Zuidwijk, Rotterdam

c.1948
Urban development plan, Nagele, Northeast Polder

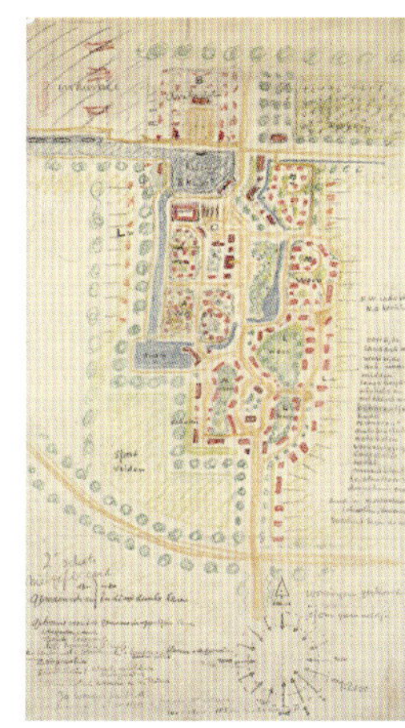

1946–9
Smit House, Puntweg 8, Kinderdijk

1949
Travels to Chicago, New York and Surinam, Curaçao

1951

Exhibition design, 'De Stijl 1917–1928', Stedelijk Museum, Amsterdam

1949–52

Home for Handicapped Children, Mgr. P. I. Verriet Institute, Salsbachweg 20, Willemstad, Curaçao

1952

Travels to Mexico

1953–4

Netherlands Pavilion, Venice Biennale

1954

Appointed Officer of the Orde van Oranje Nassau

1944–55

Teacher of architectural design at the Advanced Architecture Institute (from 1946: Academy of Architecture) in Amsterdam.

1952–55

Slegers House, Den Bruyl 35, Velp

1955

Sonsbeek Pavilion, Arnhem

1953–6

Juliana Hall and entrance to the Royal Trade Fair, Graadt van Roggenweg, Utrecht

1954–7
Housing, Hoograven, Utrecht

1957
Mondial Chair

31 March: death of Vrouwgien Rietveld-Hadders

1956–8
Van Daalen House, Fazantlaan 14, Bergeijk

De Ploeg mill, Riethovensedijk 20, Bergeijk

1957–8
Press Room, UNESCO building, Paris

Design of the 'ideal flat', Dutch pavilion for the World Expo, Brussels

Van den Doel House, Monnickendammerrijweg 31c, Ilpendam

1958
10 May – 10 August: retrospective exhibition 'Rietveld: Contribution to the renewal of architecture', Centraal Museum, Utrecht

Poster for the exhibition

1958–9
De Zonnehof Museum, Zonnehof 8, Amersfoort

1959–60
Van Dantzig House, Harddraverslaan 60, Santpoort

1961
Founding of the Rietveld, Van Dillen and Van Tricht Partnership

15 November: registers at the address of the Rietveld Schröder House, Prins Hendriklaan 50, Utrecht

1958–63
Academy of Art, Onderlangs 9, Arnhem

1961–3
Van Slobbe House, Zandweg 122, Heerlen

1963
5 July: receives Silver City Medal from the City of Utrecht with the inscription: 'Zijn bouwen is bewaren en scheppen tevens' (His architecture is both conservation and creation)

1956–67
Fine Arts Academy, Gerrit Rietveld Academy, Fred. Roeskestraat 96, Amsterdam

1958–67
Auditorium for a cemetery, Vijfhuizerweg, Haarlemmermeer

1964
Receives an honorary doctorate from Delft Technical College

Made an honorary member of the Association of Dutch Architects

25 June: Rietveld dies in the Rietveld Schröder House in Utrecht

1963–73
Vincent van Gogh Museum, Paulus Potterstraat 7, Amsterdam

Bibliography

The sections on Gerrit Rietveld and the Rietveld Schröder House are a good starting point for information; the 'Consulted works' section gives additional sources on both Rietveld and the context in which he worked.

Gerrit Rietveld

Baroni, D., *I mobili di Gerrit Thomas Rietveld* (Milan, 1977). Published in English as: *Gerrit Thomas Rietveld Furniture* (London, 1978) and *The furniture of Gerrit Thomas Rietveld* (New York, 1978)

Blotkamp, C. (ed.), *De beginjaren van De Stijl 1917–1922* (Utrecht, 1982). Published in English as: *De Stijl: the formative years* (Cambridge/London, 1982)

Blotkamp, C. (ed.), *De vervolgjaren van De Stijl 1922–1932* (Amsterdam/Antwerp, 1996)

Brown, Th. M., *The Work of G. Th. Rietveld, architect* (Utrecht/Cambridge, 1958)

Brown, Th. M., 'Mondrian and Rietveld: The divining rod and the compass', in *Nederlands Kunsthistorisch Jaarboek* 19 (1968), 205–14

Bless, F., *Gerrit Thomas Rietveld 1888–1964. Een biografie* (Amsterdam, 1982)

Docter, R. (ed.), *De mooiste ruimte die ik ken. Het Nederlandse Biënnale–paviljoen van Gerrit Rietveld in Venetië/The Most Beautiful Space I Know: The Netherlands Biennale Pavilion in Venice by Gerrit Rietveld/Lo spazio più bello che io conosca: Il padiglione creato da Gerrit Rietveld per la Biennale di Venezia* (Rotterdam, 1995)

Kuper, M., [untitled], in Visser and Labesque 1993, 12–18

Kuper, M. 'Gerrit Rietveld', in C. Blotkamp 1996, 195–240

Kuper, M., *Rietveld als meubelmaker. Wonen met experimenten 1900–1924* (Utrecht, 1983)

Kuper, M., 'Rietveld and de Gooise schoonheidscommissies', in Kuper and van Zijl, 1988, 71–93

Kuper, M. 'Rietveld at Work: Recollections of Colleagues, Pupils and Clients' in Oku 2009, 220–7

Kuper, M. and I. van Zijl, *Gerrit Th. Rietveld. Het volledige werk* (Utrecht, 1992). Published in English as: *Gerrit Th. Rietveld: The Complete Works* (Utrecht, 1992) and in French as: *Gerrit Th. Rietveld: L'oeuvre complet* (Utrecht, 1992)

Kuper, M. and I. van Zijl, *Rietveld Schröder Archief* (Utrecht, 1988)

Kuper, M., W. Quist and H. Ibelings, 'Gerrit Th. Rietveld. Casas/Houses', in *2G Revista Internacional de arquitectura/International Architectural Review* (2006), no. 39/40

Mulder, B., *Gerrit Thomas Rietveld. Schets van zijn leven, denken and werken* (Nijmegen, 1994)

Oku, K., *The Architecture of Gerrit Th. Rietveld* (Tokyo, 2009)

Onna, E. van and N. van Onna, *Gerrit Rietveld Mien Ruys in Bergeijk* (Veldhoven, 2008)

Rodijk, G. H., *De huizen van Rietveld* (Zwolle, 1991)

Slothouber, E. (ed.), *De Kunstnijverheidsscholen van Gerrit Rietveld/The Art Schools of Gerrit Rietveld* (Amsterdam, 1997)

Troy, N., *The De Stijl Environment* (Cambridge, 1983)

Vöge, P., *The Complete Rietveld Furniture* (Rotterdam, 1992)

Zijl, I. van, *Rietveld in Utrecht* (Utrecht, 2001)

Rietveld Schröder House

Anon, 'Schröder Huis', in *Kwadraatblad* (promotional publication of the de Jong & Co printing company) (Hilversum, 1963)

Mulder, B. and G. J. de Rook (eds.), *Rietveld Schröder huis 1925–1975* (Utrecht/Antwerp, 1975)

B. Mulder and I. van Zijl, *Rietveld Schröderhuis* (Bussum, 1997)

Overy, P. et al., *Het Rietveld Schröder Huis* (Houten, 1988)

Zijl, I. van, *60 + 20 = de geschiedenis van het Rietveld Schröderhuis* (Utrecht, 2005)

Zijl, I. van and B. Mulder, *Het Rietveld Schröderhuis* (Utrecht, 2009)

Consulted works

Writings by Gerrit Rietveld

[untitled], in *De Stijl* 7 (1927) 79/84, 46

'Aanteekening bij kinderstoel', in *De Stijl* 2 (1919) 9, appendix XVIII

'Architectuur', in *De Nieuwe Stem* 14 (1959) 8/9, 560–72

'Curaçao', in *Katholieke Gezondheidszorg* 20 (1951) 5, 198–9

'De nieuwe school', in *de zomerkrant*, Instituut voor Kunstnijverheidsonderwijs (1955), 3 and 4

'De stoel', in *De Werkende Vrouw*, 1 (1930) 9, 244

'Een nieuwe plattegrond voor een volkswoning', in *Bouwkundig Weekblad* 62 (1941) 27, 226–8

'Een nieuwe volkswoning', in *De 8 and Opbouw* 12 (1941) 9, 122–7

'Het interieur', in *Bouwkundig*

Weekblad 66 (1948) 25 and 26, 188–201 and 206–209

'In Memoriam architect P. J. Klaarhamer', in *Bouwkundig Weekblad* 72 (1954) 13/14, 101

'Inzicht', in *i 10* 12 (1928) 17/18, 89–90

'Korte rede van G. Th. Rietveld bij gelegenheid van het erlenen van het eredoctoraat in de technische wetenschappen door de senaat van de Technische Hogeschool te Delft', speech given on 11 January 1964 in Delft, in: Bless 1982, 246–8

'Nieuwe zakelijkheid in de Nederlandse architectuur', in *De Vrije Bladen* 9 (1932)

'Over architect Oud', in *Forum* 6 (1951) 5/6, 132–4

'Over de vorm van het meubel', in *De 8 and Opbouw* 8 (1937) 21, 198–9

'Tweede min of meer herhaalde lezing tijdens de architectuur-tentoonstelling in het Centraal Museum te Utrecht', speech given in 1958. In: Bless 1982, 220–39, esp. 223–4

'"Vakverrotting"', in *Bouwkundig Weekblad* 56 (1935) 47, 489.

'Verbouwing van den schouwburg "Kunstmin te Dordrecht"', in *De 8 and Opbouw* 12 (1941) 5, 61–5

Books

Tentoonstelling van Architectuur, Schilderkunst en Beeldhouwkunst (Amsterdam, 1928)

Adelaar, D. et al., Willem van Leusden, *Essays over een verhard romanticus* (Utrecht, 1990)

Bakema, J. B. et al., *Rietveld-tentoonstelling. Bijdrage tot de vernieuwing der Bouwkunst* (Utrecht, 1958)

Barr, A., *Cubism and Abstract Art* (New York 1936) (reprint: New York, 1974)

Bekkers, W. M. J. et al. (eds.), *Bredero's Bouwbedrijf. Familiebedrijf – mondiaal bouwconcern – ontvlechting* (Amsterdam, 2005)

Berlage, H. P., *Gedanken über Stil in der Baukunst* (Leipzig, 1905)

Bijleveld, M. van et al., *M. F. Duintjer. Strak, helder, open – architectuur als drager van een nieuwe samenleving 1908–1983* (Rotterdam, 2007)

Blotkamp, H. et al., *S. van Ravesteyn* (Amsterdam/Utrecht, 1977/8)

Boer, T. de et al., *M. R. Radermacher Schorer 1888–1956. Minnaar van het 'schoone' boek* (Amsterdam, 1998)

Boterenbrood, H., *Weverij de Ploeg 1923–1957* (Rotterdam, 1989)

Broekhuizen, D., *De Stijl toen/J. J. P. Oud nu* (Rotterdam, 2000)

Brugman, T., *Spanningen* (Amsterdam/Antwerp, 1953)

Brummelen, J. van and E. Slothouber, *De Rietveld academie. Een akademiegebouw als model* (Hilversum, 1984)

Bruin R. E. de et al. (eds.), *Een paradijs vol weelde. Geschiedenis van de stad Utrecht* (Utrecht, 2000)

Clarijs, J., *'t Spectrum. Moderne meubelvormgeving en naoorlogse idealisme* (Rotterdam, 2002)

Dresden, S., *Over de biografie* (Amsterdam, 2002)
Droste, M., *Bauhaus 1919–1933* (Groningen, 1990)

Eliens, T., *H. P. Berlage. Ontwerpen voor het interieur* (Zwolle, 1998)

Eliëns, T. and M. Halbertsma, *Volmaakt verchroomd: d3 en het avant-garde meubel in Nederland* (Rotterdam, 2007)
Ex, S. and E. Hoek, *Vilmos Huszár (Huszar) schilder en ontwerper 1884–1960* (Utrecht, 1985)

Forty, A., *Words and buildings: A vocabulary of modern architecture* (London, 2000)

Frank, J., *Die internationale Werkbundsiedlung Wien* 1932 (Neues Bauen in der Welt series, VI) (Vienna, 1932)

Friedman, M. (ed.), *De Stijl 1917–1931* (Amsterdam, 1982)

Gouwe, W. F. (ed.), *Ruimte. Jaarboek van Nederlandsche ambachts & nijverheidskunst 1929* (Rotterdam, 1929)

Gropius, W., *Internationale Architektur* (Bauhausbücher 1) (Munich, 1925)

Heer, J. de, *De architectonische kleur. De polychromie in de puristische architectuur van Le Corbusier* (Rotterdam, 2008)

Hemel, Z. and V. van Rossem, *Nagele. Een collectief ontwerp 1947–1957* (Amsterdam, 1984)

Hinte, E. van, *Wim Rietveld industrieel ontwerper* (Rotterdam, 1996)

Hitchcock, H.-R., *Architecture: Nineteenth and Twentieth Centuries*, 10th ed. (Kingsport, 1985)

Hitchcock, H.-R. and P. Johnson, *The International Style*, 3rd ed. (London/New York, 1995)

Hoek, E. (ed.), *Theo van Doesburg oeuvrecatalogus* (Utrecht/Otterlo, 2000)

Huygen, F., *Designkritiek in Nederland. Een essay* (Rotterdam, 1996)

Huygen, F., *Martin Visser* (publication for the oeuvre prize of the Netherlands Foundation for Visual Arts, Design and Architecture) (Amsterdam, 1998)

Idsinga, T., and J. Schilt, *Architect W. van Tijen 1894–1974* (Den Haag, 1987)

Ibelings, H., *Nederlandse architectuur van de 20ste eeuw* (Rotterdam, 1995)

Jans, J., *Bouwkunst en cultuur* (Amsterdam, 1934)

Kuipers, M. (ed.), *Toonbeelden van de wederopbouw. Architectuur, stedenbouw en landinrichting van herrijzend Nederland* (Zwolle, 2002)

Leeuw Marcar, A., *Willem Sandberg. Portret van een kunstenaar* (Amsterdam 1982; revised and expanded, Rotterdam, 2004)

Linssen, C. et al., *Het gaat om de film! Een nieuwe geschiedenis van de Nederlandse Filmliga 1927–1933* (Amsterdam, 1999)

Moorsel, W. van, *Nelly van Doesburg 1899–1975* (Nijmegen, 2000)

Mulder, B., *Vier x Rietveld* (Amersfoort, 1991)
Nagtegaal, C., *Truus Schröder-Schräder. Bewoonster van het Rietveld Schröderhuis* (Utrecht, 1987)

Orchard, K. and I. Schulz, *Kurt Schwitters und seine Freunde/ Kurt Schwitters en de avant-garde* (exhibition catalogue) (Hanover/Rotterdam, 2006)

Ottenhof, F. (ed.), *Goedkope arbeiderswoningen* (Rotterdam, 1936)

Petersen, A. and P. Brattinga, *Sandberg* (Amsterdam, 1975)

Rasch, H. and B. Rasch, *Der Stuhl* (Stuttgart, 1928)

Rebel, B., *Het Nieuwe Bouwen. Het functionalisme in Nederland 1918–1945* (Assen, 1983)

Reinhartz-Tergau, E., *J. J. P. Oud. Architect. Meubelontwerpen and interieurs/Architekt. Möbelentwürfe und Inneneinrichtungen* (Rotterdam, 1990)

Rens, H. van, *Gerrit Rietveld Teksten* (Utrecht, 1979)

Roodenburg-Schadd, C., *Expressie and ordening. Het verzamelbeleid van Willem Sandberg voor het Stedelijk Museum 1945–1962* (Rotterdam, 2004)

Ruys, M., J. Ruys and Th. Ruys, *Het vaste plantenboek* (Amsterdam 1950)

Semper, G., *Der Stil in den technische und tektonische Kunsten* (Munich, 1860–3)

Spaans-van der Bijl, T., *Utrecht in verzet 1940–1945* (Utrecht, 1995)

Speidel, M., *Bruno Taut retrospective: Natur und Fantasie 1880–1938* (Berlin, 1995)

Stahl, G. (trans. and intr.), *On Vision and Colors by Arthur Schopenhauer and Color Sphere by Philipp Otto Runge* (Princeton, 2010)

Taut, B., *Die neue Wohnug. Die Frau als Schöpferin* (Leipzig, 1920)

Timmer, P., *Metz & Co. De creatieve jaren* (Rotterdam, 1995)

Vegesack, A. von and M. Remmele (eds.), *Marcel Breuer, design and architecture* (Weil am Rhein, 2003)

Venneman, J., and M. de Kroon (eds.), *De Mondial. Rietvelds stoel voor de wereld* (Culemborg, 2006)

Verrips, G., *Dwars, duivels and dromend. De geschiedenis van de CPN 1938–1991* (Amsterdam, 1995)

Visser, M. and S. Labesque (eds.), *Het beeld van Rietveld* (Rotterdam, 1993)

Vreeze, N. de, *Woningbouw, inspiratie & ambitie. Kwalitatieve grondslagen van de sociale woningbouw in Nederland* (Amsterdam, 1993)

Wagt, W. de, *J. B. van Loghem 1881–1940. Landhuizen, stadswoningen en woningbouwprojecten. Beelding van levenshouding* (Haarlem, 1995)

White, M., *De Stijl and Dutch modernism* (Manchester/New York, 2003)

Wilk, C., *Marcel Breuer: Furniture and interiors* (New York, 1981)

Wilk, C. (ed.), *Modernism 1914–1939: Designing a new world* (London, 2006)

Woud, A. van der, *Het Nieuwe Bouwen Internationaal/ International. CIAM Volkshuisvesting/Housing Stedebouw/Town Planning* (Delft, 1963)

Zijl, I. van (ed.), 'Truus Schröder: tentoonstelling per post' (Utrecht, 1998–9)

Chapters in books

Benton, T., 'Modernism and Nature', in Wilk 2006, 310–39

Blotkamp, C., 'Theo van Doesburg' in C. Blotkamp 1982, 14–46

Blotkamp, C. and C. Hilhorst, 'De dissidente kunstenaars: Bart van der Leck, Vilmos Huszár en Georges van Tongerloo', in C. Blotkamp 1996, 311–62

Bock, M., 'Cornelis van Eesteren', in C. Blotkamp 1996, 226–68

Buiter, H. 'De moderne stad 1907–2000', in Bruin 2000, 435–557

Esser, H., 'J. J. P. Oud', in C. Blotkamp 1982, 125–54

Gill, R., 'De sporen van Rietveld op Curaçao – 45 jaar later', in *De Horen en zijn echo. Verzameling essays [voor] Henny E. Coomans* (Amsterdam, 1994) 141–4

Harmsen, G., 'De Stijl en de Russische revolutie', in Friedman 1982, 44–9

Hoek, E., 'Piet Mondriaan' in C. Blotkamp 1982, 47–82, 58

Mácel, O., 'Marcel Breuer – "inventor of bent tubular steel furniture"', in Vegesack and Remmele 2003, 52–115

Oorthuis, G., 'Een denkbeeldig geraamte van lijnen', in Slothouber 1997, 105–16

Santen, B. van, 'Bredero's Bouwbedrijf, 1921–1947', in Bekkers 2005

Stam, M. 'Het vraagstuk der arbeiderswoning in verband met de steeds veranderende grootte der gezinnen.', in: Ottenhof 1936, 17–25

Straten, E. van, 'Theo van Doesburg', in C. Blotkamp 1996, 13–66

Verhoeven, T. H. G., 'Stedelijk leven in een stroomversnelling (1851–1917)', in de Bruin, 2000, 415 and 416

Wever, P., and S. van Schaik, 'De Mondial – Rietveldstoel voor de wereld' (typescript published in slightly modified form), in Venneman and de Kroon 2006

Wilk, C., 'Sitting on Air', in Wilk 2006, 230

Articles in periodicals

'Architekt G. Rietveld: Pui N. V. Goud and Zilversmids Compagnie Amsterdam' and 'Architekt G. Rietveld: Intérieur N. V. Goud and Zilversmids Compagnie Amsterdam', in *De Stijl 5* (1922), 2

'Holland und die Baukunst unserer Zeit', in *Schweizerische Bauzeitung* 82 (1923) 18, 225–9

'Boutiques 1921', in *L'Architecture Vivante* (autumn/ winter 1925)

'Huizen van glas and staal', in *Utrechtsch Provinciaal and Stedelijk* newspaper (5 October 1931)

'Heerenhuizen te Utrecht. Rietveld heeft met één slag een deel van het publiek gewonnen', in *De Telegraaf* newspaper (27 October 1931), 9

'Nieuwe bioscoop in aanbouw', in *Utrechtsch Dagblad* (November 1936)

'Vreeburgbioscoop heropend, in *Utrechtsch Dagblad* (December 1936)

'G. Th. Rietveld geb. 1888', in *Goed Wonen* 11 (1958) 6, 130–4

'Prof. Granpré Molière and dr. Rietveld erelid B.N.A.', in *Bouw* 19 (1964) 13, 448

Badovici, J., 'Entretiens sur l'architecture vivante. Maison à Utrecht (Pays-Bas) par T. Schröder et G. Rietveld', in *L' Architecture Vivante* autumn/winter (1925) 28–9; esp. 31–3

Bakema, J. B., 'De vrije vorm', in *De 8 and opbouw* 12 (1941) 8, 105–7

Bekaert, G., 'G. T. Rietveld leeft voort', in *Streven* 17 (1964)

Beusekom, A. van, 'Gerrit Rietveld and zijn "periodiek in briefvorm" 1931–1932', in: *Jong-Holland* (1991) 1, 33–51

Bibeb, 'Wij maken maar een achtergrond. Gesprek met architect Rietveld', in *Vrij Nederland* (19 April 1958)

Bill, I., 'Lebensgestalter. Ein Gespräch in der Wiener Werkbundsiedlung', in an unknown illustrated magazine (1932, held as a clipping at the Rietveld Schröder Archive).

Boeken, A., 'Eenige opmerkingen over de winkelverbouwing Kalverstraat 107 te Amsterdam. Arch. G. Rietveld', in *Bouwkundig Weekblad* 43 (1922) 49, 476

Boeken, A., 'De winkelverbouwing Kalverstraat 107 te Amsterdam. Arch. G. Rietveld', in *Bouwkundig Weekblad* 44 (1923) 45, 455

Boot, C., 'Mart Stam. Kunstnijverheidsonderwijs als aanzet voor een menselijke omgeving. Dessau–Amsterdam' in *Wonen/TABK* 11 (June 1982), 10–21

Breuer, M., 'Die Möbelabteilung des Staatliches Bauhauses in Weimar', in *Fachblat für Holzarbeiter* 20 (1925), 18

Breuer, M., 'Metallmöbel und moderne räumlichkeit', in *Das neue Frankfurt* 2 (1928), 1

Broek, van den, J. H., 'Vragen aan Rietveld', in *De 8 and Opbouw* 4 (1933) 22, 191–2

D[oesburg], Th. v[an], 'Aanteekeningen bij een leunstoel van Rietveld', in *De Stijl* 2 (1919) 11, appendix XXII

D[oesburg], Th. v[an], 'Schilderkunst van Giorgio de Chirico en een stoel van Rietveld.', in *De Stijl* 3 (1920) 5, 46

Doesburg, Th. van, 'Der wille zum Stil', in *De Stijl* 5 (1922) 2, 23–32

Doesburg, Th. van, 'Tot een beeldende architectuur', in *De Stijl* 6 (1924) 6/7, 78–83

Doesburg, Th. van, 'Data and Feiten (betreffende de invloedsontwikkeling van "De Stijl" in het Buitenland) die voor zich spreken', in: *De Stijl* 7 (1926–7) 79/84, 53–71

Eyck, A. van, 'De bal kaatst terug', in *Forum* 13 (1958) 3, 104–11

Gruyter, W. J. de, 'Bouwkundige tentoonstelling van den Utr. Kunstkring', in *Utrechtsch Provinciaal and Stedelijk Dagblad* (22, 23 and 24 October, 1929)

Ibelings, H., 'La fama de Rietveld/Rietveld's fame', in Kuper 2006, 30–3

Kloos, J. P., 'Zomerhuisje aan de Loosdrechtsche plassen, Architect G. Rietveld', in *De 8 and Opbouw* 12 (1941) 8, 103–5

Kroon, B., 'De geboorte van het Rietveld Schröder Huis', in *De Tijd* 29 (November 1974) 24–6

Kuper, M. and M. van Schijndel, 'Der Sitzgeist', in *Jong-Holland* 3 (1987) 2, 4–11

Kuper M. et al., 'Gerrit Th. Rietveld. Casas', in Kuper 2006, 88

Meijer, J. de, 'Vakverrotting', in *Bouwkundig Weekblad* 56 (1935) 44, 463

Meulen, J. N. van der, 'Museum and school van Kunstnijverheid te Utrecht', in *Oud-Utrecht*, 66 (1993), 96

Quist, W., 'Honrade, ambable e inflexible/Honest, gentle and uncompromising', in Kuper 2006, 23–24

Schröder, T., 'Wat men door normalisatie in den woningbouw te Frankfort a/d Main heeft bereikt', in *De werkende vrouw* 1 (1930) 1–2, 12–14

Staal, A., 'Vragen over de "vragen aan Rietveld"', in *De 8 and Opbouw* 5 (1934) 1, 8

Tussenbroek, O. van, 'Drie stoelen van G. Rietveld', in *Binnenhuis* (1 March 1928), 71

Audio

Oudsten, F. den and L. Büller, interviews with Truus Schröder (tape recordings in the Rietveld Schröder Archive) (1982)

Rietveld, G., Guided tour of his retrospective at the Stedelijk Museum Amsterdam (Stedelijk Museum Amsterdam, sound archive of the audiovisual department, no. 1999-006, 41' 52") (6 March 1959)

Archives

Bauhaus Image Archives (Bauhausbilderarchiv), Hochschule für Architektur und Bauwesen, Weimar

The Han Schröder Papers, 1950–92 (Special Collections, Virginia Polytechnic Institute and State University, Blacksburg, VA)

J. J. P. Oud Archive, Netherlands Architecture Institute

Rietveld Archive, Netherlands Architecture Institute

Rietveld Schröder Archive, Centraal Museum, Utrecht

Index

Numbers in italics refer to illustration captions and chronology

Phaidon Press Limited
Regent's Wharf
All Saints Street
London N1 9PA

Phaidon Press Inc.
65 Bleecker Street
New York, NY 10012

phaidon.com

First published 2010
Published in paperback 2016

ISBN 978 0 7148 7320 6

This book was published with the support of the Dutch Foundation for Literature.

A CIP catalogue record for this book is available from the British Library and the Library of Congress.

Designed by Wim Crouwel, assisted by Remco Crouwel

Printed in China

The author would like to thank the Centraal Museum and Phaidon Press for their contribution in the making of this book.

Gerrit Rietveld's work is © Gerrit Thomas Rietveld, c/o Pictoright, Amsterdam, 2009. Images not solely credited to the Rietveld Schröderarchief are listed below by page, and abbreviations are used throughout: RSA=Centraal Museum, Rietveld Schröderarchief, NAI=Nederlands Architectuurinstituut, t=top, b=bottom, l=left, r=right, c=centre. Archief Verriet Instituut: 154b; AVIODROME Luchtfotografie, Lelystad: 171; Badisches Landesmuseum: 44tr; Bauhaus Archiv: 207t&b; Bildarchiv Österreichische Nationalbibliothek: 95bl; Bureau Monumenten, Archeologie, photo Han van Gool: 181b,231tr; CM: 22tl,23t,194r; CM and Stedelijk Museum Amsterdam, photo Stedelijk Museum, Amsterdam 2009: 28,29tl,222tr; Centraal Museum, loan Moolenbeek: 58b; CM/loan Nederlands Architectuurinstituut: 134t; CM/loan private collection: 195b; CM/photo Axel Funke: 21b,222l; CM/photo Ernst Moritz: 27bl,34tr,35b,36tl,tr&br,44br,45c,54t,78tl&tr,80t,92t,97t,99tr&br,100,101tl,108b,111bl,113bl&tl&tr,131br,134b,136b,138l, 173t,184t,197br&tr,222br,224tr,227tl,225tl,230ctl; CM/photo Hans Wilschut: 48,49,51,71,50,62tl&tr&bl,63,65,66,67; RSA/photo Axel Funke: 176tr; RSA/photo Cas Oorthuys: 175t,183br,229bl; RSA/photo Ernst Moritz: 83bl; RSA/photo Eva Besnyö: 85b;121br&tl,122bl&br,123bl&tl&tr,226br,227cbl; RSA/photo Fridtjof Versnel: 187,231br; RSA/photo Jaap d'Oliveira: 103t; RSA/photo Jan Versnel: 17tl&b,158tr,168,169b,170b,171t&b,172b,173b,174,175b,178b,184b,230cbl&bl&cbr,230tl,231tl; RSA/photo Jannes Linders: 158b,229tr; RSA/photo Museum of Modern Art, New York: 162; RSA/photo Nico Jesse: 89,128t,142b,145b,227ctl; RSA/photo Stedelijk Museum Amsterdam: 185b,230br; RSA/photo Ton Roelofsma: 177t,179,231cr&bl; RSA/photo ulkoja: 182b,231cl; RSA/photo Violett Cornelius: 166t,229cr; Collection Bertus Mulder: 39t; Collection Bertus Mulder, photo Ernst Moritz: 24bl; Collection Erven Schelling Amsterdam, photo RSA: 27tr; Collection Ms. M. Fernhout: 81br; Collection Nationaal Archief Curacao, photo F. Fischer: 155t,229cl; Collection Osaka City Museum of Modern Art: 24br; Het Utrechts Archief, photo E.A. van Blitz: 223br; Kröller Müller Museum: 202t; Limburg Antiquairs : 24t; Maria Austria Instituut, photo Ad Windig: 114; Maria Austria Instituut, photo Jan Versnel: 117br,120br; NAI: 39c,86b,101tr,104b,111tl,117bl,121tr,125,126tl,133tl,137,142t,146b,149,150,152,153t,154tr,178t,185tr,195tr,202b&c,228bl&cbl,230tr&ctr, NAI/photo Ernst Moritz: 197tl; NAI/photo Eva Besnyö: 81bl&123br; NAI/photo Jan Versnel: 177b; NAI/photo Particam: 163bl; Photo AVIODROME Luchtfotografie, Lelystad: 153b; private collection: 182t; Rijksbureau voor Kunsthistorische Documentatie: 23b, Stedelijk Museum Amsterdam: 64tr&bl&br,34tl,97c,98,101bl,132tl,133tr,145t,224cl,226cr.